Jonathan Clements

ANIME
A History

A BFI book published by Palgrave

For Andrew Partridge

First published in 2013 by
PALGRAVE

on behalf of the

BRITISH FILM INSTITUTE
21 Stephen Street, London W1T 1LN
www.bfi.org.uk

There's more to discover about film and television through the BFI. Our world-renowned archive, cinemas, festivals, films, publications and learning resources are here to inspire you.

PALGRAVE in the UK is an imprint of Macmillan Publishers Limited, registered in England, company number 785998, of 4 Crinan Street, London N1 9XW. Palgrave Macmillan in the US is a division of St Martin's Press LLC, 175 Fifth Avenue, New York, NY 10010. Palgrave is a global imprint of the above companies and is represented throughout the world. Palgrave® and Macmillan® are registered trademarks in the United States, the United Kingdom, Europe and other countries.

Cover illustration: Shiori Abe – http://sa2hanadi.tumblr.com. Originally used at Scotland Loves Anime, 2013
Designed by couch
Set by Cambrian Typesetters, Camberley, Surrey & couch
Printed in China

This book is printed on paper suitable for recycling and made from fully managed and sustained forest sources. Logging, pulping and manufacturing processes are expected to conform to the environmental regulations of the country of origin.

British Library Cataloguing-in-Publication Data
A catalogue record for this book is available from the British Library
A catalog record for this book is available from the Library of Congress

ISBN 978–1–84457–390–5 (pb)

CONTENTS

ACKNOWLEDGMENTS

This book began life as a PhD dissertation at the Faculty of Applied Design and Engineering at what was then Swansea Metropolitan University – now part of the University of Wales. My tuition fees were paid by Skillset Screen Academy Wales (now Media Academy Wales), although the time to write would not have been possible had not my literary agent, Chelsey Fox, secured a book contract with Rebecca Barden at the British Film Institute. Jerome Mazandarani of Manga Entertainment and Andrew Partridge from Scotland Loves Anime made sure there was work for me on many below-the-line matters, which helped pay the bills. Gemma Cox at *NEO* magazine, Cheryl Morgan at *Salon Futura* and John Clute at the *Encyclopedia of Science Fiction* also threw me writing jobs that helped feed the hungry maw of the doctoral research. The final draft was completed while I was on secondment to China on behalf of the University of Jyväskylä's Department of Computer Science and Information Systems.

Several parts of this book have had incarnations in other forms. I first publicly tested my notions of ownership and access before an audience at the University of Edinburgh, where I was invited to speak by Yōko Matsumoto-Sturt. Joseph Steiff allowed me to put my testimonial materials to early use when he asked for a book chapter on anime for *Sherlock Holmes and Philosophy* (2011). An early version of part of Chapter 3 first appeared as an article in *animation: an interdisciplinary journal*, where it benefited immensely from suggestions and comments by Suzanne Buchan, Kim Joon Yang and two anonymous readers. An early version of Chapter 6 appeared in *Mechademia*, at the end of a process in which discussions with Christopher Bolton, Wendy Goldberg, Frenchy Lunning and Frederik L. Schodt led to its improvement. At the instigation of Stuart Picken and Helen Parker, some other parts of Chapter 3 were given as a speech to the Japan Society of Scotland, again in Edinburgh. I gained unprecedented access to much obscure material courtesy of the 62nd Locarno Film Festival, for which I was an animation consultant, and where my stay in Switzerland was made trouble-free through the arrangements of Carlo Chatrian, Olmo Giovannini and their colleagues. Although little of it appears here, I would also like to mention the groundwork done on the overseas anime business in my 1995 Master's dissertation at the University of Stirling, which bought me access to Swansea in the first place, and would not have been possible without a rare British Academy scholarship. I have also been blessed with mouthy and combative students at my workshops on the structure of modern anime at Swansea itself, as well as the Irish Film Institute, the Glasgow Film Theatre, the Edinburgh Film House, Screen Academy Wales, Anifest in the Czech Republic and several corporate clients.

This book is an odd hybrid in that it was accepted as a doctoral proposal and as a book proposal at the same time. It has hence benefited doubly from the peer-review process, and the British Film Institute's two consultants, Rayna Denison and Andrew Osmond, steered the course of the research, not only in their comments on the original proposal, but also in subsequent reviews of the manuscript, ultimately turning them into unofficial supervisors. Their ideas were responsible for many changes, tweaks and asides that have measurably improved this book, although I did not take all their advice. In particular, I have wilfully clung to several sources and concepts derived from history in order to elucidate what I regard as common errors of practice in the film studies community. On occasion, this may appear like I am reinventing a few wheels, but I strongly feel that some writers on anime could do with a reminder of how the cart actually rolls. At the publishers, Sophia Contento and Belinda Latchford diligently carried this book from manuscript to print, adding all sorts of unexpected whistles and bells, including korrekt spellingz and many person-hours of screen-grabbing, to the overall package's demonstrable benefit.

Other individuals who have helped in some way include Felicity Blastland, Martin Capey, Kelvin Donne, Erica Fothergill, Raz Greenberg, Paul Hazel, Dina Iordanova, my thesis supervisor Barry Ip, Frederick Litten, Helen McCarthy, Joe Peacock, Jayne Pilling, Hannah Raybould, Mark Schilling, Ellis Tinios and Tochigi Akira.

My thanks to those figures from the Japanese animation industry who have spoken personally to me or answered email interviews about their careers and experiences: Ishii Katsuhito (Nice Rainbow), Itano Ichirō, Kamimura Yasuhiro (Gainax), Katō Kunio (Robot Communications), Kitayama Shigeru (Victor Japan/Flying Dog), Koike Takeshi (Madhouse), Maki Tarō (Pioneer), Miki Shunichirō, Nakayama Yoshihisa (Kyoto Animation), Nishimura Satoshi, Noda Fūko (Studio 4 Degrees C), Oiji Shunsuke (Sunrise), Onodera Keiichi (Pioneer/Geneon), Sadamoto Yoshiyuki (Khara), Satō Yumi (Brain's Base), Takahashi Ryōsuke (Sunrise), Takeda Yasuhiro (Gainax), Yamada Naoko (Kyoto Animation), Yamaga Hiroyuki (Gainax), Yokoyama Shūko (Aniplex). I have rarely quoted from our conversations, because this work is documentary in nature; however, they were invaluable in driving the investigation forward and assessing my research partway.

Online sources have also been of great use. In particular, the work of two bloggers, Ben Ettinger and Catherine Munroe Hotes, have regularly challenged my own *nescience*, while the Anime News Network, particularly Justin Sevakis and Zac Bertschy's ANN podcasts, has constantly fed me new ideas and information.

The library of London's School of Oriental and African Studies offered strong support in background materials on Japan and film, but I was left to rely largely on my own supplies for much of the material on anime itself. Amazon Japan was a priceless resource, both for new books and for secondhand rarities. Because Japanese resellers usually refuse to mail secondhand books to foreign addresses, I relied upon a mail drop in Yokohama at the home of the Tamamuro family, where Tamamuro Sachiko, Matsuda Akiko and Matsuda Naomi kindly forwarded many obscure books to Europe. My colleague Tamamuro Motoko has worked without complaint on many difficult readings, clarifications and translations to ensure that my conclusions are solid. Matthew Johnson and his family are probably still wondering what I thought I was doing when I turned up at their house at Christmas and demanded to watch all the credits, and *only* the credits, of their Rankin/Bass DVDs.

My son Alexander is probably the first and last child in the twenty-first century to grow up watching 1930s propaganda cartoons, and developed an odd obsession with Hatsune Miku while we watched her DVD concerts together. His grandmothers and aunts in the Clements, Mäki-Kuutti and Parkkonen families have often watched over him while his father was writing. His mother, Kati Clements, has offered unfailing support to an author at work; I doubt this book would have been completed without her help.

INTRODUCTION
What do we talk about when we talk about anime?

Although *anime* is the most common modern term for animation in Japan, it was not coined until the middle of the twentieth century. Common terms for animation in earlier periods included *senga* ('line art') or *kuga* ('flip pictures'), alongside the archaic *dekobō shin gachō* ('mischievous new pictures'), *chamebō-zu* ('playful pictures') and later, more popular terms such as *manga-eiga* ('cartoon films') and *dōga* ('moving pictures') came into use (Ōtsuka 2001: 29; Tsugata 2007a: 57).

The historian Tsugata Nobuyuki's (2011b: 30) most recent return to the question of 'What is anime?' pushes its notional origin late in the twentieth century. He identifies three sudden expansions in 'anime', as:

(0)   *Astro Boy* and its influence, 1963–
(1)   *Space Cruiser Yamato, Nausicaä of the Valley of the Wind*, and their influences, 1974– and 1984–
(2)   *Neon Genesis Evangelion* and *Princess Mononoke* and their influences, 1995– and 1997–.

Here, Tsugata reframes *Tetsuwan Atomu* (1963, *Astro Boy*) from his earlier works (Tsugata 2004: 151; 2005: 76–7, 181–2; see also Masuda 2007: 119) as a 'zeroth' period of development because although he recognises its vital importance in the evolution of the medium, he now wishes to define anime not merely as 'Japanese animation', but as a particular *kind* of Japanese animation, that diverges in the 1970s by fastening itself to other objects and processes, including but not restricted to: foreign interest, transgression, visual cues, merchandising and integration into a media mix. However, Tsugata is not providing an answer. His article 'Anime to wa Nani ka?' [What Is Anime?] is framed as a question, and ends with consideration of 'the grey zone' of all those inconvenient exceptions that do not fit within his parameters, such as whether or not digital performance capture should be included (Tsugata 2011b: 21). Tsugata's argument introduces a new distinction: that between 'Japanese animation' (i.e. animation that comes from Japan), and 'anime', which he confines within a parameter broadly bracketed by his own life. 'Anime', for Tsugata, comprises the TV cartoons that he watched as a child, and everything that came after them. 'Japanese animation' is the older or more obscure material that he often writes about as an adult, but also occasionally 'full' animation films.

Even if we wish to speak of anime within Tsugata's parameters, as a late twentieth-century phenomenon, we must understand the nature of its historical construction (Miyao 2002: 193), which requires treatment of the preceding decades, and the technologies, relationships and precedents established within them. Even if we begin a history of anime in 1963 or 1974, we must first comprehend (to borrow a phrase), the 'end of anime prehistory'.

It was as a result of such arguments, that Clements and McCarthy chose to assign their definition of 'anime' to the broadest possible of compasses: '*Anime* refers to animation from Japan' (Clements and McCarthy 2006: 30). This definition can still fall apart at a quantum level, depending on how much we want to quibble about the nature of 'animation' and to what extent it can come 'from Japan'. But we should accept, as does Foucault in *The Archaeology of Knowledge*, that *all* disciplines, all 'objects of knowledge' will similarly collapse under their own weight if subjected to such a degree of deconstruction and hypercriticality (Foucault 2002: 231–2; see also Ellis 1989: 94). However, the definition from Clements and McCarthy, *The Anime Encyclopedia: A Guide to Japanese Animation since 1917* (2006) at least delineates 'animation' and 'Japan' as two crucial categories, and allows for any study of it to at least consider the history of animation in Japan before Tsugata's 'zeroth' date of *Astro Boy* in 1963.

The name of the Association of Japanese Animations (sic, AJA hereafter) contains, perhaps inadvertently, a plural, as if to remind readers that Japanese animation is not necessarily about painted acetate cels, but also digital works, sand animation, stop-motion puppetry and claymation. There is far more to a Japanese animation 'industry' than the group of artists who are most often considered at its core (AJA 2008 I: 20). *Dōga*, the Japanese term usually translated as 'animation', is used specifically to refer to inbetweening in the AJA's manual, and is only the halfway point in the AJA's own list of the multiple processes required in the creation of a cartoon (AJA 2008 II: 49). Just as Mori Yasuji once likened animation production to an 'orchestral ensemble' (Kanō 2004: 127), we might consider that, in addition to animation itself, there are such diverse tasks as storylining and storyboarding, music, sound and voice-acting, marketing and advertisers, toy tie-ins and TV ratings, video duplicators and website managers – many other occupations that feed into the process of creating a Japanese cartoon, and in facilitating viewers' access to it. The AJA even includes some tasks entirely devoid of original animation content, such as the localising of foreign cartoons into Japanese, in its overview of the sectors of the 'Japanese animation industry' (AJA 2008 II: 136). Following this argument, the industry in Japan has already celebrated its centenary, since its inception would date not from the first screening of domestically made cartoons in 1917, but from the first screenings of foreign cartoons around 1912 (Haraguchi 2000: 16; Tsugata 2007a: 56) or even the first Japanese sight of pixillated camera trickery as early as 1903 (Koga 2011: 47).

Tomino Yoshiyuki (2002: 60) admits that at Mushi Pro in the mid-1960s, it was common for staff to claim that 'only the animators were human beings', disregarding the contributions of production assistants, painters or tracers. In 1980, Ishiguro Noboru wrote a semi-fictional producer's diary, outlining a series of incidents that were just as much part of the anime industry as tracing images on a cel. These situations included the frantic morning scramble to complete an animatic reel sufficient for an afternoon sound-recording session, and the striking image of a courier arriving at Narita Airport, only to discover in a moment of panic that his luggage has gone missing, along with the 500 urgently needed cels it contained from a South Korean subsidiary (Ishiguro and Ohara 1980: 220, 222; see also Tada 2002: 197–219). When we speak of Itano Ichirō climbing into the cockpit of an American fighter jet to research dogfighting; Yamamoto Eiichi demanding his fair share of the royalties for a song on the *Jungle Taitei* (1966, *Jungle Emperor*) album; Rintarō ringing a manga artist's doorbell in the pouring rain to argue about a change in the script, we are still speaking of the Japanese animation industry, of its workers and its scandals, its successes and failures, its legends and its traditions. This book is a history of the Japanese animation industry because it recognises the participation of those with many other skills, including but not limited to producers, writers, composers and financiers.

This book employs a historiographical approach, less concerned with anime 'texts' themselves than in their existence in (or apparent absence from) historical memory, what other researchers might call their 'significance' (Staiger 1992: 24) or their 'artistic heritage' (Postlewait 2009: 18) – not merely their showings in box-office sales reports and TV ratings, but in their influence on sets of creatives in particular generational locations, and on the anime that followed.

This is not a book that dwells on, say, gender roles in *Kyojin no Hoshi* (1968, *Star of the Giants*), or manifest camp in *Shinseiki Evangelion* (1995, *Neon Genesis Evangelion*) – although I hope someone writes both of those. This is a book concerned with how *Star of the Giants*, *Evangelion* and a number of other anime fit within a continuum of a century's film-making, how they came to be, who the makers thought were watching, and how they transformed the nature of subsequent productions. Some, like the forgotten works of the 1940s 'Shadow Staff', no longer exist. Others, like the seminal broadcast of *Astro Boy* have a rose-tinted, modern heritage at odds with elements of their initial reception. Others, like a digitally composited episode of *Koshika Monogatari* (1983–5, *The Yearling*) in 1983, represent landmark events in anime history that largely passed viewers by, unnoticed. Still others, like the well-known *Evangelion* enjoyed a *contextual* significance (coincidentally broadcast at the same time as the studio inaugurated its first online message board) that played an arguably forgotten role in its impact.

Consequently, this book draws on Japanese-language materials that elude those 'New Critics' who focus solely on the texts themselves. A historiography of anime begins with simple lists (some purportedly 'complete') of Japanese cartoons, and broadens to include their nature, their staff and the available recollections of the participants in their production. The chief materials utilised comprise dozens of industry memoirs and testimonials, often with conflicting perspectives and agendas. Other sources include what Barbara Klinger (1997: 116) perceptively characterises as the 'particularly rich terrain' of exhibition sources (the manner in which the works were packaged and presented for their audiences as synchronic *events*) and distribution (the materials generated by the political economy of sales and marketing). Although there are asides regarding parallel developments in the non-Japanese industry, treatment of anime abroad is only considered where it impacts the constitution of production within Japan.

Despite occasional efforts by foreign distributors and reviewers to characterise it as a specific filmic mode – sci-fi, or erotic horror, or Oscar-winning family films – anime is not a 'genre'. It is a *medium*, albeit one that can benefit from being parsed in terms of Jason Mittell's work on genre, as a 'discursive genealogy' (2001: 8–9) impacted by changes in technology, delivery systems and cultural context. The nature of Japanese animation has been subject to periodic ruptures that transform it radically, but do not so much supplant existing forms as add to them. There are many 'lost valleys' in the anime world, where genres or modes that once ruled the airwaves continue to survive, marooned in isolated pockets but still watched by ageing or marginalised audiences, or persisting as the sole vestiges of once-dominant forms. Some of them contain actual dinosaurs.

There is always more to say. New testimonies come to light; old archives are unearthed; new developments offer fresh perspectives for reconsidering previous events; sometimes new attitudes even demand them. In recent years, database software and online search engines have transformed the speed with which scholars and consumers alike can access Japanese film. Access to works about anime in the English language has also improved. Most notably, several scholars are already pursuing work in areas related to those in this book. Ian Condry brings anthropological fieldwork into anime production houses, with his *The Soul of Anime: Collaborative Creativity and Japan's Media Success Story* (2013), published in the same week I delivered the manuscript of this book. Marc Steinberg has approached the post-1960s era in *Anime's Media Mix: Franchising Toys and Characters in Japan* (2012), drawing on work that articulates anime as an integral part of a 'media ecology' that lures viewers away from consumption of narrative and into *participation* in an environment of images and merchandise. Beyond studies of themes and content already undertaken by Susan Napier (2006) and Marco Pelliteri (2010), there are also two significant works on elements of the anime production process: Hu Tze-yue approaches anime as transnational cultural capital in *Frames of Anime: Culture and Image-building* (2010) and Thomas Lamarre deals with philosophical matters concerning the *space* of anime and its implication for the moving image, in *The Anime Machine: A Media Theory of Animation* (2009). There is, however, no full-length *history* of Japanese animation available in English – an omission that this book seeks to remedy, articulating 'anime' as a succession of conceptual systems that form and change throughout the latter half of the twentieth century and into the twenty-first, in reaction to 'the permanence of problems, the continuity of tradition or the mechanism of influences' (Foucault 2002: 62).

Cinema studios seize the high ground of exhibition, only for newly arrived animators to flourish in commercials and on TV. TV, in turn, becomes a saturated market, only for new avenues to be found in video. This book considers such an ever-branching genealogy of innovations, as each disruption forces the less secure or less established elements of the Japanese animation industry to find new ways of surviving. In doing so, we will periodically see epitomes of each new system, in the form of studios or creators who flourished at a particular time.

HISTORIOGRAPHY AND PRACTICE
Allan Megill's *Historical Knowledge, Historical Error: A Contemporary Guide to Practice* (2007) assesses several issues that can compromise not only sources but also the historians who interpret them. Megill (2007: 33) cautions against 'four ways of evading history', or errors of practice that might damage our understanding of the past.

1   Historical **nescience** – the ignorance or rejection of history.
2   The **aesthesis** of History – the identification of history only with sublime or beautiful objects.
3   History as **tradition** – the concentration on the promotion of one's specific group or outlook.
4   History as **memory** and **commemoration** – the honouring of 'our' dead.

Thomas Postlewait, in *The Cambridge Introduction to Theatre Historiography* (2009), independently reaches similar conclusions by drawing on similar sources, including earlier work by Megill himself. Megill's issue of *aesthesis*, for example, can be seen in Postlewait's (2009: 80) warning against 'the seductive appeal of certain kinds of anecdotes and stories, which tend to simplify yet distort the nature of historical events'. Similarly, he identifies the attitudes of some historians themselves as essential contributors to what Megill would call errors of *tradition*, such as 'the inclination to accept the testimony of key participants in an event because their versions of what happened are consistent with our preconceived narratives of what we want the event to represent'.

In other words, if enough authorities claim that, say, 'Tezuka's revolution' in production methods shook the foundations of the anime world in 1963 with the broadcast of *Astro Boy*, such an idea is liable to become locked into the discourses of subsequent scholars. Those later writers who suggest that it was hardly much of a 'revolution' (Sugiyama 1999: 115–16), that it was an effect, rather than a cause (Oguro 2004c: 2) or even that it was not really 'Tezuka's' to begin with (Miyazaki 2009: 196) risk being drowned out beneath the sheer volume of prevailing assumptions.

Postlewait (2009: 81) concedes that there may also be areas where methodology and narrative tempt historians to reject elements that do not fit well with the story they intend to tell, thereby creating new outbreaks of what Megill would call *nescience*: 'the determination to disregard the details in the sources that fail to align with not only our favourite anecdotes, statements and descriptions, but also our organizing narrative and general assumptions'.

In the above-mentioned dispute over 'Tezuka's revolution', for example, it is worth noting that the dissenters are pursuing individual agendas. Sugiyama is writing a book chapter whose stated aim is to prove the paramount influence of the Tōei studio, even upon its rival Tezuka Osamu. Serikawa Yūgo (interviewed by Oguro) is obliquely suggesting that the style of anime was developed under his watch at Tōei and merely copied by Tezuka. Miyazaki Hayao is writing a magazine article designed to prevent people from associating him with Tezuka in any way in the immediate days after Tezuka's death.

This leads us back to where we started, with a sense that the broadcast of *Astro Boy* in 1963 was probably an event of great consequence for Japanese animation, worth examining further. In doing so, however, we will see that while sources largely agree that there *was* an 'anime revolution' in 1963, they are in chaotic disagreement about what form that revolution actually took, and are still arguing about it four decades later (Tsugata 2007b: 251–6).

Chapter 1 examines what little evidence remains of the animated works pre-dating the Great Kantō Earthquake of 1923, as visualised through an interpretative frame that contrasts testimonials of industry figures with legal discourses over the control of the new medium of film. Chapter 2 narrates the transformation of Japanese animation from an artisanal diversion to an industrial profession, within the context of changes in film technology up to the 1930s. Chapter 3 addresses issues of memory and forgetting in testimonials of Japan's 'Fifteen Years War' from 1931–45, which saw animation enjoy unprecedented leaps in investment and output, so long as it subscribed to the political agenda of the militarist government. It includes bonus details on the immediate post-war experiences of one Japanese animator, Mochinaga Tadahito, who found himself repurposing his skills in the service of the Chinese Communists. Chapter 4 similarly examines a supposed hiatus in chronologies of Japanese animation, contrasting an official record of remarkably few completed productions against testimonials of fervid competition over funding and resources during the tense period of the US occupation and its aftermath. With an ever-expanding archive of extant content, Chapter 5 employs testimonials concerning labour issues at Japanese studios in the 1950s – one well known to posterity, the others far more obscure, with an artistic heritage that can only be properly visualised through the construction of a new chronology, using the interpretative frame of work for hire for foreign clients.

It is only with Chapter 6 that we reach the supposed origin of 'anime', with Tezuka Osamu's *Astro Boy*, approached here through the contrast of rival accounts of its controversial genesis, along with quantitative data regarding its actual impact. Chapter 7 offers another interpretative frame, contrasting the rare occasions that animation appeared on the cover of Japan's *TV Guide* in the 1960s and 1970s, with 'trended change' as new technologies affected production processes. Technology comes to the fore again in the long 1980s in Chapter 8, as the impact of video is assessed at multiple levels of the processes of production, distribution and reception. Chapter 9 outlines the 'discovery' of anime outside Japan, and the effect that this multinuclear, polysemic event had on expectations and processes within the domestic industry in the closing years of the twentieth century. Chapter 10 returns to technology, with a final chronology that approaches testimonials of modern anime in terms of digitisation, from the first consideration of computer technology in 1974 to the shutdown of the analogue broadcast signal in 2012. The Epilogue considers the prophets and doomsayers of the 'anime business' as it begins its second century.

ANIME AS OBJECTS

For a large part of the process that takes it from creator to consumer, intellectual property is less an entertainment event, and more like a magical commodity that, if fed the right conditions, somehow spits out revenue. It is these featureless monetising boxes that are traded at film markets, sold on to third parties and bundled in deals to broadcasters and video distributors. Sometimes, they are briefly unpacked and tinkered with, through the addition of a new voice track or mastering in a new format. Inevitably, however, they are returned to a dormant status, as 'things' to be swapped and hyped, pushed and sold. Such an attitude is anathema to most viewers (or 'audiences' or 'end users'), and to the many cultural critics who focus on the content rather than the form. It is, however, a tangible part of the life of creative works.

If anime is an object, the people who interact with it can be visualised on a chain (see figure overleaf), from *ownership* of the intellectual property, through the *authorship* and *production* of the work, through its *distribution* to theatres, TV channels or rental stores, its *exhibition* through, for example, cinema screenings or TV broadcast, through its eventual *access* by the viewer.

This not only helps produce Barbara Klinger's 'desired, *Rashomon*-like effect' (1997: 110) of using multiple perspectives to bring a work's significance into focus, it also brings other works into consideration that might not normally be regarded as typical of 'Japanese animation', despite clear connections to the chain. *Final Fantasy: The Spirits Within* (2001) is only owned by the Japanese – paid for with Japanese money, but made in the US. *Rudolph the Red-Nosed Reindeer* (1964) is only *produced* by the Japanese, made in Japan for export to foreign markets. Disney's *Snow White and the Seven Dwarfs* (1937), the cartoon that the Japanese call *Shirayuki-hime*, is localised and *exhibited* by the Japanese, but not made by them. And if, somewhere in Japan at this moment, an Internet user is watching an untranslated foreign web cartoon online; the existence of that cartoon within the framework of Japanese animation is merely one of *access*. However, all of these objects might be considered somewhere in an appraisal of 'the Japanese animation industry'.

Although not made in Japan, the 1950 localisation and distribution of Disney's *Snow White and the Seven Dwarfs* (1937) still made it part of a 'Japanese animation industry'

THE OWNERSHIP–ACCESS CHAIN

Ownership: e.g. rights holders, literary estates, investors, sponsors, production committees and, sometimes, original creators.

Authorship: e.g. writers, and in some cases, artists and directors.

Production: e.g. animators, inkers, tracers, key artists, set designers, programmers, cameramen, digital compositors, sound engineers, actors, musicians, colourists, duplicators, inbetweeners – all the remaining agencies of a work's initiation. In cases of international distribution, production elements may return later in the process, in localisation, adaptation, translation, dubbing or subtitling.

Distribution: e.g. business-to-business sales and transport of film objects, buyers and sellers of territorial rights, marketing and promotion, postal workers, video stores, online shops. A 'distribution' step may also be obstructive, such as the obstacle presented by customs authorities or censorship.

Exhibition: e.g. cinema owners, TV broadcasters, film festival organisers, individual owners of private TV sets, mobile phones or computers. Whoever provides or manages the signal to the screen on which the anime is viewed.

Access: the viewer, whoever it may be that stares, gazes or glances at the screen. Not necessarily the owner of the screen, or even the original intended viewer.

Klinger (1997: 115–18) observes that the nature of each of these processes creates different categories of data, many of which are employed in the compass of this work. Production accounts, distributor marketing and exhibition sales data are only the most obvious – there are also the promotional behaviours of the personnel at the time, and their reminiscences in later life, as well as 'intertextual' elements such as the influences of other media, and historical contexts, including but not limited to legal influences on a production or its release, or economic conditions that might incentivise or hamper it. Everyone that interacts with anime in some way, however small, from screenwriters to shelf-stackers, from censors to cinema ushers, can be assigned a place somewhere on the ownership–access chain. This encourages us to consider all aspects of an object's existence, not merely those facets, usually of authorship or access and reception, which have most often been accorded 'epistemological authority' by other critics (Lobato 2012: 4). This can even include extra-legal elements not part of the owners' sanctioned process, what Ramon Lobato calls the 'informal economies' of film distribution, such as piracy, torrenting or fansubbing (unlicensed translation), any of which can constitute invisible elements of production or distribution (Lobato 2012: 43–5).

Theoretically, the highest point on the ownership–access scale is authorship, which is to say that of the original creator. This, however, is almost sure to be subsumed in ownership and production, since animation usually requires many participants: authors, artists, storyboarders, directors, key animators, inbetweeners and colourists. The rights of authorship, as enshrined in Japanese law, cover many potential areas of an anime's creation, including authorship of the original script, the music, the images, the photographs that may have been used as reference material and even the programming code used to create modern computer animation (Ushiki 2011: 203). It might also be difficult to establish who the true 'author' is, since so many aspects of Japanese animation are established structurally and industrially before a text is written.[1]

There are, however, some cases in which a true authorship can be argued. In the title of his book on Tezuka Osamu, Tsugata Nobuyuki uses the term *anime sakka* or 'animation author' in Japanese, which might be better rendered in translation as 'anime auteur'. True anime auteurs are rare, although there are some cases to be made, for example, such as Tezuka himself, who not only created the original texts, but had invasive and distinct influence on the staff that collaborated to bring those works to life (Tsugata 2007b: 229).

However, most of the staff on any given property are liable to be working 'for hire' or after the signature of a copyright waiver. It is hence likely that regardless of the authorship of the original idea, the ownership of an animated work will rest in a holding company or production committee of several interested parties. It might even be possible to argue that authorship itself is a matter of evolution, as useful memes and practically inspired tropes, developed in the early days of anime, establish high-concept *norms* which later committees merely shuffle and refine.

Successive, descending levels of the ownership–access continuum involve varying degrees of access to the material. In most cases, lower levels are merely renting access to the material, in the form of cinema prints or master-tapes distributed to foreign territories that are supposed to be returned to the true owner at the end of a licence period. A cinema theatre, for example, has merely rented the right to participate by exhibiting them for a set period. Similarly, TV companies only borrow the tapes, soundtracks and negatives they use for a foreign-language edition, and are expected to return them eventually. In the case of *Astro Boy*, when the bankruptcy of the original Japanese owner made it impossible to determine who should receive the returned materials, it became the duty of the American sub-licensor to destroy them instead (Ladd with Deneroff 2009: 187).[2]

As Klinger also observes (1997: 112), film works might also be regarded in a diachronic context, as long-term entities with changing significance, not merely as synchronic instants frozen in a particular moment of their original release. The significance of Ōtomo Katsuhiro's *Akira* (1988), for example, varies wildly with one's position on the ownership–access chain – for those involved in its production in the late 1980s, it might be reasonably regarded as a money pit, seemingly without any hope of recouping its investment; for those involved in its foreign exhibition in the 1990s, a rare, landmark cinema event and a flagship for Japanese animation; for those in its distribution in the 2000s, a long-term, blue-chip investment that offers steady returns. At the level of access, there is a similar variety of possible diachronic perspectives, from the fans who regard it as an unquestionable classic, to the enthusiasts for whom it is the only Japanese animation they have knowingly watched, to the younger generation of anime viewers, who kick against established tradition and decry it as overrated or dated – its originality and groundbreaking status eroded through a modern reception tainted, perhaps, by a surfeit of imitators, or through viewing it on a small screen, deprived of the majesty of its initial theatrical exhibition.

We might also discern an implicit additional level – access is both physical and cognitive. Merely because a viewer is able to see a Japanese cartoon, a 'preferred reading' cannot be immediately assumed. Has the text been translated? Is it subtitled or dubbed, and even if so, how faithful is that translation to the original? Hence, at the lowest level of the continuum, notions of simple access unpack once more into content, and transform into complex issues of audience and reception.

ANIME AS EVENTS

When the anime object is finally unpacked and accessed, be it in a cinema, on a TV screen, a cellphone or a laptop, it is not merely a text. For its original audience, it is also a moment in time – perhaps twenty-five minutes just after dinner on a Friday in 1963, or a ninety-minute movie on a rainy day in 1978. We should not forget its temporality, which is to say its position in time as part of an ongoing process (Webster and Mertova 2007: 32).

For discussions of audience, reception and even influence, it can be productive to consider anime as *events*, leading us to interpret, in the manner of Janet Staiger (1992: 81), not a text, but 'a historical explanation of the event of interpreting a text'.

Nagayama Yasuo's *Sengo SF Jiken Shi: Nihonteki Sōzōryoku no 70-nen* (2012, *An Event History of Postwar SF: 70 Years of Japanese Imaginative Power*), for example, describes the development of Japanese fandom in terms of a culture created through the discourse of notable real-world happenings. Instead of focusing on the content of books, films or comics, Nagayama investigates the impact of conventions, press conferences, media scares and magazine launches, as moments in time that unite the culture of fandom, disseminate its core texts and generate its own sense of tradition.

Similarly, the historian and the critic miss something if they consider anime solely in terms of a scholar's reaction to its content, in whatever format it is first presented to them. More often than not, that format is a world away from the manner in which an anime was experienced by its original audience. Postlewait's account of historiography in the performing arts argues that all 'texts' have a double identity that needs to be understood as both performative actions and representative events (Postlewait 2009: 150) – shades here of what in film studies might be called meaning and significance (Staiger 1992: 24).

The performative action is what actually happens in the text – the activity of the characters as viewed by the audience. The representative event is the impact of the text on the world around it – the way it is remembered by the audience in the realm of 'artistic heritage'.

A critic's personal reaction to a text can be far removed from that of its original audience or implied audience, or any of the multiple possible 'readers' – Staiger (1992: 24) suggests up to fifteen different kinds. The performative action in *Hatsune Miku Live Party* (2011), for example, is nothing more than a pop concert. However, its representative event, the mannerism of a live pop concert performed by an animated character with a human backing band and a human audience, is far more important to understanding its significance in anime history and the attention it receives.

Hatsune Miku in concert (2011) includes the performance of her singing, but also the performance of her live band and the audience's 'performance' of accepting her as real

In the years before 1983, the majority of anime viewers had no choice but to watch Japanese animation as 'events'. In theory, repeat viewing was possible at cinemas through the purchase of another ticket, but for many anime viewers, particularly on TV, an anime was a one-time appointment. On TV, its 'artistic heritage' was often transient, creating expectations for recurring plots or dramatic rituals that would be revisited seven days later, or experienced in colour at a cinema during the next school vacation. Moreover, rose-tinted memories cause cartoons watched in childhood to be remembered as magical, golden experiences – a useful fiction that has fed the modern retail industry in childhood favourites, but also led to much disappointment when old shows are held up to modern scrutiny, or remade by over-enthusiastic former fans, now grown up and turned into producers.

As Timo Linsenmaier (2008: 4) has argued, it is vital to consider animated texts in context. A propaganda movie loses much of its impact when considered outside the interpretative frame in which the propaganda was deemed necessary. Our experience, as contemporary, foreign viewers, of the reception of anime, will always be compromised – the original Japanese implied viewer becomes a narratee, the person to whom the original text was narrated, but not necessarily 'us', the new viewer. In much the same way as Klinger characterised modes of viewing in *Beyond the Multiplex: Cinema, New Technologies and the Home* (2006), anime viewed on a Blu-ray, at the viewer's discretion, without commercial breaks or sponsorship announcements, stoppable and repeatable at will with optional hypertexts, is not the way that anime was consumed for the bulk of its initial appearances. In the case of TV cartoons, there is a world of difference between, for example, an eighteen-year-old American downloader in 2013, who torrents an entire anime series, fast-forwards through the credits and binges an entire season in a single evening, and a seven-year-old Japanese child in 1975, experiencing a single much-anticipated viewing, one episode a week, with no recourse to review or repeat, scattered with exhortations to buy the toys and lunch-box tie-ins, possibly with occasional interruptions by a mewling sibling or distracted parent.

Nor is it always correct to regard the Western viewer as the final viewer. Some anime are deliberately premiered abroad for promotional purposes, in order to increase the chances that the eventual Japanese release can begin with notifications of European film festival awards, or DVD extras that show footage of foreign fans. Beyond the obvious marketing strategy, we might also see the ghost of auto-orientalism, as a Japanese film company seeks overseas validation in order to imply global success. But this, too, adds an intriguing eddy to the oscillations of watcher and watched – some foreign filmgoers are encouraged to give a new 'performance', that of an enthusiastic reception, that forms an integral metatext to an anime on its eventual Japanese release.

ANNALS, CHRONICLES AND DATA FILES

The historiography of Japanese animation begins with quantitative data – lists of cartoons as theatrical events or as retail objects. Although Japanese works on anime rarely have an index, many include a timeline that might be said to comprise the most basic possible structure of anime history (e.g. Tsugata 2005: 239–53). These timelines might be termed 'annalistic', for their resemblance to the year-by-year chronologies of important events to be found in Chinese dynastic histories or similar medieval European documents. However, as noted by Hayden White in *The Content of the Form: Narrative Discourse and Historical Representation* (1987: 6–7) even the simple assembly of names and dates in such annals creates an implied narrative, and an implied editorialisation on the part of the compiler.

Compilers of annals are also obliged, by the simple constraints of space, to list only those events that they deem to be of major importance. Inevitably, this becomes a matter of seeking out the 'first' of any new development – the first cel-based cartoon, the first talkie, the first stereo mix, the first episode of a new show – creating in turn 'an ahistorical debate that never confronts the "why" of its development' (Standish 2005: 25). Fixation on the 'first' in any form or content is often less instructive then a general sense of its 'trended change' – which is to say as part of an overall transformation of practices and conditions, generally in answer to shifts in technology or market perceptions.

White identifies a second, more detailed form of historical chronology, which he calls the 'chronicle'. In expanding the basic data of the annalistic form, perhaps by running congruent timelines of domestic and foreign developments, or occasional editorial asides, the chronicle form 'often seems to wish to tell a story, aspires to narrativity, but … usually is marked by a failure to achieve narrative closure' (White 1987: 5). The most influential and enduring form of such chronicles in the anime world is the two-volume *The Art of Japanese Animation* (Animage 1988, 1989) which aimed to present a year-by-year, and work-by-work, account of the entire Japanese animation world, from 1917 to 1988. *The Art of Japanese Animation* books contain just enough synopsis and analysis to qualify as a cusp of qualitative rather than quantitative data and, and were also illustrated with a single image for each entry, allowing a more immediate appreciation of issues of colour, style or characterisation, even for researchers who could not read Japanese.

A chronicle that lists not only the films, but also the names of the people that worked on them, allows the reader to build up a picture of entire careers, as revealed by the simple recurrence of certain names. Long out of print and out of date, the two books were nevertheless a huge influence, and their shadows can be glimpsed in much subsequent research.

Other chronicles offer new avenues for appraising the anime industry. Some depict each TV series as an independent timeline, allowing readers to immediately assess which shows were enjoying their first runs concurrently (e.g. Yamaguchi 2004: 212–23). However, there appears to be no account which currently also includes second-runs, syndications and other repeats, which substantially increase the amount of anime available to a hypothetical viewer on any given day.

Still other chronicles contrast anime 'firsts' with developments in animation outside Japan, and also with other world events that may throw some light on the surrounding zeitgeist. Most remarkable among these is a thirty-five-page effort by Tsugata Nobuyuki (2004: 206–41), which lists anime achievements alongside concurrent 'events' including, but not limited to, the rise of the miniskirt, the handover of Okinawa, several plane crashes, the rise of the Internet game, the fall of Saigon and the reunification of East and West Germany. His inclusions might initially seem little more than a frivolous exercise in local colour, but each of them has echoes and resonances in anime itself in everything from tropes to content. Of course, this is precisely what White means when he speaks of 'implied editorialisation'. In deciding to record miniskirt fashion as the sole noteworthy world event in 1967, Tsugata not only accords it equivalent weight to, say, Adolf Hitler's rise to power in 1933, but also implies a teleological focus that this event is a signifier with some meaning for the study of anime. All readers bring their own subjectivities – we might observe that the miniskirt seems to have reached Japan rather late, some three years after it was first named in London by Mary Quant, which tells us something about Japan's position regarding global fashions. Or we might speculate that the appearance of such a high hemline may have made some small contribution to glimpses of girls' underwear in subsequent anime, and hence an influence to some degree on the nascent field of 'fan service', that would come to dominate many anime genres in the twenty-first century. However, Tsugata offers no annotations on his choices – instead they read more like his notes for another book. Tsugata's assembly of his chronology invites discourse, in the sense that it invites consideration of his motivations and inferences; such chronologies are merely the opening phrases of an ongoing conversation about the nature of both content and form.

MAGAZINES, DATA FILES AND DATABASES

The primary sources used to construct the first two editions of *The Anime Encyclopedia* (Clements and McCarthy 2006: 755–6) included several large Japanese film reference listings, including the VHS and laserdisc-centred *Animesoft Kanzen Catalogue* (Takefuji 1993) and the DVD-based *Anime DVD Kanzen Catalogue* (Inoue 2000a). These works were distilled into a 3,000-line spreadsheet that could be sorted by titles, year or location of further information, itself the basis for the 900-page book, which offered a substantial sense of the breadth of the anime medium. While these materials afforded unprecedented access to details of Japanese animation, they were, by definition, restricted to works that had been released on formats that could be rented or purchased by general consumers.

It was only with the second edition of *The Anime Encyclopedia* that its authors began to add entries on films that had been lost or only privately screened, using materials such as the appendices on obscure or unexhibited works in *The Art of Japanese Animation II* (Animage 1989: 137–42). Such considerations led to the addition of important animators such as Kawamoto Kihachirō (Clements and McCarthy 2006: 328–9, 334–5) whose short festival films had fallen through the cracks in earlier methodology. Such a belated inclusion demonstrates the likelihood of recurring issues of nescience in our understanding of anime, born in part from the limitations of the source material. By understanding the types of source material available, we can armour ourselves to some extent against further errors of practice.

Japanese film magazines, particularly after the publication of *Kinema Junpō* (*Cinema Fortnightly Bulletin* or the *Movie Times*) in 1919, established enduring journals of record in which some indication might arise of the progress and reception of animated films in Japan. However, many of the earliest publications can be infuriatingly vague, neglecting to mention staff and even misremembering titles (Tsugata 2007a: 102–3), particularly for those many animated films that did not fit a publication's aesthetic sense of what a film should be – narrative, fictional, shown to paying audiences. As noted by Okada Emiko (Animage 1989: 144), this attitude persisted through to the ninety-minute mixed-genre programmes introduced in the 1930s and a part of Japanese media for the next three decades:

> The problem was that the titles of animation films shown were not published. And how unfriendly, surly and unsympathetic they were when I enquired by telephone! [The theatre managers] did not even know the *titles* of the pieces shown back then.

The historiography in periodicals of Japanese animation as anything other than a subset of Japanese film was sparse before 1977, the year that saw the appearance of *OUT*, the first of several subculture magazines that accorded ample column inches to animation (Komaki 2009: 10). Although *OUT* folded in 1995, its many successors, particularly *Animage* (founded 1978) and *Newtype* (founded 1985) have performed a dual function, appealing to general readers with their glossy full-colour spreads, but consistently filling their cheaper monochrome sections with interviews and hard data; many of the memoirs and testimonials in the bibliography of this book began as serialised columns in such magazines. Both *Animage* and *Newtype* excel at statistical compilations of names, dates, facts and figures, occasionally republished in book form. They form much of the basis of the large anime encyclopedias and guides, which in turn have been plundered for many contemporary online sources, both in Japanese and other languages.

During the 1980s and 1990s, both *Newtype* and *Animage* periodically republished inhouse databases as bonus booklets included with certain annual round-up issues, originally as part of a special giveaway diary – the *Newtype* chronicles titled variously as the *Animationary* or *Almanac*, and the *Animage* version as the *Pocket Data Notes*. Although credited to the editorial staff, many of these 'data files' are the work of a group of researchers who are responsible for much contemporary descriptive design of anime productions – including Haraguchi Masanobu, Oguro Yuichirō and Watanabe Yasushi. Their work has provided a firm, empirical foundation for any later scholars attempting to establish a historical account of Japanese animation (e.g. Tsugata 2005; Tsuji 2008).

Both these forms seemed to fade at the turn of the twenty-first century, as online sources overtook them, although simple migration online is no proof of better data. Far from it, as Megill (2007: 213–14) notes:

> The most insidious, yet at the same time often unremarked, feature of the communication and information technologies that are increasingly dominating our world is how they foster the illusion that the whole of reality is either displayed before us right now, or *could* be displayed before us, if the reach of the technologies and our connectedness to them were only slightly better than they are at this moment.

Online data enclosures such as the Japanese Movie Data Base (JMDB) and the Agency of Cultural Affairs Japanese Cinema Database (Bunkachō Nihon Eiga Jōhō System, or JCD for short) often offer flexible opportunities for hunting down recurring staff or obscure titles. The JCD in particular, although it can be infuriatingly exacting in its demands for input search parameters, can be readily customised, first to show only works tagged as 'Animation', and then to order them chronologically, creating some seventy-five pages of data, each in turn expandable to individual pages on specific films.

There is one notable print successor to the *Newtype* and *Animage* books, which itself draws upon their online descendants at the 'allcinema' database. This, the largest and most comprehensive of all print compendia, is the 1,000-page *Anime Sakuhin Jiten* (Stingray and Nichigai Associates 2010), often referred to by its editors' preferred English title *Dictionary of Animation Works*, or the abbreviation DAW. However, the *Dictionary of Animation Works* is primarily concerned with the relationship of cartoons to their source material, and hence directs much of its scholarly efforts towards listing original novels, plays and comics, rather than further details of the cartoons that they inspire. Conversely, it also includes animation in Japan at the level of access rather than production – which is to say, it handily encompasses foreign cartoons that have been distributed in Japan, giving their Japanese titles and release details.

A reader might be forgiven for thinking that the massive chronological appendix in the *Dictionary of Animation Works* would be the ultimate, all-inclusive chronicle of animation in Japan, stretching from 1917 to 2009 (Stingray and Nichigai Associates 2010: 891–955). But, of course, it is not all-inclusive by any means – it does not acknowledge the existence of an animated film unless a film has been completed and seen, and hence ignores, for example, many films made during the Occupation era but not publicly screened. Conversely, the JCD, surpassing the terms of its own mission statement, includes entries for dozens of films that are not only lost, but were only ever seen by a tiny audience of military personnel (Clements and Ip 2012). Despite this, like all publications of any kind, it is never quite complete, and continues to frustrate the user with glaring omissions either in inclusion, or in the tagging that makes inclusions apparent and accessible.

STUDIO HISTORIES AND STAFF NARRATIVES

A 'grand narrative', writes Megill (2007: 162), is 'the story the world would tell, if the world could tell its story'.[3] This is, of course, an impossibility, like a 1:1 scale map, a theoretical absolute that no sane investigator can hope to attain. There is always another angle or additional consideration; admitting this is something Megill (2007: 163) regards as 'epistemologically responsible'.

At the turn of the twenty-first century, several Japanese publishers began producing detailed, large-format studio histories and filmographies for many of the major players in the anime business (e.g. Sunrise 1997; Tokyo Movie Shinsha 1999; Tatsunoko 1999; Nippon Animation 2001). The studios themselves are credited as the 'authors' of these books, often bearing the subtitle of 'data files' or 'complete works', and all heavily illustrated to an extent that would have been impossible without full studio sanction. We might call these 'the stories that the [studios] would tell, if the [studios] could tell [their] story', but to do so would be to assume that corporations are any less performative, subjective or nescient than their employees – beyond the demands of selling *a* story, not *the* story, they lack Megill's 'epistemological responsibility'. Such books provide valuable data about staff lists and broadcast times, but also give a performance that is predictably self-serving and relentlessly positive – an analogue to some extent of the 'publication bias' of scientific scholarship, where successful experiments are far more likely to be written up than failures. Moreover, these books are fan-centred, visually oriented and domestically focused. They parse 'anime' as the *medium* that Japanese viewers see on domestic TV sets, forgetting the many works for hire for foreign clients that constitute much below-the-line revenue in the anime *industry*. Even as master narratives of each studio, such books omit large parts of the picture.

The Animation Filmography of Osamu Tezuka (Tezuka Productions 1991), for example, has the appearance of a history of the sister studios Mushi Pro and Tezuka Pro, but is actually a *commemoration* of Tezuka himself. As a result, it is biased towards anime based on Tezuka's works, and neglects to mention, for example, the significant involvement of his company in the 'American' cartoon *Frosty the Snowman* (1969). In other cases, such omissions are *aesthetic* or concerned with a studio's inner *tradition* – Tokyo Movie Shinsha, for example, does not benefit from mentioning its involvement in the 'French' cartoon *Ulysses 31* (1981), and hence confines it to a brief note in the cheaper monochrome pages of its own history (Tokyo Movie Shinsha 1999: 152), saving the more appealing colour sections for works on which the studio can still turn a profit in contemporary sales and merchandise.

If lists of anime events and objects identify the edifice of Japanese animation, then the words of the production staff are its 'enunciative modalities', allowing us in turn to form the concepts and strategies of anime history as a whole. But we should remember that these participants may still be unreliable witnesses. Since this book is particularly interested in participants *in* the anime industry, it is only natural that the bulk of the enquiry is directed at works by and about those same participants.

Although discussion of the anime world outside the perspective of animators, artists and directors is rare in the English-speaking world, there is a growing body of literature on the subject in Japanese. Books by screen-writers, for example, have long emphasised their own contribution to anime productions (e.g. Toriumi 1987; Tsuji 1996; Hoshiyama 2007; Ubukata 2009). Voice actors have become the default 'celebrities' of the anime world since the late 1970s, and while there are several detailed memoirs (e.g. Ikeda 2007; Furuya 2009), their testimonials are also a ubiquitous feature of monthly magazines. Some actors also graduate to production roles, such as Nomura Michiko (Oguro 2006: 112–26). It has been argued that much anime has been 'producer-led' since the 1950s (Takahashi 2011a: 56), and this has been supported by several producer memoirs and testimonies (e.g. Yamazaki 2005; Suzuki 2008b; Ishikawa 2009; Kinema Junpō 2011b). An intriguing recent trend articulates the anime industry from an economics or management perspective (e.g. Funamoto 1998; Tada 2002; Masuda 2007; Masuda 2011) and even through the changing nature of training practices and edu-cational outreach (Murasawa 2011), from the early need to mentor staff, to modern attempts to monetise the teaching of animation itself. There have also been steps towards the self-commemoration of anime historiog-raphy, with such publications as the *Animage* twentieth-anniversary history (Animage 1998), or an editor's memoir of the magazine *Animec* (Komaki 2009).

But prolificacy is no guarantee of insight, and insight is no guarantee of prolificacy. Ōtsuka Yasuo, a man whose sole directorial credit was on a forgotten promotional cartoon for a dairy company, is not a name likely to be known to the average foreign viewer, even though his influence in the anime industry is profound and long-standing. As a witness to the early days of post-war animation, and a teacher and lead animator at Studio Ghibli, Ōtsuka is intimately involved with the anime world. Now published under the imprint of Studio Ghibli itself, his *Sakuga Asemamire* (2001, *Sweating over Animation*) is one of the prime sources for the history of 1960s and 1970s anime. He is also the author of one of the best books about the anime industry, concerned largely with a film that does not exist. Otsuka's meticulous *Little Nemo no Yabō* (2004, *The Prospect of Little Nemo*) treats the 1989 release of the troubled animated feature *Little Nemo* as a non-event, preferring instead to track the complex paths of production of the film it could have been, through roads not taken, failed pilots, abortive directions and departed staff.

There are other influential figures whose lack of published memoirs renders them shadowy – Yabushita Taiji is only mentioned in others' writings; Nishizaki Yoshinobu is rarely seen at all, largely because of the legalities and gag orders surrounding his prolonged court battle with Matsumoto Leiji. Tezuka Osamu is seen everywhere, in multiple autobiographies and biographies, theoretical discussions, hagiographies and polemics. And yet Yokoyama Ryūichi, who beat Tezuka to the airwaves with the first anime TV series, hardly mentions animation at all in his own autobiography. Depicted by others as a daffy but loveable dilettante, Yokoyama's memoirs treat his animation work as subsidiary to his true vocation as a manga artist, although as explored in Chapter 4, this tells us more about Yokoyama's feelings at the time he wrote his memoirs than at the time he set up the company, when he had appreciably higher hopes. What little commentary Yokoyama does pro-vide is often contradicted by more exacting accounts from other witnesses. For more rigorous details of Yokoyama's rise and fall in animation, a paradigm that foreshadowed Tezuka's in many ways, we must instead turn to books written by his former colleagues – a dismissive aside by Mochinaga Tadahito, for example, or the fond recollections of Suzuki Shinichi, whose own, modest memoirs include a substantial account of life at Yokoyama's studio Otogi Pro (Mochinaga 2006: 100; Suzuki 2008a: 107–37).

Aside from studio histories, biographies or data files, the most solidly academic enquiry into anime in the twen-tieth century was a collection (Misono 1999) that attempted to establish a grounding in the history of television anime, recognising in the process the importance of 1950s cinema features for the prehistory of TV. A decade later, particularly after the conferral of Miyazaki Hayao's Oscar, and the realisation that anime, a subaltern sector of the Japanese media, was the nexus of a global business worth $6.59 billion per year (Kataoka 2011: 152), there was a rush of new scholarship in volume form. *Animation no Eiga-gaku [Animation Film Studies]* (Katō 2009) was concerned with all animation, only focusing on Japanese animation for a few chapters. The later *Anime-gaku [Anime Studies]* (Takahashi and Tsugata 2011), represents the first broadly successful attempt to discursively construct 'anime studies' as an object of knowledge, delineating Japanese animation as a field of academic enquiry in and of itself, rather than as a subset of film, business, culture, media or any other discipline.

There have also been several interview collections designed as preliminary oral histories of anime (e.g. Oguro 2006; Kanō 2004) in which the animators are enjoined to speak for themselves. Notably, it is the animators who are usually sought in such enterprises, which is to say directors or key artists; other members of creative staff, such as screenwriters or producers, are rarely approached, although there are exceptions (e.g. Oguro 2006: 282–97). There is an issue here of commemoration and nescience – it is rare indeed that we find a publication like *Gainax Interviews* (Hotta 2005), which diligently documents not only the celebrity creatives at a studio, but some below-the-line business managers and production coordinators.

Academic enquiry into anime occasionally arises in film, animation and media journals, although the first port of call for the Japanese-reading researcher is liable to be *Animation Kenkyū* (the *Japanese Journal of Animation Studies*), published annually by the Japan Society of Animation Studies. However, as the names of both publication and institution imply, *Japanese* animation is not the prime field of enquiry, but rather the investigation of animation by Japanese scholars. Hence, the journal has been rather less use for an enquiry of this nature than one might hope, particularly since its most prominent contributors, such as Tsugata Nobuyuki, have already republished some of their best research in improved volume form. For a dedicated journal about Japanese animation, one must look instead to the Anglophone world, in *Mechademia: An Annual Forum for Anime, Manga and the Fan Arts*.

The context and receptions of the publication of Kurosawa *et al.*'s *Anime wa Ekkyō suru* (2010, *Anime in Transition*), may turn out to be more important than its actual content. The book comprises one volume in the publisher Iwanami Shoten's series *Nihon Eiga wa Ikiteiru* (*Japanese Film Is Alive*), and its inclusion alongside seven companion studies on topics such as documentary or the director's art is a provocative, proportional statement about the modern relevance of animation to Japanese media and film studies. Moreover, five of the book's eleven chapters are by foreign scholars, suggesting that American, Korean and Chinese researchers still seem more willing to embrace Japanese animation as a worthy subject of enquiry. Arguably, this points to a sense of auto-orientalism, in which Japanese editors appeal to external authorities for validation of their own research interests in what some might still regard as an unworthy field of study. However, Murasawa Masataka suggests (2011: 294) that some Japanese scholars may even be discouraged by the aesthetic or performative quality of the subject title on their resumés, reluctant to select the simplistic, even childish term アニメ 'anime' on course applications, when compared to the more classically invested, academically persuasive titles such as 映画学 'film studies'. He also notes (2011: 302–3) the inherent impracticality of 'anime studies' as a discipline; studios place greater value on industrial training than on academic qualification, and hence do not encourage or necessarily reward scholarly enquiry.

SOURCES AS PERFORMANCE

Why do the makers of anime discuss the making of anime? In a keynote speech, 'Performance in and of Animation' at the Society for Animation Studies Conference, Glendale, California (2002), Donald Crafton suggested that historians of animation should consider issues of 'performativity', not only within the texts themselves, but within the presentation of self by the participants and studios.[4] This was seized upon by Hu Tze-yue (2010: 85) as an idea that could be applied to studies of films in production.

> Crafton narrows it down to two essential prepositional properties of classical animation, distinguishing **performance *in* animation** as 'performances represented by artist animators,' and **performance *of* animation** as 'the practice of creating animated film'. (my emphasis in bold)

The Phantom Ship (1956) begins not with animation, but with the animator

Hu applies these categories specifically to the production of Tōei's *Hakujaden* (1958, *Panda and the Magic Serpent* a.k.a. *Panda and the Magic Serpent*),[5] but they can be mapped onto many parts of the Japanese animation industry. Just as Walt Disney became a metatextual live-action character in some of his own cartoons, playing the avuncular inventor demonstrating his newest characters and contraptions, Japanese animators can become performers in and of their own work. Ōfuji Noburo's *Yūreisen* (1956, *The Phantom Ship*) begins with a shot of the artist's hands at work, cutting the cellophane that will form the basis of the first animated image. It can be argued, as Crafton or Hu would have it, that the performance begins with the animator's presence, just as much part of the film as the supposed 'opening shot' that follows of a ship at sail. The decision to include the sight of Ōfuji at work is a creative one, and possibly also a promotional one – a reminder to the audience that what they are seeing has been painstakingly constructed by hand, and they should savour not only the content, but also its form.

In pointing to the degree to which a source can itself be a 'performance', Crafton and Hu were siting their work within what Peter Burke (2008: 97) has called 'the rise of *occasionalism*' – his term for the study of cultural history through participation in events and rituals, including the consumption of texts and self-identification within communities of fans. Itself drawing on Erving Goffman's *Presentation of Self in Everyday Life* (1959), and alluding to several more recent authors who have focused on acts of identity and performances of consensus, Burke's concept offers rich potential for the visualisation of the anime industry as an all-inclusive community of participants in every stage on the chain of ownership and access (see figure on p. 6), each demonstrating a 'flexible response' to different situations, and each giving a performance of their own (see also Burke 2005: 49; Nagayama 2012).

Sometimes, these performances take the form of a literal, textual appearance, in the manner of Winsor McCay's participation in *Gertie the Dinosaur* (1914) or Walt Disney's introductions – such as the stilted, stiffly formal address by Ōkawa Hiroshi that begins the trailer for *Hakujaden*, or the demonstration of animation processes by Ōfuji Noburō in *Shikisai Manga no Dekiru Made* (1937, *How to Make Colour Cartoons*).[6] This, it seems, was only one of an entire subgenre of *Making of …* films about Japanese animation. PCL valorised its output with Ōishi Ikuo's ten-minute hybrid animation/live-action film, *Talkie no Hanashi* (1936, *The Story of the Talkie*).[7] Kimura Hakusan's *Hassei Manga no Dekiru Made* (1940, *To Make a Talking Cartoon*)[8] similarly combined live action and animation in a film about the making of an animated film. These performances of production continued after the war with Nichiei's *Manga-Eiga no Dekiru Made* (1951, *To Make a Cartoon Film*) and an identically titled two-reel film made by Tōei Dōga in 1959. Since the advent of video, *Making of …* featurettes have become a common component of press kits and DVD extras – often, the former is repurposed to create the latter.

Such performances are often part of the marketing machine that accompanies an animated text, or a director's appearance at public events and in interviews. Nor are they necessarily dependable representations of the performer's actual contribution – Max Fleischer played the role of the animator in *Out of the Inkwell* (1918), although the actual animation was done by his off-camera brother Dave (Crafton 1982: 298).

As Hu suggests, there are many kinds of 'performance' connected to a film, including the image that the studio wishes to present, the public face of the film-makers, the private attitude of the staff, and the implied audience for the work itself. We can see such performances in many aspects of the Japanese animation industry, from the claims of one company to be 'fan-friendly', to the claims of another to be responding to audience demands, to the assertions made by marketing men about the intent or success of the artists' aims. The very nature of the entertainment business encourages a performative component in interactions with the media. Press releases push 'unique' selling points that are not really unique; *Making of …* documentaries breathlessly insist that a longstanding production technique has been invented especially for a certain film, essentially claiming a false 'first' to add to a work's artistic heritage. The best journalists will always question the nature of the narrative they are being fed to bulk out their news items – the less skilled, less committed journalists simply parrot the party line.

There are other elements behind the scenes. The late Kon Satoshi once granted an interview to a researcher studying his work, but only after the payment of a ¥50,000 fee. Another famous director, still living, once spoke forthrightly to an interviewer about the anime business, only for 'his people' to insist later that he had not said things already caught on tape. Anime audiences, and, indirectly, later academic researchers, are often shielded from such intrigues, but also unaware of the influence they might have on the information that is then imparted.

And, of course, such performances carry over into written accounts of the animation business – there are scores to be settled, axes to be ground, boasts to be made and colleagues to be thanked. Was the guest on the festival podium an actual participant in the creation of the work on display, or simply the fastest runner in the marketing department when the offer of a ticket to a foreign festival came up? In fact, such 'performance' might often be the catalyst for many of Megill's bugbears in 'evading history' – commemorating the wrong participants; simply forgetting crucial staffers (i.e. nescience); singling out only the tradition of one's in-group, or concentrating only on the aesthesis of stirring stories or studio-approved anecdotes.

Drawing on Hayden White's *Metahistory* (1973), Thomas Postlewait argues (2009: 98) that historians of the performing arts often face a temptation towards a 'mode of emplotment', mapping a particular narrative style onto the story they decide to tell. We must be watchful for the anime narrative that decides to tell the entire story in a single mode that might elbow information aside if it inconveniently breaks the spell. Sometimes, this is rather obvious, as in the case of Ōwada Hideki's tongue-in-cheek manga dramatisation of the creation of the *Gundam* series, *Gundam Sōsei* (2009, *The Genesis of Gundam*), which openly tells outrageous lies about the development of the TV show for satirical effect. In other cases, it might be understandably tactful, such as when a eulogy to a dead animator only mentions his successes.

When Mori Yasuji (1984: 151) coins the medical condition of 'Anime Syndrome', we might perceive a desperate, noble call for mercy from over-worked animators who risk ruining their health for the sake of industry deadlines. And yet, awash with industry testimonials about late nights, sleeping at desks and frayed nerves at studios with impossible deadlines, how should we process the revelation that staff at one well-known studio were observed playing mah-jong for three weeks of every month, before dashing off their allotted episode of *Astro Boy* in the remaining handful of days before it was due (Ishiguro and Ohara 1980: 104)? Is the appearance of hard work itself merely another facet of performance? There is, after all, no narrative force or attention-grabbing drama in a production diary that reads: 'We had the right amount of time to do it all, and finished nicely on schedule.'

If possible narratives *in* anime can be 'emplotted' as romance, tragedy, comedy or satire, then narratives *of* the anime industry can similarly fall into these modes. Furthermore, 'performance' can be considered as a locus where Megill's problems of historical practice arise as immediate, contemporary issues, not in what *has* happened, but in what is happening right now. Today's reportage and interviews are, after all, tomorrow's testimonials, and will form the basic materials of future historiography. When a new magazine article or website gushes about a 'groundbreaking new anime' or slates 'the worst anime ever', to offer two admitted extremes, Megill's historical issues are nascent and manifest in the present moment. Nescience and memory, tradition and commemoration each exercises unseen influences on what is reported about contemporary events. Such issues of practice can affect the comprehension of the reporter who forgets a director's name; they drag down the value of the journalist who does not know what questions she should be asking; they can compromise the integrity of academic research that is ignorant of production processes and influences.

Writers perform in collaboration with their readers, in private, often unspoken agreements that the topic under discussion is something about which both are enthusiastic, or should be. It is an acknowledged truth that industry personnel give interviews as part of the promotional process for their film; a media interview's primary purpose is to *sell* a film to audiences, and this will assuredly skew the information imparted. Moreover, journalists have their own agendas; they are rarely neutral chroniclers, but active agents in the presentation of their subjects. Their interviewee is a genius whose every word is sacrosanct and infallible; the film under review is a disaster of epic proportions, made by a bunch of obvious idiots – such claims, and the myriad variations of approval and disapproval that lie between them, can amount to a 'mode of emplotment', not in a historian's treatment of the sources, but in the original sources themselves. Historians themselves, in collating material on past events, become 'witnesses' whose testimonies may be used by other researchers, and who may themselves skew later interpretations of those same events (Postlewait 2009: 269). Such issues can exert influences on the material over which academics later pick and scuffle.

Moreover, the writer is usually presenting an entirely separate performance – that of the clever writer. Here is an exchange originally in Japanese between the director Hayashi Shigeyuki (generally known simply as Rintarō) and the anime historian Oguro Yūichirō, who is interviewing him:

RINTARŌ: *Astro Boy*'s … first episode went on air on the 3rd January, didn't it?
OGURO: I think it was New Year's Day.
RINTARŌ: No, it was something like the 3rd, surely?
OGURO: It *was* New Year's Day.
RINTARŌ: New Year's Day? But if I remember rightly, Tezuka-san was still saying around the 30th
December that he 'wanted another shot at the audio' …

(Oguro *et al.* 2009: 34)

Here we see the dual elements of performance and historical memory in contention. Rintarō is giving a long interview for a book that bears his name, dedicated to his life's work, and bearing the brand of Madhouse, the studio he co-founded. The Japanese being spoken on both sides is carefully nuanced, with Rintarō implying he is unsure of his initial pronouncement, and Oguro, the interviewer, offering him a gentle escape route by pretending not to be sure himself. It is only when Rintarō shows signs of clinging to the erroneous date that Oguro pulls out the big guns, and says categorically: '*Gantan desu yo*' (It *was* New Year's Day).

This is an odd exchange to leave in a book. Editorially, it pulls focus away from the nominal subject, Rintarō, into an assertion that Oguro knows the story better than the man he is interviewing. As Oguro is the editor of the book in which the interview appears, his decision to include the exchange might seem boastful and self-serving. However, Oguro might have included this exchange as an oblique assertion of narrative and editorial reliability; it demonstrates that in the event Rintarō makes an error, we can be sure that our well-informed interviewer will flag it for us. In other words, he shows us this error almost happening, in order to reassure us that others will not.

Oguro may also have decided to leave in the exchange in order to humanise his subject. The interview with Rintarō covers his whole life and takes up over 100 pages – around half the book, in fact – and it could be a perfectly understandable decision to include slips, false starts and little eddies of conversation in order to impart yet another performance – inserting the reader into the conversation itself, as if one is having a friendly chat with a goodnatured celebrity. This, too, is a performance, and if it is Oguro's intention, it cleverly dramatises what might otherwise be a long chronicle of names and dates.

We value Rintarō's testimony, but we must check it against quantitative data – as Oguro does here, by stating outright that the first episode of *Astro Boy* was broadcast on 1 January, as indeed it was. We concede that both Rintarō and Oguro may be involved in their own performances, but we look beyond that to the details most pertinent to a history of Japanese animation.

MEMOIRS AND TESTIMONIALS

Such shortcomings in personal accounts lead us to consider the faults of a testimonial, which is to say a first-person, subjective account of certain events by a participant in them. Most accounts cited in this study come from participants in the anime industry; only a few from scholars, critics or figures from other sectors. As a result, we must read such texts with the understanding that the authors have an inimitable grasp of immediate events and situations, but possibly not of their relationship to the broader world of anime. Many works cited are memoirs, which is to say, recollections of parts of a subject's own life, framed in hindsight by the later relevance of the events described. A smaller subset are autobiographies, in which the anime industry forms part of an individual's account of their entire life – in particular, many manga artists are apt to recount their dabblings in the anime industry in brief, but only as a chapter or an appendix to a life focused on other matters. Interviews, particularly those conducted during a production or as part of its marketing, are better described as testimonial, as they lack the opportunities presented by hindsight to refashion and reframe a subject's recollections, for good or ill. It seems sensible to also file press junket interviews, when a subject is merely hyping their newest work, as testimonial in nature, as biased arguments for the value of a particular text.

Even if a production interview is conducted after a film is completed, it cannot treat the 'story' of the event it describes in its entirety. Of course, the very nature of a memoir makes it more likely for an author to deal with matters of reception or heritage, but it is still likely to be skewed by the author's desire to validate his or her own memory.

As with American accounts of Disney and his successors, many media personae have a performative element that must be weighed and assessed. Tezuka Osamu was ever the driven genius, and presented himself as such to his readers and staff. Two decades after his death, the executors of his estate at Tezuka Pro keep his memory alive with remakes and reappraisals that have been so successful that some observers assume that Tezuka invented anime. This rather ignores the contribution that many of Tezuka's staff surely made to the style that came to be known as 'his' alone (Tsugata 2007b: 234), or indeed the opprobrium heaped upon Tezuka by many industry veterans in the 1960s, who held him responsible for a decline in industry standards in order to accommodate the demands of TV broadcasting (Miyazaki 2009: 193–7; Ōtsuka 2001: 96).

Meanwhile, Tomino Yoshiyuki, whose work in the anime business spans six decades beginning with *Astro Boy*, frequently embraces his reputation as *Minnagoroshi* Tomino ('Kill 'em All' Tomino), playing up to his persona as a crotchety ogre in magazine columns on the anime business, and requiring the researcher to repeatedly question how far his tongue is in his cheek. Okada Toshio (2010: 243) likens early press interviews with Tomino to wartime propaganda, carefully redacting his more provocative or unwelcome statements, but also notes that more recent coverage invests Tomino with credibility in direct relation to his fluctuating media profile, as either visionary or delusional, depending on his current position in the ratings. Conversely, a full tenth of Tomino's memoir of *Gundam* is devoted to his loving adoration of his wife, subverting his usual image as a prickly tyrant (Tomino 2002: 239–76).

There are also issues of reliability. Sometimes this is a simple matter of facts and figures, such as when Rintarō is unable to remember the precise broadcast date of the first episode of *Astro Boy* (Oguro *et al.* 2009: 34). In this case, he is corrected by his interviewer, but such a moment serves to remind the researcher that interviewees can, and will make mistakes. They are not academics revising, rewriting and subjecting their every thought to peer review. They are often old folk trying to remember things that happened forty years ago. Errors can vary from simple slips of memory, to guesses masquerading as memory, to self-delusion to matters of true nescience – things about which the interviewee was ignorant both at the time of the events being recalled, and at the time at which the testimony is recorded.

Yamazaki Keishi, a minor figure at Tokyo Movie Shinsha whose role was often tediously managerial, nevertheless writes one of the most dramatic and informative accounts of the anime industry, leavened with amusing anecdotes and backstage gossip, and frequently backed by sales figures and TV ratings. However, when the otherwise dependable Yamazaki writes eloquently and persuasively of the origins of sports drama in anime (Yamazaki 2005: 92), he is seemingly unaware that he is repeating a paradigm already established in the 1920s (Wada-Marciano 2008: 63). Similarly, he offers a detailed account of the origin of the groundbreaking visual style of *Star of the Giants*, relying on references to script conferences and planning logistics (Yamazaki 2005: 100–1), a story contradicted elsewhere in favour of an impetus from the animators themselves (Hikawa 1999: 189–91). Such testimonial flaws present two problems: there is firstly the epistemological issue that merely by being present for the production, Yamazaki is not automatically an expert about its every inspiration and implication. But there is also the phenomenological issue, that Yamazaki is crucial to our understanding of the production; even if his view is mistaken, it can nonetheless be an accurate reflection of what his production staff believed to be true at the time. It is a subjective truth, but not a historical one (Denzin 1989: 23).

Similarly, Yamamoto Eiichi, whose industry account is peppered with verifiable facts, still occasionally suffers from an understandable degree of subjectivity, brought on by the intense pressures of working at Mushi Pro. He notes the arrival of *Sennin Buraku* (1963, *Village of the Immortals*), which he calls the 'second TV anime series', inadvertently assuming that *Astro Boy* was the first, and forgetting entirely not only the existence of Yokoyama Ryūichi's earlier *Otogi Manga Calendar* (1962) (Yamamoto 1989: 123) but also the stop-motion animation prepared for export by Mochinaga Tadahito (Minakawa 2009b: 225). Moreover, Yamamoto presents his entire account as a 'fictional truth', only revealing at the very end of the book that his memories of the anime business are intended as repetitions of facts, and that only his digressions into his personal life are fiction (Yamamoto 1989: 347).

Such is the nature of the multiple sources available to the researcher in Japanese animation historiography, and which may be brought to bear in an account of its ever-changing, ever-branching genealogy. In the earliest days of anime, particularly before 1923, very little survives of the texts themselves, leading us to begin only with their contexts, and the historical memory of their existence.

NOTES

1. Masuda (2007: 4) notes that the difference between complex creation/authorship and simple production/manufacture is often blurred in Japanese since the terms 制作 and 製作 are both pronounced *seisaku*.

2. In terms of anime's transnational distribution, translation and foreign-language audio tracks form a further level of intellectual property – it is sometimes a condition of the licence that these are forfeit to the Japanese licence holder at the end of the licence agreement, hence augmenting and improving the original owner's intellectual property.

3. Megill makes no mention of the anthropologist Clifford Geertz, but his phrasing seems deliberately evocative of 'the story they tell themselves about themselves', which is Geertz's summation of ritual performance in *The Interpretation of Cultures* (1973: 448).

4. Crafton had alluded to this before as a performance of 'self-figuration' (1984: 11, 347).

5. This film is more commonly known by its Japanese title so this will be used in the text.

6. JCD 34526 refers to *Katsura-hime* (1937, *Princess Katsura*), not the *Making of* that frames and contains it.

7. JCD 37841 – date supplied by the National Film Center, Tokyo, in the programme to its 2004 season of early Japanese cartoons.

8. JCD 37875 and Tsugata (2012: 36). The other two films mentioned are not in the JCD, but mentioned in the entry on the first.

1 KID DEKO'S NEW PICTURE BOOK

Early cartoons in Japan 1912–21

In December 2004, the researcher Matsumoto Natsuki stumbled across an antique box of movie paraphernalia in Japan's ancient capital of Kyoto. Among the camera parts, film canisters and other bits of junk, Matsumoto retrieved a small strip of 35mm film, comprising a mere fifty frames – just enough footage to splice into a loop. More crucially, the film contained images in red and black ink, drawn directly onto the celluloid.

If run through a projector at the early twentieth-century norm of sixteen frames per second, the scrap of film would last just under three seconds. The sequence of hand-drawn images would present an impressionistic, stylised but identifiable sequence: a boy in a beret, scrawling the words *Katsudō Shashin* (moving pictures) on a blackboard, and taking a bow (Matsumoto 2011a: 98). Scanned into a computer and looped on the Internet, it would eventually reach a worldwide audience far larger than any that could have conceivably seen it a century earlier.

The discovery of the Matsumoto Fragment was a contentious issue in the study of Japanese animation. Reported in the Japanese newspapers during the 'silly season' of summer 2005, its significance soon ballooned from a mere curio to a matter of politicised scandal. Matsumoto unwisely speculated that the fragment could be 'up to ten years older'[1] than the cartoon previously thought to be Japan's oldest, inadvertently leading the *Asahi Shinbun* to immediately assume that it had been made in 1907, and others to proclaim that the Matsumoto Fragment was even older (China Daily 2005). In the space of a few column inches, rehashing a press release at the height of summer when there was little other news worth reporting, journalists had inflated the story from that of a simple antique curio to a discovery that could rock the world of animation studies – suggesting that the medium of animated film itself might have been created in Japan.

Matsumoto never made such a claim. A few foreign anime magazines credulously repeated the hype, only for it to die down again. The nescience of the original reporters had allowed Japanese animation to briefly assert its own tradition as the original tradition, before it became clear that there was no evidence to back up the claims. The Matsumoto Fragment was old, certainly, but it could not be dated. It may not even have been screened, rendering it, to some, as less a film than a comic drawn on celluloid.

In the years since, Matsumoto has published a more detailed account of the context of his discovery. Most notable is a further description of the 'junk' amid which it was found – cardboard boxes containing toy magic-lantern kits from distant Europe, and intended for home use. The notion led Matsumoto to reconsider the rhetoric of previous 'firsts' and defining 'events' – yes, we can still hunt down the 'first' reported cartoon in Japan and the place of its first exhibition, but such a bias towards public exhibition ignores the possibility of a vibrant, unseen domestic culture of magic-lantern shows, and toys that produced animation in some other form (Matsumoto 2011a: 99–100).

It is difficult to discern an exact origin point for animation in the history of film. We might split hairs by pointing out that *all* film is animation, imparting the illusion of movement to images that are still when in their resting state – if this is the case, then the zoetrope and praxinoscope, alongside other Victorian curios, are themselves types of animation, and cinema itself is an outgrowth from this root.

Historians of pre-cinema similarly argue for the rise of the magic-lantern show as a precursor to true cartoons. Although its first arrival in Japan is unrecorded, examples certainly made it as far as China, where in the 1670s, the Italian Jesuit Claudio Filippo Grimaldi demonstrated a series of optic 'miracles' before the court of Kangxi, the Emperor of Hearty Prosperity (Mannoni 2000: 73).

Eventually, the technology of the magic lantern reached the isolated island nation of Japan, where the use of local materials and ingenuity transformed it from a simple picture show into something far more dynamic. Finding the European metal lanterns too weighty and unwieldy, Japanese practitioners made their own from more portable paulownia wood, which in turn made it easier for Japanese performances to incorporate motion (Koyama-Richard 2010: 54). The term in Japanese for a magic-lantern show varies from place to place, reflecting the itinerant nature of such performances. From the first appearance of magic-lantern shows or phantasmagoria in 1803 as *utsushi-e* ('reflected pictures') in the Edo (Tokyo) area, they were known in the Osaka region as *nishiki kage-e* ('brocade shadow pictures'), but in Shimane simply as *kage ninge* ('shadow puppets'). The materials deployed in magic-lantern shows were fragile in the extreme. Every wooden projector (or *furo*) required two lenses, and each magic-lantern plate (*tane-ita*) was painted onto the thinnest possible glass. Hence, very few artefacts have survived from the period – a gap of nescience that has led many historians to assume that Japanese cinemagoers had no frame of reference for watching pictures in the dark. But magic-lantern shows in Japan would often involve several practitioners darting behind the screen creating, in the words of the Minwa-za company director Yamagata Fumio, 'a real spectacle' (Koyama-Richard 2010: 54–5), with each lantern projecting a particular character, allowing them to appear to move and interact more like insubstantial puppets than projected slides. Nor were the magic lanterns confined to fairy tales or legends, since some were also employed for instructional purposes – commencing with their incorporation into anatomy lectures as early as 1877, but expanding by 1895 to spectacular military news events, complete with a narrator, choir and accompanying musicians, who would thrill Japanese audiences with tales from the Sino-Japanese War (Ōkubo 2011: 76, 87).

The screening of films in Japan throughout the so-called silent era coalesced around issues of a performative 'event', in which a master of ceremonies, the *benshi*, would string together the often disparate two- and three-minute reels of film with an ongoing patter of elucidation, humour and interpretation. Particularly in the earliest days of cinema in Japan, when the form of the new entertainment was just as exciting a prospect as the content, the *benshi* would begin by explaining how the technology of film projection actually worked. Only then would he move onto the content of the upcoming films, giving advance notice of the nature of the next film, including any warnings that might be required about fearful moments or incidents of odd foreign behaviour, such as kissing (Greenberg 2001: 7; Katō 2006: 211).[2]

Japan gained its first dedicated movie theatre, the Denki-kan (Electric Pavilion) in Asakusa, Tokyo in 1903 (Standish 2005: 18). Such an event is an important milestone in the development of early cinema, since the presence of 'fixed sites' (Elsaesser 1990: 161) suggests an immediate rise in demand for product to fill them. Although there were 300 Japanese movie houses by 1916, the vast majority of them were concentrated in the Tokyo and Osaka metropolises. The cinematic experience in the countryside remained in the hands of travelling shows that performed in tents. In all cases, the *benshi* was a critical conduit of meaning and entertainment. Intertitles were largely absent from Japanese film before 1920, rendering foreign works hard to follow without a live interpreter.

The *benshi* was hence more than a mere announcer or narrator, although he also performed those roles. He was the cinema's barker and town crier, its warm-up man and the literal interpreter of the film. To many audience members, the *benshi* was the star (Greenberg 2001: 8; Katō 2006: 214). A good *benshi* could send the audience home praising a spectacular night's entertainment, even if the films on show were little more than reel-ends and cast-offs; a bad one could turn the greatest of films into a dull evening out. There are stories of *benshi* in tuxedos and tails, adding a touch of class to the local picture house, and instilling a sense of occasion among moviegoers. There are photographs of *benshi* attired as the movie stars they are voicing, imparting an immediate, third-dimensional impact to the films they presented by dressing up as, say, Charlie Chaplin (Bernardi 2001: 101). When the inaugural issue of Japan's first film magazine *Katsudō Shashin Kai* (*Moving Picture World* or *The Cinematograph*) appeared in June 1909, it was a *benshi*, not a movie star, who graced the cover (Fujiki 2006: 68).

The *benshi* style pre-dated the moving pictures themselves. Similar narrators had long been a feature of Japanese puppet theatre, where onstage musicians accompanied a man who performed the voices of the characters. The term was also applied to the itinerant storytellers of the *kamishibai* (paper theatre), a tradition that persisted until the 1950s, who could set up their stands in streets and parks, and tell a story by slotting card pictures in and out of a frame like a proscenium arch, sometimes mounted on the back of a bicycle. The *kamishibai benshi*'s performance was supposedly free, but only children who bought sweets from him got to sit at the front (Nash 2009: 80).

The notion of a *benshi* was not foreign to Western audiences – before the rise of the intertitle in France around 1903, cinemas employed a *bonimenteur* to talk audiences through the 'silent' presentation.[3] Some of the earliest practitioners of film in America and Europe used it as part of a hybrid performative event, and promised 'prologue presentations' by live acts that ensured every time-slot would precisely fill the requisite two hours (Balio 1993: 27; Crafton 1997: 75–6).[4] Others made the film and live presentation symbiotically reliant upon each other. Perhaps the most famous of such hybrid performances was that of the cartoonist Winsor McCay, who presented a one-man show in which he acted the role of a dinosaur tamer. The part of Gertie the Dinosaur was 'performed' by a sequence of drawn images shown on film on a screen behind McCay. *Gertie the Dinosaur* in its original incarnation, was a 'vulnerable' text designed as part of Winsor McCay's vaudeville act. McCay himself would stand on stage and interact with Gertie in the manner of a lion-tamer, coaxing her into performing tricks, throwing her an apple and finally walking behind the screen and 'into' the picture, as a cartoon McCay that rode off on his dinosaur (Crafton 1982: 111). In Japanese terms, McCay functioned as a unique and exclusive *benshi*, presenting a film that originally could not exist without his personal presence.

McCay was prevented from presenting *Gertie* in its original intended form by a conflict-of-interest issue with his new employers at the Hearst Corporation, who wished to limit his public appearances. As a result, the edition of *Gertie* that has survived is a retooling of the original footage, with a newly filmed framing device in which McCay the eccentric artist wagers that he can make the dinosaur come to life. He is hence preserved as a performer of his own work, and the performance of his animation, the making animate of Gertie the Dinosaur, is part of the new story. In this reversioning of *Gertie the Dinosaur* (also 1914), the dinosaur animation takes up five minutes from a total running time of twelve (Crafton 1982: 117).

Such performance *in* and *of* animation has been a feature of the medium since its first appearances on film. In 1896, Georges Méliès, under the stage name of *le dessinateur express*, undercranked the camera that filmed him drawing caricatures of celebrities, in order to give the impression of 'lightning sketches'. A decade later, J. Stuart Blackton's *Lightning Sketches* (1907) presented Blackton himself at work before zooming in on the blackboard as the characters came to life (Crafton 1982: 50, 55). Animation in the West hence began as it did in Japan, with its origins obscured in the ferment of sideshows, vaudeville acts and 'trick films', as part of a cinema of attractions. Such trick films made their way to Japan during the very earliest days of cinema; the film historian Koga Futoshi has persuasively demonstrated that a 1903 poster for an event at the Kado-za theatre in Osaka, the *Tennen-shoku Katsudō Daishashin* (*Natural-coloured Moving Great Pictures*) bears Japanese artists' renditions of at least eight of Méliès' films stretching from *Le Livre magique* (1900) to *Les Trésors de Satin* (1902) (Koga 2011: 48–50).[5] A year later in 1904, the Kabuki-za, in competition with nearby picture houses that were showing reportage from the Russo-Japanese War, fought back with a gloriously eclectic selection of otherwise unidentified movie reels, including one called *The Haunted House in the Ruins of Napoleon's Palace* (Dobson 2005: 78). This may have been one of the many 'haunted house' trick films that had already flooded the European market. Although none of these films are 'animation' in the strict sense of drawn images given implied motion, several contain pixilation (time-lapse), stop-motion or visual effects that utilise elements of the process we now call animation.[6] In 1905, these films reappear alongside a number of identifiable later Méliès works in a Japanese catalogue of magic-lantern slides and moving-picture shows (Koga 2011: 57). Both appearances predate the establishment of Japan's first true film magazine, *Katsudō Shashin Kai* in 1909, and hence hail from a period lacking a journal of record that might document or confirm their actual contents.

In animation's first decade, it largely obscured its artifice. Blackton's *The Haunted Hotel* (1907) differed from numerous 'trick film' predecessors in presenting lingering close-ups of some of its pixilated hauntings, making it impossible for the audience to assume that standard live stagecraft tricks were being employed. Instead, they were left to ponder the nature of the special effects (Crafton 1982: 17). Even Blackton's *Humorous Phases of Funny Faces* (1906), one of the 'first' true animated films, seems to have sited itself within a preexisting magic-lantern tradition of 'humorous transformations' (Crafton 1982: 35).

But, as Crafton notes himself, audiences soon grew wise to such sleight of hand. The very possibility that film could be viewed repeatedly only increased the chances of its allure fading. Jokes wore out faster, and innovations soon grew old. As noted by Grainge *et al.* (2007: 5), audiences were nowhere near as gullible or naïve as 'cinematic myth' suggests, and artistic heritage is arguably often at odds with the true reception of such works. Far from running in fear from the sight of a train steaming towards the camera, audiences had already become inured to certain filmic and narrative techniques, even in the days before cinema, thanks to magic-lantern performances and similar sideshows. Hase Masato (2010: 38) goes so far as to suggest that the story of audiences running from the on-screen train was a rumour put about by the film's distributors in order to create a buzz of expectation. In other words, he points to a possible error of practice – that posterity has confused a text of distribution (the hyperbole of hucksters), with an account of actual reception.

The expense of animation, then a costlier and more time-consuming application than live action, incentivised many early animators to pad out their animation sequences with live-action framing devices – such as the scientist in Émile Cohl's *Les joyeux microbes* (1909) who invites the viewer to peer through his microscope at the animated creatures dancing on the slide (Crafton 1982: 70). This in turn encouraged early animators to make their artifice part of the performance, appearing in their own works in order to showcase the effort involved in creating the animation in the first place.

Similar issues shadow the history of cinema in Japan, where an ongoing tradition of sideshows and theatrical 'events' often hybridised the appearances of early films. The term in Japanese for such fortean spectaculars, eye-openers or wonders is *misemono* – literally 'see-world-thing', an independently reached corollary to the European 'cinema of attractions' (Gunning 1990: 56–7), and occasionally classified with the English term 'attractions', even in Japanese (Iwamoto 2011: 218).

There is no indication as to whether animated special effects formed a part of any of the fad in *rensageki* (chain performances) of the 1910s, in which live actors on a stage would alternate with pre-shot location footage projected on a screen in the same theatre (Bernardi 2001: 22; Katō 2006: 222).[7] Neither wholly part of the traditions of cinema nor theatre, such dramatic 'events' have faded from memory and are now difficult to reconstruct. On 24 June 1905, the Kabuki-za theatre played home to the bizarre spectacle of the 'Kineorama' of the Russo-Japanese War. Despite the implicit promise of film footage from the war in Manchuria, the 'Kineorama' was revealed to be 'a six-inch-deep large tank filled with water, behind which was displayed a crudely painted backdrop'. The story of the Russo-Japanese War was then presented as a form of puppet/model theatre, demonstrating the ingenuity and also the varied content to be found in supposed 'sideshows' and 'puppet shows' of the pre-cinema era (Dobson 2005: 77).

The first mention of something that *appears* to have been a cartoon in a Japanese cinema theatre is an otherwise unidentified film with the Japanese title *Kimyō-naru Bōrudo* (*The Board Becomes Strange*), shown at Tokyo's Yachiyo-kan theatre on 2 August 1907, which *may* have been a screening of Blackton's *Humorous Phases of Funny Faces* (Haraguchi 2000: 16). The earliest mention in Japanese sources of a work described as a cartoon is the screening of something called *Nipparu no Henkei* (*The Nipper's Transformations*) on 15 April 1912 at Tokyo's Teikoku-kan theatre (Tsugata 2007a: 56; Litten 2013: 2), believed to be a retitling of Émile Cohl's *Les Exploits de feu follet* (1911, *Will-o'-the-wisp's Exploits*). However, as 'events', these screenings are slippery and elusive. We rarely have more than a couple of fragments of each event to draw upon – either an unspecific audience reaction or a misleading promise on a poster. Reception and artistic heritage is difficult to establish, since many early cinema events seem to have comprised a grab-bag of whatever reels the exhibitors could scrape up, shoved through the projector – the form, of the spectacle of moving pictures, usually deemed more worthy of note than their content. Moreover, typology was often defined in retrospect, as in the case of a group of films recorded in contemporary accounts as *Dekobō Shin Gachō* (*Mischievous New Picture Books*) but otherwise unknown (Yamaguchi and Watanabe 1977: 8).

There remains some argument about the identity of the films. Frederick Litten (2013: 5) suggests that the first was Charles Armstrong's *Isn't It Wonderful!* (1914), contesting the claims of several Japanese scholars that the films were a group made by Émile Cohl. However, there appears to have been some contemporary confusion, accidental or otherwise, concerning the relationship of the *Dekobō* films to each other. *Dekobō* in Japanese can be translated as 'mischievous', and carries with it an implication of confusion and surreality that seems applicable to several of Cohl's early works, particularly his *Fantasmagorie* (1908). However, the *-bō* suffix might also be interpreted as an indicator of a boy's name. As a result, some patrons, and possibly some exhibitors, began regarding the unrelated animated films as the ongoing adventures of a single character called 'Kid Deko', described as 'a boy who likes doing mischievous things' (Tsugata 2007a: 57). Patrons were lured back to successive screenings with the implication that later, and, presumably, unrelated films were further adventures of the nonexistent 'Kid Deko', subtitled with names such as the 'Adventure Chapter' or 'Magic Chapter' to suggest an ongoing serial (Miyao 2002: 195). Some of the cartoons may even have been parts of an actual series, since John Randolph Bray's *Colonel Heeza Liar* films (1914 onward) undoubtedly made their way to Japan in the mid- to late 1910s. Although their first screening dates are unknown, they were prominent enough by July 1917 to be named and cited, in hindsight, as a leading influence on local Japanese animators (Tsugata 2007a: 98).[8]

At a first glance, moviegoing demographics might seem to be ideally suited to a cartoon audience, with domestic film output largely aimed at 'nursing mothers … and snot-nosed brats' (Standish 2005: 65), while 'educated' audiences favoured foreign films – of course, all cartoon films were also foreign at this time, but the caricaturisation of human beings in cartoons may have allowed a negotiated, localised reading among Japanese audiences. In other words, it has always been easier to believe that cartoon characters are locals, as many of them do not have identifiable ethnic characteristics. However, it was the very concentration of audiences among juveniles and the working classes, groups now associated with the rising popularity of 'Kid Deko', which concerned the authorities. 'Mischief', in particular, was not something that should be encouraged, even among children. What concerned the authorities, and particularly the Ministry of Education, was not confusion so much as *carnivalisation* – the ridicule of the overlying order under the cloak of harmless fun (Miyao 2002: 203). We might also note that similar issues had begun to trouble the American authorities (Grieveson 2007 [1999]: 34–5), and that stories of moral panic in, for example, Chicago in 1906 and 1907, may have reached Japan along with the films.

The rise of cinema in Japan was concurrent with early developments in socialism and anti-establishment thought. Left-wing agitation had been on the rise since the Second Japanese Socialist Party Conference in 1907, with radical developments and pamphleteering calling for overhauls in women's rights, labour laws and even the imperial system itself (Keene 2002: 691–2). Behind the scenes, albeit largely unspoken in documentation of the period, was a growing concern among government officials that the imperial heir, the future Taishō Emperor, was mentally unstable and liable to bring the Japanese throne into disrepute. The highest-profile incident was the arrest, prosecution and eventual execution of a dozen anarchists who had intended to blow up the Emperor. This in turn, led to the realisation at the Ministry of Education (Monbushō) that the new media had a great power for good or ill, and that it was in the interests of the government to steer these new means of communication along the 'right path' (*zendō*) (Standish 2005: 135).

With pressures mounting on both sides, it is easy to see why the authorities might have demonstrated a particular hypersensitivity to film, particularly when its interpretation was not a matter of record, but a matter of live spin provided at the whims of a *benshi*. The risk was made clearest in 1908, when the police refused to permit the exhibition of the French live-action film *Le Règne de Louis XVI* (1905), on the grounds that it contained an anti-monarchist message, and depicted scenes of the people storming the palace. However, instead of mothballing the film, its distributor simply renamed it *Hokubei kidan: Gankutsu-Ō* (*A Strange Tale of North America: The Cave King*), while the resident *benshi* claimed that images of rapier-wielding aristocrats in pompadours actually depicted wealthy Wild West bandits, brought down at the end by the cooperation of the police and concerned citizens (Hirano 1992: 13; High 2003: 173).[9] Faced with such subversions, the Tokyo police department began introducing a system for regulating *benshi* through official licence applications (Fujiki 2006: 68–9).

THE FIRST JAPANESE ANIMATED CARTOONS

In the midst of this growing concern, foreign animation began to form a distinct subset within the materials on show at the metropolitan picture houses. In particular, the French cartoons of Émile Cohl seem to have swiftly made their way to Japan after he parted ways with the Gaumont studio. Cohl's works often gave the impression of having been drawn in white chalk on a blackboard, although they were actually made in India ink on white rice paper, traced and retraced over a lightbox but then developed with a reverse negative to create white lines on a black background (Crafton 1982: 61).

However, these secrets of the production process eluded Japanese animation's 'first' practitioner, who does not seem to have realised how Cohl produced his images. It is difficult to tell, since the lack of any extant examples of the work of Shimokawa Ōten (1892–1973)[10] renders his output almost entirely invisible. None of his five films has survived, and there is little detail as to their running time or places of exhibition, if indeed some were ever exhibited at all. We only have 'artistic heritage' to draw on for evidence of Shimokawa's work, but the heritage itself derives largely from Shimokawa's own self-commemoration. There is no mention of his first film, *Imokawa Mukuzō Genkanban-maki* (1917, *Imokawa Mukuzō the Doorman*)[11] in the contemporary film magazine *Katsudō no Sekai*, leading some scholars to suggest that he may even have made the whole thing up (Tsugata 2003: 15). There is a certain temptation to read into Shimokawa's own account a degree of bluster and deliberate vagueness, as if he were hoping to elbow his way into histories long after the fact. Seventeen years after he supposedly gave up on animation, he revisited his memories of the period in the film magazine *Eiga Hyōron*, noting that he was 'probably' the first Japanese animator, on the grounds that, at the time he was working, he had no knowledge of any other practitioners and 'no idea' about works from abroad (Yamaguchi and Watanabe 1977: 9).

Shimokawa does appear to protest a little too much that he, as an active member of Japan's cartooning establishment, based in Tokyo, should not only have somehow heard nothing of animated films, domestic or foreign, over the previous several years, but also made no attempt to conduct further research into them before starting work. However, in setting up this unlikely creative vacuum, Shimokawa is able to make a claim for himself as a solo innovator, divorced from any other artistic context or influence.

> Therefore I had to consider everything myself. First I drew pictures in succession with white chalk on
> a blackboard … . When I wanted to move a character's hand, I erased that part and redrew it.
> (Yamaguchi and Watanabe 1977: 9)

If Shimokawa truly were thrown in the deep end at the Tenkatsu studio's instigation in 1916, then it is entirely possible that he might have stumbled along through trial and error, interpreting garbled reports both of images on blackboards such as the 'lightning sketches' of Méliès or Blackton, but also the white-on-black imagery obtained by Cohl via a more devious reverse-negative process, far less likely to have occurred to an artist with no experience of film. Either through dissatisfaction with his own product, or through unreported criticisms and commentary from his colleagues, Shimokawa had turned by late spring 1917 to a new production method, drawing in black ink on white paper, and covering with white paint any part of the image that needed to be redrawn. Apparently independently, Shimokawa seemed to be following a developmental pattern already prefigured by his colleagues in France and the US. Cohl and McCay 'both used mechanical shortcuts and photography assistants' (Crafton 1982: 137). We know, for example, from the descriptions of pre-existing techniques included in John Bray's patent application for zinc-etched backgrounds, that assistants were already employed in 1913 to trace the unchanging parts of backgrounds onto new paper sheets, leaving the lead artist to animate only the parts that changed from frame to frame (Crafton 1982: 145).

Similarly, Shimokawa hired a camera assistant, Shibata Masaru (1897–1991), and dabbled in the application of machinery that would automate some parts of the drawing process. It is Shibata's memoirs, of being the cameraman on Shimokawa's 'third' work, *Chamebō Shin Gacho: Nomi Fūfu no Shikaeshi no Maki* (1917, *Playful New Picture Book: The Revenge of Mr and Mrs Flea*),[12] which supply third-party confirmation that Shimokawa's pioneering efforts were not entirely fictional. Shibata recalled the existence of the film and the method employed by Shimokawa at the time, which seemed to be in imitation of the chalk-and-blackboard technique found in Blackton's *Humorous Phases of Funny Faces*. Thereafter, Shimokawa drifted into a new method utilising a background that he would print in large quantities, on which he would draw a new foreground image for every frame. The film historian Tsugata Nobuyuki suggests that Shimokawa may have only turned to this technique in his fifth and last film *Chamebō-zu: Uotsuri no Maki* (1917, *Playful Pictures: Fishing Chapter*)[13] before giving up on animation as a medium – it seems that the several months he spent tinkering with the technique proved neither fruitful for him nor his patrons at Tenkatsu (Tsugata 2003: 16).

According to claims made by Shimokawa in 1934, he made five short animated films for the Tenkatsu studio, between late 1916 and autumn 1917, after which point he gave up the experiment, complaining that the effort was damaging his eyesight (Tsugata 2007a: 100). Several of the short films seemed to have reused the Mukuzō character already employed by Shimokawa in his magazine caricatures. The majority of these films appear to have been made with the aid of a blackboard and chalk, and one, *Dekobō Shin Gacho: Meian no Shippai* (1917, *Mischievous New Picture Book: Failure of a Great Plan*), is mentioned in the March 1917 issue of *Kinema Record*, described as a 'second line-drawing (*senga*) trick in which Mukuzō ends up trapped in a hole after trying to drag a pig out of one'. Tsugata Nobuyuki, although he expressed doubt as to the very existence of *Imokawa Mukuzō the Doorman* in 2003, now regards *Kinema Record*'s reference to *Failure of a Great Plan* as the 'second film' as sufficient indication that there must have been an earlier film preceding it, and in turn has recently come to invest Shimokawa's other claims with far greater credibility (Tsugata 2007a: 99).

The most interesting thing about Shimokawa's brief foray into animation is the nature of its failure. Despite his initial drive, neither he nor his sponsors at Tenkatsu seem to have regarded the effort involved in animation to be truly worth the returns. He walked away from animation as the new medium faced increasing pressures from the authorities, which other creatives would find newer and more enduring ways to meet.

ZIGOMAR AND THE CREATION OF CINEMA

Locally made animation in Japan arose during a period of vibrant debate about the nature of cinema – the first time in which cinema was generally regarded as a distinct art form in its own right. The incorporation of cinema and cartoons as mere elements within the wider field of sideshow entertainment seemed to persist until 1911, when cinema itself was foregrounded as the focus of a new moral panic, in the wake of an allegedly harmful foreign import that glorified the activities of a live-action French master-thief (Miyao 2002: 193).[14] *Ji-Go-Ma* (1911, *Zigomar*) was a film for which the audience reception seems to have taken the distributors by surprise. A late work by the director Victorin Jasset, it was initially shelved by Japanese distributors, partly because of the scenes that appeared to glorify larceny, but largely because it was regarded as rather dull. It was eventually released to plug a gap caused by a late shipping of another film, only to garner unexpected box-office receipts, particularly among juvenile audiences (Makino 2001b: 49; Fujita 2011: 399).

Zigomar was soon followed by its French sequels, and by several Japanese works that purported to be continuations. To the horror of the Ministry of Education, Japanese children were reported 'playing' games in which they and their friends imitated the actions of the French criminals. Inevitably, newspaper reports began to associate juvenile delinquents with the film, assigning the name 'Zigomar gangs' to disaffected youth, and hence implying that juvenile gangs had been inspired by the film. By 1912, newspapers were suggesting that *Zigomar* was merely one of several dangerously influential narratives consumed by impressionable youths, and that the nature of film itself made cinema a potentially dangerous and subversive blight on society. The *Asahi Shinbun* proclaimed with hand-wringing fretfulness:

> Even if one can say that every villain is the product of a serial author's imagination, it cannot be denied
> that, once he appears in a work of the moving pictures, the sense that one is touching the real thing is
> more prominent than with one's feeling in watching theatre. (Gerow 1996: 61, quoted in Miyao 2002: 202)

Zigomar's popularity, and allegations of copycat activity among Japanese youth, was sufficient to rouse the interests of an anti-cinema lobby spearheaded by the Teikoku Kyōiku-kai (Imperial Education Association). In a whirl of claims and counterclaims, a national education policy report highlighted 'lantern slides, moving pictures and general storytelling' as areas that required government regulation (Makino 2001b: 50). In targeting 'general storytelling', the report appears to focus on the activities of the *benshi*, whose live presence at film events afforded them the opportunity to control the interpretation of texts that might otherwise seem innocuous. In the case of *Zigomar*, its sequels and many Japanese imitators in the three years that followed (Hirano 1992: 14), the authorities were concerned with the consequences of lionising criminals, particularly among juvenile audiences. Some *benshi* were derided as 'unfit in language and attitude', and the report made the unlikely rec-ommendation to 'encourage all to as best possible not show moving pictures to children' (Makino 2001b: 54).

Fortunately for early animation, even the authors of the report seem to have realised that this was an unre-alistic aim, immediately conceding that less draconian measures might achieve similar effects: the careful selection of the films to be exhibited, and the discouraging of film exhibition for children at any time other than at weekends and public holidays. These guidelines were formalised in October 1911 as the Regulations for Inspection of Magic Lantern and Moving-Picture Shows (Gentō oyobi Katsudō Shashin Film Shisa Kitei), altered from 'recommendations' under the outgoing Katsura administration of 1911 into 'regulations' under the incom-ing Saionji administration of 1912. Further issues of content in the guidelines proscribed large areas of cinematic content. The examples given in Makino Mamoru's work are from the Osaka region, but similar rules were soon in force all over Japan, and included demands for film-makers to avoid depictions of adultery or cruelty, glorification of criminal acts, and *anything that would promote mischief among children* (Makino 2001b: 54). Such demands must have seemed crippling to early animators, and may have influenced the number of early Japanese cartoons that emphasised an educational or instructional component. Although the composition of Japanese films in their first decade of production seems little different from that of their Western counterparts, extant works show a palpable number of folk tales and parables, as if in the hope that these would encompass some sort of homily or epigram.

By 1917, there had been another perceptible shift. Whereas 'moving pictures' had once been subordinate to magic lanterns, half a decade later it was moving pictures alone that attracted the full attention of the auth-orities. As the title implies, the 1917 Tokyo Moving Pictures Entertainment Industry Control Regulations (Katsudō Shashin Kōgyō Torishimari Kisoku) now regarded moving pictures as the chief attraction at theatres. The regu-lations stipulated a number of new rules from which we can deduce that the role of the *benshi* remained significant, and a rising concern about the corrupting influence of motion pictures. The power of censure was relocated from small local stations to municipal police headquarters. This supposedly allowed for the imposi-tion of universal directives less likely to be subjected to varying interpretations from place to place, but also afforded the police other areas of control to enforce, including three-part separation of audiences into men-only, women-only and combined male-female seating, limitations on the size of screen, mandatory registration of *benshi* and the imposition of age restrictions, recognising that some films would be unsuitable for the under-fifteens. It also seemed to leave animators stuck with an impossible task – making children's films in a medium in which children's films were increasingly discouraged (Katō 2006: 225).[15]

Drawing on the 1996 PhD thesis of Aaron Gerow, Miyao Daisuke notes that 'cinema was constructed dis-cursively between ... two sites of knowledge' – production and regulation (Miyao 2002: 202). In other words, film texts or events, including animation, were generated by the twin agencies of their production staff and the demands of the authorities. But it would be a fallacy to assume that such a relationship was entirely adver-sarial. The Ministry of Education was only opposed to the wrong sort of films, such as the much-feared *Zigomar*, and several other tales of assassins, rebels and revolutionaries. Just as the *Asahi Shinbun* had recognised the immense power of cinema, the very interest of the authorities in regulating film contained within it an impli-cation not of censure, but recognition of great potential. It only remained for canny film-makers to navigate the perilous clauses of the regulations in order to produce films that might meet with the approval of the auth-orities. Artistic competence was not an issue among the early animators – those who became animators were already artists (Lamarre 2009: xxxix). However, those animators who found enduring success in the 1920s needed to find a way to embrace the dual tensions of art and commerce.

The bipartite classification of films, into those that were suitable for children and those that were not, soon took its toll in an industry where film-makers favoured the larger audience sector that could be guaranteed to both have the money for tickets and not invite police interference. By 1920, the number of child-friendly entertainment films, including cartoons as a large subset, had fallen drastically (Katō 2006: 226). It would seem that for many of the pioneer animators, it was simply not worth the risk to painstakingly assemble a film one frame at a time, only to risk being told after its completion that its target audience would be denied any chance to see it.

Kōuchi Junichi was an animator who demonstrated very clearly how *not* to do it, with a film that would cause him so much trouble that he left the business for several years. His second film, *Chamebō: Kūkijū no Maki* (1917, *Playful Boy's Air Gun*)[16] was the first animated film to become a victim of the new censorship regime, with a report that 'felt that the film would encourage children to misbehave' (Miyao 2002: 201). We might contrast Kōuchi's spectacular own goal – even the title is enough to set off alarms with any parent or teacher – with the greater artifice shown in Ōishi Ikuo's *Usagi to Kame* (1918, *The Hare and the Tortoise*). As the title makes immediately obvious, *The Hare and the Tortoise* is based on *Aesop's Fables*, a series of classical morality tales known to the Japanese since the early 1600s. Moreover, Ōishi's work was not even a film for viewing in public cinemas, but an advertising vehicle for Morinaga Milk Chocolate (Haraguchi 2000: 30) – it is debatable whether it even fell under the auspices of the regulations at all, since they were aimed at physical theatres, not stores where a projector might be set up. Candies seem to have been sold to audiences in the same manner as at *kamishibai* – in the sense that the film itself is simply an event that lured in audiences, who were then invited to buy chocolate once in the auditorium. The 'event' of *The Hare and the Tortoise* might have comprised a venue for selling chocolate, but its basic text seems entirely wholesome and benign.

ANIME AND PURE FILM

There is a ready temptation to impose a narrative of 'emplotment' on Japanese cinema in the 1910s, dividing it into hard-pressed film-makers and censorious authorities. However, the period saw many film-makers and government figures in strong agreement about the potential of the new medium, and the need to divorce it from its unwelcome ties to ossified tradition. A group of young cinematographers, known to posterity as the Pure Film Movement (*Jun Eiga-geki Undō*), published polemics and reviews in contemporary journals complaining that film remained beholden to the traditions and tropes of the Japanese theatre. The Pure Film Movement held that too many directors were treating cinema simply as a gimmick, and refusing to recognise its potential as an entirely new medium (Bernardi 2001: 30).

The vision presented by the Pure Film Movement was one of an art form whose practitioners were reluctant to lift themselves from the assumptions of the past. Too many films in the 1910s, it was claimed, were unimaginative restagings of scenes from kabuki, presented in a single, long, locked-off take, and adhering to traditional theatrical gesture, performance and even gender – using the traditional *onnagata* female impersonators rather than actual actresses (Bernardi 2001: 13). To critics such as the future film director Kaeriyama Norimasa (1893–1964), contemporary films were dragged down by the limitations of the old media, without properly exploiting its potential. After all, film could liberate the viewer from the proscenium arch and leap between exotic locations; it could introduce undreamt-of special effects. In order to achieve this, film needed to cast aside middle-aged men dressed as teenage geisha; it needed to find more naturalistic actors, and develop scripts that played to its strengths, instead of making it little more than a pale shadow of a live kabuki performance.

To the theorists of the Pure Film Movement, the *benshi* were part of the problem, rendering the new medium of film unnecessarily subordinate to live performance (Katō 2006: 222).[17] Since so much of the high-earning material of the 1910s cinema had come from America and Europe, Japanese film-makers could recognise the potential to make money exporting locally made films. That, however, would require a film that was intelligible to non-Japanese audiences and, in the days before sound, more reliant on intertitles that could be swapped out with local languages (Gerow 2010: 113). The Pure Film Movement came to see the *benshi* as the last true barrier towards 'Pure Film', since like Winsor McCay and his performing dinosaur, these impresarios required a film to be incomplete without them. Narrating a film live was easier when the shots were long and predictable, and where there were few sudden jumps or surprises. Dialogue and narrative were easier to fit into extended pauses rather than rapid sequences. And when there were no intertitles to steer the audience's understanding of a story, the audience required a *benshi* as an interpretive crutch (Katō 2006: 215).

The debate over Pure Film also dragged animation into its compass, at first under the assumption that, as a genre without any local precedents, it could not fail to aspire to an international outlook. This was certainly the tone of the exhibition of early films by the animator Kitayama Seitarō, whose venture making cartoons for the

Nikkatsu Mukōjima studio in May 1917 was reported as a 'new enterprise in Japan' in the pages of *Katsudō no Sekai* (Yamaguchi and Watanabe 1977: 10).

Kitayama's first cut-paper animation *Saru Kani Kassen* (1917, *The Battle of the Monkey and the Crab*)[18] was shown in two Asakusa cinemas, including the Denki-kan, Japan's first dedicated cinema theatre, a venue renowned for screenings of exotic foreign films. Miyao Daisuke writes that the innocuous one-reel cartoon should be considered not merely as an achievement in animation, but as part of the evolving discourse on Pure Film, accomplishing 'equivalence with foreign fare' in terms of its production and exhibition, and eschewing a *benshi* in favour of intertitles to explain key points of the narrative (Miyao 2002: 199).[19]

However, the ideology of the Pure Film Movement is not entirely clear. Surely a dream of export might be just as easily fulfilled by distributing uniquely Japanese images as by sights of interchangeable modernity? The story of *The Battle of the Monkey and the Crab* was just as traditional, and hence presumably hidebound, as a kabuki play, and yet it appeared to suffer no censure for this. In fact, *Hanahekonai: Meitō no Maki* (1917, *Hanahekonai: A New Sword Chapter*),[20] released by Kitayama's rival Kōuichi Junichi, not only clung to indubitably Japanese content, but received critical praise for doing so:

> The subject matter is particularly interesting. Japanese animation should use Japanese subjects. The interest of this animation film lies in its use of a purely Japanese subject, 'a sword', from which it makes a comedy.
> (cited in Miyao 2002: 200)

Why was the Pure Film Movement so indulgent of traditionalism within the content of Japanese cartoons, while decrying it in live action? Miyao suggests that perhaps the Pure Film Movement overlooked animation because it was widely agreed that animation could never aspire to the 'realism' demanded of live-action film. He also notes that 'traditional subjects represented pedagogical authority' (Miyao 2002: 201), allowing animation to flourish in a sector of film that was largely outside the scope of the Pure Film Movement's concerns. While Pure Film concerned itself with drama and realist documentary, animation in the late 1910s and throughout the 1920s favoured folk tales and allegories as a means of appeasing a censor that was otherwise hostile to the very idea of children watching films.

KITAYAMA SEITARŌ AT NIKKATSU MUKŌJIMA

There is some debate over when Kitayama Seitarō saw his first animated film. His colleague Yamamoto Sanae claimed in his own memoirs that he and Kitayama saw an 'American import' cartoon called *Fleischer no Dekobō Gachō* (*Fleischer's Mischievous Picture Book*) in 1915 at the Teikoku-kan in the Tokyo cinema district of Asakusa, in the company of their fellow artists Mineta Hiroshi and Yamakawa Kunizō. He goes on to claim that he and the three artists began discussing making their own animated films the following day (Tsugata 2007a: 153–4). However, as Tsugata Nobuyuki notes, this account is riddled with historical problems, starting with the alleged date of 'Taishō 4' (1915), which he regards as more likely to be a misprint for 'Taishō 6' (1917). However, that does not deal with the largest problem in Yamamoto's account, which is that the Fleischer brothers' *Out of the Inkwell* film series was not even released in America until 1918, at least a year after Kitayama and his colleagues claimed to have seen it. Yamamoto probably saw something with 'Dekobō' in the Japanese title, but not something by the Fleischer brothers. Yamamoto's memoir is rich in peripheral details – the ever-present chirping of the cicadas in what was presumably summer; the four men strolling to the Asakusa cinema in their straw boaters – but he appears to have entirely misremembered the title of the film that first inspired them. Nor can he simply have misremembered the date, as the commencement of Kitayama's animation work is firmly established as 1917. Tsugata admits defeat, and concedes that the four artists saw an otherwise unidentified cartoon in Asakusa, probably in 1917, which inspired them to attempt to replicate the process themselves.[21]

Kitayama's own memoirs record that he saw numerous foreign cartoons in 1916, which inspired him to offer his services to the film studio Nippon Katsudō Shashin (Japan Moving Pictures, or Nikkatsu for short) in 1917.

It was this deal that led to an impressive outburst of productivity, resulting in twenty-two short films, mainly on folk- or fairy-tale themes, between 1917 and 1918.

Nikkatsu had been founded in 1912 as part of a cluster of entertainment companies with connections to *yakuza* organised crime (Standish 2005: 36). Kitayama worked under the studio official Makino Shōzō, a prominent figure in early Japanese live-action film, who, according to Kitayama, found the atmosphere at Nikkatsu's Tokyo branch as stultifying and dull as he did (Tsugata 2007a: 142).

Notably, although Kitayama's output during his Nikkatsu period extended to twenty-two animated films, these did not represent the core of his duties with Nikkatsu. Instead, he continued to make his cartoon films largely in his spare time, while concentrating on what he called 'art titles' for live-action films under the technical director Fujiwara Kozaburō (Tsugata 2007a: 128). His first work in this capacity was *Ikeru Shikabane* (1918, *The Living Corpse*)[22] an adaptation of the Leo Tolstoy story of the same name, directed by Tanaka Eizō. From his description, from a surviving photograph of Kitayama at work, and most notably by the use of the English term 'art titles', these seem to have been direct copies of the illustrated intertitles first seen in American films around 1915 (Salt 2009: 148) – intertitles with an illustration or calligraphic flourish to add a touch of class, spruced up with a more aesthetically pleasing name in order to impart a certain perceived value. They were drawn on cards and then photographed in natural daylight outside the studio before being spliced into the film (Tsugata 2007a: 131). As a shot fired in the ongoing war against the dominance of the *benshi*, an 'art title' definitely had a certain marketing cachet, but Kitayama immediately began applying his skills in new and interesting ways.[23]

Japanese cinematographers already understood that film had a greater potential than that of simply replicating whatever scene the lens was pointed at. Foreign films had already established the potential to add graphics, either as opening or closing credits, or as intertitles within the body of the film itself (Salt 2009: 64). They also established the possibility of using 'tricks'. The earliest of such tricks were in-camera effects such as iris fadeouts or pixilation – to novice moviegoers, even a simple cut between two different locations could be parsed as a 'trick'. Kitayama went a step further with his Nikkatsu work, by featuring animation specifically as a special effect, swiftly applying himself to skills at the periphery of animation and graphics, to augment the studio's live-action output. In Oguchi Tadashi's film *Nogi Shōgun, Aa Nogi Taishō* (1918, *Shōgun Nogi, or rather General Nogi*),[24] Kitayama added on-screen titles – not *intertitles* as seen in previous films, but titles overlaid upon the screen image itself – reading 'A Great Star Falls' at the moment of Nogi's suicide. The term 'great star', or *kyosei*, is a poetic Japanese term for a 'great man', although Oguchi's *mise en scène* takes the term literally, lingering on the stars in the night sky, one of which suddenly bursts into animated effulgence, before tumbling to Earth as a meteor. In the same director's live-action film *Kuni no Home* (1918, *Glory of the Nation*),[25] Kitayama overlaid an animated effect to create the mist-like white ghost of a deceased guardsman (Tsugata 2007a: 138).

It is only amidst such below-the-line work that Kitayama continued his output of actual cartoons, usually comprising one- or two-reel works, and largely based on fairy-tale themes, although some, such as *Yume no Jitensha* (1917, *The Dream Bicycle*) were originals. As the strictures of the new Moving Pictures Entertainment Industry Control Regulations began to bite, Kitayama's narrative cartoon output adhered largely to worthy folk tales known to Japanese educators, including *Urashima Tarō* (1918),[26] *Shita-Kiri Suzume* (1918, *The Cut-Tongue Sparrow*) and *Kintarō* (1918).[27]

In the eyes of at least one of Kitayama's handful of staff, such films were immensely difficult to turn into a profit. The animator Yamamoto Sanae wrote:

> Many people came to the cinema and they were popular, but the production tempo was just too slow. Unless completing at least 300-*shaku* [five minutes] of film per week, it was not profitable. It took at least 16 drawings in order to animate a figure to take a single step. So, in order to tell a story, we needed to draw enormous amounts of art and shoot every single one against a background, which was very time-consuming. It required patience. *We realised that it was impossible to make entertainment films.*
> (Yamamoto, quoted in Tsugata 2007a: 174–5; my emphasis)

Yamamoto's observations bear a close resemblance to those of his colleagues in other countries, who similarly found themselves far down the cinema pecking order. Since narrative cartoons were not long enough to form the central pillar of a programme, they were forced to subsist in the margins, as peripheral and hence easily jettisonable extras. Some distributors simply regarded animated films as not worth the effort. In one infamous story, Lewis Selznick contemptuously offered a young Paul Terry a fee that was less than the value of the film stock for his cartoon *Little Hermann* (1915). 'When Terry protested, Selznick is said to have informed him that the film was worth more before he had drawn on it' (Crafton 1982: 148).

If it seems odd that Kitayama and his staff should be decrying entertainment films even as they produced films of some kind at a rate of up to three a month, that is because, on those rare occasions where Kitayama's films show up in the historical record at all, they do so as obscure narrative films for children. But just as Kitayama was earning a modest living making titles and graphics under the Nikkatsu umbrella, he had also found a new revenue stream for animation that was to prove far more lucrative than 'entertainment films', and which made their continued production possible in the years 1917 and 1918.

According to Kitayama, the idea came from his Nikkatsu boss Makino Shōzō, who had spotted a loophole in the regulations. If the authorities admitted that film was a unique and powerful medium, and that it was open to abuse, then surely the best possible way to use film for good was to do so in the considered service of the authorities.

Makino somehow secured a contract with the Ministry of Communications (Teishinshō) to produce several public-information films utilising animation. The first, commissioned by the Department of Postal Insurance, was *Itazura no Post* (1917, *Mischievous Post*), presenting a cartoon sequence of obstacles and dangers facing a letter on its way to a customer. He followed this in October of the same year with *Chokin no Susume* (1917, *Recommendations for Your Savings*), which, despite being a public-information film, was premiered at the Opera-kan in Asakusa as if it were an entertainment film.

'By contrasting a diligent person who saves money and a lazy person who does not', wrote the reporter for *Katsudō Shashin*, 'this film suggests that your later life will be better if you save' (Tsugata 2007a: 134). Kitayama believed, and no source has yet contradicted him, that these films marked the first use of animation for instruction or advertisement in Japan. Notably, despite any cartoonish elements or comedic narrative, they were also plainly not intended for children – while children might have enjoyed them, it is difficult to imagine infants needing advice about postal insurance or savings bonds. Despite the eternal assumption that animation is largely a children's medium, Kitayama's chief financial successes in it in the 1910s, and indeed in the 1920s, were aimed at a markedly adult audience.

Although animation had been used in advertising in Europe as early as 1899, with Arthur Melbourne Cooper's stop-motion *Matches Appeal* (Crafton 1982: 223), the parochial and time-sensitive nature of advertising had rendered export pointless. Nor was animated advertising or instruction of much appeal in America before World War I. John Bray himself only openly recognised the potential of educational films in 1919, when the processes already in place for military instruction were readily retooled for industrial clients, particularly in the automotive industry (Crafton 1982: 159–60). But such films were not exported. As a result, all previous animated films seen in Japan before 1917 had been narrative entertainment films, perhaps explaining the staging of Kitayama's premiere as theatrical event worthy of comment and critique. His next work for the Department of Savings, *Chiri mo Tsumoreba Yama to Naru* (1917, *Even Dust Piled Up Will Become a Mountain*), does not show up in any theatrical listings, suggesting that it was toured in town halls and public meetings, rather than with the same sense of occasion as its predecessor.

Kitayama's new venture seems to have been part of a much broader push on the part of the Ministry of Communications to engage both audiences and creatives in instructional film-making, which included a scriptwriting competition, for which the winning script *Yama no Kyōdai* (1918, *Mountain Brothers*) was produced as a live-action film. A second script, *Gatten Tokubei* (*Tokubei Understands*) was reported in the June 1919 issue of *Katsudō Hyōron* as entering production at Nikkatsu under Kitayama's directorship, and supposedly involved a series of comedic situations explaining how savings were best protected and utilised in the events of earthquakes and fires (Tsugata 2007a: 118, 135). However, although the magazine reported *Tokubei Understands* as a fully animated production, it also claimed that it was up to ten times longer than Kitayama's usual output, with an estimated length of thirty minutes. It seems more likely either that the purported length of 2,000 *shaku* (600 metres) was a misprint for 200, and that Kitayama's work formed only one reel within a larger, live-action whole. Like most Japanese films from before 1923, there is no extant copy of *Tokubei Understands*, so its mention in *Katsudō Hyōron* is the only evidence that it even existed at all. While there is space on Kitayama's production slate for something the size of *Tokubei Understands* to have been made following the completion of his one-reeler *Tarō no Banpei: Sensui-kan no Maki* (1918, *Tarō the Guardsman: The Submarine*) in August 1918, Kitayama's own memoirs point to a much more diverse below-the-line working schedule in the same period. Instead of mentioning *Tokubei Understands* which, as the longest Japanese cartoon made up until that point, would have surely established a prime place in his memoirs, Kitayama writes of an overwhelming set of demands for more animation piecework on other, unnamed, films, many of which were jobs separate from his obligations at Nikkatsu:

> Film producers from other companies, learning that I worked for Nikkatsu … doing animation (*senga*) and subtitles (*jimaku*), started to bring all sorts of jobs to me. These jobs started to take increasing amounts of my time so that on occasion I had problems meeting my obligations at Nikkatsu. I was a freelance at Nikkatsu, so should have had no issue with other work in my spare time. But I came to feel bad about it, as I came to think that it was Nikkatsu that had led me to such work in the first place … . Takamatsu Toyojirō … in particular was a very keen producer, who insisted that it was unthinkable to make commercials or instructional films without animation. As a result, animation was used heavily in so-called 'advertising' (*senden*) and 'educational' (*kyōiku*) films, so much so that there were hardly any that did not include it. (Kitayama, quoted in Tsugata 2007a: 140–1)[28]

Reading between the lines, Kitayama was less troubled over his loyalties to Nikkatsu than over his loyalty to Makino Shōzō, the man he had to thank for his burgeoning career. Notably, Makino Shōzō resigned from Nikkatsu in 1919, supposedly in reaction to the ongoing pressures over censorship and copycat criminal behaviour among young audiences. However, just as Makino had recognised the potential of educational film as a revenue stream in 1917, he seemed as keen to exploit the idea in a new venture, setting himself up as the manager of a company in 1920 dedicated solely to 'educational' films (Standish 2005: 134). The departure of Makino from Nikkatsu seemed to trouble Kitayama far less, and within a few months, he had followed his former boss into independent production, with many of his early instructional films made for Makino's new venture. Crucially, however, Kitayama was no longer one of many technicians working for Nikkatsu. In 1921, he became the boss of his own dedicated animation studio, Japan's first, the Kitayama Eiga Seisaku-sho – translated as the Kitayama Film Production Works or more romantically, the Kitayama Film Factory.

NOTES

1. Matsumoto's speculation was not 'unwise' in itself – in fact, as he later explained (Matsumoto 2011b: 100–1), he very carefully dated the years of manufacture of all the peripheral materials found *in situ* with the fragment, in order to deduce the earliest *possible* point in time when such a group of items could be assembled. However, an academic should have perhaps anticipated the likely journalistic response to such speculations, which immediately chose the most eye-opening and spectacular possibility, no matter how unlikely.
2. Katō (2006: 211) outlines the changing expectations of a *benshi*'s role, from one of delivering a prologue (*maesetsu*) before the start of films at the beginning of the twentieth century, to one of delivering an ongoing narrative (*nakasetsu*), that began to gain prominence after 1903. Katō suggests that the practice of a ten-minute warm-up before the showing of a film reel had largely died out by 1917, but plainly it was the rise of the *nakasetsu* performances of narration during films that propelled *benshi* to greater heights of showmanship, beginning in 1903 and reaching a peak in 1917; the Tokyo police began forcing *benshi* to apply for licences after 1920 (Fujiki 2006: 71, 78). Notably, 11 per cent of the *benshi* at their 1917 peak were women. By the time of the first issue of *Kinema Junpō* in July 1919, the cover images depict foreign movie stars, not domestic narrators – an early sign of a steep decline in the reception of *benshi*, as actors

permanently eclipsed them in the artistic heritage of film. Considering the matching dates, it would seem fair to suggest that the concern of the authorities and of the Pure Film Movement seems to have grown during the rise of the *nakasetsu* style, as *benshi* begin to present an even more active danger to the narrative integrity of films, and risked subordinating the filmed medium entirely to the presentational skill of the live narrator. Examinations for *benshi* were suspended in 1936, seemingly as a result of the virtual disappearance of the profession (Fujiki 2006: 80).

3. Ezra (2000: 27); Elsaesser (1990: 165) notes the existence of similar 'lecturers' in the Anglophone world, but suggests they had faded away by 1906.

4. Balio (1993: 27) suggests that the use of live acts in American cinemas was also a weapon against the competition from vaudeville, as most audiences would opt for the superabundance of a night of combined live and cinematic entertainment, rather than a night of live entertainment alone.

5. *Tennen-shoku* is translated here as 'natural-coloured' but can also mean 'spontaneous' or 'technicolour' (Nelson 1974: 36). Here, as in its appearance in the studio name Tennen-shoku Katsudō Shashin (Natural-coloured Moving Pictures), or Tenkatsu for short, I feel that the intended meaning is closer to 'lifelike', 'vibrant' or 'real' (as opposed to 'painted'), but to adopt that translation would be pushing the text too far.

6. Barry Salt (2009: 51) regards academic coverage of trick films to already be 'excessive … especially in view of the fact that they proved a dead-end as far as the cinema is concerned', but admits on the next page that trick films are the direct ancestor of 'single frame filming', and hence of animation itself.

7. The *rensageki* form was resurrected with the advent of television (Clements and Tamamuro 2003: xv) and its vestiges may arguably be seen in modern news programming that switches between live studio broadcast and pre-recorded footage.

8. Could the 'Kid Deko' films have actually been instalments in Bray's *Colonel Heeza Liar* sequence? Although the *-bō* suffix might be applied to a priest as easily as a child, the moustachioed colonel does not resemble either dictionary definition. Moreover, he was identifiable enough to Japanese authors by 1917 to be described as 'Hiiza Taisa' (Colonel Hiiza), suggesting that he was a figure distinct from 'Kid Deko'.

9. *Gankutsu-Ō* contains within it another resonance for Japanese audiences. Since 1901, it was known in Japanese as the title of Dumas' *The Count of Monte Cristo*, which itself was adapted into an American silent movie in 1908. Possibly, there may have been a deliberate attempt here on the part of the distributors to confuse the two film works. Makino (2001b: 61) claims that the three-character title (*Gan-Kutsu-Ō*) was itself an aesthetic echo of the tripartite Japanese title of *Zigomar* (*Ji-Go-Ma*), although this rather seems to be putting the cart before the horse, as *The Count of Monte Cristo* was known by that title in Japanese for a decade before the release of *Zigomar*.

10. Notably Shimokawa's pen-name, Ōten or sometimes Hekoten, uses the character 凹 or *heko*, meaning 'concave'. Paired with *deko*, or 'convex', it makes 凸凹 *dekoboko* 'rugged' or 'rough', and possibly 'zany' (Nelson 1974: 60). It does seem like a remarkable coincidence that Shimokawa's own pseudonym seems so closely linked to the contemporary *Dekobō* signifier for animated films, although possibly that may have been his intention all along.

11. DAW 66.

12. DAW 462.

13. DAW 462.

14. Standish (2005: 133) notes that the Japanese film historian Sakuramoto Totomio reached similar conclusions in 1993.

15. Although the Japanese text specifies the dividing line is at age fifteen, a Japanese child is considered to be 'one year old' at birth. In British terms, the dividing line of the regulations is at age fourteen.

16. DAW 462.

17. Ironically, however, film-makers who considered themselves 'Pure' still relied on the *benshi* to narrate their films in the days before sound (Dym 2001: 145).

18. DAW 304.

19. Considering the work that Kitayama subsequently found in the next couple of years, it may be fair to suggest that to certain members of the audience, the presence of the intertitle content, not the animation form itself, was the most powerful and inspiring part of the cinema event.

20. DAW 613. Miyao calls it *Shintō no Maki* (*New Sword Chapter*); I follow the title used in both DAW and in Animage (1989: 5). But see Matsumoto (2011a: 97) for discussions of variant titles.

21. Tsugata (2003: 18) suggests yet another date, of summer 1916, which either represents his best guess at the time, since revised, or an error by his English translator when faced with the notoriously confusing Japanese dating system that numbers years by the year of the reigning Emperor. 'Summer' is not open to debate – the cicadas take care of that – the year 1917 is still questionable. Tsugata's more recent book on Kitayama favours 1917, but if so, Kitayama and his three friends somehow managed to crank out ten cartoons in the latter half of the year. Surely it is more likely that they began work in 1916 and exhibited their first work in early 1917, thereby allowing themselves a full year of output to achieve the rate of ten cartoons in twelve months? His chronology (Tsugata 2007a: 118, 277) seems to support 1916 as the year of inspiration, rather than 1917 as claimed in his main text. Tsugata gives 20 May 1917 as the date of the first completed Kitayama film, *The Battle of the Monkey and the Crab*.

22. JCD 31785.

23. Salt (2009: 118) distinguishes between purely decorative 'art titles', which are as described in my main text, and 'illustrated titles', an earlier fad in the 1910s. Illustrated titles were abandoned because a film that relied on an element of illustration within its intertitles became prohibitively expensive to export, since 'translation' did not merely involve swapping out the intertitles, but entirely redrawing the artwork.

24. JCD 31872. Salt (2009: 148) notes that such superimposed titles were developed early in cinema history, but fell out of favour when film-makers realised that they were immensely harder to swap out for foreign markets than simple intertitles. As with tinted film (see Chapter 2), it would seem that this new development was shelved until new technology arose that either removed the problem or brought down the cost of fixing it. In the case of subtitles, that would presumably be the widespread availability of dedicated optical printers in the mid-1930s – see Salt (2009: 231).

25. JCD 31832.

26. DAW 82.

27. DAW 217.

28. The term *senden* can also be translated as 'propaganda', although the meaning of propaganda itself has shifted in the past century to almost exclusively negative connotations, which it did not have in the 1920s. See Taylor (2003: 4).

2 THE FILM FACTORIES
Animation technique and technology 1921–37

During the 1920s, Japanese animation transformed from the largely artisanal, small-scale productions of its inception, to the industrialised output that characterised its move into profitability. The period saw the rapid adoption, seemingly from American models, of several basic film technologies that would be standard throughout much of the twentieth century, but also a drift away from the medium of entertainment, in search of richer pickings to be found in the educational and instructional sectors.

There are two dates in the early 1920s that mark clear turning points in the fortune of Japanese animation. One is the foundation of Japan's first dedicated animation studio in 1921, although neither the name of Kitayama Seitarō's 'film factory', nor its majority output in graphics and subtitles, suggest that its participants regarded their labours as particularly noteworthy at the time. In hindsight, we define Kitayama Eiga Seisaku-sho as Japan's first animation studio, although this does not appear to have been the primary contemporary self-identification of its staff.

A far more drastic event in the history of Japanese film is the Great Kantō Earthquake of 1 September 1923, which levelled much of the Tokyo and Yokohama region. Striking minutes before midday, the earthquake upended thousands of lit cooking stoves, causing greater damage in its aftermath as raging fires spread through the ruins of wooden and paper houses. In his memoirs, the animator Yamamoto Sanae recalled dazed, bedraggled refugees fleeing the disaster area, and the burning fires giving way to eerie, pitch-black nights without electricity (Tsugata 2007a: 191). In a climate of national calamity and reconstruction, the film business was as badly hit as every other sector. The earthquake destroyed every studio in the Tokyo area except for Shōchiku Kamata, and the process of rebuilding took years – Nikkatsu was not reopened in Tokyo until 1934 (Wada-Marciano 2008: 5). Tokyo benshi were laid off in droves, in the expectation that the entertainment business would take five full years to recover. Some fled to provincial theatres to continue their trade; others found a new niche in the market as roving 'oral newspapers', delivering news in speech form while the printing presses were reconstructed (Dym 2001: 147).

Some companies, including Kitayama Eiga, relocated to the Osaka region, but in terms of content, the disaster of the earthquake served to distance the industry from the traditionalist leanings of the Tokyo theatrical and benshi interest groups. With good reason, the Kantō Earthquake marks a watershed in many histories of Japanese film, not only as a great tragedy, but also as a liberating influence that freed the surviving film-makers from tradition (Makino 2001c: 78–9). Joanne Bernardi (2001: 27) goes so far as to call it the 'final catalyst' in the modernisation of Japanese film, and notes that, despite the unspeakable destruction in 1923 and the levelling of much of the city, Tokyo's count of cinema theatres had leapt from 112 before the earthquake to 178 only three years afterwards.

The earthquake itself was less damaging to Japanese animation in the long term than the ensuing fires, which destroyed almost all evidence of domestic cartoons before 1923. The amount of material that survives post-quake is demonstrably greater, and allows a wide enough selection of material to pursue much more intensive studies of form and content. It is thus easier to study Japanese animation post-Kantō Earthquake, particularly within the content-based systems popular in film studies.

Tsugata Nobuyuki (2012: ii) notes that the earthquake also created an unexpected and largely forgotten eddy in the time-stream of Japanese animation history, in which the Kansai region around Osaka and Kyoto became the 'centre' of the industry for the next three decades, only ceding primacy to Tokyo with the foundation of Tōei Dōga in 1956. Yamaguchi Yasuo (2004: 50) points to the Great Kantō Earthquake as a watershed in generational location, believing that the changes in staffing brought by the pressures of the new era meant that a different kind of animator gained prominence. Takahashi Mitsuteru has suggested (Takahashi and Tsugata

2011b: 253) that this is not merely a statement of general opinion, but of identifiable, attitudinal fact, affecting everything from the expectations of staff to their sources of inspiration:

> The reconstruction in the wake of the Great Kantō Earthquake saw the rise of what might be called a second generation of animators, including Yamamoto Sanae, Murata Yasuji, Ōfuji Noburō, and Masaoka Kenzō. And the great influence on this generation was the work of Disney and the Fleischer brothers.

Takahashi adds (Takahashi and Tsugata 2011b: 253) that the same period saw a palpable influx of Disney and Fleischer cartoons, sufficient for him to term it a '*Mickey Mouse* and *Betty Boop* boom'. The earthquake had no direct influence on these films, which were surely already on their way from the United States. However, they formed part of the general context in which this 'second generation' of animators worked – forming both the animation events that spurred them, and the representative works that inspired them. Takahashi sees only the Japanese distribution and reception end of this alleged boom – at the production end in America other variables were at work, not least the increased concentration on children's entertainment as a means of generating ticket sales and concession trades in the wake of the Great Depression – Mickey Mouse Clubs first convened as Saturday-morning events in post-Depression US cinemas (Crafton 1997: 258). Meanwhile, Japanese cartoons engaged in a series of discourses with American material, often playing in imitation of or reaction to the newest arrivals. Some Japanese cartoons of the period attempt to imply a relationship to or a belittling carnivalisation of Hollywood 'originals', such as the Betty Boop-like damsel in distress to be seen in Kataoka Yoshitarō's *Ban Danemon: Shōjōji no Tanuki-bayashi* (1935, *Ban Danemon: The Monster Exterminator*). Ōfuji Noburō's *Baguda-jo no Tozoku* (1926, *The Thief of Baguda Castle*) parodies the Japanese title of the Douglas Fairbanks vehicle *The Thief of Bagdad* (1924), although the story was entirely different (Ogata 2010: 1).

   Kitayama remained the most successful Japanese practitioner, largely because his work was never in competition with the accomplished new cartoons arriving from abroad. While Japanese output in narrative, fictional cartoons was sparse for many years, Kitayama's production of informational, educational and instructional films grew stronger than ever – government contracts, it seemed, were unaffected by the disaster.

The title of the samurai story *The Thief of Baguda Castle* (1926) attempted to imply a nonexistent relationship to *The Thief of Bagdad* (1924)

PRODUCTION: ANIMATION METHODS

The earliest known account of how Kitayama worked can be found in the February 1918 issue of *Katsudō no Sekai*, which 'takes a look at Nikkatsu's Cartoon Factory' (Manga Seisaku-sho), or rather, Kitayama's office. Kitayama's camera set-up was constructed on a framework roughly the same size as a modern set of bunk beds. The camera itself was mounted on the upper 'bunk', in a fixed position, aiming down at the lower bunk. The image was placed on the lower level under a hinged glass sheet to prevent the component papers moving. Two 40–50W electric lamps at either side provided light.

For filming, one animator would operate the camera by climbing a ladder and turning the camera handle once to generate an exposure of two frames. A second animator would kneel before the lower bunk, ready to switch out the papers and add the next scene. The filming area beneath the glass was 30cm^2 – roughly the size of the screen of a modern laptop. The focal distance from the camera to the filming plate was 90cm (Tsugata 2007a: 117–18).

Kitayama's 1918 set-up is remarkably similar to the rostrum camera set-up used industry-wide until the 1990s. Moreover, although Kitayama and his pair of assistants were generally working with paper, they were already using separate sections for foreground and background. The glass plate might compress the paper firmly together and effectively render it as merely two-dimensional, but even in 1918, there was already a thin 'third' dimension to consider. Within a decade of Kitayama's primitive arrangement, Ōfuji Noburō had already refined it to include several glass planes, each separated from the other by a few inches. As Thomas Lamarre notes (2009: 23–4), this effectively prefigures the technology, if not the application, of the 'multiplane' camera patented by Disney in 1940 and 'first' used in Japan by Mochinaga Tadahito in 1941. While Ōfuji did not demonstrably exploit the potential of a multiplanar image, he had already built much of the apparatus that it required. In his memoirs, Kitayama briefly noted a series of minor refinements to the production set-up between the original Nikkatsu work and the establishment of his own studio three years later.

> Tools also were improvised after much effort. The wooden frame was replaced by an iron frame; the camera that once was fixed in place became movable both vertically and horizontally. [Effects such as] OL [overlap] and FI [fade in] became possible and techniques improved enough to enable us to produce something similar to modern animation. However, the basic production method remained primitive. We had to draw every single movement and no colours were used except black and white, and eventually an intermediate grey. (Kitayama, quoted in Tsugata 2007a: 167)

Kitayama's account of his production is a valuable document, but as the reference to 'modern' animation suggests, it was written in 1930, some time after the events described. It is hence not a testimonial, but a memoir, parsed in terms of how the animation business looked to him in hindsight. Tsugata (2007a: 168) identifies this as a crucial issue in the historiography of the development of the Japanese animation business, because of the reliance in Kitayama's 1930 'memories' on examples and diagrams lifted from the American book *Animated Cartoons: How They Are Made, Their Origin and Development* (1920) by Edwin G. Lutz.

Lutz's manual drew heavily on the developments and techniques of John Bray's studio, which itself had taken swift steps to industrialise the process of animation along lines proposed in general labour terms in *Principles of Scientific Management* (1911) by Frederick W. Taylor (Crafton 1982: 163–4). It is impossible to pick apart Kitayama's text sufficiently in order to determine how many of his innovations at Nikkatsu and Kitayama Eiga were truly 'improvised' before 1920, and how many were copied from foreign sources. It is entirely possible that Kitayama and his staff independently created the technologies they used in the early 1920s. However, owing to Kitayama's reliance on foreign illustration sources in his later memoirs, such as a camera-stand diagram blatantly lifted, lettering and all, from Lutz (1920: 203), it is also possible that much of Kitayama's 'memory' of the early 1920s is actually a reconstructed image of the late 1920s, by which time his set-up may have incorporated alterations suggested in Lutz's book – a book which was undoubtedly in his possession by the end of the decade.

There is an interesting question as to when Japanese animation transferred from, to use Thomas Elsaessar's terms (1990: 155) a largely amateur, artisanal production process, into an organised, commercial, industrialised process.

It is unanswerable in part because some animators remained, or indeed, remain artisans to this day, working solo or in small groups. However, elements of industrialisation, a division of labour and a uniformity of tasks can be discerned as early as 1918. In the same memoir, Kitayama boasts:

> Shimokawa [Ōten] and Kōuchi [Junichi] apparently had many contacts and studied the medium, but because their production cost was very high for the standard of the time, they stopped producing after 23 films. I considered making films economically and put that into practice, so I could make dozens of films one after another. (Kitayama, quoted in Tsugata 2007a: 174)

The tone certainly sounds like that of an 'industrial' animator bragging of his tailorised labour processes, although if it is, Kitayama comes across as rather a ludicrous figure, since two additional staff members hardly make a 'factory', while the rarity of acetate cels in Japan at the time would have forced Kitayama to copy only the outward appearance of Bray's process, rather than the interior techniques made possible by cels. There is no mention here of an awareness of full or limited animation or other economies, although it does seem that tensions over art and commerce were already arising in the Japanese animation business only two or three years after the appearance of the first film. Placing an emphasis on industrial quantity rather than artistic quality, Kitayama successfully completed a project roughly every month.

Nor does Kitayama's triumphalist tone sit well with claims made in the press in 1917, when Nikkatsu Mukōjima announced to *Katsudō no Sekai* that 'they will be producing and distributing one or two cartoon comedies every month' (quoted in Yamaguchi and Watanabe 1977: 10). There is no question about it – if someone at Nikkatsu's Mukōjima studios was making a promise about cartoon output, the only animator they could have meant was Kitayama. And while Kitayama certainly managed a regular output of animated films in the years that followed, only a tiny handful of them were the 'cartoon comedies' promised in 1917. It seems that if he did make a dispassionate commercial decision to eschew fiction in favour of instructional films, he did so only *after* he had discovered the same limitations of the field that scared off his competitors. Perhaps, even, someone made the 'discovery' for him, and he related it only in hindsight; the potential of instructional animation was a major theme in Edwin Lutz's *Animated Cartoons*, and formed the bulk of its closing chapter (1920: 253–61).

Kitayama's tone of ridicule towards his competitors suggests that they failed where he had succeeded, simply through inadequate budgeting. As noted in Chapter 1, Shimokawa and Kōuchi faced several other problems that hampered their progress, not the least Shimokawa's relative lack of interest in the medium, and Kōuchi's damning encounter with the censor after his inadvisable release of a cartoon about a boy and an air rifle, as well as unspecified 'business difficulties' with his backer (Tsugata 2003: 17). However, it seems unfair for Kitayama to parse such problems among his competitors as some sort of proof of his superior working methods, particularly when his methods added only a couple of extra staff members.

At the time that Kitayama was writing off Kōuchi as an also-ran in the animation world, Kōuchi was actually returning to the field, having set up a new company, Sumikazu Eiga, in 1923, working out of his home (Animage 1989: 13). After early, hesitant steps in entertainment, Kōuchi embraced the field of public-information films in much the same manner as Kitayama himself, demonstrating a particular acumen for films with a political message, including *Kokka o Sukue* (1925, *Your Country Needs You*), *Yosan Seiji* (1925, *Budget Politics*) and *Shisei Sasshin* (1925, *Reform of the Municipal System*) (Yamaguchi 2004: 47).

In other words, Kitayama's pronouncements in 1930 present a difficult issue with his testimony. Ultimately, it does not much matter where Kitayama got his ideas from, but in consideration of the degree to which Japanese animation is a replication in whole or part of a foreign process, it is of interest to the historian.

Tsugata contends that even if Kitayama did not innovate any particular process or device in Japan, his division of labour was a vital development in the history of Japanese animation (Tsugata 2007a: 255–6). For Tsugata, this was a crucial step, splitting the labour into just enough component parts, and hence speeding it up just enough to take animation from a painstaking, labour-intensive hobby to a business that could turn a profit. This seems a little unfair on Shimokawa Ōten, since he, too, was 'dividing' the labour on his films by late 1917, with the hiring of a camera assistant. But what separates the division of labour on Shimokawa's films from that on Kitayama's is the nature of the labour that could be divided. Shimokawa still had to draw every single frame himself. Kitayama was able to split the same artistic work between two or three people, allowing him not only to turn around finished film swiftly enough to turn a profit, but also to split his output between urban centres.

Many years later, in 1958, when Yamamoto Sanae was secure in his position at the Tōei Dōga studio, he offered a different version of events, subtly undermining the notion of Kitayama Seitarō as the solo pioneer of Japanese animation in the 1920s.

> The research was conducted by three people, and so the profit should have been divided equally between them, which is what caused the trouble. Kitayama was multitalented and very smart; he negotiated with the filming studio and did all the managerial tasks, so naturally he became the boss. The other two did not like it, and they went their separate ways. (Yamamoto, quoted in Tsugata 2007a: 176)

Tsugata Nobuyuki suggests that this is a reference to Mineta Hiroshi and Yamakawa Kunizō, the other two artists present at the unidentified 'Fleischer' screening that started it all, who stayed out of the animation business thereafter because Kitayama's rapid expansion in staff and output dominated the market and made it impossible to compete. One cannot help but wonder if the two unhappy collaborators in Yamamoto's piece are actually Yamamoto himself and his fellow Kitayama alumnus Kanai Kiichirō, since both eventually went their own way, too.

But if Tsugata's interpretation is correct, then it actually works in Kitayama's favour. If his methods allowed him to dominate a market in which others' hesitant steps had only led to failure, then his managerial skills were surely a vital component in his success. As with other anime entrepreneurs later on – particularly Tezuka Osamu – considering that the participants in the animation industry are all working with broadly the same materials, conditions and technology, perhaps it is indeed a reasonable assumption that whatever it was that made Kitayama Eiga a success, Kitayama himself and his bluntly commercial approach was a major factor.

Kitayama's achievements did not merely 'scare off' competitors. They also encouraged them, with several of his staff members spinning off animation companies of their own during the 1920s. When Kitayama departed for Osaka after the Kantō Earthquake, he was able to leave his assistant Yamamoto Sanae in Tokyo, where Yamamoto continued to work as a 'branch' of Kitayama Eiga, producing the films *Usagi to Kame* (1924, *The Hare and the Tortoise*), *Yūbin no Tabi* (1924, *The Mail's Journey*) and *Tonshi Hakashi* (1925, *Doctor Ready-wit*). Yamamoto subsequently broke with Kitayama, establishing his own animation company, the Yamamoto Cartoon Film Production Works (Yamamoto Manga-Eiga Seisaku-sho) in 1925 (Yamaguchi 2004: 50). Kitayama's other leading assistant, Kanai Kiichirō, had already left in 1923 to establish the Tokyo Graphics Film Works (Tōkyō Senga Film Seisaku-sho), where he worked individually on such films as *Issun Boshi* (1928, *Tom Thumb*), and also in collaboration with his former colleague Yamamoto on several cartoons in the late 1920s and early 1930s (Tsugata 2007a: 160–1).

Yamamoto Sanae's recollection of Kitayama's filming process is a quaint glimpse into the logistics of a very different age. Notably, his testimony draws our attention to the different frame-rates of a hand-cranked era, and the power considerations of working in the early days of electricity:

> For a character taking one step, we would divide the sequence into 16 frames, and then animate the 16 frames in one second. The character walks in small increments. In order to show that in each frame, we required a light box [*tōsha-ki* – literally: 'projection desk']. We had to make the tools to copy an artwork using special papers. First of all, we had the light box made. The best thing to use was electric light, but at the time there was no power supply except at night. It was impossible to use artificial light during the day, except in large factories. After three or four o'clock, the sunlight was too weak for us to draw. We would start again after five when the power came on. (Yamamoto, quoted in Tsugata 2007a: 125–6)[1]

Tsugata Nobuyuki notes that there is no provision within the 1918 article for the production of Kitayama's actual artwork. The 'animation production room' as described is a 'six-mat' area, little more than nine square metres, with walls covered in blackboards to allow for the production schedules to be constantly updated and checked off. Allowing for at least one window and somewhere for the shelves used to store artwork, there is little space left for an artist's desk or materials. Yamamoto confirms this in his own memoirs, claiming that Kitayama would draw the artwork himself at home, and then bring it into the studio each day (Tsugata 2007a: 125).

This, too, foreshadows conditions common in later years in the animation business. Animation 'studios' are rarely the monolithic, clearly identifiable buildings that we might associate with an American movie lot. Instead, they are more likely to be rooms within an anonymous office building, or even spaces set aside in private residences. This very anonymity, however, also gives the animators flexibility. Kitayama's 'Cartoon Production Studio' at Nikkatsu amounted to little more than the camera and its frame. Every other aspect of the production process could be swiftly moved or reconstructed at a new venue. This seems to have given Kitayama a degree of mobility, not only in the setting up of the Kitayama Film Production Works in 1921, but in the ease with which he could relocate its entire production capacity to Osaka after the Kantō Earthquake in 1923.

EXHIBITION: VENUES FOR INSTRUCTIONAL FILMS

Following the establishment of a Film Recommendation System in 1921, which marked cartoons as one of three areas of development, the Ministry of Education began offering subsidies and incentives to animators for the production of educational films, and the 'production of films for pedagogical purposes' (Miyao 2002: 203). By 1925 this had transformed into an annual appropriation, effectively guaranteeing audiences and revenue to any animators who would produce films that met the requirements of government education. In fact, it is possible to argue that the first thirty years of the Japanese animation business represented a period in which such 'invisible' productions comprised the majority of Japan's animation output, with occasional narrative stories as exceptions rather than the rule. Such a point is particularly relevant if we consider that even some of these narrative cartoons were really instructional or promotional films in disguise, such as Kitayama's *Kinrō no Ari* (1930, *The Industrious Ant*), intended as a parable of value in moral education, or Ōishi Ikuo's *The Hare and the Tortoise*, commissioned to promote Morinaga Milk Chocolate.

We might compare such incentives in Japan with their American equivalent, the 'captive audience' enjoyed by animators at Warner Bros. in the 1930s, who knew that their cartoons were sure to be block-booked onto the schedule as part of a night at the movies for Warners cinemas. As noted by Chuck Jones, this in turn fostered a safe and reliable industry among the animators, and removed an element of financial insecurity (Lewell 1982: 134). In a similar fashion, the rise of a captive audience and guaranteed educational market lured many Japanese animators away from narrative films and into documentaries and instructional animations, including such adult topics as Yamamoto Sanae's *Baidoku no Denpa* (1926, *The Spread of Syphilis*) and Kitagawa Tetsuo's notorious *Dorei Sensō* (1931, *Slave War* – see below). The chief benefit of such government contracts was that payment was guaranteed – in an era where cartoons were not yet long enough to form a main cinema attraction in their own right, animators were usually reliant on fickle audiences or parsimonious cinema managers, whereas informational films had alternative audiences in town halls and colleges. However, this same benefit also kept much instructional animation out of the traditional journals of record in the Japanese film business. In an issue that also troubles record-keeping elsewhere (e.g. Anthony *et al.* 2009: 5), the historiography of animation often takes notice only of extant or completed, screened dramatic/fictional works. This can lead to odd counterintuitive gaps in the available Japanese data, such as the apparent eight-year hiatus from 1918–26 in the *Anime Sakuhin Jiten* (*Dictionary of Animation Works*), the largest book ever published on Japanese animation, which misleadingly implies that no animation was created in Japan at all during those years (Stingray and Nichigai 2010: 891). In fact, Kitayama alone was completing a new animation project almost every month, demonstrating a business acumen that largely eluded the more artistically minded pioneers who had preceded him (Tsugata 2007a: 174).

Kitayama was the most prolific of the instructional animators. The Kitayama Film Production Works in Tokyo produced many educational films, beginning with *Kiatsu to Mizuage Pump* (1922, *Air Pressure and the Water Pump*). Kitayama's work achieved early attention, and indeed imperial praise, when he was hired in

1922 to prepare explicatory graphics to accompany a lecture by Dr Kishi Kazutaka on a proposed new scheme to generate power by incinerating garbage. City councillors had previously rejected the scheme when it had been demonstrated with a scale model at a power station, but somehow assented when it was presented as a cartoon. According to Kitayama, his animation swayed the audience more than any models or diagrams could, and the scheme was put into action (Tsugata 2007a: 178–9). This achievement, or at least the myth of its efficacy, bolstered by words of encouragement from Prince Higashinomiya, would secure Kitayama and his colleagues more government contracts in the years that followed, including Yamamoto Sanae's *The Mail's Journey*, commissioned by the colonial governor-general's office in Korea, and Kitayama's science-education film *Shokubutsu no Seiri* (1924, *The Physiology of Plants*). Kitayama also obtained a contract from the Lion Brand toothpaste company to contribute to a feature-length documentary, written by a celebrated lecturer on dentistry. Tsugata Nobuyuki argues (2007a: 178) that the lost film *Kōkū Eisei* (1923, *Oral Hygiene*) represented a new genre in Japanese animation, as it was intended neither for entertainment nor advertising, nor even 'education' in the usual sense, but as an instructional film. According to Kanai Kiichirō, a worker at Kitayama Eiga:

> Before the Great Earthquake we worked on a nine-*maki* scientific *senga eiga* called *Oral Hygiene* for Lion Brand Toothpaste's Kobayashi shop. It must have set a new record for the length of animation up to that point. (Kanai, quoted in Tsugata 2007a: 178)

Two of the terms in the Japanese quotation are ambiguous and problematic. The term *senga eiga* would normally be translated as 'animation' but was also used in relation to graphics and intertitles. Kanai does not specify if *Oral Hygiene* was entirely animated, partly animated, or if its *senga* elements were a series of still images. For all we know, it could have been a work more similar to a modern-day slideshow or PowerPoint presentation than a cartoon. Similarly, *maki* is a counting word for rolled objects, and can mean either nine reels of film or nine chapters of a text. Kanai's text implies that *Oral Hygiene* was a single, integrated film, but other extant descriptions make the *maki* sound less like reels than chapters. Nor do other descriptions match Kanai's own count; the Lion Brand archives list only eight parts to *Oral Hygiene*. However, a history of Japanese dentistry mentions a ninth part, noting that the complete *Oral Hygiene*:

> is a very long film – 12-*maki* altogether, 7000 feet long. Production started in 1922 and was completed in August 1923. Originally it was planned to release the film in Tokyo, but due to the Great Kantō Earthquake on 1st September 1923, it was screened at the Osaka Public Hall on 29th and 30th November 1923. It was a so-called science film to spread knowledge of dental hygiene, handling 'Nutrition and Chewing, Dental Caries and Infection Deciduous Teeth, The Permanent First Molar, Formation of Dental Caries, Prevention of Dental Caries, Family Oral Hygiene, and Social Dentistry Facilities'. **At the end there was a cartoon called *Kōkū Sensō* (*Oral War*).** (quoted in Tsugata 2007a: 184–5, my emphasis in bold)

The final sentence suggests that only the ninth chapter was a cartoon in any true sense of the word, although it is unclear how long that chapter was. Seven thousand feet of film is feature-length, approaching two hours. If Kanai's 'eight-*maki*' truly were eight reels, it is remotely possible that the grand finale of *Oral War* ran for four reels, or roughly thirty minutes, but that would have put it a decade ahead of its time. It seems more likely that *Oral War* amounted to merely one or two reels, closing a feature-length documentary that otherwise comprised eight topics depicted in live footage and drawn graphics. Kanai's claim to have worked on a Japanese cartoon of record-breaking length might still be true, but in 1923 that record was probably a mere eight minutes (Animage 1989: 5).

Tsugata Nobuyuki faithfully includes *Oral War* in a list of 'productions by Kitayama Seitarō' (Tsugata 2007a: 147), and reports its length as eight reels, but we should remember that, as with his work at Nikkatsu, Kitayama made no claim to be working exclusively on animated works. As a result, although *Oral War* is listed as a production by Kitayama's company, there is no reason to assume that it was entirely animated, or even that the reels counted on Kitayama's own production slate represented the entire length of the film.

CONTENT AND THEMES: FROM FOLK TALES TO SPORTS

Despite the behind-the-scenes supremacy of instructional and educational animation, the public face of cartoons still relied upon narrative stories. By 1928, a drive to encourage consumption of the right sort of films in younger viewers led to the first Children's Film Day, a Tokyo-based film festival. The Children's Film Day served as a deadline, target or nexus for some animators, and an impetus to supply completed films that could then go on provincial tours. In addition to themes from myths and folklore, animation in the 1920s also recognised new, modern subjects. Kimura Hakusan's *Nonki-na Tōsan Ryūgū Mairi* (1925, *Carefree Father in the Palace of the Dragon King*)[2] rests upon the post-earthquake publishing phenomenon of the *Nonki-na Tōsan* manga by Aso Yutaka, and, unlike the earlier comic spin-off *Imokawa Mukuzō*, seems to have gone into production without the consent of the creator (Animage 1989: 6).

More immediately notable among the modern cartoons is an ongoing interest in sports, reflecting Japan's increasing participation in the international community in the first three decades of the twentieth century. Japan first took part in the Olympics in Stockholm in 1912, but only sent two athletes (Guttman and Thompson 2001: 117). By 1928, however, Japan's presence was not only more substantial, but 'played as radio drama in Japan, where listeners were enthralled with the first success of Japanese Olympians abroad' (Wada-Marciano 2008: 62).

> Modern sports became linked paradoxically with modernity and tradition through the literature of national sports associations, which invoked mythic masculine images of bushidō (the warrior's code of Japanese chivalry) virtues reinvented as a modern tradition. Indeed, there were two discursive responses to the problem of modern sports' compatibility with Japanese traditions. The first to appear was a mythic Japanese spirit to assert that modern sports were played with a different emphasis in Japan. The second was a reinvention of Japan's traditional sports, like judō and kendō, as modern collegiate institutions, with an emphasis on quantifiable achievement. (Wada-Marciano 2008: 65)

This in turn led to the *wakamono sports eiga* (youth sports films), a definable genre in Japanese live-action movies throughout the 1920s. It also appeared in cartoon form, beginning with Murata Yasuji's *Dōbutsu Olympic Taikai* (1928, *Animal Olympic Games*).[3]

The sports genre involved a new environment – a placeless, modernist setting based on the towering foreign stadiums where real-world Japanese athletes were competing against foreign powers. This 'stateless' (*mukokuseki*) environment has been described by Mitsuyo Wada-Marciano (2008: 36) as a cosy form of foreign location with Japanese qualities, in that the 'use of foreign atmosphere creates … a liminal site for *imagined* Otherness'. Sports offered Japanese cartoon characters the first chance to interact with foreign characters, in some cases literally, as in the sight of Mickey Mouse and Betty Boop cheering on the lead character in *Mabō no Dai Kyōsō* (1936, *Mabō's Great Race*), and to do so in an environment that may have been competitive, but was, once again literally, a level playing field.[4]

There is, then, a certain irony in the fact that the Japanese cartoons exported in this period traded on their traditionalist appearance. The first, and apparently only film of Kitayama Seitarō to be exported abroad was *Momotarō* (1918),[5] which was dispatched to France with great fanfare with the help of the Association Franco-Japonaise, amid another set of aspirational promises, faithfully repeated by the February 1919 *Katsudō no Sekai*, to the effect that 'henceforth, all cartoons produced by the [Nikkatsu Mukōjima] studio will be exported to France' (Tsugata 2007a: 175). In fact, there is no evidence that any more were, leaving the foreign limelight in the 1920s largely domi-

Unlicensed foreign fans cheer on the
Japanese hero in *Mabō's Great Race* (1936)

nated by Ōfuji Noburō, whose cartoons found international acclaim in France, where their distinctive *chiyo-gami* (coloured paper) look helped mark them as 'uniquely' Japanese products. His later *Kujira* (1927, *Whale*) was exhibited in France and the Soviet Union (Miyao 2002: 200).

OWNERSHIP: SMALL-GAUGE CAMERAS AND THE PROLETARIAN FILM LEAGUE

Japanese amateur film, which is to say, the arrival of technology that made film feasible for individuals rather than organisations, began in 1923 with the arrival in Japan of the first small-gauge cameras, Charles Pathé's Pathé Baby and George Eastman's Kodascope (Makino 2001a: 38). Although expensive, such devices nevertheless put some form of film-making within the grasp of wealthy hobbyists – most notably the camera collector Tezuka Yutaka, whose love of his Pathé Baby would lead him to buy home-screening copies of films featuring Charlie Chaplin and Mickey Mouse, and whose son Osamu would write in later life of trips to the store to buy film for his own amateur projects (Tezuka 1997: 17–19). The small-gauge cameras also led to a minor flurry of amateur film magazines and film clubs. These clubs served to unite a new group of would-be film-makers, and would lead indirectly to several small-scale animation productions alongside live-action film projects. In particular, we might note the work of the animator Ogino Shigeji (1899–1991) who began working with a 9.5mm Pathé Baby camera on short works such as *Hyakunen-go Aru Hi* (1932, *One Day 100 Years Hence*) and *Felix no Meitantei* (1935, *Felix the Famous Detective*),[6] with an average output of a couple of films every year, for the next forty years (Tsugata 2010b: 26–7). However, the likelihood of any such films reaching a wide audience in the 1930s was largely destroyed by changes in Japanese legislation.

In 1925, the Japanese government passed the Public Security Preservation Law (Chian Iji Hō), a directive aimed at quelling left-wing dissent, which mandated a prison sentence of up to ten years for joining any association opposed to private property or the alteration of the 'national identity' (*kokutai*) (Sharp 2011: 39). The latter was usefully vague – since the authorities defined what the *kokutai* was, the new law effectively allowed them to define any dissent as a threat to the status quo as a threat to 'national identity'. The law led to the founding of a new unit of Special Higher Police (Tokubetsu Kōtō Keisatsu), a 'thought police' in all but name, with special units for dealing with, among others, Koreans, labour disputes, surveillance of foreigners and, most directly associated with the film world, censorship.

It was within this hostile political climate that the Proletarian Film League of Japan (Nihon Puroretaria Eiga Dōmei – Prokino for short) briefly struggled to mount an alternative to the culture films of the prevailing order, by using newly available small-gauge cameras, particularly 9.5mm and 16mm formats, to chronicle workers' lives, labour disputes, strikes and May Day parades (Sharp 2011: 200). Some members of the league also made animated films, with patchy records remaining of the existence of several films made between the years 1930 and 1932, including *Fuzai Jinushi* (date unknown, *The Absentee Landlord*),[7] *Alibaba Monogatari* (1930?, *The Story of Alibaba*) and *Issun Boshi* (date unknown, *Tom Thumb*).[8] Initially, the Prokino films were avowedly instructional, as typified by *Ajita Prokichi Shōhisha Kumiai no Maki* (1930, *Ajita Prokichi's Consumer Union*), which exhorted audiences to pool their spending power in order to cut out the middleman between customer and producer (Tsugata 2010b: 25). The leading character, Ajita Prokichi, seems intended as a mascot for the movement, with a name that recalls the Japanese pronunciation of 'agit-prop', but also a title with phrasing that implies other episodes of Ajita's activities are coming soon. The Prokino movement appears to have intended to make several more films of 'abstract disputes', only to find that audiences expressed a greater interest in practical advice, as per other instructional animations of the era. Prokino's output continued with Soviet parables, such as *Sankichi no Kūchū Ryōkō* (1932, *Sankichi's Mid-air Journey*),[9] in which a bird tells an awestruck child about a utopian society 'in the north', but for preaching more subtly, particularly to middle-class audiences, the group turned to an antiwar message.

Entotsuya Perō (1930, *Perō the Chimney Sweep*) was commissioned as a children's parable, funded by the Kyoto 'studio' Dōei-sha (Children's Films) but actually the work of several members of the league (Tsugata 2010b: 25). Shot on 16mm and using stop-motion to animate shadow puppets, it was originally intended as Dōei-sha's entry in the children's film events (*kodomo eiga kai*) held annually as markets for new works. Instead, however, it was screened as part of a night of Prokino films, alongside two features and a May Day documentary (Makino 2001a: 40). It depicted a chimney sweep in a land at war, praised for alerting the authorities to approaching enemy forces. However, Perō comes to realise that the enemy are only retaliating against aggression initiated by his own side, in a war that eventually ruins his home village and has him openly proclaiming his opposition to 'imperialist ideology'.[10]

The most notorious production of the Proletarian Film League was Kitagawa Tetsuo's *Slave War* (1931, *Dorei Sensō*),[11] a three-reel agit-prop piece, shot on 16mm, in which the imperialist bourgeoisie were depicted as pigs in suits, on a constant search for new markets to exploit, enslaving the peasants of China, who eventually fight back in a revolt. Extant stills reveal a scrappily drawn, low-quality work, lacking the unity and simplicity of image of *Perō the Chimney Sweep*. However, *Slave War*'s problem lay in the unity of its *script*, which ignored the government-approved tone of pan-Asianism, and instead implied that the Japanese themselves were also imperialists, exploiting Chinese coolies to no lesser an extent than the hated Western powers. Although the polemic of the film was aimed specifically at the British, it made it clear that the French and Japanese had made little attempt to stop the predations of the British in Asia. The 'heroes' of *Slave War* were not the Japanese, coming to the aid of their Asian cousins, but the workers of Guangdong in South China, who rise up against all oppressors (Animage 1989: 13).

The film's event was as controversial as its contents, with reels sneaked around Japan and screened as underhand exclusives after the police proclaimed the film itself to be 'Wanted' (Hu 2010: 65). Possibly as a result of a partial seizure during a raid, the film was put in the hands of the Special Higher Police, who returned it two months later in a state 'so unintelligible that it became known, even outside the movement, both for its creative use of animation and as an example of the excesses of Japanese censorship' (Nornes 2003: 38–9). The butchering of *Slave War* was the last straw for Prokino, which avoided animation thereafter, although some of its members, most notably Seo Mitsuyo, would eventually end up selling their skills to the establishment.

The Proletarian Film League was disbanded by 1934, amid mounting government controls on all films, as the arts themselves were co-opted even deeper into the apparatus of militarist society. In the decade that followed, the left-wing propaganda of the league was swamped by a tidal wave of right-wing propaganda, as the culture films were deployed in the promotion and shaping of the Japanese war effort.

SOUND AND MUSIC

The advent of recorded sound in Japanese film came close on the heels of its adoption in American cinemas, and it fell subject to the same conflicts over rival formats and the expense of installation. *Benshi* and live musicians, of course, were strongly resistant to films with sound, although the advent of sound was initially regarded as something of a boon for the live performers. By the end of the 1920s, 'two-thirds of the world's 57,341 cinemas were outside the United States' (Crafton 1997: 418), and silent films were readily repurposable for foreign audiences. The arrival of sound brought the inescapable fact of foreign films complete with foreign soundtracks, leading the international film business to confront new issues in alternative soundtracks and subtitling, even the possibility that soundless films would need to remain a permanent feature of export markets.

In 1927 the American journal *Film Daily* published Thomas Edison's account of his failed Kinetophone format, a synchronised sound auxiliary that had already been superseded by 'phonofilm' technology:

> We took the voice on a phonograph record and arranged the talking machine so that it could be operated from the projection room of the theatre. The phonograph was placed down in front of the screen, and it worked fine. I had hardly set the machine to working, when a Japanese man nearly went crazy over it. He asked what I would take for the invention. I really did not think much of it, and thought that $2,000 or $3,000 would have been a pretty fair price. Before I could make a price, however, he up and offers me $50,000 for the rights. Did I give them to him? Certainly I did. As soon as I caught my breath after the jolt. (Edison, quoted in Crafton 1997: 57)

Edison's quote is odd because it implies that the Japanese would have had the technology for talking pictures years before the first talking features in Japan, which were, depending on how one counts, either Josef von Sternberg's *Morocco* (1930), screened with its original English dialogue and Japanese subtitles, or Mizoguchi

Kenji's *Furusato* (1930, *Hometown*), which included a recorded theme song, selected sound effects and scraps of dialogue (Katō 2006: 238–9). Japan's first 'official' talkie, containing a spoken soundtrack from beginning to end, was Gosho Heinosuke's *Madam to Nyōbō* (1931, *The Neighbour's Wife and Mine*), which added to its exotic flavour with sly in-film references to recent American movie successes (Yamaguchi 2004: 54).[12]

If the advent of sound were delayed in Japan until the 1930s, and slow to spread even then, it was partly because of the problems of installation and competing formats that made it a costly risk in other countries, but also because of the increased resistance of the *benshi*, who viewed the new development as a threat to their livelihood. The expense of sound equipment usually meant that the top-end theatres were the first to install it, thereby threatening the jobs of the most experienced *benshi*, those with the greatest ability to mobilise opposition among their colleagues (Dym 2001: 150).

The arrival of sound brought immense pressure to bear on the *benshi*. Some tried to bellow their interpretation live as the soundtrack played, which was both frustrating for the individual *benshi* but lucrative for the profession as a whole, as it required extra *benshi* to take up the shortfall caused by lost voices (Crafton 1997: 423). In 1929, Japanese *benshi* went on strike, in protest at the growing hegemony of sound. However, there was also a growing dominion of *benshi*, with leading men as the main focus of each theatre's celebrity cult, additional voice players taking up the shortfall on matinees and lesser films and female *benshi* who increasingly added spice to romantic comedies by taking over the female roles (Fujiki 2006: 77). In the struggle of the *benshi* to match everything that the cinema medium threw at them, we see an analogue of the similar pressures faced by Hollywood's silent-movie stars in the switchover to sound. It was no longer enough for a *benshi* to simply explain the plot. The *benshi* had consistently emphasised their own performance, to the extent of becoming true 'voice actors' over the later silent films. Now they faced increasingly rapid cutting from shot to shot, and competition from partial, and then entire soundtracks. Audiences in the 1920s and 1930s became increasingly accustomed to female characters on screen, soon played by actual women, and then even voiced by them. As if to deliberately make life difficult for the *benshi*, some of these characters began to burst into song (Katō 2006: 241–3). By the mid-1920s, the smarter *benshi* were finding other outlets for their talents, as *kamishibai* storytellers or in the new medium of radio. Some even stepped in front of the camera, competing with screen performers for acting jobs in Japanese films (Dym 2001: 151) and as the pioneers of an all-new profession, providing the Japanese-language soundtracks for foreign films (Crafton 1997: 424).

The impact of sound on animation was threefold. At a local level, talkies without *benshi* required either a completely new soundtrack – then, as now, a costly endeavour – or the simpler solution of subtitles, which generally fell under the purview of the same 'graphics' (*senga*) departments where early animators, or rather, those men who had the potential to become early animators, had gravitated. Kitayama Seitarō's first credit for 'subtitles' (*jimaku*) was for the on-screen message in *General Nogi* (1918), and he implied in his memoirs that subtitles formed a large part of his work for Nikkatsu on otherwise unmentioned live-action jobs (Tsugata 2007a: 140). Like Kitayama, other early 'animators' similarly earned much of their living not from the art of animation but from the craft of graphics, most notably Murata Yasuji (1896–1966), who left his previous job as a cinema technician to become a subtitler at Yokohama cinema in 1923 (Yamaguchi 2004: 51). Murata's first animated film, *Giraffe no Kubi wa Naze Nagai* (1927, *Why Is the Giraffe's Neck So Long?*) followed four years later.

The change in technology also facilitated a flourishing in shorter subjects, particularly one- and two-reelers from America in which music, rather than dialogue was the prime sound component. Shorter films, within the running time of a three-minute phonograph record, could be played in tandem with a phonograph, which had the additional benefit of not requiring a complete rewiring of the theatre – even in remote provincial theatres, a phonograph could be brought in for the event and then removed to the next venue. Although synchronisation issues made such 'record talkies' more vulnerable than composite film prints which contained a soundtrack on the film itself, the novelty of their arrival created a brief boom in 'record talkies'. In America, D. W. Griffith's silent film *Dream Street* (1921) was the first to employ phonograph sound (Crafton 1997: 58), while the Fleischer brothers were fast behind with their cartoon *Come Take a Trip* (1924), which boasted of a twenty-five-second opening song sequence (Haraguchi 2000: 32). The Fleischers would follow this with thirty-six *Song Car-Tunes* (1924–7), each using an animated bouncing ball to encourage an American theatre audience to sing along.

Similarly, the fact that early sound projects favoured short subjects produced a new demand for cartoons, particularly those that could be related directly to the release of a specific record. Ōfuji Noburō's *Whale* was made available in a version intended to be synchronised to a Victor Records release of Rossini's *William Tell Overture*, beginning a strong connection between the Japanese music and animation industries that endures to this day. Another of Ōfuji's films, *Kuro Nyago* (1928, *Black Cat*) was synchronised directly to a jazz record via the Eastphone sound system. The three-minute film, made using cut-paper animation, features a cat that accosts human beings in a forest. It dances for their entertainment, first solo, then with a fellow cat, and then in a chorus line with all the humans present.

There are several moments of 'dialogue' in *Black Cat*, although since both its form (pieces of animated paper) and content (a talking, dancing cat) are unreal, this very lack of naturalism plays to the film's advantage. Whereas human characters in a live-action film would be only too obviously out of sync if the phonograph and film were even a second out of step, the simplistic animated figures of *Black Cat* gain considerable leeway through their very simplicity. When a human character speaks, he has only two mouth positions, open and closed. The lead cat has three: open, closed and *very* open – this last a sort of yawn used for moments of increased volume. However, there is no attempt at lip synchronisation, nor might we expect any. The on-screen characters are no more or less 'animated' than the characters of the contemporary Japanese puppet theatre, which were not expected to move their lips either.

The fact that some films now came with their own phonograph soundtrack did not mean that all animators discarded the *benshi*. Some cartoons continued to be 'silent' films – which is to say, not silent at all, but requiring the live participation of musicians and a narrator. It is tempting to speculate who the intended *benshi* were; it seems unlikely that many early cartoons were manufactured in such quantities as to require armies of narrators. Surely it is more likely that, as with Winsor McCay and *Gertie the Dinosaur*, many such early animations were intended to be accompanied by their individual creators. Ōfuji's *Kokoro no Chikara* (1931, *Power of the Heart*) has characters that break the fourth wall, turning to invite audience approval like vaudeville actors or cheeky puppets. But for them to do so with maximum dramatic impact, the *benshi* would have needed to be ready with split-second calls and responses; we should not assume that every production was as seamlessly timed as the one that is included in the 2010 Kinokuniya DVD release. The chances of it being so, however, would surely be greatly increased if the *benshi* were Ōfuji himself.

In the same vein as the Fleischer brothers' singalong shorts, many early Japanese cartoons were plainly intended to include yet another participant: the audience itself, although this feature is not always acknowledged in modern versions. During the 2010 Kinokuniya DVD presentation of *Kaeru Sanyūsha* (1933, *Three Frog*

Possibly the most widely seen animation in
the 1930s, the singalong *National Anthem*
(1931) shown in cinemas before other films

Heroes), the subtitles to a song appear on screen but are ignored by the modern
benshi. A song is clearly being sung, but in this version it is only a ghost. The
text, in such cases, remains vulnerable, in the sense that we can never be sure
how Ōfuji expected it to be performed, or indeed how theatre managers would have
presented it on those inevitable occasions when the original creator was not present to advise. It is unclear, for example, if Ōfuji expected audience participation
in some of his three-minute musical cartoons. At least in the DVD synchronisation
presented in modern formats (Zakka Films 2008; Kinokuniya 2010) of *Mura Matsuri*
(1930, *Village/Harvest Festival*) and *Haru no Uta* (1931, *Song of Spring*), the on-
screen lyrics also appear *as* the song is sung, but too quickly for an audience to read
them.[13] They work as a visual adornment, along with other decorations such as
dancing notes and characters, but they do not seem to function as an *aide-mémoire*
for viewers who hope to join in with the song. Viewers would need to know the
song before the film started, although such foreknowledge of movie content was
commonly encouraged in early Japanese cinema (Kitamura 2010: 170), and may
have been part of the context, intended as a means of ensuring advance record sales
before the listeners also became the viewers.

Similarly, the DVD (Digital Meme 2007) of Ōfuji's *Kokka Kimigayo* (1931,
The National Anthem: His Majesty's Reign)[14] which would surely have demanded
audience participation to extend to standing and singing along, also delivers its lyrics
a beat too late for the expectations of modern karaoke, seemingly in keeping with
the intentions of the original film-makers. According to Tochigi Akira from the
National Film Centre in Tokyo, *The National Anthem* was made expressly for this
purpose, to be sung at most if not all film screenings, and hence liable to have
been one of the most widely seen pieces of domestic animation in the 1930s.[15]
However, at the speed at which it has been run on every occasion I have seen it,
it has limped along at a dirge-like pace that seems far too slow.

Soundtracks and film in such 'record talkies' were supposedly foolproof, with
carefully marked points for synchronisation, but this does not take into account the
possible variations in film or phonograph speed that might arise at different venues.
The exactitude required for singalong subtitles seems to have eluded early animators, although this may not have been a large issue in the case of *The National
Anthem*, which viewers would have been expected to know anyway. Notably,
by the time of *Momotarō Umi no Shinpei* (1945, *Momotarō's Divine Sea Warriors*),
the issue of audience participation had clearly been resolved or at least refined, with
the film's centrepiece 'A-I-U-E-O' song presented with a degree of clarity and
pace that makes it ideal for a juvenile audience.

Developments in sound proceeded rapidly in the 1930s, establishing many
of the norms that persist to this day in industry terminology. Like Kitayama Seitarō,
Masaoka Kenzō started out as a technician in live-action film, working as an art
director at Makino Shōzō's newest venture, Makino Eiga. By 1929, he was working as part of the educational film unit at Nikkatsu, where he drifted into animation
with *Sarugashima* (1931, *Monkey Island*),[16] the first of a two-part series of exotic
desert-island settings and high-seas adventures. Thanks in part to contacts within
the Nikkatsu organisation and subsequently, the Shōchiku chain, Masaoka's films

Benkei vs Ushiwaka (1939) matched its animation to pre-recorded dialogue

were swiftly distributed, inspiring him to establish his own studio, Masaoka Eiga (Masaoka Films), in Kyoto. The company's first work was commissioned by Kido Shirō, the chairman of Shōchiku, as Japanese animation's first 'true' talkie, with a soundtrack fully integrated into the film itself. The first 'voice actors' (*seiyū*) credited in the *Animage* chronology of Japanese cartoons appear in *Chikara to Onna no Yo no Naka* (1933, *In the World of Power and Women*).[17] The film is no longer extant, so we can only guess at its content, although advertising and contemporary reviews plainly indicated it to be an 'adult' work, laden with bawdy humour. The comedian Furukawa Roppa provided the voice of a hen-pecked salaryman, whose wife, played by the Takarazuka Theatre star Sawa Ranko, becomes convinced that he is conducting an affair with an office typist. Eventually, the women are exhorted to settle matters with a boxing match, which turns to tickling.

In the *World of Power and Women* featured dialogue that was recorded after the animation had been made. Other films swiftly built on its technical achievements, with the first optical soundtrack, physically integrated into the film itself, appearing that same year in Ōfuji Noburō's *Numa no Taishō* (1933, *Boss of the Swamp*). Masaoka would not top his own achievement again until 1939, when he pre-recorded his own voice and that of his wife as the leading characters in *Benkei tai Ushiwaka* (1939, *Benkei vs Ushiwaka*). Such pre-scoring, as opposed to after-recording, offered the animators better chances to refine the animation to match existing dialogue, but it was likely to have been a refinement which escaped many audiences.[18]

CEL ANIMATION

Another of the achievements of *In the World of Power and Women*, also liable to have been lost on the public, concerned the physical materials of its construction. Previous animators had relied on various formats of cut paper, either as dark silhouettes, brightly coloured *chiyogami* paper scraps, or white sheets with the the the ink-and-turpentine base perfected at Kitayama Eiga. Masaoka's film may have been the first Japanese cartoon to employ transparent cels, heralding the arrival of a transformative technology in Japanese animation (Yamaguchi 2004: 55). If it was not, then the first identifiable and extant cel animation was close behind, in the form of Masaoka's *Chagama Ondo* (1935, *Dance of the Teakettles*).[19] According to Tsugata Nobuyuki (2004: 109), Masaoka's innovations in sound and picture made him a key figure in the development of Japanese animation, who played a vital role in transforming the industry from one in which a simply moving picture was regarded as noteworthy, to one in which animation was truly established as an art and craft.

Cut paper still had its benefits. Ōfuji Noburō's reliance on cut paper allowed him to make some elements only once, and then to re-pose rather than redraw them. The paper-cut samurai, carrying an *omikoshi* shrine, who lurch into frame at the beginning of Ōfuji's *Village/Harvest Festival* seem to be the same samurai who previously carried a similar shrine across Ōfuji's earlier *Mikan-bune* (1927, *Satsuma Ship*). Like many later animators working under pressure, Ōfuji could potentially store pre-existing artwork, and sneak it out again – three years is a long time in the world of children's entertainment, particularly when viewing was only ever likely to be in public on single, unrepeatable occasions. Similarly, Yamamoto Sanae's *The Tortoise and the Hare* depicted a hare with separately sectioned eyes and nose, and involved a repetition of three similar cut-paper pieces to create a loop of 'running' (Tsugata 2007a: 173).

Animation cels, however, had the additional benefit of a translucency an order of magnitude above that of the tracing paper that had previously been common in animation. It was not *quite* transparent, as animators soon discovered when too many stacked one upon the other led to a murky, deadening effect on the lowermost cels. However, it was certainly more translucent than paper and, although it took longer to dry, it was more hard- wearing, to the extent that cels could be 'washed' in acid and reused a limited number of times, thereby reducing costs.[20]

Celluloid, and later tri-acetate cellulose, was first employed in animation in Europe and America in the 1910s, where the material became the subject of several heated lawsuits. John Randolph Bray recognised the potential of celluloid in animation, suggesting that it might have a better translucency than paper, in his 1915 patent application for the animation process. However, his wording inadvertently excluded celluloid itself from the application, allowing his rival and later business partner Earl Hurd to patent the use of celluloid the same year. Bray then patented the idea of employing cels for backgrounds in 1917 (Crafton 1982: 154). Both Hurd and Bray, and it seems, many of their contemporaries preferred to use cels only for foreground action, sticking to paper for backgrounds (Crafton 1982: 150). It may seem odd that early animators took so long to wake up to the potential of celluloid, as it had been an essential basis for photography for many years. However, it was also in short supply, particularly when competing against wartime requisitions for nitro-cellulose in gun cotton, and early animators may have also been discouraged by the simple expense.

As a result, celluloid was not widespread in animation in Europe until the 1930s (Crafton 1982: 255), and even rarer in Japan until 1934, when the Fuji film corporation began manufacturing it domestically at its factory in Odawara. Cels were not an immediate panacea for animation ills. Just as tracing paper was prone to buckling (or 'cockling') due to heat or damp, animation cels ran a similar risk of halation effects – in which light would be smudged or scattered by imperfections or dust on the surface of the cel. These imperfections could be caused by poorly made or poorly kept cels, inadequate paint-drying provisions, deformation or simple wear and tear, particularly when cels were frequently reused after being washed with acid. As a rule of thumb, cels were regarded as waste materials if they had been recycled more than five times (Ushio 2007: 195–6).

Adoption of the cel was fast and widespread after the Odawara factory brought the local price down. Ichikawa Kon recalls his days as an assistant animator at J. O. Studios, working on a series of five-minute samurai comedies called *Hana yori Dangosuke*. The production process began with a script, and then the recording of music, sound effects and dialogue, to which the animators then synchronised the drawing, Masaoka's prescoring process seemingly already having found favour with other studios. With acetate cels still rare, Ichikawa's work was done on tracing paper, which was then traced directly onto film by an all-female staff of inkers (Ichikawa and Mori 2001: 24). Cels, however, would soon become the default medium for Japanese animation during the 1930s and for the next sixty years, except for a few dissenters such as Ōfuji, who continued to use paper or cellophane when it suited him, and occasional stop-motion animators or art-house pieces that engaged rarer methods such as sand or paper collages. Although the size of the frame would fluctuate with the nature of new delivery systems, from widescreen cinemas to squarer televisions, the basic technology of cel animation was fixed in Japan in the 1930s. Although it was refined on several occasions, particularly through the introduction of the multiplane camera (see Chapter 3) and xerography (see Chapter 7), the process itself underwent very little alteration until the 1990s.

Notably, the adoption of the cel brought with it the 'perf[oration] and peg' system of sprockets and holes, used by Raoul Barré from 1912 onwards in Europe, and presumed to have been exported worldwide with the cel itself (Crafton 1982: 194). Perforations and pegs ensured that every cel was held in precisely the same position, in order to allow for only intended alterations from frame to frame. However, despite the presence of perforations and pegs on pre-war animation cels in Japan, the animators themselves often seem to have relied merely on paperclips or bulldog clips for keeping their original contact sheets in place. This practice seemed to have been acceptable until the late 1950s, when a horrified Jimmy Murakami, newly arrived from America, berated staff at Tōei Dōga over their failure to use perforations and pegs (Osmond 2001). Japanese animators, however, seemed to have retained faith in their ability to judge register by the naked-eye registration, possibly because of the longstanding use of registration lines (kentō) in Japanese woodblock printmaking (Tinios 2010).

COLOUR ANIMATION

Japanese cartoons in the period remained monochrome, although the potential of colour was a very real feature of film discourse. John Randolph Bray's first colour film experiment, *The Debut of Thomas Katt* (1920) was far ahead of the Japanese film industry, but also far ahead of the adoption of the Technicolor process, which first gained attention in animation with Disney's Silly Symphony *Flowers and Trees* (1932). However, it is worth mentioning that the Matsumoto Fragment itself, that 'first' scrap of Japanese images drawn on film made some time before 1917, actually involved both red and black ink. Certainly by the mid-1930s, Japanese cinemas were playing colour shorts as accompaniments to the live-action main features. The technical superiority of foreign cartoons seemed to give them the edge over local products. In particular, early anime memoirs include several references to the compelling explosion of colour that Disney's Silly Symphonies brought to otherwise monochrome nights at the movies (e.g. Tsuji 1996: 8–9; Mochinaga 2006: 62; Suzuki 2008a: 82). None of the young audience members could have known that Disney in the early 1930s had a monopoly on the Technicolor process, which was not available to other studios, even in the US, until after 1934 (Telotte 2008: 47–8).

Claims of 'colour', both figurative and literal, had been a common feature of Japanese film since its inception, playing at first on the ambiguous meaning of *tennen-shoku* – spontaneous, natural or colourful – found on many posters and titles. 'Colour' was also implicit in the term *chiyo*, which literally meant 'thousand years' or 'for ever and ever', but served to describe *chiyogami*, the gaily patterned sheets used for paper-folding, decoration and as the raw materials of the early paper-cut animation of Ōfuji Noburō.[21] Ōfuji's Chiyogami Eiga-sha (Coloured Paper Film Company) continued trading under that name, even in the 1930s when much of its work was instead completed on acetate cels. This is likely to have been a matter of keeping things simple, although the name may have served an additional marketing purpose, conveying the impression, however misleading, that Ōfuji's work was 'colourful' in an age that was still monochrome. In the case of *Ō-Sekisho* (1930, *The Barrier*)[22] and *Song of Spring*,[23] Ōfuji offered an alternative to black-and-white film by presenting his work on film stock that had been tinted a garish, vibrant crimson/pink. It was, to be fair, no less 'monochrome' than black-and-white film, but would surely have been striking to contemporary audiences. Such films were not unknown in silent cinema, with pink- or yellow-dyed cartoon films known to have been in existence as early as 1917, some seemingly sold to private consumers as novelty toys (Matsumoto 2011a: 117). Such tinting was also not uncommon on foreign 'black-and-white films'; it seems most likely that Ōfuji's tinted cartoon was most directly inspired by a similar process used extensively on Lotte Reiniger's feature-length animation *Die Abenteuer des Prinzen Achmed* (1926), which was first screened in Japan in June 1929 under the title *Achmed Ōji no Bōken*.[24] However, such tinted films seem to disappear from the Japanese record after the early 1930s, presumably for the same reason that they fell out of use elsewhere; once an optical soundtrack was added to the physical film, an all-over wash of dye would not only colour the film, but mutate the sound produced by the optical track, which needed to be black/white monochrome in order to function correctly (Salt 2009: 199). Notably, both the aforementioned Ōfuji tinted prints were 'record talkies', synchronised to a phonograph, where such optical soundtrack problems would not be an issue.

Donald Crafton observes that many American critics of cinema expressed a drive toward colour as the natural progression from the increased 'realism' brought by sound. Just as sound added an immediacy and truth to on-screen images, it accentuated other areas for improvement, such as the absence of colour and the two-dimensional presentation (Crafton 1997: 249). Colour film remained an expensive gimmick, and its early

Princess Katsura (1937) showcased colour film-making, but only as part of a Making-of documentary that was longer than the film itself

appearances in Japan often highlight the artifice of its own creation. Ichikawa Kon reported experiments at J. O. Studios in the early to mid-1930s, in which the staff laboriously painted reds, blues and yellows by hand, frame by frame, onto a film. He notes that the film was screened and pronounced a success, but implies it was a private apprentice piece, and never intended for public viewing (Ichikawa and Mori 2001: 25).

Ōfuji Noburō's two-minute short *Princess Katsura* was included within, and seemingly made expressly for, Ogino Shigeji's five-minute introduction to cel animation, *How to Make Colour Cartoons*. It was also a cunning way of stretching a two-minute cartoon into a five-minute running time, effectively by including a *Making of …* that was longer than the film itself.[25] It remained, however, an obscure stunt, and the true advent of Japanese animation in colour would be delayed until after the end of World War II, particularly with the widespread availability of acrylic paints in the late 1950s.

CONCLUSION

By 1937, Japanese animation had accreted technologies of production essentially unchanged for the next fifty years. However, we might note that transformations were just as radical at the level of exhibition, with changes to audience expectations of a night at the movies, and of the 'purification' of film from a hybrid performance to a standalone medium. Distribution also formed an important factor, in the negative sense that censorship and legislation presented ever more powerful barriers to films unable to meet the criteria of the increasingly authoritarian government. Although the period witnessed a brief flourishing in independent production, film-making became largely impossible without the consent and, increasingly, financial backing of the authorities – an issue that would colour Japanese animation for the next decade.

NOTES

1. Yamamoto uses the term *tōsha-ki* (投射机) rather than 投射器 , which is pronounced the same but means 'projector'.

2. Clements and McCarthy (2006: 166) file it as *Dreamy Urashima*, the title under which it was exhibited at a modern Tokyo film event.

3. Clements and McCarthy (2006: 607) call it the 'first identifiable sports anime', as opposed to earlier races in cartoons that were not specifically sporting events.

4. The idea of a *mukokuseki* (stateless) aesthetic, that makes things appear alluringly, but safely, foreign in order to appeal to Japanese markets, is an interesting forerunner of Tezuka Osamu's much later *mukokuseiteki* (denationalised) aesthetic as noted in Chapter 6, which makes things appear alluringly, but safely un-Japanese in order to appeal to foreign markets. See for example Tsuji (1996: 292); Chun (2007: 279); Minakawa (2009b: 197, 240). The playing field wasn't actually that 'level' – in *Mabō's Great Race* nobody seems to mind that the Japanese protagonist defeats the foreign athletes by cheating!

5. DAW 803.

6. JCD 37813. As the name implies, it was a parody of Sullivan's character Felix the Cat. *One Day 100 Years Hence* does not currently have an entry in the JCD.

7. JCD 37799.

8. JCD 34469.

9. JCD 37822, date supplied in Tsugata (2010b: 25).

10. That, at least is the synopsis in Tsugata (2010b: 25). The synopsis in Animage (1989: 12) is almost entirely different, and claims that a grateful bird gives Perō a magical egg, which hatches soldiers that he puts to use in his country's war effort, much to his eventual chagrin. After seeing a ruined village, Perō destroys the egg and becomes a peaceful farmer.

11. JCD 37800.

12. My title translation is based on that of Sharp (2011: xxv).

13. The film also appears in the Digital Meme 2007 box set, but with a newly recorded soundtrack containing no lyrics.

14. JCD 37791.

15. Tochigi Akira, personal communication.

16. JCD 38420. At time of writing (8 February 2012), the JCD currently misfiles *Monkey Island* with the same title as its sequel *Kaizoku-bune* (1933, *The Pirate Ship*), found at JCD 38424.

17. Animage (1989: 14); DAW 458; JCD 22306 and 37830 – bafflingly, it is listed twice.

18. Modern anime industry terminology distinguishes between four types of sound recording. An *afureco* (after-recording) is dialogue post-synchronised to a newly made animated cartoon. This is, supposedly, the default setting of modern Japanese animation, although many *afureco* sessions seem billed as such for marketing purposes, since such an event is an opportunity to assemble the entire cast for a photo call, even if the animation has only been 'completed' as far as the animatics (Clements and McCarthy 2006: 672, 708). *Atereco* (substitution recording) refers to the replacement of a foreign-language voice track with Japanese dialogue. *Prereco* (presented recording) refers to recording dialogue before the animation is made, particularly prevalent in puppet animation and in animated work executed in Japan as work for hire for American studios. A final nuance is the more modern term *mitereco* (visual recording), which refers to filming the voice actor at work in order to use the actor's movements and expression for artistic reference (Yamamoto 1989: 254; AJA 2008 II: 132).

19. JCD 34453. Minakawa (2009a: 35) implies, seemingly through an accidental juxtaposition of unrelated phrases, that Masaoka's later *Spider and the Tulip* (1942) was the first Japanese cel animation. It was certainly a widely seen and conspicuous use of cel animation, since the characters were integrated with backgrounds composed of real tree branches.

20. Crafton (1982: 184) reports 'cel-washing' as a low-echelon task at American animation studios as early as 1916.

21. Nelson (1974: 156) gives the definition 'gaily coloured'; I might suggest 'myriads' as a more precise translation of the original sense.

22. JCD 37765.

23. JCD 37792.

24. DAW 20.

25. It is included as an extra on the 2010 DVD *Animation no Senkakusha Ōfuji Noburō: Kokō no Genius [Animation Pioneer Ōfuji Noburō: Isolated Genius]*.

3 THE SHADOW STAFF
Japanese animation at war 1931–48

In addition to Korea, a colony since 1910, Japan already enjoyed numerous rail and mining concessions in north-eastern Asia, largely inherited from the Russians in 1905. In 1931, Japanese officers made a bid for greater glory, orchestrating a bogus 'terrorist' attack on a Japanese railway line, and then 'retaliating' with overwhelming force. Japanese troops occupied several urban centres, and by February 1932, had installed the deposed Last Emperor of China, Henry Puyi, as the nominal ruler of the puppet state of Manchukuo. The Chinese resistance began immediately, plunging Japan into armed conflict on the Asian mainland that would last for the next fifteen years.

To the Japanese, the era from the Manchurian Incident to the atomic bombing of Nagasaki was a 'Fifteen Years War', escalating most markedly in 1937 with the outbreak of open hostilities between Japan and China, and in 1941, with the infamous attack on Pearl Harbor.

Isolde Standish (2005: 81, 143) has noted the multiple functions of film in the period as an instrument of national policy in Japan, as an attempt to maintain a largely invented tradition of the 'family state' (*kazoku kokka*), but also to foster austerity measures, steer national opinion and 'correct' the supposedly dangerous ideas to be found in foreign films. She also notes the influence of similar national film policies in fascist Italy and Nazi Germany, as well as the horror of Japanese delegates at the League of Nations in 1933, who reported that Japan was made to look quaint and backward in a montage of images from member states (Standish 2005: 140).[1] This last challenge, of exporting more acceptable images of Japan to the outside world, seems to have fallen by the wayside after Japan's exit from the League of Nations that same year, although Japanese propaganda images continued to be employed within Japan's immediate sphere of political influence, particularly in the colonies of Korea and Taiwan, and Japanese-occupied territory in Manchuria and along the Chinese coast.

The pinnacle of such entertainments would come in two parts: Seo Mitsuyo's widely seen five-reel children's cartoon *Momotarō no Umiwashi* (1943, *Momotarō's Sea Eagles*), and its more accomplished nine-reel sequel, *Momotarō Umi no Shinpei* (1945, *Momotarō's Divine Sea Warriors*), which eluded many audiences due to evacuations from urban areas at the time of its release. Both were commissioned by the Ministry of the Navy, and both have understandably dominated subsequent discussion of Japanese animation in the 1940s (e.g. High 2003: 422–3; Akita 2004: 258; Komatsuzawa 1994: 191–5; Mochinaga 2006: 98–9).

CONTENT AND THEMES: MODERNITY AND MILITARISM

Katō Teizō's ten-minute animated short *Ō-atari Sora no Entaku* (1932, *The Plane Cabby's Lucky Day*)[2] is set in the future year of 1980. It features a social divergence, seemingly inspired by that in Fritz Lang's *Metropolis* (1927), in which humans dwell in skyscrapers while the Earth's surface has been ceded to anthropomorphic animals. A taxi driver on a long fare is forced to stop in the clouds to repair his plane, where one of the local birds informs him of a nearby island that possesses rich treasure. However, despite a fascination with futurism, including images of aerial traffic control and food cooked in seconds, *The Plane Cabby's Lucky Day* is a film object that can only be retrospectively placed within a tradition of the development of Japanese science fiction. Its original context is far more concerned with the development of Japanese imperialism: the grotesqueing of other races as literal lower orders, and the implication that a colonial mindset, with a will for overseas plunder, would find rich resources for the taking. Its most cunning subtext lies in the offhand manner in which a 'long fare' both incorporates and localises the South Seas within the compass of Japanese power, presenting unidentified Pacific islands as enduring, albeit distant and backward, additions to the Empire.

The Plane Cabby's Lucky Day (1932)
imagines a future where the South Pacific is
regarded as a distant suburb of Tokyo

Sora no Momotarō (1931, *Momotarō of the Sky*) is similarly concerned with territorial politics and logistics. A simple good-versus-evil narrative is subsumed within a discussion of Momotarō's decision to go to war in order to protect penguins and seals on a distant, ice-bound South Sea island. Despite the distance (10,000 km), Momotarō agrees to save them from the predations of 'a ghastly eagle'. The film's political message lies in its assumption that territories in the South Seas are not only within Japan's sphere of interest, but that their occupants demand Japan's intervention against the actions of the [American] eagle. Its educational content is oblique, limited to the suggestion that Momotarō's traditional companion, the pheasant, is excluded both from the action and from the awarding of medals because 'he can't swim'. A surprisingly large part of the film is taken up with Momotarō's journey to the south, which requires two refuelling stations, one staffed by a rabbit and a turtle, while the furthest is manned by a penguin and a grumbling sperm whale. The title character swiftly returned in *Umi no Momotarō* (1932, *Momotarō's Underwater Adventure*), which repeated many of the same tropes, but with submarines fighting sharks instead of planes fighting eagles.[3]

During the 1930s, military hardware and concerns even creep into ostensibly benign children's cartoons, such as the machine gun that comedically rivets a door in *Mabō no Kinoshita Tokichiro* (1938, *Mabō as Tokichiro Kinoshita*) or the trench periscope utilised in *Kangaroo no Tanjōbi* (1940, *Baby Kangaroo's Birthday Surprise*).[4] Kataoka Yoshitarō's *Osaru no Sankichi Bokūsen* (1942, *Sankichi the Monkey: The Air Combat*), is purportedly a comedy about monkeys fighting off an aerial attack by bears in aeroplanes. However, even in its supposed humour it concentrates with grim focus on the logistics of dogfighting and flak batteries, and it ends on the chilling note that, while the bears have been defeated, other enemies still lurk in the skies.

THE IMPACT OF THE 1939 FILM LAW

Japanese film-makers gained a new structure of exhibition in 1936, with the official commencement of ninety-minute mixed-genre theatrical programmes in small cinemas or 'news theatres' (*news eigakan*). The perceived need for variety in these week-long programmes created a new desire for animation, particularly at New Year, when some cinemas mounted an all-cartoon programme for children on vacation (Animage 1989: 144). However, Japanese cartoons were still forced to compete with foreign imports for slots on the news-theatre programmes.

The Film Law (*Eiga-hō*), proclaimed in April 1939 and enforced with fifty-eight last-minute additional articles in October of the same year, had wide-ranging implications for all films in Japan. Among many prescriptive measures (Hirano 1992: 15), it demanded that all cast and crew be licensed, and it fixed the requirements of an evening at the cinema, insisting on a programme that included newsreels and 'cultural films' (*bunka eiga*) – worthy documentaries designed to 'nourish the national spirit' (Sharp 2011: 63). Fu Poshek (1997: 68) translates the term as 'propaganda shorts', which might appear provocative at first, but is highly applicable, particularly in the early twentieth-century sense of 'propaganda' as 'simply … the means by which the converted attempted to persuade the unconverted' (Taylor 2003: 4).

The power of the government censor was relocated from that of post-production to *pre*-production approval, while the authorities now interfered directly in the physical content of films. In an intensification of the proscriptions of the 1925 Public Security Preservation Law, films were expressly forbidden from questioning the power

Momotarō of the Sky (1931) teams legendary heroes and animals with the technology of modern imperialist expansion

of the imperial family or the national constitution, from damaging the interests of the Empire, from 'hampering' enlightenment of Japanese subjects and the development of Japanese culture. Clause 7 was particularly spiteful, insisting that no films should be 'notably inferior in production technique' (Hirano 1992: 15). Henceforth, by imperial fiat, all films made in Japan had to be active contributors to national policy. And, somehow, good. Meanwhile, heavy restrictions were placed on foreign films. Imports of new foreign films largely ceased (Hirano 1992: 207), while many of those already in circulation were soon found to contravene censorship directives on issues, including but not limited to: descriptions of individual happiness, images of women smoking, sexual frivolity and the use of foreign words (Hirano 1992: 16).

The effective phasing out of foreign works did not necessarily have the desired effect. Tsuji Masaki (1996: 8–9) writes of his youthful disappointment with the disappearance of American cartoons from cinema programmes, turning a child's visit to the cinema into little more than a newsreel, followed by a self-consciously worthy *bunka eiga* documentary, but now lacking the reward of a closing cartoon. However, this new gap in the market created new opportunities for Japanese animators. Arguably, for the first time since cartoons had come to Japan, domestic animators now had a captive audience for domestic cartoon products, even the 'entertainment' cartoons that Yamamoto Sanae had said were impossible to make. All they had to do was meet the criteria of the militarist state.

Tezuka Osamu, a schoolboy in the late 1930s, recalled film prints transported by car around his neighbourhood, and screened in local halls.

> When I was at elementary school, I would go to every one of these screenings. There would be a cartoon film beforehand. A Japan-made five-minute cartoon film, but I found these more interesting than the main features that followed. The main features were usually dull. As the teachers selected them for instructional purposes, I am sure they were probably educational, but they were also worthy, dark and didactic. And when I think about it, the films became immensely nationalistic and martial. (Tezuka, 1997: 15)

The nine-year-old Tezuka records the titles of some of these sanctimonious live-action features, but oddly does not note, or perhaps simply does not recall, the cartoons he saw. By that time, animation was reflecting similar propagandist influences, with films such as *Sora no Shanghai Sensen* (1938, *The Aerial Battle over Shanghai*) and *Sora no Arawashi* (1938, *Sky Eagles*), in which Japanese animal pilots shoot at images of Popeye and Joseph Stalin in the clouds. Other films of the period were subtler in their anti-Western message. Arai Wagorō's *O-Chō Fujin no Gensō* (1940, *Madame Butterfly's Fantasia*) retold the ending of Puccini's opera, with its emphasis on the heroine's abandonment by the feckless foreign cad Pinkerton.

It is during the war years that we also see the diverse directions taken by the 'second-generation' animators of the late 1920s. Five years after he disappeared into police custody after the seizure of his erotic cartoon

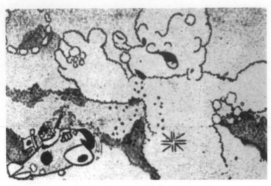

Sky Eagles (1938) pits characters from Japanese folklore against icons of the enemy media. The term 'eagle' (*arawashi*) meant 'ace' in wartime Japan

The Aerial Battle over Shanghai (1938) made light of Japan's invasion of China

Cool Ship, Kimura Hakusan returned with *Arawashi* (1938, *Eagles*),[5] a ten-minute cartoon featuring a Japanese aerial attack on a Chinese army base. Meanwhile, the Animage *Art of Japanese Animation* (Animage 1989: 23) traces a line of apprenticeship from Kitayama Seitarō, through his assistant Kanai Kiichirō, to Kanai's younger brother Satō Kinjirō, who flourished in the 1930s as the founder of the Satō Film Production Works (Satō Eiga Seisaku-sho).[6] Satō and his long-time collaborator Chiba Yōro were much in demand during the last decade of Japan's 'Fifteen Years War', producing their long-running *Mabō* series (see Table 3.1), which pitted a mischievous Japanese boy and his animal friends against the forces of Western imperialism, with walk-on roles for Churchill and Roosevelt. The titles alone show an inexorable drift from the wholesome promotion of sports and health into outright military propaganda.

TABLE 3.1: THE MABŌ FILMS 1936–43

YEAR	FILM
1936	*Mabō no Dai Kyōsō* (*Mabō's Great Race*)[7]
1936	*Mabō no Tōkyō Olympic Taikai* (*Mabō's Tokyo Olympics*)[8]
1937	*Mabō no Shōnen Kōkūtai* (*Mabō's Boy Aviation Squadron*)[9]
1938	*Mabō no Tairiku Hikyō Tangun* (*Mabō's Mainland Undercover Spies*)[10]
1939	*Mabō no Muteki Kaigun* (*Mabō's Invincible Navy*)[11]
1940	*Mabō no Kinoshita Tokijirō* (*Mabō as Kinoshita Tokijirō*)[12]
1941?	*Mabō no Shiken Hikō* (*Mabō's Experimental Plane*)[13]
1942	*Mabō no Tekketsu Rikusen* (*Mabō's Mighty Landing Force*)[14]
1942	*Mabō no Tairiku Senbutai: Circus no Maki* (*Mabō's Mainland Pacification Squad: Circus Chapter*)[15]
1942	*Mabō no Tairiku Senbutai: Hizoku Taiji no Maki* (*Mabō's Mainland Pacification Squad: Bandit Extermination Chapter*)[16]
1942	*Mabō no Nankai Funsenki* (*Mabō's War Chronicle of Tough Fighting in the South Seas*)[17]
1943	*Mabō no Rakkasan Butai* (*Mabō's Paratroop Detachment*)[18]

Largely forgotten in the post-war period, the popular Mabō character became progressively more martial as the Fifteen Years War wore on

Notably, the Olympic-themed *Mabō's Great Race*, in which Mickey Mouse and Betty Boop cheer the Japanese hero across the finish line, is only a minute and a half long, whereas most of the remaining films, made with army or navy funding, run at around ten minutes. Budgets appear to reflect Japan's military rise and fall, with running times that climb to a height of seventeen minutes in 1942, before dropping to only five in 1943 as resources were presumably reallocated to the great enterprise of *Momotarō's Sea Eagles*. The militarised *Mabō* films carnivalise the danger of conflict, presenting warfare in China as an excit-

ing adventure for Japanese boys and their talking-animal friends. Moreover, the Japanese are depicted as agents of pan-Asian goodwill, saving grateful girls from Manchurian robbers, 'exterminating' bandits who threaten peaceful Chinese farmers and protecting beleaguered South Sea islanders from attacks by British soldiers. In addition to the *Mabō* films, the Satō studio's output extended to other areas of the Japanese Empire, including *Mori no O-isha to Hakui Yūshi* (1943, *The Forest Doctor and the White-clad Hero*),[19] shown in Taiwan, which focused less on the military heroes than the medics who tended their wounds. Standish (2005: 112) suggests that the implied audience for all such cartoons was not merely the children themselves, but that they were also intended to 'allay the fears of parents who might have been hesitant in allowing their young sons to transfer to the various military academies'.

Such narrative cartoons are remembered because they left a record of their existence, not only in the minds of impressionable young audiences, but in terms of posters and press coverage from the period of their exhibition. However, the Japanese navy also invested heavily in animation for a much narrower audience of military personnel; these films are not remembered, because they were not seen by general audiences, and seemingly wilfully forgotten by many of their creators.

THE LOST WORKS OF THE SHADOW STAFF

In 2007, a small Japanese publisher released the second volume of the autobiography of one of the minor figures of Japan's television animation era, Ushio Sōji. Ushio clearly did not trust his own celebrity enough to depend on it for the success of his memoirs, preferring instead to frame his text as a commemoration of the significantly more famous Tezuka Osamu. In publishing terms, this is perfectly understandable as a means of appealing to an audience wider than a small number of animation historians; in historical terms, it allowed Ushio to insert powerful, unprecedented revelations, of immense value in the assembly of a narrative history of Japanese animation. In asides presented out of chronological order, Ushio delivers information that helps reassert historical actors and activities thought to have been 'dead and gone' – a type of 'repressed memory' (Megill 2007: 42–3).

Possibly, since Ushio died before the book was printed, his estate may have been unaware of the volatile nature of the information that he was sharing, which would permit others to throw traces of data elsewhere into sharp historical relief. In his book, Ushio recalls the foundation in 1939 of a Special Film Unit (Tokubetsu Eiga-ban), formed by the amalgamation of the Tōhō Cultural Film Department and the film company Nihon Eigasha.[20]

[The unit] comprised about thirty people. Our task was to secretly make four reels on level bombing theory and ten reels on practical bombardment. This 'Shadow Staff', including me, was under the direct supervision of the executive director Masutani [Rin] and the director Mori [Iwao].[21] (Ushio 2007: 237)

According to Ushio, a 'practical' component involved him climbing aboard an Akatonbo (Dragonfly) training biplane in order to watch military exercises in Ise Bay. Since there was no way a film-maker could get a bomber's eye view without actually sitting at the bombardier's station, Ushio was eventually made to operate it himself, sighting a five-metre square target in the sea below, and then releasing the lever with a shout of 'Tei!' (bombs away). He made many sorties, sometimes as many as four a day, until his proficiency at dropping dummy bombs was considered to be good enough to animate the experience for others. The Japanese Cinema Database does not give a year for his *Bakugeki Riron* (1940–1, *Principles of Bombardment*) films, but Ushio specifically dates his training with the Suzuka Air Squadron to a one-year period from autumn 1939, placing the notional production somewhere around 1940–1. Ushio further notes that his film had been used to instruct the navy pilots who attacked Pearl Harbor, implying it was completed and being screened by mid-1941 (Ushio 2007: 237).[22]

The Japanese Cinema Database lists twenty-one lost 'animated' films made by this unit, later known as the Tōhō Aviation Education Materials Production Office (Tōhō Kōkū Kyōiku Shiryō Seisaku-sho), and one further film that utilises the same animation staff without carrying the unit's name on its credits. The data are patchy in the extreme, based largely on descriptions of objects (the number of reels or the titles on lost canisters) rather than content. According to Ushio, these works were only '80 per cent animated', with introductory portions in live action, giving way to graphic representations of concepts, schematics and instructions (Ushio 2007: 193). Staff records, completion dates and participant records for the films are partial at best, although the available titles, locations, crewmembers and topics permit sorting into eight broad categories (see Table 3.2 – complete details in Clements and Ip 2012).

TABLE 3.2: THE WORKS OF THE SHADOW STAFF 1940–4

GROUP	SERIES	FILMS
A	*Industrial Science.*	Five films made by unidentified staff for the Ministry of Munitions. Undated.
B	*Principles of Bombardment.*	Four films made by Ōishi Ikuo and Sagisu Tomio, with the co-operation of Naval Aviation Ōi Division Headquarters, the Suzuka Air Squadron and the Ministry of the Navy. 1940–1?
C	*Naval Aviation Combat.*	Two films made by Ōishi Ikuo and Matsuzaka Yoshihito for the Kasumigaura Air Base. 1943.
D	*Ship Identification.*	Two films made by Karasawa Hiromitsu with the presumed co-operation of navy headquarters and the Combined Fleet. 1944?
E	*Torpedo Essentials.*	Two films made by Nakazawa Hanjirō with the co-operation of the Ōita Squadron and the Naval Aviation Office. 1944.
F	*Wireless and Radar.*	Two films made by Nagamura Eiichi, possibly at Yokosuka Air Base. 1944?
G	*Unsorted.*	Four films on the subject of dive-bombing, landing tactics, impact assessment and aerial combat essentials. Undated.
H	*Other.*	One film not classified as a production by the Tōhō Aviation Education Materials Production Office, but plainly utilising at least two of its staff (Ōishi Ikuo and Sagisu Tomio) in key roles.

Considering that the instructional films listed run to approximately sixty-six reels, it is possible that twice as much Japanese animation was produced in the war years for instructional purposes as was for entertainment. However, in terms of the 'aesthesis of history' (Megill 2007: 33), they are inconveniently fragmentary, not 100 per cent animated and not designed to be entertainment – they are mere instructional tools, not works of art.

Film lengths in this period were often given in reels instead of metres or minutes, and hence it is difficult to determine precisely how long these films were. A reel can hold up to eleven minutes of film, although several cartoons released during the period crammed up to twelve minutes onto a single reel, presumably for ease of portability (Tsugata 2007a: 186). But given an average running time of eight minutes per reel,[23] some of the Shadow Staff films were longer than their better-known counterparts in the 'entertainment' sector. In the case of the Group B film *Bakugeki Riron: Danchaku-hen* (1942, *Principles of Bombardment: Impact*),[24] with a listed size of six reels, this implies a likely running time of around forty-eight minutes. Such a length would still make it longer than the following year's *Momotarō's Sea Eagles*. Moreover, at eight reels, and with a presumed completion date of 1944 or earlier, Nagamura Eiichi's Group F film *Mugen Riron: Sankyoku Shinkūkan* (*Principles of the Wireless: Triodes and Diodes*)[25] could have been a reasonable contender as the 'first feature-length' Japanese cartoon, ahead of the actual record holder, Seo Mitsuyo's 1945, *Momotarō's Divine Sea Warriors*.

As they were made for a small and secretive audience of Japanese military professionals, the Shadow Staff films were never officially distributed in theatres, and hence have no official release date or presence in filmographies. They are, for example, entirely absent from the relevant pages in general chronologies of Japanese animation (e.g. Yamamoto 2004: 183; Stingray and Nichigai Associates 2010: 892) and from the putatively 'complete' published history of the parent studio (Galbraith 2008: 37–59). Similar issues arise in the study of American films from the same period, many of which are also either lost, neglected or edged out of company histories and retrospectives (Shull and Wilt 2004: 15).

The Disney studio, whose work on *Victory through Airpower* (1943) is well known, produced many less widely seen films in the period, including the Donald Duck short *The New Spirit* (1942), promoting the payment of taxes (Shull and Wilt 2004: 125–6). Notably, Disney's 'hidden' output of instructional animation was even higher than that of its Japanese counterparts, at five times its pre-war annual productivity: '204,000 feet of film, 95 per cent of it for government contracts', as against a previous peak of 37,000 feet (Solomon 2009: 146). Disney embarked upon ventures in instructional film-making, after 'tests revealed that trainees learned faster and had better retention when material was presented in animation, rather than live action or illustrated lectures' (Solomon 2009: 145). Beginning with *Four Methods of Flush Riveting* (1941) for the Lockheed corporation (compare to the Industrial Science series in Table 3.2), Walt Disney soon moved into films promoting the purchase of war bonds. By 1942, Disney had been classed as an 'essential industry', churning out 'scores' of forgotten films under the auspices of the War Manpower Commission. According to Marc Davis, one of the Nine Old Men:

> Many of the films were fully animated, although some were diagrammatic ... They had one series they called *The Rules of the Nautical Road*, thousands and thousands of feet that they turned out, done very simply, on what various lights meant and so on. But we really animated many of those things: I did some animation as well as story work on them. We used top-flight people when they were available. (Solomon 2009: 146)

As Charles Solomon notes, with a running time of 207 minutes, *The Rules of the Nautical Road* was 'longer than *Snow White* and *Pinocchio* combined' (Solomon 2009: 146). The studio's wartime *magnum opus* was an unnamed Beechcraft aviation maintenance and repair manual that ran for six hours.

America's closest equivalent to the Tōhō Aviation Education Materials Production Office was Major Rudy Ising's 'Fort Roach', the 18th Air Force Base Unit (First Motion Picture Unit) in Culver City, California which 'turned out more animated footage than any of the other Hollywood studios' (Solomon 2009: 147). Artists also served by drawing insignia and logos and, in the case of Dick Kelsey, by making the models used for pre-attack presentations.

The American industry, unlike its Japanese counterpart, also produced some films that were both instructional and entertaining. The films of the Shadow Staff, born from a twenty-year tradition of Japanese educational films for adults, and intended for a restricted audience, seem to have been bluntly, humourlessly informational.

ANIME

Compare this with the *Private Snafu* series made by Warners from 1943–6 for the American army, born from a tradition of films that had to succeed on their own merits *as* entertainment. Mainly directed by an uncredited Chuck Jones, with scripts from Theodore Geisel ('Dr Seuss') and Phil Eastman, and the voice of Mel Blanc, *Private Snafu* similarly united a group that would go on to post-war fame in their homeland (Shull and Wilt 2004: 82). Like the works of the Shadow Staff, *Private Snafu* was intended solely for military personnel but, unlike the Japanese equivalent, it was played for laughs. Its exclusivity was encoded internally, with 'sex and vulgarity' designed to establish that the films were not intended for an audience of children. Moreover, *Private Snafu* educated its audience with a negative dialectic, discussing matters such as hygiene, sanitation and weapons maintenance by showing the title character getting things wrong, with humorous consequences (Shull and Wilt 2004: 84).

Hence, some American cartoons in the war period, both public and restricted, appear to have maintained their tone from pre-war days, while the Japanese industry maintained the pre-existing split between the publicly seen entertainment cartoons, now made mainly for children (Mochinaga 2006: 98–9), and instructional films, not 'entertaining' at all, now made solely for adults in the military. This division, however, also seems to have been reflected among the staff rosters, maintaining ongoing associations of pre-war personnel and companies, now obscured beneath wartime umbrella organisations. The divergence between the 'entertainment' animators and the 'Shadow Staff' would become irreversibly distinct as the war progressed and the former were encouraged to put their names to ever longer and more accomplished works. This change was, at least partly in reaction to two foreign cartoon films – one suppressed and exhibited in secret for only a dozen people, the other widely distributed in Japan in the vacuum left by the prohibition of new American imports. Between them, they inspired the Japanese military to pour increased funding into Japanese animation.

THE RECEPTION OF *FANTASIA* AND *PRINCESS IRON FAN*

In 1941, a dozen men assembled in a private Tokyo screening room. They included the animator Ōishi Ikuo, who had once imitated *Felix the Cat* in his *Ugoki-e Kōri no Tatehiki* (1931, *Moving Picture Fight of Fox and Tanuki*), the animator Seo Mitsuyo, who had already found acclaim with his *Norakuro* series, the model-photographer Tsuburaya Eiji and the animator Ushio Sōji. The select group had been called together to see an item that had been seized in the South Pacific by a Japanese navy patrol before the official outbreak of hostilities. Hidden in the hold of a raided American transport ship, a number of canisters of film had been brought back to Japan for inspection, and then prepared for viewing.

The film was Walt Disney's *Fantasia* (1940), screened in secret so that the animators of wartime Japan could know their enemy (Ushio 2007: 193–5). *Fantasia* itself would not be distributed in Japanese cinemas until 1955, but had a powerful effect on its tiny, invited audience. Ushio Sōji, then working as an animator under his real name of Sagisu Tomio, sat in the dark and wept at the finale (Ushio 2007: 195). We only know this because it is his account of the screening some sixty-six years later that confirms not only the existence of the confiscated film print (seized along with a copy of *Gone with the Wind*, 1939), but also the convoluted route it took to Japan and the identities of some of the audience members. Before the posthumous publication of Ushio's memoirs, the clandestine *Fantasia* screening was hinted at by industry personnel, but never confirmed. It was shown only to the topmost animation directors – even their deputies were not privy to it, although some had heard that it took place (Mochinaga 2006: 96).

Quite inadvertently, this stolen copy of *Fantasia* may have been one of the most powerful tools of American propaganda. The majority of the men in the screening room were makers of short, black-and-white documentaries and instructional films; they could not have competed with *Fantasia* on equal terms, even if they had wanted to. None of the Japanese viewers was aware of the film's expense to its American producers. *Fantasia* had cost almost $2.3 million, but had found its distribution severely curtailed by the build-up to war. By 1941, it had only recouped a fifth of its production costs, and looked set to be a flop – in fact, it did not go into profit until 1969. Considering the poor reaction to Disney's earlier *Pinocchio* (1940) and the prohibitive price of

Fantasia, many of Disney's backers were dealing with the unpleasant prospect that the previous success of *Snow White* had been nothing more than a 'tremendous fluke' (Barrier 1999: 273, 279). In short, the cartoon business was nowhere near as lucrative as it first appeared, but the Japanese did not know that.

Fantasia was also a dramatic narrative, an aesthetically pleasing experience. It could be viewed as entertainment, without the martial undertones of many Japanese films from the same period, all of which were now made under the auspices of the 1939 Film Law. To a general audience, music, song and an unfolding story were surely of greater aesthetic impact than dispassionate recitations of facts. *Fantasia*, like the handful of Japanese dramatic narrative cartoons released in cinemas in the 1940s, encouraged a 'fundamental orientation ... of delight and admiration' (Megill 2007: 34).

A less expensive, but arguably even more influential film had also arrived from China. *Tieshan Gongzhu* (1941, *Princess Iron Fan*) was completed by the Wan brothers in occupied Shanghai, and eventually released in Japan on 10 September 1942.[26] Presumably, it was not banned as a foreign film because of the underlying implication that Shanghai was successfully occupied, and hence no longer 'foreign' – it was first screened in 'Chinese' Shanghai, then in the 'Japanese' sector of the city in February 1942, and subsequently made its way to Japan proper (Komatsuzawa 1994b: 226). This is particularly ironic, since the Wan brothers originally intended it as a protest against the Japanese, seeding the film with images of 'the brutal reality of the daily violence in a country crippled by war' (Quiquemelle 1991: 180). Fortunately for the animators, they had been able to cut the film's original closing line, 'Get the final win in the anti-Japanese war', before it fell into Japanese hands (Lent and Xu 2003: 65). Oblivious to this hidden history, distributors screened a cut version of *Princess Iron Fan* in Tokyo, and inadvertently inspired local film-makers to emulate its achievement.

Princess Iron Fan was an enormous achievement in wartime film-making – truly feature-length, drawing on a rich folkloric tradition, with comedy, fights and even the chance to sing along with the aid of a Fleischer-style bouncing ball. At least one print of the film even had patches of colour, since the Wan brothers had painstakingly drawn fire effects in red ink directly onto the celluloid (Lent and Xu 2003: 64).

The press and audience response surrounding it, in China and Japan, focused on it as a landmark cartoon, although it is readily apparent to the modern viewer that the majority of the film's sequences are heavily rotoscoped. Human movement is fluid and realistic, because the human movement has been shot in live action to serve as a baseline for the 'animation'. As in Disney's *Snow White*, the true 'animation' is only to be seen at the peripheries of such tracing, in some of the animal characters and in elements not present in the original live footage. The film even playfully acknowledges this, such as in a moment where the character of Pigsy absentmindedly detaches his own ear and uses it as a fan, as if admitting that he is really a man in a mask. In an odd sense, *Princess Iron Fan* is 'full' animation, but only because full animation through rotoscoping actually proves less labour-intensive and difficult than accurately blocking, drawing and compositing the images would be in a 'limited' sense.

Princess Iron Fan's reception in Japan was mixed. It was one of the last great cartoon events of the war years, released in the late summer of 1942, before wartime deprivation truly began to bite. It also appears to have been carefully retooled to appear more 'Japanese', listed in many sources with a slightly different title, and featuring a Japanese soundtrack supplied by former celebrity *benshi* turned radio announcers, such as Tokugawa Musei, whose name was bigger on the Japanese posters than that of the Wan brothers.[27] There was also a growing realisation among audiences that their enjoyment of the film was actually a subversion of its original intent, and that they were actually watching *anti*-Japanese propaganda. The teenage Tezuka Osamu (quoted in Komatsuzawa 1994b: 228) noted: 'I clearly understand that this is a work of resistance. It is clearly a satire, saying that if the Chinese people work together they can overcome the Japanese Army which has invaded and attacked their country.'

Since it did not receive a Japanese release until almost a year after it was completed in China, it is fair to assume that producers, including officers of the Imperial Japanese Navy, viewed it well in advance of its official exhibition to Japanese audiences. Hence, Japanese producers had many months to react to *Princess Iron Fan* before audiences saw the film – possibly the film was only granted a general release once the navy was sure it could muster a suitably impressive response.

MOMOTARŌ'S SEA EAGLES: PRODUCTION

The most palpable form of this reaction was the decision to make 'Japan's first feature-length cartoon film', *Momotarō's Sea Eagles*, although its claim to be 'feature-length' was a matter of promotional hype rather than actual fact. None of the children in the auditorium was sitting with a stopwatch, but squabbles over the alleged feature status of the film regularly arise among critics.

'Feature-length' is a powerful signifier in the history of cartoons, equivalent to breaking the sound barrier or landing on the Moon.[28] This is not necessarily a matter of production logistics, although the staffing requirements for a feature film certainly imply an increase in industrial capacity likely to result in further productions, and hence further revenue – a pipeline of possible future projects, and a likely labour pool of trained staff. However, the true impact of a feature-length status is a matter of exhibition and distribution. As Disney had already worked out by the 1930s, cartoons were fated always to be second-string features as long as they were not the main attraction of a night at the movies. *Momotarō's Sea Eagles* was not Japan's 'first feature-length' animated film. It does not qualify as such under the auspices of even the most forgiving of motion-picture academies,[29] although it has been pointed out that the myth of its feature-length status was almost as powerful as a true feature-length would have been (Gerow 2008: 10). It was certainly billed as such, and feted as the main attraction in theatres.

The film was commissioned for the Navy Ministry Public Affairs Office, sponsored by the Ministry of the Navy, and directed by Seo Mitsuyo. Much of what we know about its production comes down to us through the memoirs of Seo's assistant Mochinaga Tadahito, who was officially in charge of backgrounds and visual effects (Mochinaga 2006: 92).

Despite the willingness of the Navy Ministry to fund the film, amounting to an eventual cost of 200,000 yen, staffing levels were still critically low. The company Geijutsu Eiga-sha (GES) was offering low pay rates, and animators were rare, so that Seo and Mochinaga eventually created much of the animation on their own. Moreover, the navy had developed unreasonable expectations following the successful completion of the live-action film *Hawaii-Malay Okikaisen* (1942, *The War at Sea from Hawaii to Malaya*) in a mere six months, including substantial modelwork from Tsuburaya Eiji. As a result, the film's liaison and unofficial producer Lieutenant Commander Hamada Shōichi expected all production to be completed in three months. Seo estimated a more realistic production schedule at 'six or seven months' (Komatsuzawa 1994: 193).

As production got underway, there was an ominous indicator of how the war effort was truly progressing, when a squadron of B-25 bombers, the infamous Doolittle Raiders, descended on a surprised Tokyo on 18 April 1942: 'One of the bombers flew low in the sky above the studio and then disappeared out in Tokyo Bay. It disturbed our work for the day' (Mochinaga 2006: 92–3). The Doolittle raids took place eleven months before the premiere (25 March 1943), suggesting that if Mochinaga truly was dragged from his work to watch an American bomber overhead in April 1942, the production must have slipped a little further than the seven months originally promised.

Seo Mitsuyo's average daily output was sixty images, in a rough form that was corrected by Hashimoto Tamaki as she traced his originals. Although Seo's co-workers regarded this at the time as an incredible speed, it would soon be accepted as merely an average daily workload for Japanese animators, equivalent to that of American animators working for Disney (Ōtsuka 2001: 28; but see Ushio 2007: 205; Minakawa 2009a: 275). Another woman, Tsukamoto Shizuyo, was in charge of what Mochinaga calls 'colouring', as even monochrome film required five different tones of paint.[30] All in all, with Mochinaga himself struggling to produce backgrounds to match the foreground images, the staff kept up with Seo's pace, even though it usually meant shooting the day's illustration at night. This last job was also Mochinaga's, and he often found himself waking up the following morning, having fallen asleep beside the camera stand (Mochinaga 2006: 93).

WORKING CONDITIONS AND THE MULTIPLANE CAMERA

It was the camera stand that made the greatest difference to *Momotarō's Sea Eagles*, designed by Mochinaga himself for the company's previous production, *Ari-chan* (1941). A simple rostrum platform, suitable for holding an image flat while a camera shot each frame from above, was already commonplace in the Japanese animation industry. Nor were Japanese animators strangers to multiplane camera stands, as GES's rivals at Yokohama Cinema were already known to be using one to make *Kogane-maru*, also in production at the time.

It is likely that both Mochinaga and the Yokohama Cinema animators were less 'inventing' their multiplanes than copying the ones already seen elsewhere. Variants of the multiplane had been in operation since Lotte Reiniger's *Die Abenteuer des Prinzen Achmed*, through the Fleischer brothers' use of three-dimensional model sets behind cels in the 1930s in their related Stereoptical Camera. But the prime example was that found at the Walt Disney studios from 1937, in the Silly Symphony *The Old Mill* and for the feature *Snow White and the Seven Dwarfs*. US patent 2,201,689 was granted to Disney for the 'Art of Animation' camera on 1 May 1940, which was next employed to notable effect in the opening sequence of *Bambi* (1942). While *Bambi* was not seen by Japanese audiences until after the war – in fact, not released in Japan until 1951 – the technology involved in making it must have surely come to the attention of Japanese animators.

Like Disney's multiplane camera (Telotte 2008: 63), Mochinaga's created the 'illusion' of depth by using *actual* depth. Standing three metres in height, so tall that GES staffers had to remove part of the floor to get it in the studio, it allowed for the furthest cel to be a significant distance away from the lens, and hence made parallax seem much more realistic. It also allowed the inclusion of three-dimensional objects or real items – tree branches, for example – in the background, further adding to the sense of depth within the image.

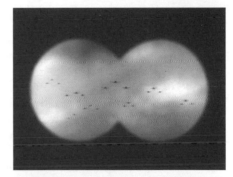

Such a set-up was sure to generate high levels of murkiness in the background of its images, which Mochinaga offset by differentiating the amount of light concentrated on each cel or pane of glass. Whereas the Disney multiplane had adjustable lamp settings and used long exposures to compensate for low light, Mochinaga's required artificial light on each level, making it remarkably difficult for anyone except Mochinaga to control, as he alone seemed to have mastered the studio's German-made luminosity meter. Mochinaga's design had five levels, including the uppermost on which the camera was placed, allowing for four filming planes: close-up or extreme foreground, midshot, long shot and background (Animage 1989: 23). The first two levels were lit by double 150W lightbulbs, the long shot by two 300W bulbs and the furthest level by a powerful doubling of 600W bulbs. In *Ari-chan*, Mochinaga had even experimented with lighting 'effects', with a moonlight scene chiefly lit by a single powerful light source, positioned as spotlight behind the image of the Moon itself on the background pane.

The work of Mochinaga's multiplane camera is obvious at several moments in *Momotarō's Sea Eagles*. Mochinaga himself picks out certain key shots of 'the aircraft carrier rolling on the waves, planes flying through dense cloud, Oahu island seen between the clouds, dive-bombers and friendly planes seen through the rotation of the propeller from inside an aircraft' (Mochinaga 2006: 94).

Momotarō's Sea Eagles (1943), despite not quite being feature length, was a main event in cinemas for school outings

The Navy Ministry agreed to bankroll the film regardless of the cost, and crucially provided help in sourcing celluloid – nitrocellulose, or 'gun cotton', was in far more pressing demand for the manufacture of ammunition. Even with the navy's help, cel supplies were so low that the film-makers were still obliged to recycle their old cels by washing them in acid. As Seo recalled (quoted in Komatsuzawa 1994: 193–4):

We washed them five times and kept using them. When we would do that, the cels would get warped or otherwise damaged. When you put as many as three cels that have lost their transparency together, it becomes impossible to see the background. So we established a rule to only stack two cels together. The thickness of old cels is uneven, so the middle becomes depressed and warped. When held against a flat glass, for shooting, the edges of the cel warp into waves. The people who see this film usually ask, 'The edge of the screen is a little whitish. What were you trying to do with that?' Nothing, really: that is halation resulting from the warping of the cel.

The resultant film was oddly paced, as Seo and Mochinaga had made the framing scenes of take-off and landing first, then interpolated the comedy business, subplots and the titular sea eagles (a lost chick and a helpful mother bird). The film, however, was exactly what the navy wanted, and screened to an ecstatic group at the ministry, including Emperor Hirohito's brother, Prince Takamatsu. It was soon released to wide acclaim, and to Mochinaga's great chagrin – his memoirs recall his mixed feelings over the successful completion of a propaganda film that was fit for purpose. Even though he told himself that Disney was making a film in which Donald Duck sank a Japanese warship, he could not help noting that the euphoric reaction to *Momotarō's Sea Eagles* could only have increased navy enlistment:

I heard that many youths volunteered for the flying corps and that while they were on duty they died on air raids. I wonder whether the film that we made influenced their decision to volunteer … I thought, in the future I only wished to make a film that would *benefit* the young, difficult though that might be. (Mochinaga 2006: 95)

MOMOTARŌ'S SEA EAGLES: ACCESS AND EXHIBITION

There has been some confusion around the multiple Momotarō films of the period. Modern histories of Japanese animation often elide the success of the 1943 film into the achievement of its 1945 sequel, made by Seo Mitsuyo after he had left GES and many of his former colleagues behind. *Momotarō's Divine Sea Warriors* is undoubtedly a better film – better animated, better written, far more entertaining and boasting a more persuasive propaganda message. It was also the first truly feature-length Japanese cartoon, at seventy-four minutes, designed to just outstrip the Wan brothers' *Princess Iron Fan*.

Although *Momotarō's Sea Eagles* has been overshadowed by the accomplishment of its follow-up, it is fair to say that few, if any Japanese boys would have been persuaded to enlist by the 1945 sequel, which was far less of a box-office success. In part, this was because it was completed in the closing days of the war, with the Doolittle Raiders now followed by swarms of land-based bombers from newly occupied islands, in turn devastating Japanese cities and reducing many cinemas to rubble. The decline in venues was accompanied by an even more drastic decline in available audiences; government had passed the Decisive War Emergency Measures, which conscripted boys over twelve and girls over fourteen into factory work, while younger children were evacuated to the countryside, and hence unable to swell admissions (High 2003: 411).

Instead, it was the 1943 *Momotarō's Sea Eagles* that was the defining Japanese propaganda cartoon of the war era. It was the keystone achievement of Japanese animation in the war period, and with takings more than three times higher than its production budget, a remarkable success compared to the fortunes of the Disney studio during the same period, when its features were running up huge debts (Barrier 1999: 279–82).

Much of the contemporary excitement was based on reviews and word of mouth for *Momotarō's Sea Eagles*, with eventual box-office takings approaching 700,000 yen, and a reported audience of 1 million (Akita 2004: 258). Mochinaga himself recalled complaints from cinemas that the sheer volume of juvenile patrons was wrecking the seats, and that he heard children at play imitating Momotarō's attack order: 'Torpedo squadron, bomber squadron, fighter squadron! Take battle positions!' (Mochinaga 2006: 98–9). It was also *Momotarō's Sea Eagles*, rather than the later, longer film, that made it out to the Japanese colonies, where it was seen, for example, in Taipei by the young Kotabe Yōichi, later an animator at Studio Ghibli (Kanō 2004: 58).

However, we might also inject a note of caution into breathless reports of stellar 'box office'. *Momotarō's Sea Eagles* was a 'hit' fuelled by compulsory school outings arranged by an authoritarian educational establishment. In other words, while it is filed by modern histories as a narrative entertainment film, its mode of exhibition bore a far greater resemblance to the instructional films of the 1920s and 1930s. It does not appear to have attracted attention from adult members of the public, or even from older teens. Suzuki Shinichi, a boy in Manchuria who would grow up to become an animator himself, noted in his own memoirs:

> I have no recollection of my parents taking me to see any movies, although I do remember the teachers at my school gathering us together and taking us to see cartoons. We saw films such as *Fuku-chan's Submarine* and *Momotarō's Sea Eagles'*. (Suzuki 2008a: 64)

If such films were 'hits', they appear to have had audiences solely comprising school-age children, which perhaps explains the theatre damage Mochinaga recounted. Mori Yasuji, who was born in 1925 and hence already in his late teens in 1943, reports his own childhood love of animation, but does not recall seeing any cartoons at all between 1942 and the end of the war (Mori 1984: 62, 101). Eighteen years old at the time of the release of *Momotarō's Sea Eagles*, Mori seems to have had no opportunity to see it, despite his avowed obsession with animation.

Wartime screenings seem to have been an odd throwback to the glory days of the *benshi*, recalling the times when a master of ceremonies in military uniform, and clutching the portrait of the Emperor, would begin each movie event with a restatement of loyalty to the throne (Fujiki 2006: 79). One film historian recalled:

> I remember trooping off with the rest of my fourth grade class to see the *Sea War From Hawaii to Malaya* at a downtown theatre in December 1942. Before the show a naval officer gave us an inspirational speech. Then we had a lecture from our principal. Upon returning to school, we sat down to a writing assignment on The Greater East Asian War and Our Firm Resolve as the Nation's Youth. (Yamamoto Akira, quoted in High 2003: 388)

The screenings of *Momotarō's Sea Eagles* seem to have been similarly arranged, with the film an integral part of an overall 'event' highlighting loyalty, patriotism and national unity.

FUKU-CHAN'S SUBMARINE (1944): AUTHORSHIP AND PRODUCTION

With Seo distancing himself from GES to work at Shōchiku on *Momotarō's Divine Sea Warriors* (Gerow 2008: 11), and GES itself merged with Asahi Eigasha, Mochinaga was offered a job directing a new cartoon, *Fuku-chan no Suisenkan* (1944, *Fuku-chan's Submarine*) to be based on the *Fuku-chan* manga by Yokoyama Ryūichi. Mochinaga himself regarded the suggestion as 'absurd', and wrote that Seo must have praised him to the navy to an unrealistic degree. Regardless, despite Mochinaga's protestations of his own lack of experience, he was put in charge of the submarine project.

Largely eclipsed in the post-war era by his younger rival Tezuka Osamu, Yokoyama was a manga celebrity in the early twentieth century. His *Edokko Ken-chan* (*Little Ken the Tokyo Kid*), running since 1936 in the *Asahi Shinbun*'s Tokyo edition, had been one of the first manga to be adapted into a live-action film (1937). Its mission statement seemed to be almost the antithesis of propaganda; in the wake of the 'Ni-Ni-Roku' attempted coup on 26 February 1936, *Little Ken the Tokyo Kid* had been rushed back into print in the newspaper, on the understanding that its gentle humour would help persuade the populace that the status quo had been restored (Yokoyama 1997: 78). The titular Ken was an average Japanese boy, although readers favoured the antics of a supporting cast member, a mischievous street urchin called Fukuyama Fukutarō. As the star of the spin-off *Fuku-chan*, running in the *Asahi Shinbun*'s national edition from October 1936, the character would find enduring fame in manga form until 1971, becoming the mascot of Waseda University and, in the war years, being put to militarist use. Yokoyama was drafted into the Japanese military on 1 January 1942. The chief nature of his wartime service was as a poster and propaganda artist in Singapore and Malaya that same year, but he returned to Japan to both continue the wartime serialisation of *Fuku-chan* in the *Asahi Shinbun*, and to contribute to the production of two cartoon films based on his work.

After the presumed success of Masaoka Kenzō's obscure one-reeler *Fuku-chan no Kishū* (1941, *Fuku-chan's Surprise Attack*),[31] the Navy Ministry was keen to commission two more cartoons extolling the joys of maritime life. One, the one-reeler *Uwanosora Hakase* (1944, *Professor Sky-Above*), was dreamt up by Yokoyama and director Maeda Hajime in a Tokyo bar, and made by an eighteen-strong team over a period of eight months. It was a co-production between the Navy Ministry and the newspaper's sister company Asahi Eigasha, but has not survived (Animage 1989: 26). The second production, seemingly running concurrently, was the more ambitious five-reeler *Fuku-chan's Submarine*),[32] Mochinaga's directorial debut.

The issue of who did what on *Fuku-chan's Submarine* is problematic. The script is credited to a film critic, Shigeno Tatsuhiko (High 2003: 471). The *Animage* history of Japanese animated films claims that the key animation was largely in the hands of Yokoyama himself. Mochinaga's own memoirs tell a different story, portraying Yokoyama as a preoccupied celebrity, easily distracted and far more interested in the wire-controlled car he had just brought back from occupied Singapore. At their first meeting, Yokoyama proclaimed that he 'knew nothing about animation', but that he would be happy to draw as much as required (Mochinaga 2006: 100). Sequestered in an office in Yugawara for a week with the rest of the production team, Yokoyama proved difficult to motivate, and eventually only produced a quarter of the illustrations for which Mochinaga had been hoping.

'Mr Yokoyama', wrote the director diplomatically,

> came up with plenty of ideas, but did not draw. He would make a little progress at the urging of his friend Mr Maeda [Hajime], but he was a popular man, concerned with the ongoing serialisation of *Fuku-chan* in the *Asahi Shinbun*'. (Mochinaga 2006: 101)

For Yokoyama's part, the production and reception of *Fuku-chan's Submarine* is barely mentioned in his own memoirs. It only occurs twice: once when he misremembers it as a 'pre-war' cartoon, and again in 1951 during a meeting with Walt Disney in America, when the famous studio head claimed to have seen the film, and a star-struck Yokoyama happily took the credit for it (Yokoyama 1997: 133, 143).

As seemed commonplace on navy-funded productions, the team was invited to see military technology up close, in this case during a research trip to the naval base at Kure, where its members lived briefly among naval officers, and were permitted to come aboard the submarine *I-157*. Mochinaga's team observed the crew supplanting their meals with fresh flying fish retrieved from the deck, and would incorporate this sight into the film's memorable cookery scene (Mochinaga 2006: 103).

For Mochinaga, the production was rendered difficult by staff attrition through military conscription – Mochinaga himself was called up partway through production, but was awarded a waiver at the navy's insistence. His staff laboured under the 'Rising Sun' naval ensign on the wall, along with the famous 'Z' signal of Admiral Tōgō, understood by all navy personnel to mean: 'The fate of the Empire depends on this battle. Let each man do his utmost.' The same flag can be seen piously raised by the ship's crew in *Momotarō's Sea Eagles*.

Mochinaga found himself competing for resources with his colleagues both on the rival production of *Professor Sky-Above* and the animated instructional films in production for private military use, accentuating tensions between pre-existing staffers of Asahi Eigasha, and new arrivals like him from the former GES. As he skirted on the edge of physical collapse, the navy arranged for a taxi to take him to work, but this luxury was soon suspended due to lack of fuel (Mochinaga 2006: 105–6).

Logistical considerations also affected the film itself. Mochinaga was keen to use something he called a 'dovetail stand' (*mizuochitai*), possibly an analogue of Disney's 'process projection' (Telotte 2008: 73), which would allow him to incorporate underwater effects and modelwork in the backgrounds. He cites lack of time as his main reason for abandoning the idea; by the time the stand was built, Mochinaga was operating the multiplane camera with only two assistants, and was having enough difficulty simply exposing the film (Mochinaga 2006: 104).

RIVALRIES AND CONNECTIONS

Resources were still limited, and personal connections still strong. The Tōhō staff were supposedly working together, although some noted a distinct rivalry between employees of the former Asahi Figa-sha and the former GES. Matters came to a head when two entertainment cartoons were in concurrent production, as well as ongoing Shadow Staff work. Mochinaga, who was then directing *Fuku-chan's Submarine*, felt that the competition for resources was won by the other two projects, the cartoon *Professor Sky-Above* and 'photography for military instruction' (*gun no kyōzai no satsuei*). He compared the struggle for resources to the historical Battle of Minato River, and considered his own production to have barely survived the pressure (Mochinaga 2006: 105).

Many film-makers in the war period had to deal not only with a lack of resources, but also with a growing sense of paranoia and hysteria among the authorities. Scientific fact was not welcome where it contradicted the received wisdom of the Japanese state, such as in the case of *Fuji no Chishitsu* (1940, *The Geology of Mt Fuji*), an unmade documentary that dared to suggest that the great symbol of the permanence of the Emperor was actually in a state of 'ceaseless evolution and transformation' (High 2003: 129–30). Not long after Ushio had been permitted to spend day after day dropping bombs from a biplane, his colleague Yamamoto Kajirō (not in the Shadow Staff) found himself forbidden from setting foot on a genuine Japanese navy carrier to research his live-action film *The War at Sea from Hawaii to Malaya*. Already resigned to using Tsuburaya Eiji's modelwork for the aerial sequences of combat with Allied fighters, Yamamoto was forced to base his sets and models on images of *American* carriers taken from photoshoots in *Life* magazine. On a visit to a Japanese airbase, he was reminded of his position in the pecking order when he saw a counter-espionage cartoon, warning that 'domestic spies' included intellectuals, journalists and persons connected with the movie industry (High 2003: 384).

Possibly, Yamamoto was just unlucky. The Shadow Staff appeared to enjoy a unique access to military secrets, not shared by other film-makers in Japan's war effort. In *Momotarō's Sea Eagles*, drawn-out sequences of take-off and landing seem informed by an animator's actual, physical presence on an aircraft carrier, at the very least for a day's observations of shipboard protocol and technology. It has been claimed that Seo spent 'hours studying documentary footage of war planes' for the sequences in *Momotarō's Sea Eagles* (High 2003: 472), but he may have also seen life on an aircraft carrier firsthand. His former assistant, Mochinaga Tadahito, was certainly permitted to spend some time on a navy vessel as part of his research for *Fuku-chan's Submarine* (Mochinaga 2006: 101–2) and the depiction of a parachute jump in Seo's later *Momotarō's Divine Sea Warriors* is also curiously precise. Although the paratroopers are cartoon animals, their behaviour on the aircraft, their hooking up of their ripcords to the overhead rail, and their nervous silence amid the roar of the engines all seem informed by real-world experience, or at least, intensive study of live-action documentaries shot *in situ*.

The propaganda animators certainly watched the documentaries of their live-action colleagues very closely, and even acknowledged them with their choice of titles. The live-action films *Umiwashi* (1942, *Sea Eagles*), and *Sora no Shinpei* (1942, *Divine Sky Warriors*) both appear to be referenced in the later anime titles *Momotarō's Sea Eagles* and *Momotarō's Divine Sea Warriors*, hence the use of these title translations here, rather than the slightly different versions in circulation elsewhere. The latter film also draws heavily on the live-action *Malay War Record* (1942) for its sequence in which Momotarō argues with the demons – framed in imitation of General Yamashita's harangue against General Percival after the fall of Singapore (High 2003: 125, 368, 372).

However, if there were any sense of camaraderie among the ranks, the film-makers remained at odds with their military patrons. Already depicted in propaganda as suspicious individuals, and suffering from increasing pressure from contradictory authorities, producers at the Tōhō unit began to play the supply officers at their own game. Sure that the military procurement officers would be ignorant of animation production methods, producers at Tōhō deliberately overestimated the amount of film required for animation by a factor of 300 per cent, claiming that the excess had been used on bad takes and deleted scenes (Ushio 2007: 237). This was a blatant lie – owing to storyboarding and shooting frame by frame, animation was actually prized for allowing its film-makers to conserve film stock. The extra film acquired was then secretly utilised in live-action films, including *Kawanakajima Kassen* (1941, *The Battle of Kawanakajima*), *Ahen Sensō* (1943, *The Opium War*) and Kurosawa Akira's 1943 film debut *Sugata Sanshirō*.

In the closing days of the war, hostilities sought the animators out. Ill and exhausted after the high-pressure production of *Fuku-chan's Submarine*, Mochinaga Tadahito returned to his home to discover that it had been destroyed in an Allied bombing raid. With a pregnant wife and dwindling food supplies, he fled to his parents' home in Manchuria. Ōishi Ikuo was even less fortunate: returning from a location scout in the Caroline Islands, he was killed aboard ship during an enemy attack on 4 December 1944.

As for the productions of the Shadow Staff, of those that had survived the fire-bombings of the closing days of the war, many were destroyed in the autumn of 1945. Ushio recalls (2007: 209–10)

> anything reminiscent of the wartime era, anything that reeked of connections to the military, was either shredded or burned and buried. Anything considered harmful by the Occupation authorities was fair game for destruction. I was disconsolate when I heard that films I had put my heart into, and animation I had completed with new technology, these treasures had been buried in a deep pit.

Time may have obscured Ushio's memory of the precise date, and indeed the nationality of the figures that destroyed his work. Only too aware of the significance of propaganda films to vengeful victors, the Tōhō studio is known to have pre-emptively destroyed several films before the Americans could arrive at the Sōshigaya building where much of the Shadow Staff's output had been produced (Hirano 1992: 42, 211), and there is no reason to believe that the works of the Shadow Staff itself were not considered similarly sensitive. There was undoubtedly a mass burning of 'harmful' movie materials by the Occupation forces, but that was not until April/May 1946, when US soldiers lit pyres of propaganda by the banks of the Tama River on three occasions (Hirano 1992: 43). In theory, at least one copy of each film was preserved and sent to archives in Washington, from which they were largely returned to Japan by 1967. However, many of the films have simply disappeared.

A CHINESE INTERLUDE

The involvement of Japanese animators in wartime propaganda did not end with the surrender of Japan. In the case of one in particular, Mochinaga Tadahito, it continued for several further years.

Fuku-chan's Submarine had its premiere on 9 November 1944. Wartime fervour seems to have been replaced by a longing for simple relief: although the film's plot supposedly turns on the sinking of enemy freighters and the struggle of a cartoon crew to carry out repairs at sea, young audiences amid wartime deprivation warmed most conspicuously to the scenes of plentiful food and the jaunty 'Song of the Submarine Kitchen' (Animage 1989: 26). With air raids now a constant danger, and his own house destroyed in bombing, Mochinaga sought safety away from Japan.

His decision to leave for Japanese-occupied Manchuria was not as odd as it may initially sound. He had grown up there, as the son of an employee of the Manchurian railway. His wife's father and siblings were already in Manchuria, and refuge with them presented a far safer option than merely relocating elsewhere in a Tokyo under bombardment. Mochinaga believed, rightly, that food would be marginally easier to find in Manchuria. Most crucially, his wife was pregnant with their second child.

Mochinaga ignored the advice of Ōmura Einosuke, a producer at the former GES, who argued that the war was sure to be over 'within three months', and that hence the situation would change for the better (Mochinaga 2006: 110). Mochinaga's memoirs omit the unspoken subtext – that the end of the war was sure to mean a Japanese surrender, Allied Occupation and possible purges of known propagandists. In that regard, the very success of *Momotarō's Sea Eagles* may have been a contributing factor in Mochinaga's decision to leave the country.

Mochinaga's memoirs refer to Manchuria in inverted commas throughout, as if acknowledging its artificial status. He arrived at Changchun (or *Shinkyō*, 'New Capital', as the Japanese then called it) and immediately contacted a former colleague from GES, who secured him a meeting with the director Kimura Sotoji at the Manchurian Film Association (Manchukuo Eiga Kyōkai, or Man-Ei). Kimura offered Mochinaga work on his film in progress *Su Shaojie* (see Yamaguchi 2006: 498) although, since it was unreleased, this was presumably an unfulfilled plan to assign him to post-production graphics or credits (Mochinaga 2006: 118). Mochinaga was hired to work under Sasaya Iwao in the Man-Ei art department graphics section, literally 'line art' (*senga*). With production stalled on *Su Shaojie*, Mochinaga was instead tasked with organising text, on-screen maps and animated graphs for the documentary *Kita-Man Nōgyō* (1945, *North Manchurian Agriculture*). He notes (2006: 121) that this was not his official job, but that Morikawa Nobuhide, who had been assigned the task, needed to be taught every step of it.

The war soon came to Manchuria. Food shortages like those in Japan began to bite, and in August 1945, less than a month after arriving, Mochinaga and his fellow workers were called into the Man-Ei dining hall to hear the Japanese Emperor's surrender broadcast on the radio. He recounts (2006: 127–8) an abortive plan to set fire to the studio, but that the Japanese were talked out of it by their Chinese co-workers, who already regarded the studio plant and machinery as property of an as-yet undetermined Chinese successor state. The Japanese army had already fled, leaving them with 'nothing but bayonets and bamboo poles' (Mochinaga 2006: 124; Satō 2004: 325).

Instead, the Japanese commandeered a fire truck and prepared to run for home. They made it as far as Fengtian before the Soviet Occupation shut down any chance of further movement. However, Mochinaga was soon rehired at what had once been Man-Ei, soon to be rebranded as China's Northeast Film Company (Dongbei Dianying Gongsi).

From September 1945 to April 1946, the location of Man-Ei was under Soviet stewardship. Its employees were offered the chance to return to work as the nucleus of the new Dongbei studio, which was expected to be handed to the Chinese government, as soon as the Eighth Route Army and the KMT had settled who would make up said government (Kitaoka 2009: 39).

Mochinaga was provided with papers identifying him to the Russians as '*Kitaskaya Kino*', that is, as a Chinese film worker. In a convenient oversight, the Soviet bureaucracy does not seem to have allowed for the possibility that a worker in Chinese film might not himself be Chinese. Instead, Mochinaga was put to work on Russian films, overseeing subtitling for the Chinese, Korean and Japanese markets. Subtitling was a skill that reused Mochinaga's experience in graphics, and he soon dragged several fellow Japanese nationals into the work – including Oshiro Noboru, a famous manga artist, who was found at a nearby refugee camp.

Mochinaga's work involved materials cannibalised from the former Man-Ei. His artists wielded carbon sticks worn down to stumps, and a rare Askania camera with seventy lenses, including a precious telephoto. The camera had a colourful history: left in Japan by Richard Angst after the filming of *Die Tochter des Samurai* (1936), it had been requisitioned by the South Manchuria Railway Company, and eventually ended up at Man-Ei. When the Russians departed, they took it with them.

One unknown Soviet film, which Mochinaga calls *Yukai-na Renchū* (date unknown, *Pleasant Company* or *Jolly Fellows*), featured an opening sequence in which an animated cow dashes on screen and writes the title with its tail. Mochinaga reanimated the sequence to remove the Cyrillic script, so that the title was now written in Chinese or Korean. He notes that the film was also shown in Japan in this version, but with the Chinese-title variant, as the Mandarin characters (*Yukuai Lianzhong*) were cognate with those used in Japan. He also began work on a cartoon of his own, *Mekakushi-sareta Roba* (*The Blindfolded Donkey*), but offers no other information on it (Mochinaga 2006: 138).

DEMOCRACY NORTH-EAST AND *THE EMPEROR'S DREAM* (1946–7)

Mochinaga's brief spell working for the Soviet industry ended with the arrival of the Chinese army, or rather, armies. Mochinaga and his staff retreated to Hao Gang when Changchun came under attack from the Nationalist Chinese, now fighting the Communist Chinese for control of China. Mochinaga admitted to his Japanese nationality, but he had the good fortune to be in the hands of one of Communist China's most progressive and POW-friendly organisations – for almost a decade, the Eighth Route Army had proclaimed itself to operate a policy of good treatment for prisoners of war, in the hope that they would switch sides (Kushner 2006: 133). The Eighth Route Army hence permitted Mochinaga and several other Japanese film-makers to labour under the new regime (Kitaoka 2009: 51). Mochinaga would later claim that he felt he had little choice but to remain in

China, as the journey home was unquestionably perilous, and had as its destination a Japan that was sure to be gripped by shortages of food, clothing and housing (Satō 2004: 333, 336). After August 1946, with the frontline in China's ongoing civil war moving to the south, repatriation from Manchuria became feasible, and many Japanese nationals willingly began the journey home, but Mochinaga elected to stay in China – possibly because of his fears of persecution during the US Occupation.

Dongbei was eventually amalgamated with the Yan'an studio, comprising Party faithful from Mao Zedong's wilderness base. All filming, live and animated, was hampered in the immediate post-war period by the absence of film stock. Mochinaga estimated that by 1946 there were only 20,000 feet of unexposed film left in China: enough for a mere 210 minutes of filming. Moreover, the available film comprised differing varieties: Japanese panchromatic stock and newly arrived Russian orthochromatic stock. The materials were practically incompatible and unreliable – Mochinaga reports (2006: 162–3) on a red flag shot with mixed stock, which left it occasionally, and embarrassingly, indistinguishable from a white one.

By June 1946, the Japanese had reassembled in the Manchurian town of Xingshan. Mochinaga's group was one of several assigned to *Minzhu Dongbei* (*Democracy North-East*), the first of a newsreel series recording land reform in Manchuria and the ongoing conflict between the Chinese civil war factions. Japanese expatriates, including Kimura Sotoji and Uchida Tomu, were among the crews. Unsure of what they should be filming, they had shot a large amount of footage, and were reprimanded for wasting precious film stock. Even though Party film-makers from Yan'an were among them and just as complicit, the Japanese were blamed for the misuse of resources. Mochinaga, however, avoided censure through his concentration on map graphics and singalong subtitles. Filming extremely limited animation, one frame at a time, he did not waste an inch of precious celluloid (Kitaoka 2009: 55). Unknown to Mochinaga, his first two newsreels were also exported to Prague for the World Festival of Youth and Students, where they were exhibited in July 1947 (Gao 2003: 1).

The Japanese workers' skills might have saved them from Russian prison camps, but were of little help in the harsh competition over resources in the immediate post-war period. While Chinese nationals seized the film work, the marginalised Japanese were assigned lowly illustration commissions for the nearby Dongbei Medical College and the Bureau of Coal Mining. In both cases, they were given the task of painting propaganda posters and large images of Mao Zedong and General Zhu De, at which they so excelled that they were soon hired to produce similar portraits for other Communist institutions, including ones of Mao and Stalin for the Eighth Route Army itself, in such quantities that Mochinaga lost count. It was hence, with outrageous historical irony, that the portrait of Chairman Mao that led the Xingshan Communist parade on May Day 1947 had been painted by former Japanese propagandists. One of Mochinaga's assistants, Chiba Momoe, would eventually marry a Chinese cameraman and remain in Beijing, where she continued to paint propaganda posters for the Communist regime (Mochinaga 2006: 164, 210; Satō 2004: 341).

New Chinese recruits continued to crowd out the Japanese in editing, filming, sound recording and performance. However, the skills of the Japanese animators remained unchallenged by locals. The heartland of the Chinese animation industry was concentrated in the south in the area around Shanghai, far behind the enemy lines of the Chinese civil war. 'In the north-east, there were no Chinese animators at all' (Satō 2004: 347).

Mochinaga's animation work continued invisibly on the *Democracy North-East* newsreels, where he was called upon to animate battle diagrams showing the course of the civil war. With materials still in short supply, he foraged for supplies and made his own ink and gelatin. Through contacts established through his mother, who was running a creche for the local medical college, he liberated formalin to serve as a preservative in his new paints, and mixed low-quality industrial glue with zinc powder. He travelled as far as Harbin in search of gum Arabic, and was overcharged for a bottle of powdered glue. He settled for casein but, as it was made from dairy products, it would soon go stale. As a result, he was forced to mix his own paints with a pestle and mortar (Mochinaga 2006: 167–8).

For his next assignment, Mochinaga was shown a propaganda comic drawn by Hua Junwu. The images depicted the US General George Marshall, festooned with weapons and operating a puppet in the likeness of Chiang Kai-shek, leader of the Chinese Nationalists. In addition, Mochinaga was provided with a photograph of Marshall, and ordered to deliver a thirty-second puppet sequence.

To make the face, I started off with *papier-mâché*. I soaked newspapers in hot water, tore them into small pieces and simmered them in a pan. I wrung them out, added plain flour and glue to make them hard and made face and limbs. I nailed thin strips of leather for the joints to complete it. (Mochinaga 2006: 169)

With film stock still in short supply, Mochinaga could not afford to shoot the marionette sequence live. Instead, in order to use only the exact number of frames allotted, he replaced the leather joints with stiffer sockets and animated the sequence one frame at a time, with the strings above the marionette merely left in shot for artistic effect.

The sequence appeared as part of the third episode of *Democracy North-East*, in a segment called *Fanshen Nian* (*The Year of Uprising*). The stop-motion sequence was greeted with accolades far outweighing its role in the newsreel, leading the Dongbei studio news director, Chen Bo'er, to comment that puppetry was a fondly remembered entertainment in the region, which had died out since the advent of the Japanese and Man-Ei's cinema output. Hence, she ordered a stop-motion two-reeler, which she resolved to write herself and leave to the Japanese to animate (Ehrlich and Jin 2001: 8).[33] Mochinaga borrowed two French-made dolls from Kimura Sotoji, and disassembled them to discover wooden bodies connected by iron sockets around brass spheres. His Chinese technicians attempted to recreate the joints, but had difficulty creating exact spheres. Eventually, Mochinaga was left with a 100 ball-and-socket joints of variable quality, all handmade. He used the best ones in his 'lead' marionettes, and hoped the reject joints would not be noticed among the 'extras'. Of greater concern to Mochinaga was the news that the People's Liberation Army had surrounded the real-life Chiang Kai-shek on all sides, causing Mochinaga to work twenty-four-hour shifts out of fear that the film would not be finished before the war was over.

Huangdi Meng (1947, *The Emperor's Dream*) ran to twenty-six minutes, and was credited to Chen Bo'er as scriptwriter and director. It played in Chinese cinemas on the same bill as the fourth instalment of *Democracy North-East*, and featured four vignettes based on Chinese opera, each played as a satire on Chiang Kai-shek's Nationalist government. Mochinaga notes that many of the other staff were Japanese, including himself, the art director Hazumi Mitsuo, his assistant Oda Kenzaburō and the camera operator Kiga Shingo (Mochinaga 2006: 172; Yamaguchi 2006: 386–7).

TURTLE IN A JAR: SCAVENGING MATERIALS

At the time, stop-motion animation appears to have been a stopgap measure for Mochinaga. He certainly returned to cel-based animation as soon as the opportunity arose, when he made the twelve-minute cartoon film *Wengzhong Zhuobie* (1948, *Turtle in a Jar*). A satirical view of American investment in China's Nationalist faction, it depicts Chiang Kai-shek as the eponymous creature, who, it is implied, will be easy for the Chinese to hem in and catch – the title is the Chinese idiomatic equivalent to 'shooting fish in a barrel', hence its listing in some sources under the title *Go after an Easy Prey*. The script is credited to Zhu Dan; the directing credit is Mochinaga's Chinese name: Fang Ming.

Supplies were no less scarce, but Mochinaga appears to have won the trust of his Chinese masters. He was able to scavenge some 0.8mm cels from the local theatre, where he presumed they had been intended to stand in as fake window glass in a stage set. Much thicker than usual for animation purposes, frequently brittle and marred by an amber discoloration, the cels also required Mochinaga to reformulate his homemade paints, which had been mixed for drying on paper rather than celluloid. Mochinaga's main problem would be humidity, insofar as cels had to dry by a natural process of evaporation. He hence experimented with new mixtures of paint and honey, as well as glycerine, and bought a secondhand hair-tension hygrometer that could give him reliable humidity readings in the drying room. It was, however, lacking the all-important human hair, and Mochinaga had heard that Asian hair would not work properly.

On a second scavenging trip to Harbin, he acquired pens and some chemicals from a pharmacist whose Japanese lettering was still visible beneath the new Chinese sign. He also pestered a redheaded girl in a Russian café to give him the vital strand of hair for his hygrometer. Back in Xingshan, he built drying shelves out of plywood, and calibrated the hygrometer by setting its 90 per cent reading against a soaked cloth. He then put his staff to work on the film, with all the crew working without shoes, in order to prevent static electricity building up when the cels were handled (Mochinaga 2006: 188–9).

Turtle in a Jar was completed and screened in 1948, shown in cinemas alongside the ninth instalment of Democracy North-East. A playful cartoon set alongside pious announcements of revolutionary successes and proletarian concerns, it received a truly rapturous reception, resulting, at one reported screening, in the audience demanding not one, but three encores in a single night (Satō 2004: 349). Thereafter, Mochinaga relocated to Changchun, the old site of Man-Ei. With the liberation of Beijing in 1949, he continued to work on Chinese newsreels, and also in film preservation in Changchun, where he found complete prints of Princess Iron Fan and, ironically, his own Momotarō's Sea Eagles, which remain in the Beijing Film Archives to this day.

As a delegate at the first Beijing Cultural Production Conference in 1950, Mochinaga first met the Chinese animator Te Wei. Both men had worked in wartime propaganda, and were soon co-opted into the newly established Shanghai Film Studio. Mochinaga brought many of his remaining Chinese and Japanese staff south from Changchun to work in the new animation department, where his Chinese alias can be seen on the credits of several early cartoon productions and stop-motion animations for what would become known as the Shanghai Animation Studio.[34] He was also a colour-checker on China's first colour feature film, Liang Shanbo yu Zhu Yingtai (1954, Butterfly Lovers), although by the time the film was released, he had already left China. Despite all the deprivation and harsh conditions of his years in China, he returned to post-Occupation Japan before the famines and persecutions that would dominate the next decade in the People's Republic.

NOTES

1. See also Balio (1993: 35) for details of the German and Italian variants.
2. JCD 37821. Available on the Digital Meme Japanese Anime Classic Collection DVD box set, volume 2.
3. Akita (2004) appears to ignore Momotaro's Underwater Adventure, although as a Momotarō-themed war film, it should surely have been included in his article on the subject. This just goes to show how swiftly modern technology can alter our access to previously obscure films, as both were included on the Digital Meme 2007 box set, and are now readily available worldwide.
4. JCD 37877.
5. JCD 37845
6. The brothers had different surnames because the elder had been adopted as a child into the Kanai family (Tsugata 2007a: 162).
7. Not in the JCD. Included on the Digital Meme DVD Japanese Anime Classic Collection, volume 4.
8. JCD 34505.
9. JCD 34522 – the Japanese Cinema Database gives the release date as 27 October 1937.
10. JCD 37843 – allcinema gives the date of this film as 1938.
11. JCD 37866 – allcinema gives the date of this film as 1939.
12. JCD 37844 – this is the only wartime Mabō film not to be set in the Japanese Empire, instead having a samurai theme based on Japan's civil war. Included on the Digital Meme DVD Japanese Anime Classic Collection, volume 4.
13. JCD 37906, date unknown. I place it here in the assumption that Satō was making at least one a year.
14. JCD 37888.
15. JCD 37889. The Tokyo National Film Centre gives the release date as 1941. See http://www.momat.go.jp/FC/NFC_Calendar/2004-07-08/kaisetsu.html.
16. JCD 37890.
17. JCD 37905.
18. JCD 37934 – this is one of only two Mabō cartoons to appear in The Art of Japanese Animation, implying that details of the other films have only come to light in the last twenty years (Animage 1989: 25). Eight Mabō films were shown at Tokyo's National Film Centre in 2004. I use the English title translation previously employed by High (2003: 470).
19. JCD 37867. The film was lost for decades, but donated to the Museum of Taiwan History by a private collector in 2009.

20. Animation's value in military instruction had been recognised as early as 1916, when John Randolph Bray was commissioned by the War College to produce six reels for training soldiers, including: 'the operation of the mechanism of the Lewis and Browning machine guns, rifle grenades, trench mortars and various ordnance pieces, as well as how to read military maps, harness cavalry horses, etc.' (Crafton 1982: 158). Indeed: 'The industrialization of the cartoon was to a slight extent a military by-product' (Crafton 1982: 162).

21. The original text has the term 'Shadow Staff' in katakana, i.e. in 'English'. Since *maki* is a counting word for rolled objects, which can mean either reels of film or chapters of a text (Nelson 1974: 356), it is possible to read Ushio's claim here as a reference to fourteen separate instructional films, although since the Japanese Cinema Database has found evidence of thirteen reels on the subject of bombardment (Group B), we can safely assume that Ushio is referring to the four films listed. The 'missing' reel might be a film that has disappeared from the historical record, but is more likely to have been wound onto one of the other reels.

22. There is a certain irony in that, soon after Japanese animators were teaching Japanese pilots how to attack American targets, Disney staff were conscripted into making topographical models of Japanese territory for the briefing of American bomber pilots (Beier 1946: 236).

23. The *Animage* history of Japanese animation lists both reel counts and running times for eighteen Japanese cartoons released between the years 1936 and 1945. The total number of reels counted is thirty-seven, with a combined running time of 310 minutes, generating an average reel length of 8.4 minutes (Animage 1989: 20–6).

24. JCD 34581. Given the variable reel lengths, it might have even been up to sixty-six minutes, but forty-eight minutes seems more likely.

25. JCD 34583.

26. DAW 286–7. Many Japanese sources give the title as *Saiyūki*, or *Journey to the West*, a transliteration of the Chinese title of the original novel, *Xiyouji*.

27. Although Tokugawa's presence was clearly a big deal for the distributors of *Princess Iron Fan*, it doesn't seem to have interested Tokugawa himself. His three-volume memoirs mention none of his cartoon performances. At the time *Princess Iron Fan* was released, he was far better known as the radio voice reading out Yoshikawa Eiji's bestselling novel *Musashi* (1935).

28. As Hu (2010: 169) records, the Wan brothers were well aware of this, which is why their *Princess Iron Fan* was feature-length in the first place.

29. Tsugata (2007b: 23) suggests sixty-five minutes as a reasonable definition of 'feature length'.

30. Deneroff (1987: 2) offers 'opaquing' as a more semantically correct term for colouring in a monochrome era.

31. DAW 671.

32. DAW 671.

33. Despite a name that appears to me to be rather butch, the photograph of Chen Bo'er in Lent and Xu (2003: 67) is clearly that of a woman.

34. Sharp (2011: 173) states that the 'animation division' of Man-Ei was 'moved to Shanghai as part of Shanghai Film Studios and became an independent enterprise as the Shanghai Animation Film Studio, in 1956'. However, it is unclear to what degree there was an 'animation division' at Man-Ei. Considering that Mochinaga was mixing his own paints, scavenging his own cels, repurposing whatever cameras he could find and in one case, laying the concrete and sawing the wood to make the studio buildings, it is arguable that Mochinaga *was* the animation division.

4 THE SEEDS OF ANIME
Japanese animation industries 1946–62

Several animators in the post-war period successfully carried the skills and know-how of the animators of the Fifteen Years War through the lean times of the Occupation, in order to create a firm base of talent and labour. In straightforward numbers, this meant a personnel increase from 100 active Japanese animators at the beginning of the period (Mori 1984: 112), to an estimated 500 at its end (Yamamoto 1989: 28). Chronicling such transformations at the organisational and managerial levels of production also involves a consideration of the effects of the interregnum Allied Occupation from 1945–52, and problems of exhibition as short-form Japanese cartoons struggled to compete in a marketplace dominated by foreign features. The period represents an aesthetic and memorial blind spot – considered by many earlier accounts as little more than a gap between a wartime height and the recovery of Japanese animation at the turn of the 1960s.

For any author seeking to tell the story of Japanese animation as a narrative progression towards the present viewer, the completion and limited screening of *Momotarō's Divine Sea Warriors* is a technical watershed in the history of Japanese animation. With the works of the Shadow Staff disqualified by aesthetics or discounted by nescience, *Momotarō* was, and remained, the longest, most accomplished work of Japanese animation up to that point, and was not superseded, at least in terms of length, until the release of *Hakujaden*[1] thirteen years later (Clements and McCarthy 2006: 424–5, 478). The intervening period of post-war deprivation and reconstruction, labour disputes and the slow rebuilding of Japan's animation industry is hence often regarded as an inconvenient hiatus – a backward step while the industry retrenched and reformed, before it could once more continue the rush toward the reader's present. There is an inevitable temptation to regard *Momotarō* and *Hakujaden* with a form of 'extraordinarity bias', valuing their combined eighteen reels of film as somehow more significant than the eighty-two or more reels of other animation known to have been created in Japan during the thirteen years that separate them (Animage 1989: 27–38; Tsugata 2012).

The period is greatly misunderstood in animation studies, partly due to a lack of extant materials, but also because many historians have simply assumed that little of interest happened between Japan's defeat in 1945 and the release of Japan's first full-length colour feature, *Hakujaden*. The *Nippon no Anime Zenshi* [*Complete History of Japanese Animation*], for example, rushes through the period 1945–58 in just three pages, one of which is devoted to old Disney cartoons (Yamaguchi 2004: 64–6).

But it is possible to conceive of the period 1945–52 (the Occupation era) as the one in which Japanese animation confronted its greatest disruption of all, with serious threats to revenue and staffing. The industry faced an overwhelming 'colonisation' by foreign content – chiefly the works of the Disney studio, kept from Japanese audiences since the 1939 Film Law and now suddenly unleashed. However, the Tōhō studio maintained a standing group of animators, within what was its 'educational' (*kyōiku*) department until 1951, briefly renamed the 'graphics' (*zukai*) department until its disbandment in 1952. Defectors from Tōhō subsequently joined Nichidō, an independent company that had already accreted around pre-war pioneers such as Masaoka Kenzō, along with left-wing animators ejected from Tōhō during 1940s labour disputes (Tsugata 2004: 119).

SHIN NIHON DŌGA-SHA (NEW JAPANESE ANIMATION COMPANY)

The first animator to attempt any new work was Masaoka Kenzō, who established the Shin Nihon Dōga-sha (New Japanese Animation Company) in November 1945, and immediately began production with almost 100 staff. Even considering that Masaoka had been based in Japan's ancient capital of Kyoto, which had been left untouched by US bombing raids, the speed with which he began production in Occupation Japan is still remarkable (Yamaguchi 2004: 64). However, he was steered into this by the Occupation authorities, who preferred to have Japan's animators assembled under an easily identifiable umbrella organisation, rather than spread out among dozens of garrets and small studios (Hu 2010: 79).

Masaoka's first post-war work, *Sakura* (1946, *Cherry Blossoms*) featured Kyoto in the springtime, reflecting both his own desire for renewal and his enduring interest in setting animated fantasies to pre-recorded soundtracks. The dialogue-free single-reel cartoon, comprising 'fragmentary frames of an early spring' over a purloined soundtrack of Carl Maria von Weber's *Invitation to the Dance* (1819) (Hu 2010: 79) was regarded, even by its director, as a flawed work, doomed by poor materials and damaged cels (Tsugata 2004: 116). It was never commercially exhibited, although an incomplete workprint had an influential private screening in December 1945, at Tōhō's Sōshigaya studio building, for an audience of animators and would-be animators (Ushio 2007: 223).[1]

A rough cut of *Cherry Blossoms* was shown to the assembled animators, supposedly in celebration of the newly announced collaboration between Masaoka's company and Tōhō. However, Tōhō had no intention of publicly screening the film, which remained mothballed thereafter (Tsugata 2004: 116). Or rather, if Tōhō had ever intended to screen the film, it proved impossible to do so in the censorship climate – Yamaguchi Yasuo has suggested that Masaoka's attempt to present an innocent pastoral was defeated by the appropriations of Japanese traditional imagery by the propagandists of the Fifteen Years War. Far from being a harmless image, the short-lived cherry blossom (*sakura*) was now a poetic allusion to kamikaze pilots; the pretty chrysanthemum flower was an unwelcome reminder of imperial authority; while the picturesque Mount Fuji had become, in wartime, 'a strong symbol of the Japanese national polity' (Hu 2009: 252–3).

Instead, Masaoka was left to teach forty Tōhō staff how to make animation of their own, which he did in an inspiring fortnight of lectures, the Manga Eiga Tokubetsu Kyōiku Kōza (Cartoon Film Special Education Course), beginning with his demonstration of a good artist's freehand control, drawing a circle and a triangle simultaneously. Arguably, it is at these lecture events, in the last days of 1945, that we see the beginnings of the post-war Japanese animation business. A former actor with a showman's ability to hold an audience's attention, Masaoka became the vital conduit by which the experiences of the pre-war and wartime animators were not only imparted to a new generation (about half the students present) but also codified and assessed for the benefit of fellow professionals (Ushio 2007: 224). Dog-eared, battered copies of Masaoka's animation notes were still in occasional use in the Japanese industry thirty years later, where their guidelines on special effects such as rain, explosions or water remained unsurpassed (Ishiguro and Ohara 1980: 89–91, 94).

TŌHŌ AND THE NIHON MANGA EIGA-SHA

Tōhō's 'upper studio' on Sōshigaya hill, as distinguished from the more famous 'lower studio' in Kinuta, was built in 1940, and had largely served for the production of films on 'restricted military subjects' (Hirano 1992: 42–3; Ushio 2007: 210). Mori Iwao, the head of the Special Film Unit, reputedly delegated a handful of staff to bury eight war films on the grounds of the Sōshigaya facility, thereby preserving such works as *The War at Sea from Hawaii to Malaya* for posterity. However, these appear to have been live-action works – the animated instructional films were either destroyed by the Japanese themselves or burned by the Occupation forces the following spring (High 2003: 505). *Momotarō's Divine Sea Warriors*, the pinnacle of Japanese animation to this date, was burned by the Occupation authorities and considered lost – it was only resurrected in 1983 when archivists were able to recreate it from a rediscovered negative (Tsugata 2004: 114).

The film-makers were soon joined by former staff members who had fled to the countryside in the last days of the war, and returnees from rural boltholes and postings elsewhere in the Japanese empire, swamping the studio with a surfeit of staff and a dearth of projects. The numbers of animators reported as assembling at Tōhō in 1945 was greatly in excess of the dozen or so known members of the Shadow Staff. It would seem, instead, that the forty-two animators now on staff at Tōhō included many former members of the Special Film Unit, and also many of the creatives who had worked on *Momotarō's Divine Sea Warriors* (Tsugata 2004: 114).

In the chaotic days of the early Occupation period, Tōhō, like all surviving film-making institutions, faced pressure from the Occupation authorities to continue output, while submitting to an all-new censorship regime, with more staff, reduced resources and many cinema theatres destroyed by bombing (Hirano 1992: 27). This was easier for some than others – the Shōchiku studio had specialised in domestic dramas, and could soon readily repurpose its props and sets for 'democratic' romance, whereas Tōhō had made war films, now banned, its particular speciality.

In December 1945, the Sōshigaya employees held their first production meeting. The studio's unspoken intent, under conditions in which staff greatly outweighed available projects, was simply to find something to do that would both occupy the workers and not anger the Occupation authorities at General Headquarters (GHQ). Unless each work group found a means of making itself indispensable, it was sure to be made redundant. Ushio recalls: 'We had to think of projects that were in line with the GHQ Occupation policy, *in order to feed* various people including Japanese- and Western-style artists, sculptors, model-makers and animation cameramen' (Ushio 2007: 210, my emphasis).

The number of workers at this point was put at 'about 50 staff ... including 30 animators, four producers, as well as scriptwriters, directors, cameramen and lighting crews' (Ushio 2007: 210). All of the creatives mentioned in Ushio Sōji's memoir of December 1945, and indeed of the subsequent labour disputes in the next three years, are men. This is odd indeed, since memoirs of the wartime animation business mention female workers at many levels of the production process (e.g. Mochinaga 2006: 93, 100). Possibly, such women were still present, but simply unmentioned in the extant memoirs; perhaps they were shoved aside by men returning from the war – it is suspicious, for example, that Ushio's account talks of a large staff of supposedly 'experienced' animators, who apparently still needed to be trained from scratch. Certainly, there is a palpable absence of female talent from the main staff credits of the Occupation years (Animage 1989: 27–32), suggesting that one of the first manifestations of post-war reconstruction was the return of the glass ceiling. However, other evidence suggests that women were present, albeit not in the higher echelons of the staff. For example, Mori Yasuji's wife, Nui, worked as a colourist on *Poppoya-san Nonki Ekicho* (1948, *Poppoya: Carefree Stationmaster*), although only Mr Mori is mentioned on the credits (Animage 1989: 31: Kanō 2004: 163). Masaoka Kenzō was called in to help the Tōhō staff with their new mission, in what was presented as a collaborative venture between his newly founded animators' collective and the larger, more established studio. In fact, of the three films first produced through this collaboration, two were made at Sōshigaya, and Masaoka would make a third at his own facility near Ekoda station in the Nerima district of Tokyo (Ushio 2007: 212).

The resultant production slate was a deft attempt to employ as many skills as possible. One live-action documentary, *Kodomo Gikai* (date unknown, *The Children's Congress*), featured children returning to take lessons in a ruined school. However, beyond a few days on graphics and titles, such a project demanded no work from the studio's surplus of animators (Ushio 2007: 211). As a result, the producers also intervened in the ornithological documentary *Chidori* (1947, *Plovers*), in which a girl discovers eggs on a riverbank, and witnesses the parental care of the adult birds for their chicks. Shot as a live-action film by the naturalist Shimomura Kenji, the fifty-minute piece was made to include a three-minute animation sequence, in which, for reasons unknown, a cartoon Pinocchio enters the live-action frame and dances among the birds. Shimomura was put in charge of both script and direction because he had received an award from the Japanese Ministry of Education before the outbreak of the Pacific War, and hence could be trusted to produce something suitably worthy. The insertion of the dancing Pinocchio, however incongruous, found work for ten otherwise unidentified Tōhō animators under Ichino Shōji, a former member of the Shadow Staff (Animage 1989: 28; Ushio 2007: 211). The choice of Pinocchio, several years before the 1940 Disney film of the same name was released in Japan, suggests a deliberate attempt to ingratiate the animators to the American censors.

With the combination of live and cel-based filming, it is easy to see the influences of Masaoka's *Spider and the Tulip* in both *Plovers* and the other Tōhō film in production at the same time. *Muku no Ki no Hanashi* (1947, *The Tale of the Grey Starling's Tree*) was purportedly inspired by a line in Percy Shelley's *Ode to the West Wind* (1819), a poetic allegory of revolutionary change and the role of the artist in it, which finishes with the line: 'If Winter comes, can Spring be far behind?' Its subject is an ancient tree, which sits unchanging while the seasons turn around it. Part of the title was left in katakana, in order to create a pun out of *muku*, which can mean either a grey starling or an enduring purity. Billed as a 'cine-poem', the animation was greatly augmented by a full orchestral score, provided by Hayasaka Fumio, better known as the composer for the films of Kurosawa Akira. The production seems almost tailormade to occupy as many idle hands as possible, not merely in terms of the music, but also the animation itself, which mixed modelwork (the tree) with cel-based personifications of the seasons. The militarist winter figure was seen as a demonic general, supposedly inspired by Mussorgsky's *Night on Bald Mountain* (1867) – although since at least two of the animators involved, Ushio Sōji and Wakabayashi Toshirō, had been prominent among the Shadow Staff and had seen *Fantasia* at the secret 1941 screening, it would be safe to assume that the figure of winter was rather based on Disney's version of Mussorgsky's *Night on Bald Mountain*. The personification of spring, on the other hand, was imagined as a Botticelli goddess, presumably in order to draw on the skills of the Western-style painters in the team (Ushio 2007: 212). The cartoon caught the spirit of the time, conceptualising the Occupation as an unwelcome season, fated eventually to end. After the Occupation was over, Emperor Hirohito would use similar imagery in a birthday poem, commenting: 'The winter wind has gone / and long-awaited spring has arrived' (Dower 1999: 553).

TŌHŌ KYŌIKU EIGA-BU AND NIHON DŌGA-SHA (NICHIDŌ)

In 1947, with production still ongoing on the two animated films, the Sōshigaya facility was renamed the Tōhō Kyōiku Eiga-bu (Tōhō Educational Film Division). Such a remit for instructional film-making, coupled with its growing labour pool of animators, would allow the studio to bid for potentially lucrative animation contracts from one of the only immediate growth areas in post-war film-making: educational movies for the Occupation authorities. As part of a concerted effort to impose democratic values and American attitudes on the Japanese, the US Occupation authority Civil Information and Education section (CI&E) flooded the local market, not only with short educational films about life in America, modern medical care, the 'border without guns' between the US and Canada and life in democratic, consumerist society, but also with thousands of 16mm projectors on which to watch the films. Much like the works of the wartime Shadow Staff, these films have largely disappeared from the record through their non-appearance in official cinema listings. Many of them were American documentaries repurposed for Japanese viewing, for which 'animation' may have required little more than the swapping out of opening and closing graphics. However, thirty of the CI&E films produced during the Occupation period were made in Japan, and at least some of them may have included an animation component. Although many Japanese companies bid for the chance to work on these films, the CI&E officers preferred to work with just four majors: Tōhō, Daiei, Shōchiku and, in esteemed company indeed, Masaoka Kenzō's Nihon Manga Eiga-sha (Tsuchiya 2002: 198).

The latter company, however, was already heavily enmeshed in the Tōhō machine, and risked being overwhelmed by its ties to the studio whose new talents it had mentored. Hence it is no surprise that 1947 also saw Masaoka's establishment of a new company with Yamamoto Sanae and Murata Yasuji, discretely separate from the one he had established in 1945. If the names appear confusingly similar, this is possibly deliberate – many an animation historian has been tripped up by their almost matching characters. The Nihon Manga Eiga-sha (Japanese Cartoon Film Company) remained an active corporation, but was now forced to share its founder with his new creation, the Nihon Dōga-sha (Japanese Animation Company), or Nichidō for short, later Nichidō Eiga (Yamaguchi 2004: 64). The new entity appears to be an early attempt to establish a clear division between the creatives on a production and the corporation that owns the production.

As a result, on 25 September 1947, when *Plovers, The Tale of the Grey Starling's Tree* and Masaoka's own *Suteneko Tora-chan* (1947, *Tora the Stray Cat*) premiered on a triple bill at Tokyo's Hibiya cinema and subsequently toured Tōhō cinemas on a national roadshow (Ushio 2007: 215), the latter film possessed a convoluted credit list. Ownership was shared between two entities, the Tōhō Educational Film Division and the Nihon Manga Eiga-sha, whereas production itself was credited to a third – the newly established Nichidō (Animage 1989: 28–9). The message it sent was beautifully subtle – Masaoka had essentially credited his people twice for the same work, and sent a message to potential clients that the real work on *Tora the Stray Cat* had been done by his personal animation company, now touting for business. The name Tōhō is all over the production credits, as a participating studio, as the patron of the orchestra that supplies the music and even as the laboratory that developed the film.

But for any clients in search of actual animation, the credits on *Tora the Stray Cat* function as a blatant advertisement for the services of Masaoka and his people, to the exclusion of their sometime collaborators at Tōhō.

Tora the Stray Cat, however, was still assembled under impoverished conditions. Ishiguro Noboru, who had been thrilled to see the film as a nine-year-old boy, met Masaoka as an adult, and recorded his account of the production's difficulties, in which animators were, in a sense, forced to return to 1920s conditions, as there were not enough cels to go around.

> In the immediate post-war period, the price of cels was very high, which led on occasion to the use of the same cels for backgrounds and foreground animation. Fluctuation in tones was sometimes caused by the use of tea-coloured tracing paper in the backgrounds instead of acetate cels. (Ishiguro and Ohara 1980: 87)

Plovers was a worthy nature documentary with a bizarre three-minute dancing puppet interlude; *The Tale of the Grey Starling's Tree* was a piously elegiac twenty-two-minute musical meditation on rebirth and renewal. With such competition, *Tora the Stray Cat* was a calculated centrepiece, running at twenty-four minutes, with an actual voice track whose characters broke into song, 180 scene changes and conspicuously 'full' animation (Animage 1989: 28) – in the sense of twelve images per twenty-four-frame second. As an apprentice piece and calling card, it was unmistakable, and the same character would return in *Tora-chan to Hanayome* (1948, *Tora and the Bride*) only five months later, with Tōhō relegated to a secondary position on the credits, and Nichidō with top billing (Stingray and Nichigai Associates 2010: 544).

Several live-action Tōhō films from the period also indicate the ongoing presence of Tōhō animation staff. *Shin Baka Jidai* (1947, *New Age of Fools*)[2] begins with a hybrid sequence of animated special effects, in which the Tōhō logo morphs into an advertising balloon floating above the Japan Theatre. The images of the leading man Enoken (Enomoto Kenichi) and his foil Furukawa Roppa appear on a billboard, and then transform into an animated black-market trader and comedy policeman, who chase each other across town as the staff credits appear on passing trains and nearby drainpipes. Similarly, in *Muko Iri Gōkasen* (1947, *The Glorious Ship of Son-in-Lawhood*),[3] the leading man eats too many pumpkins, and experiences an animated nightmare in which he is pursued by a pumpkin monster, and in *Tanuki Shinshi Tōjō* (1948, *Enter the Tanuki Gentleman*),[4] the live-action film is bracketed by an animated prologue and epilogue, set in the enchanted word of the tanuki raccoon-dogs. None of these films shows up in previous histories of Japanese animation, because the work on them was effectively below the line, and subsumed once more into what we might today call 'graphics'. Tsuji Masaki (1996: 184) suggests that all these sequences were the work of Ichikawa Kon during the tail-end of his days at Tōhō; however, if they truly were the work of Ichikawa, it seems odd that he would not mention them in any interviews, many of which touch upon animation as his first love. Notably, in all cases, the animation component is significantly reduced from its wartime height. Tōhō featured animation in some of its films, but it was restricted to a steady rate of two or three minutes here and there, an output no longer than that of a single pre-war reel.

'EVERYTHING CAME BUT THE BATTLESHIPS'

The internal conflicts over job allocations at Tōhō were soon subsumed within larger competition over resources, itself often obscured beneath the rhetoric of union conflict throughout the Japanese entertainment industry, under the auspices of the Japanese Motion Picture and Theatrical Workers Union (Nihon Eiga Engeki Rōdō Kumiai), itself a mere cog in the machine of the All-Japan Film Employee Union Association (Zen Nihon Eiga Jugyōin Kumiai Dōmei – or Zen-Ei for short). Unions were a genie that the Occupation forces had let out of the bottle, after David Conde at CI&E had fostered their formation in 1946 in the interests of democratising Japanese industry (Hirano 1992: 213). Ushio Sōji reports (2007: 219) rumours from the animation industry that Conde was a Communist, who had already been forced out by the Americans by April 1946, purportedly for trying to steer the Japanese film industry as a whole much too far to the left.

Ushio's view, from the inside of the dispute, is that he and most of his fellow workers were simply concerned with resources and subsistence, but that Communist agitators infiltrated the union movement, turning a largely financial dispute into a political one (Ushio 2007: 219).[5] The Zen-Ei organisation made several attempts to steer conditions at Tōhō, beginning in 1946 with a fifteen-day strike that secured minimum salaries and union participation on production committees. By spring of the same year, this union of unions published a list of 'war criminals'. This was entirely at odds with the wishes of the Allied Command, which had already stated that 'the creation of propaganda is a natural by-product of war. Those who worked on such activities will not be considered war criminals' (Kushner 2006: 75). The 'war criminality' defined by the rhetoric of Zen-Ei was an attempt to apply the occupiers' stigmatising rhetoric to a conflict among the occupied. Such a witch-hunt was sure to cause trouble among the surviving animation staff, particularly those whose names were openly listed on the credits of propaganda films (Hirano 1992: 214). According to one account (Tsugata 2004: 114), of the estimated 100 animators in Tokyo in 1946, between fifty and seventy had worked in some capacity on *Momotarō's Divine Sea Warriors*, and hence might be in some way implicated.

The idea of the list had been nurtured by a faction within the post-war authorities, who hoped to rid all sectors of Japanese industry from anyone with wartime associations. This, of course, was easier than it sounded in a country that had been 'at war' for fifteen years, leading to the last, dark days that saw schoolchildren conscripted into factory work in support of the war effort. Perhaps in an attempt to get around this issue, the highest grade of crime on the list was reserved for thirty-one individuals who had actively participated not in the war itself, but in the 'incitement to war' (*sensō chōhatsu*), relocating the act of aggression and hence the crime of war along America-centric lines, to the attack on Pearl Harbor. It was recommended that these A-grade wrong-doers should be permanently prohibited from the film business. This hitlist included, of course, Mori Iwao, the nominal leader of the Shadow Staff (Standish 2005: 175). The main force of the proscriptions was aimed at producers, since they were regarded as the true helmsmen of studio policy and hence film content. Middle-ranking producers and supervising directors were classified as B-grade, and recommended for temporary suspension. Directors, screenwriters and personnel who had merely worked on wartime films, were classified as C-grade war criminals, invited to embark upon a period of self-reflection (*jiko hansei*) – itself a phrase with ominous foreshadowing of similar purges in Communist China. Isolde Standish suggests (2005: 176) that this was a reflection of the Occupation authorities' growing realisation that it would be impossible to eliminate wartime associations from all areas of public life, and that, more pragmatically, GHQ would need 'cooperation of personnel from the film industry for the dissemination of their own propaganda'. However, accusations of collaboration or war crimes did not have to come from the Occupation forces to cause tension in the studio. In the frantic post-war competition for jobs, animators with a record in war films were apt to be classified as C-grade war criminals by their own colleagues, as part of the politics of jostling for the limited amount of available work. Ushio Sōji (2007: 210) alludes to another issue, more upsetting to some of the accused animators, which was that many of those who had worked in the wartime film business had only done so in the first place as a means of dodging the draft. If this were true, and there is no reason to believe otherwise in at least a few cases, then it would have been futile to write off animators and artists as 'war criminals' because they had chosen to make films rather than shoot at Allied soldiers. The very idea that individuals could be censured for obeying 'illegal orders' in wartime was one of the central tenets of the (then ongoing) Tokyo War Crimes Trial, but arguably ran counter to the previous 200 years of Japanese government and its emphasis on unswerving loyalty. Along with soldiers, Japanese factory workers, cooks, animators and presumably, supportive housewives, were now expected to regard themselves as culpable, held to account by Japanese political agitators, but on the basis of liberal democratic principles that were arguably foreign to many Japanese (Standish 2005: 176).[6]

Several more union actions were to follow, with an industry-wide fifty-one-day general strike in October 1946, which itself led to schisms within the unions, largely between Communists and non-Communists. According to Ushio Sōji (2007: 219), the Communist Party pursued an aggressive expansion policy, signing up members regardless of their actual political persuasion, and provocatively decorating the studio with red flags. With the original union winning a closed-shop demarcation deal, a splinter group established a 'new' studio: Shintōhō, housed at the Sōshigaya building where the Shadow Staff had once worked (Ushio 2007: 210). The presence of animated footage in Tōhō films of 1947 and 1948 should be regarded in the light of these studio pressures, and the concurrent decline in output at Tōhō, which only made thirteen films in 1947, with an overall loss of

75 million yen (Hirano 1992: 222–3). It is, in fact, remarkable that the animators managed to find ways of insinuating themselves into quite so many projects, with such versatility. However, they were to encounter their nemesis in December 1947, when the previous studio head, exhausted by all-night meetings with union agitators, was replaced with Watanabe Tetsuzō.

Watanabe was a former law professor and a darling of the Occupation forces, with an impressive wartime record that had seen him imprisoned for anti-government pamphleteering – proof, if proof were needed, that some Japanese did stand up to the militarist order. He was that rarest of Occupation minions, a man with a clean wartime record and an avowed distaste for unions, who proclaimed his mission was 'to defeat the two kinds of red at Tōhō: communists and deficits' (Hirano 1992: 224). He was, however, a man who professed to know very little about Communists or films – on his arrival at the studio, he facetiously mistook protestors' rendition of the 'Internationale' for the company song, and later boasted in a press conference that the last film he had seen was *Zigomar*. Kurosawa Akira, in his own account of the strike actions (1983: 165), cannot even bring himself to name Watanabe, referring to him only as a 'notorious Red-hater', although he also concedes that Communist agitation in the unions had reached provocatively heightened levels by the time of his appointment:

> We directors were trying to explain our situation to the new president of the company. He was listening, and it began to appear that we were rousing his sympathies. Just at that moment, our attention was diverted to the huge plate-glass window of the room where we were meeting. Outside was a union demonstration, led by a big red flag. You might as well have waved a red-lined toreador's cape in front of a raging bull.

It was the beginning of the third strike, which would last 195 days. Watanabe's position was that Tōhō was 2 billion yen in arrears, with three times as many employees as was required for its current film output (Hirano 1992: 225) – precisely the kind of pressures that had led the animators to make themselves useful on productions where animation might not have been totally necessary. The union chairman protested that today's Tōhō had been formed by the forced wartime amalgamation of several different companies, and that the studio was now required for a new propaganda purpose, to educate the masses about 'civil rights' (Hirano 1992: 226). Watanabe, however, saw this as the *non sequitur* it was – neither point was an argument that would make the deficit or overstaffing go away. Instead, Watanabe fired 266 people in April 1948, including 'communist party members, sympathisers and all 42 animators' (Ushio 2007: 211). This was part of his crusade against the Japanese Motion Picture and Theatrical Workers Union, and resulted in further defections to 'New Tōhō' (Shintōhō) up the hill in Sōshigaya. The remaining staff members were hardly any more fortunate, suspended in May and then informed of the company's indefinite closure in June.

By August, staff at the rival studios had now occupied their own buildings, and stood ready to fight over the materials and machinery left in each – in the event of studio bankruptcy, the film stock, costumes, cameras and lights would all be valuable assets. In a lively section of his memoirs, Kurosawa Akira reported (1983: 165) the Tōhō faction manning the barricades, led by an actor in a cowboy hat. Meanwhile, the electricians repurposed their lamps as spotlights to ward off night attacks, and the special-effects department installed wind machines at the barricaded gates, with sacks of cayenne pepper primed in the event of an enemy assault. Fire hoses and rain machines were turned into water cannon, and paint bombs tested that could saturate targets in a sticky blue mist – Kurosawa himself had suggested blue would be less antagonistic than red. Not all protestors were as careful with their attackers' feelings as Kurosawa – more proactive agitators had prepared broken glass and sand ready to fling into the giant fans. Meanwhile, someone had made a large sign that read: 'Culture Cannot Be Destroyed by Violence' (Hirano 1992: 229).[7]

Watanabe fought back with impressive overkill: fifty trucks that unloaded 2,000 riot police, accompanied by an unspecified number of bulldozers, six armoured cars, a unit from the US First Cavalry and, as if the situation were not surreal enough already, three reconnaissance aircraft and seven American tanks. The incident became notorious in Japanese film history, in that 'Everything came but the battleships' (Sodei 1988: 146; Hirano 1992: 229–30).[8] The union backed down, and the losing side, including a platoon of animators, retreated dejectedly via the studio's back gate on 19 August (Ushio 2007: 220–1). Among the newly jobless workers was the art assistant Kawamoto Kihachirō, who spent the next few years scraping a living by making and photographing dolls, and would later make the short animation *Shijin no Shōgai* (1974, *A Poet's Life*) based in part on his experience of the strike (Yokota 2003: 36).

Some sixty workers were retained at Tōhō under Shimomura Kenji, and the facility endured as the Educational Film Unit for several further years. Perhaps meaningfully, Ushio describes them as 'employees' or 'company men' (*sha-in*), rather than specifically as 'animators' – Shimomura was a live-action director and, despite the animation component in *Plovers*, it is reasonable to assume that animation was henceforth only of secondary concern to graphics and titles under his leadership. Many of the exiles, however, swiftly joined forces with the remnants of Nichidō.[9]

THE COLLAPSE OF NIHON MANGA EIGA-SHA

Masaoka Kenzō, at least, had successfully engineered his own escape from the spat between Tōhō and Shintōhō. He already had independent facilities, and needed only rely on the studios for distribution and exhibition, rather than production. However, his eyesight began to deteriorate, so that his role in the production of new animation became increasingly an honorary one. That, at least is the way that his absence was explained to the staff, although the reality seems to have been far more prosaic.

Nihon Manga Eiga and Nichidō served as attractors for many animators, although some, like Ushio Sōji, gave up and looked for work elsewhere. However, despite escaping Watanabe's putsches, Masaoka was still subject to the same prevailing conditions that had created Watanabe's problems. The labour issues at Tōhō were symptoms of a larger economic malaise, as occupied Japan suffered rising inflation and foundering export revenues. The remedy, as organised by the US government in December 1948, was the appointment of the Detroit banker Joseph Dodge as an 'economic czar' to reform Japan's tax and administration. Enforcing a series of austerity measures that came to be known as the Nine Commandments or the Dodge Line, he curtailed loans, increased tax scrutiny, shut down many subsidies and forced through a more balanced budget. He also fixed an exchange rate of 360 yen to the dollar, severely undervaluing the yen in order to encourage exports. Dower (1999: 541) relates that 'Public works, welfare and education budgets were cut. Unemployment rose. Domestic consumption was suppressed. Bankruptcies increased among smaller enterprises, and the media began devoting attention to suicides among small businessmen.'

One of the immediate implications, in spring 1949, was a series of extensive cuts in staffing and investment all across Japan National Railways (JNR), the chief investor in Nichidō's cartoon *Poppoya: Carefree Station Master* and its sequel.[10] When Nichidō pursued payment, the JNR accountants refused to pay, on the grounds that they were unable to authorise any expenses that did not come accompanied by a written contract. According to Masaoka's claims in a 1978 magazine article, it was these pressures and disappointments, not the ongoing witch-hunts and strikes, that led to his leaving the studio and seeking new work in children's illustration, along with his colleague Kumagawa Masao (Tsugata 2004: 121).

The imagery of Kawamoto Kihachirō's *A Poet's Life* (1974) was inspired in part by the sackings and protests at Tōhō in the 1940s

His fellow animators at Nichidō continued to work on their own productions and as contractors, including for their former Tōhō masters on works for hire such as the two-reelers *Poppoya-san Nonki Kikanshi* (1949, *Poppoya: Easygoing Engineer*) and *Otenki Gakkō* (1952, *Weather School*). Such productions kept Nichidō active on small commissions with the hope, not always realised, of reliable payment. Some animators even remained the servants of two masters, like Furusawa Hideo, whose name can be seen on both Nichidō and Nihon Manga Eiga-sha productions during the period (Animage 1989: 31). However, Watanabe Tetsuzō's ongoing crusade against Communists would bring about the destruction of Nihon Manga Eiga-sha before the 1940s were over.

Seo Mitsuyo, the director of the two *Momotarō* wartime movies, had joined Tōhō in January 1948. Fully expecting longer-form competition from rival organisations, Watanabe approved production for a feature-length black-and-white cartoon from Seo, seemingly designed to 'relive the dream of the great success of his five-reel *Momotarō's Sea Eagles*' (Ushio 2007: 222). Seo's project was conceived as an anthropomorphic variation on Hans Christian Andersen's *Emperor's New Clothes*, except with a tailless fox in the lead role. The film was intended to be exhibited in the Tōhō cinema chain as a 'feature', presumably accompanied by a couple of Nichidō shorts also in production at the time, such as the one-reeler *Dōbutsu Daiyakyūsen* (1949, *Animal Baseball Battle*). Seo's *Ōsama no Shippo* (1949, *The King's Tail*) was hence conceived as Tōhō's tent-pole feature – the crucial component in creating a programme of animation that could tour on a national roadshow rather than simply bumping up the running time of someone else's feature. Without the film, there was simply not enough Japanese animation produced in 1949 to justify the price of a cinema ticket. It is hence all the more surprising that Watanabe would cancel the film before it could even be exhibited:

> It was a spectacular work using forty animators, 100,000 cels and with a production budget of six million yen. The plan was to show it in the Tōhō cinema chain. However, on seeing the completed work, the Tōhō chairman Watanabe Tetsuzō decreed from on high: 'This is riddled with Redness!' [*Naiyō ga Akagakatte iru*] It was put on the shelf and never saw the light of day. (Ushio 2007: 222)

It was a death by a thousand cuts. In October 1949, Watanabe first made the animators reduce the running time from fifty-seven minutes to thirty-three, and only then pronounced it unreleasable (Animage 1989: 31; Tezuka 1999: 120). His decision bankrupted Nihon Manga Eiga-sha, and caused three of the lead animators, Obata Toshiharu, Fukui Hidekazu and Seo himself, to quit the animation business in disgust; all subsequently became illustrators in the children's book and comics market. The fourth, Furusawa Hideo, defected to Nichidō where he already had connections (Yamaguchi 2004: 69).

FOREIGN COMPETITION

Apart from a dozen members of the Shadow Staff who had viewed a contraband copy of *Fantasia* in a secret screening in 1941 (Ushio 2007: 193–5), Japanese animators had had little access to foreign cartoons, with the exception of *Princess Iron Fan*, made by the Wan brothers in Japanese-occupied Shanghai. From the midpoint of the Occupation and in the decade that followed, this would be redressed by at least two foreign releases each year, presenting a powerful and, in a sense, unanswerable edifice of full-colour, full-animation entertainments to lure Japanese audiences away from domestic productions.

Between the end of the war and the premiere of *Hakujaden* on 22 October 1958, Japanese cinemas hosted eighteen foreign animated 'features' of varying length, largely from American studios, but also from Czechoslovakia, France and Britain. The first of these, *Gulliver's Travels* (1939), was distributed in Japan in April 1948, suspiciously close to the date that Watanabe Tetsuzō laid off several dozen Tōhō animators. Undoubtedly, he was motivated by the ongoing labour dispute, but the possibility remains that, with regard to the animators, he was simply disheartened and overawed by the competition. Since we only have the complaints of Watanabe's victims in the Tōhō purges, it is difficult to gauge how much his behaviour over *The King's Tail* was born out of anti-Communist paranoia, and how much out of a misguided hope that Seo could produce a work that could match up to the imminent releases on the way from Disney (distributed in Japan by Daiei),[11] turning to disconsolate disappointment when he merely produced something that matched up to competition in Japan.

Following the catastrophic shelving of *The King's Tail* in 1949, Japanese animation could reasonably be said to have been swamped by colour cinema films, including many features, either newly arrived from abroad or stockpiled during the wartime ban on foreign films. For a list of the films in order of Japanese release, see Table 4.1.

TABLE 4.1 FOREIGN CARTOONS IN JAPANESE CINEMAS 1948–58

YEAR OF RELEASE IN JAPAN	TITLE	COUNTRY OF ORIGIN AND DATE	JAPANESE TITLE WHEN ALTERED
1948	*Gulliver's Travels*	US 1939	*Gulliver Ryokōki*
1950	*Snow White and the Seven Dwarfs*	US 1937	*Shirayuki-hime*, literally *Princess White Snow*
1951	*Mr Bug Goes to Town*	US 1941	*Batta-kun Machi ni Iku*
1951	*Bambi*	US 1942	
1952	*Pinocchio*	US 1940	
1953	*Alice in Wonderland*	US 1951	*Fushigi no Kuni no Alice*
1954	*Dumbo*	US 1941	
1954	*Fun and Fancy Free*	US 1947	*Koguma Monogatari*, lit. *Bear-cub Story*
1955	*Peter Pan*	US 1953	
1955	*La Bergère et la ramoneur*	France 1952	*Yabunirami no Bōkun*, lit. *The Mistaken Tyrant*
1955	*Fantasia*	US 1940	
1955	*Toot, Whistle, Plunk and Boom*	US 1953	*Pukadon Kōkyōgaku*, lit. *Plunk-boom Symphony*
1956	*Lady and the Tramp*	US 1955	*Wanwan Monogatari*, lit. *Woof-Woof Story*
1957	*Saludos Amigos*	US 1942	*Latin America no Tabi*, lit. *A Latin American Journey*
1957	*Man in Space*	US 1955	*Disney no Uchū Ryokō*, lit. *Disney's Space Journey*
1958	*Make Mine Music*	US 1947	*Peter to Ōkami*, lit. *Peter and the Wolf*
1958	*The World of Little Ig*	UK 1957	*Chinsetsu Uchū Hōsōkyoku no Maki*, lit. *Chapter of the Strange Space Broadcast Office*
1958	*Goldilocks*	Czech. 1956	Japan as *Kinpatsu-musume*

(Stingray and Nichigai Associates 2010: 892–3)

We might consider the dispiriting impact that such a flood of content could have had on struggling animators, particularly since such films sprang, fully formed, onto the Japanese market, with no discussion of their crippling expense; many had yet to make back their production costs for Disney (Yamaguchi 2004: 66), and the two Fleischer films on the roster had already bankrupted their studio by the time they reached Japan (Schatz 1997: 108). Oddly, two Russian films, *The Humpbacked Horse* and *The Brave Little Deer*, are mentioned in animators' memoirs from the period, but not included in the above list (Ōtsuka 2001: 18; Kanō 2004: 125; Mochinaga 2006: 240) – presumably, they were screened privately by animation groups.

In the year that Disney's *Snow White* played in Japanese cinemas, it took the combined efforts of both the Tōhō Educational Film Office and Nichidō to release the seventeen-minute short *Kobito to Aomushi* (1950, *The Boy and the Caterpillar*). Arguably, the nadir of the Japanese animation business came not at the beginning of the US Occupation, but at its end in the years 1951–2, when Japanese cinema audiences flocked to see the

In *Gulliver's Great Activities* (1950) Japanese-speaking natives sustain a foreign giant with tax and tariffs, and are rewarded with trade and civil reconstruction

American-made *Bambi, Mr Bug Goes to Town* and *Cinderella* (1950). Sole domestic competition in this period was Ōfuji Noburō's *Whale* (1950), which may have found a bigger audience at the 1953 Cannes Film Festival than it did in its native Japan (Animage 1989: 32). In the years that followed, Japanese animation began a slow recovery, but one only discernible in hindsight – official release records chart barely one or two short films a year in cinemas, whereas later histories augment this meagre number by including semi-professional works believed to have been finished in this period, but not publicly exhibited (Animage 1989: 33–5; Stingray and Nichigai Associates 2010: 892–3).

CONTENT AND THEMES: RECONSTRUCTION AND RETRENCHMENT

Typical among the obscure anime of the period is *Gulliver Funtōki* (1950, *Gulliver's Great Activities*),[12] which takes place in a rural Europe a world away from the Japanese landscapes and imagery found in earlier cartoons. From the first image, of a European galleon in a storm, through the village sights of cows being milked and middle European houses, it evokes the West. Moreover, it does not evoke not the West as a real place, so much as the location of an earlier cartoon, drawing much of its inspiration from the Fleischer brothers' *Gulliver's Travels*.

Its message, however, is heavy-handed and preachy enough for it to be filed as propaganda, or at the very least, public information. Gulliver, the friendly giant who has been inadvertently washed ashore in this unnamed Ruritania, is at first regarded with suspicion by the natives. He soon proves them wrong, after he is fed local food (marked with the character *zei*: 'tax/duty'). Thus fortified, he helps them with large-scale projects, including river management, mining and, it is implied, industrialisation. His activities eventually create a surplus in production, which he tows away to overseas markets (the storm that wrecked him now conveniently forgotten, as he is able to wade away on foot). He returns to help them put out a fire, capping an extended metaphor for the unseen but nationwide benefits extending from taxation and foreign trade.

There are inadvertent ironies in that Admiral Yamamoto Isoroku once cautioned the Japanese against 'smiting a sleeping enemy' – the very same temptation faced by the villagers when Gulliver is washed up on their shores. It was the Japanese tax office that funded this film, although its message is resolutely America-centric – Gulliver returns with automobiles and medical supplies. There is also a chance that it is so openly derivative of the Fleischer cartoon because that was likely to appeal to the censor – no samurai or foreign devils here, only well-intentioned Japanese slavishly aping an 'American' original in a new performance of auto-orientalism. Although made under the authority of the American occupation censor, and seemingly couched in terms designed to appeal to foreign scrutineers, *Gulliver's Great Activities* delivers a message intended for the Japanese alone: that tax brings benefits. At the end, when the European villagers uncharacteristically give the 'banzai' salute in his honour, Gulliver is entreated to stay forever, although the finale draws a discreet veil over his answer.

Notably, however, the film did not feature in the cinema exhibition environment. Despite a 1950 completion date and an Eirin censor stamp, and despite surviving to the present day, most accessibly on the Digital Meme DVD box set, it is not listed in Japanese sources as ever being screened for a paying audience (absent from both Animage (1989: 32) and Stingray and Nichigai Associates (2010: 892). As far as the journals of record are concerned, and hence also as far as cinema audiences were concerned, it may as well never have existed.

THE RISE OF TELEVISION ADVERTISING

Television, known disparagingly in cinema circles as 'the brown screen' (*brown-kan*), was also exerting a powerful indirect effect on animation. The rising cost of animation, and the ever-growing adoption of television, had radically altered the requirements of a 'night at the movies', largely killing off the subsidiary programmes that had formerly offered a market for documentaries, newsreels and cartoons. Meanwhile, at an exhibition level, cinema theatres were renting their prints directly from the distributors, and hence unwilling to pay out any extra money for works that many patrons regarded as mere filler or distractions from the main event. Consequently, the number of short films on Japanese cinema programmes was in decline by the early 1960s, although longer features were on the increase. In the case of Tōei in particular, which deliberately pushed this as a selling point, it was increasingly common for audiences to expect not one, but two features, and no filler (Yamamoto 1989: 62; Minakawa 2009a: 169).

However, although Japanese animation was rare in cinemas, it had returned in the one part of the programme that could not be dropped – the pre-film commercials. Animated advertising, both in cinemas and later on television, became a new growth area in the Japanese cartoon business (Tsugata 2005: 164–5).

At the time of Japan's first official public TV broadcast in February 1953, the country only possessed 866 television sets (Clements and Tamamuro 2003: xi). The new technology grew exponentially, gaining its first commercial channel by the end of the year, a second in 1955 and two more in 1959. These commercial channels, of course, required commercials – a medium seemingly ideally suited for animation, demanding eye-catching, distinctive and memorable images. Furthermore, advertising commands high fees, on the understanding that its screen images, sure to be seen by viewers on multiple occasions, might even be required to be more robust and enduring than television programmes themselves, many of which viewers only saw once. This resulted in the arrival of a new and wealthy patron for the animated arts, in the form of the advertising corporation Dentsū. A company that thrived on heavy vertical integration, Dentsū secured slots on the airwaves by actively involving itself in the production of the programmes which the adverts were placed between, and had already seized control of '60 per cent of primetime' by the 1960s (Tungate 2007: 187). As a result, affiliates such as the Dentsū Eiga-sha (Dentsū Film Company) became active investors in new animation, most notably in a series of commercials for the Asahi brewery, that eventually led to *Beer Mukashi-mukashi* (1956, *Beer through the Ages*), a twelve-minute compilation of adverts that charted the history of beer from ancient Babylonia and Egypt, through medieval Germany, and up to its arrival in Japan in the nineteenth century on the 'black ships' of Commodore Perry (Animage 1989: 36). Written by Iizawa Tadasu, *Beer through the Ages* represented a nexus of animation talent, including stop-motion work from Mochinaga Tadahito and Kawamoto Kihachirō, and cellophane animation from the ageing Ōfuji Noburō.

Notably, *Beer through the Ages* was a commercial for a demonstrably 'adult' product. While cinemas presented an overwhelming sense that cartoons were now for children, the items featured in commercials were largely aimed at adults. A chicken winding a clock sold products for the Fukube watch company (1952); stop-motion drum majorette dolls twirled their batons to advertise Mitsuwa soap (1954)[13]; and a cel-animated samurai lusted after Momoya's jarred spices (1961).[14]

Nakai Kōichi's history of Japanese advertising regards the watershed as *Torys Bar* (1958),[15] a sixty-second commercial for a sub-brand of Suntory whisky, which capitalised on the fact that the parent company, Kotobukiya, was the sponsor of the Japanese broadcasts of the TV series *Rawhide* (1959–65). According to a history of Japanese advertising from the late 1970s, TV commercials before *Torys Bar* had been cheap and aimed specifically at children. *Torys Bar* was hailed as a trailblazer because, in the words of its designer Yanagihara Ryōhei, 'it was a cartoon that grown-ups could enjoy' – an odd claim, as if grown-ups had not previously 'enjoyed' *Beer through the Ages* two years earlier.

Torys Bar was set in a Wild West saloon, where the big-headed character of Uncle Torys would drink and carouse. The designer of the character recalled its creation at a brainstorming session at Kotobukiya in which thirty minutes were spent outlining an affable man who

> would like drinks as a matter of fact. He would be timid but at times act daringly. He would like women but have the sense of righteousness. He wouldn't show his emotions much but would be a warm-hearted person. (Yanagihara, quoted in Nakai 1991: 735)

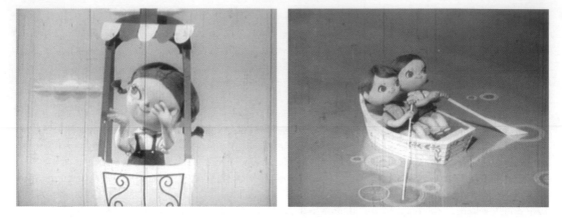

This 1961 commercial for Rohto Pharmaceuticals utilises puppet animation from Shiba Pro – Kawamoto Kihachirō's animation company

The character came first, designed for poster art sometime around 1956. The animation was a later addition, and strongly influenced by foreign animation, with Yanagihara claiming that the style of *Torys Bar* had been inspired by the staff's viewing of Disney's *Toot, Whistle, Plunk and Boom* (1953) and UPA's *Gerald McBoing Boing* (1950). However, one suspects an element here of self-fulfilling prophecy – Yanagihara's list of 'inspirations' (Nakai 1991: 735) also reads like a rundown of every foreign cartoon that could be seen in Japan in the mid-1950s. Of his 'inspirations', only *Gerald McBoing Boing* was not exhibited in Japanese theatres at the time, and that appears to have been accessed by Yanagihara through a print owned by the animation company TCJ.

We must exercise some caution with sources of the period – as often happens with puppet animation in particular, Japanese sources can often confuse animation with simple puppetry. Nakai, for example, refers in his 'Animation' section to the series of *Bunmeidō Tō Gekijo* (1961, *Bunmeidō Bean Theatre*) commercials, implying that they were animated (Nakai 1991: 469). In fact, as extant footage shows,[16] these adverts for Bunmeidō bean curd featured a dancing chorus line of singing teddy bears, but had been shot 'live', i.e. as puppetry, rather than in stop-motion. However, actual cel or puppet animation became a definite and distinctive presence in Japanese advertising of the late 1950s, and even more so after 1961, when the minimum size of advertising slots was reduced from thirty to fifteen seconds. This not only made television advertising more accessible to smaller companies, but encouraged all advertisers to find something eye-catching to throw into their fifteen seconds of fame (Nakai 1991: 706).

> By this point, commercials were usually either sixty seconds or thirty seconds, while fifteen-second slots played only a small part. When five-second slots were introduced, some producers resisted arguing: 'What can be said in just five seconds – essentially 3.5 seconds with sounds)?' However, such extreme time restriction gave birth to new ideas – the discovery of catchphrases that were suitable for an instant exposure. (Nakai 1991: 706)

Mark Tungate, in *Ad Land: A Global History of Advertising*, suggests that this concentration on 'bite-sized spots' and impressionistic slogans is some sort of manifestation of Japanese tradition, and that a mindset reared on haiku is ready to accept much shorter, compressed messages. He quotes (2007: 189) Tanaka Kunihiko of Dentsū, who claims: 'Western advertising is very rational: it's marketing oriented and strategic. Our advertising is media oriented and instinctive.' This, however, seems to be a conveniently orientalist appeal to a nebulous 'tradition' – as Tanaka admits himself on the following page, *all* advertising has subsequently gravitated to the shorter, sharper model found in Japanese commercials, a model which appears to have arisen in the first place simply because advertising space was carefully priced low in order to attract more advertisers. The more crucial issue is one of a vast and largely unchronicled market for Japanese animation, aesthetically unappealing

'Art-house' animations like Kuri Yōji's *Au Fou!* (1967) were often funded by day jobs in the advertising world

and industrially uncommemorated, which nevertheless provided significant work for many animators (Tsugata 2012). One modern researcher estimates that more than 70 per cent of commercials in the 1950s used animation to some degree (Tsugata 2011b: 24). Such support would, in turn, eventually become something of a patron of the arts. In particular, the advertising animators Kuri Yōji, Yanagihara Ryōhei and Manabe Hiroshi, collectively known as the Sannin no Kai (Group of Three), hired out Tokyo's Wakatsuki Hall on 26 November 1960 to show a one-hour programme of short 8mm films. This became a periodic showcase, expanding to an 'animation festival by 1964, with the last iteration in 1971 screening over fifty films' (Animage 1989: 154–5).

OTOGI PRO

The companies that worked in advertising tended to be small two- and three-man operations, including TCJ (Television Corporation of Japan), San Ad and the puppet outfit Shiba Production. Although they earned a living, they were not considered artists, since adverts were the filler between actual content. Ironically, the adverts were often considerably more accomplished, and better funded than the 'entertainment' cartoons of the period. They were also more widely seen – *Torys Bar* might have only lasted sixty seconds, but a viewer who saw it once a night, every night, would have sat through a feature film's worth of content in barely eight weeks. It is salutary to compare such inadvertent access with the relative difficulty audiences had in seeing other Japanese animation in the cinema.

On those occasions where an institution's works are hard to find, or obscure in the first place, and its staff dispersed to more famous and enduring studios, then artistic heritage becomes vulnerable. In the case of the artist Yokoyama Ryūichi, his self-identification as a manga artist skewed the content of his memoirs strongly in favour of the medium that made him famous and wealthy. Conversely, his animation company Otogi Pro is dismissed in his memoirs in only a few desultory lines (Yokoyama 1997: 152), despite it being one of the key independent studios of the period, a crucible of several great talents and the maker of Japanese television's first animated series. Ironically, there is more about Yokoyama's animation career in Tezuka's memoirs (Tezuka 1999: 200–3). The reasons for this present a delicate exercise in interpretation, in which we might reasonably cite Yokoyama himself as an unreliable witness.

Yokoyama cherished ambitions of becoming an animation studio boss like Walt Disney, whom he had met in 1951. With Japanese still restricted from travelling abroad during the Occupation, Yokoyama had pulled strings to get himself assigned to cover the San Francisco Conference as a journalist, and then spent two days at Disney's studios (Yokoyama 1997: 139–43). A comfortably well-off artist with influential family connections, who had enjoyed bestseller status in both the pre- and post-war periods, Yokoyama had already seen his work adapted into several media, including live-action cinema and post-war radio. The year after the critical success of his experimental cartoon *Onbu Obake* (1955, *Piggyback Ghost*),[17] Yokoyama started his own animation studio, Otogi Pro, which flourished in the late 1950s and early 1960s, and continued to exist, at least on paper, into the 1970s.

'He had a dream to make Otogi Production as big as Disney', noted his former assistant Suzuki Shinichi, 'but he was a daydreaming comic artist and not a businessman. One felt that it started off as a hobby for him, and finished as one, too.' (Suzuki 2008a: 124). Although Yokoyama was a manga celebrity, and his name was associated with several wartime films, his ability as an animator had already been called into question (see Chapter 3).

> It is not unusual in the world of animation for the artist of an original comic to take the credit for the work of the animators. Indeed, it is often part of the plan, since an adaptation of a comic capitalises to some extent on the pre-existing fame of its creator. (Crafton 1982: 83)

Yokoyama, however, remained an unknown quantity. He was undoubtedly a 'brand', but his active animation experience has been estimated at a mere three seconds of completed animation (Minakawa 2009a: 84).

Although Yokoyama's 'studio' was officially called Otogi Pro (Fairytale Productions), it was widely known among his staff as 'Tatami Productions', because much of the work was done on the *tatami* straw mats of a room in Yokoyama's house. However, considering the parlous state of the Japanese animation industry at the time, Yokoyama the wealthy dilettante performed a useful function by deciding to add a 16mm camera to his collection of toys. Never one to cut corners, he also invested in colour film, and called in numerous favours with famous friends.

As a result, his twenty-five-minute film *Piggybank Ghost* shows up in film listings as a bona fide film release, despite only being exhibited once at a special, star-studded screening at the Bungei-kan in Tokyo (Animage 1989: 35). As a performative action, there is very little to the film. As a representative event, we should bear in mind that on the occasion of its premiere, attended by such luminaries as the author Mishima Yukio and the actress Takamine Hideko, it was the Japanese animation *event of the year* – the longest Japanese cartoon to be publicly exhibited in over a decade, and in full colour to boot. On 26 December 1955, *Piggyback Ghost* was arguably the state of the art in Japanese animation, and the fact that the public were subsequently denied access to it assuredly did it no harm. Its artistic heritage was confined to the polite praise of high-powered opinion-formers, sufficient to secure Yokoyama a contract for a follow-up with wider distribution prospects. It would enjoy this place in the sun for three years, until its impact, and indeed its place in history, was largely wiped out by the release of Japan's first genuine full-colour, full-length animated feature, Tōei Dōga's *Hakujaden*.

Yokoyama followed with the eighteen-minute *Fukusuke* (1957), for which he took on extra help and upgraded to an old 35mm Askania camera, which could not track upwards or back, but was instead in a fixed position on a wooden box. The animator Suzuki Shinichi reported that on his first trip to the house to work at Otogi Pro, Yokoyama answered the door wearing a *yukata* bathrobe and a beret, which supposedly never left his head. Suzuki and his fellow animator Machiyama Mitsuhiro were installed upstairs in a single eight-mat room, where they not only ate and slept, but also carried out much of the studio's work (Suzuki 2008a: 111).

Suzuki had joined Otogi Pro in the hope of learning the animator's trade, but soon discovered that Yokoyama had had only a peripheral involvement with the previous films that bore his name, and that his fellow animator Machiyama's sole previous animation experience had been working for Yokoyama on *Piggyback Ghost*. Yokoyama understood the principles of animation – drawing, tracing, colouring, filming – but had no direct experience of more industrial elements of the process, such as production-line techniques or quality controls. Yokoyama's management of the studio often extended to simply pointing at a page from his published *Fukusuke* children's book, and demanding that it be 'animated' by the end of the day. As a result, Suzuki found the experience to be entertaining, but somewhat 'haphazard' (*tesaguri*):

> When I started working for Otogi Pro, all I had was Mr Yokoyama's drawings, and I believed that was how one made animation. Every day Mr Yokoyama would say 'today we're doing this', and give me a drawing of, for example, a frog on tracing paper which he would ask me to 'move like this'. I drew the movement and showed that to Mr Yokoyama. If he said 'That looks fine', I traced that onto a cell. I rubbed ink sticks and, because it needed to be a little viscous to stay on the cels, I experimented with additives like starch syrup in the ink … . Shot lengths were also an approximation. Even if the produced artwork exceeded the scheduled length, that was fine. When all was done and Mr Yokoyama approved it, I put a cross through that part of the *Fukusuke* picture book with a red pencil. That meant the scene was done. (Suzuki 2008a: 114–15)

This fumbling working method, described by its participants variously as a 'cottage industry' or 'improvisational jazz', was brought to a close during the production of *Fukusuke* by the arrival of Maeda Hajime, the producer with whom Yokoyama had worked on *Professor Sky-Above* during the war.

Maeda reintroduced rigorous practices that seemed to have been in use during the war era, including the exposure (*satsuei*) sheet, better known in modern animation as a dope sheet, listing the number of frames to be shot per image, the nature of the image and whether it was sectioned with separately moving hands, feet or other parts, and any other special instructions for the animators. An older, wiser Suzuki (2008a: 117–18) describes the dope sheet as the 'lifeline of animation', and plainly welcomed its arrival at Otogi Pro, where previously Yokoyama had decided on the number of frames to shoot on a seemingly random basis, and not known if his hunches were right until the rushes came back from the developer.[18]

Maeda told the artists that his more industrial methods would not guarantee a work of art, but that they would at least prevent an otherwise inevitable waste of materials, time and manpower spent creating artwork that did not adequately convey the story. However, despite the imposition of a stricter schedule, the animators at Otogi Pro still seemed to be improvising a lot of their materials. The animators were obliged to use offcuts of unexposed film from other productions, suggesting that even the profligate Yokoyama was not entirely free with his money. However, with staff that did not understand the meaning of the emulsion numbers on the canisters, Otogi Pro often found its productions assembled on varying film stock with colours that fluctuated from shot to shot. Meanwhile, Yokoyama's wife, eight children and even next-door neighbours were occasionally drafted in as extra labour. Suzuki (2008a: 119) recalls:

> We did not know which paint to use for the cels, so we used poster colours mixed with some Pentel paints to add oil. Even then, the cels repelled the paint, and when they dried, the paint would crack. … Because we mixed two types of paint, dark tones would come out uneven … . The filming itself was also done amateurishly, so even when we got large halation effects, I thought that there was nothing we could do about it. Everything was experimental. That was Otogi Pro.

Beggars, however, could not be choosers. Since Tōhō had laid off all its own animators, the studio paid for Yokoyama's cottage-industry effort and toured it in Tōhō cinemas all over the country. Yokoyama did not make any residuals on the roadshow, but seems to have been well compensated nonetheless, later claiming that *Fukusuke* was the only one of his animated works ever to turn a profit (Suzuki 2008a: 123).[19]

The animation sequences from *I Am Two* (1962) have largely escaped anime historians because the film is filed as 'live action'

Unaware that *Fukusuke* would be seen with hindsight as his company's high point, Yokoyama expanded his staff to twenty, recruiting several future big names such as Yamamoto Eiichi, Saitō Hiroshi and Okada Emiko. Yamamoto Eiichi started working for Otogi Pro straight out of high school in 1958, and stayed for two years (Yamamoto 1989: 10). Despite the shambolic nature of Otogi Pro's working practices, the young Yamamoto still regarded it as a good option when compared to the Tōei studio, then enmeshed in labour disputes of its own (see next chapter) or Ōfuji Noburo's small and idiosyncratic Chiyogami Eiga-sha. With a degree of revulsion, Yamamoto noted that the only other option would be to work for one of the 'trifling' companies making television commercials (Yamamoto 1989: 17).

Yokoyama's own apparent disinclination to remember his animation days has hidden much of Otogi Pro's work from posterity. In the early 1960s, his most widely seen piece of animation was tucked away inside Ichikawa Kon's live-action film *Watashi wa Nisai* (1962, *I Am Two*, a.k.a. *Being Two Isn't Easy*). There are, in fact, three moments of 'animation' within *I Am Two*. One is a simple graphic overlay near the climax, presenting the face of a departed grandmother within the disc of the full moon. Another is a very brief pixilation sequence in which the child-narrator ponders escaping from his playpen. This is shown with the aid of a substitute doll that 'climbs' in limited stop-motion. The most noticeable sequence of animation is a forty-second cel-based dream sequence in which the moon transforms into a banana and a sailboat. However, this sequence is accomplished and fit for purpose, a far cry from the slapdash 'jazz' assembly line reported several years earlier by Suzuki Shinichi.

Otogi Pro was plainly learning from its mistakes. Yokoyama was credited as the 'director' of *Otogi no Sekai Ryokō* (1962, *Fairytale World Tour*), but the seventy-six-minute cinema feature, constructed out of seven shorter films, is more likely to have been the work of his 'assistant' Suzuki Shinichi. The staff credits include some powerful names, including Yamamoto Eiichi, just about to leave for pastures new, and Tokugawa Musei, the last of the great pre-war *benshi*, still lending authority to films with his celebrity voice (Animage 1989: 42).

Otogi Pro's pinnacle came in 1962, when the TBS television channel broadcast the first of what would be 312 episodes of the animated series *Otogi Manga Calendar*. Each episode lasted only three minutes, and was almost swamped by advertising and sponsor announcements that often took up another sixty or eighty seconds. Nor was every episode animated, since the content of each piece varied with the nature of the topic under discussion – each episode was an enquiry as to what happened 'on this day in history', and was sometimes illustrated not with animation, but with archive footage and collages. However, many episodes were animated and it is this, or its obscure predecessor *Instant History* (1961), from which it may have plundered some footage (Animage 1989: 4), which is regarded as the 'first animated television series' in Japan. Animation had been 'on television' since 1953, but with the broadcast of Yokoyama's history lessons, a new opportunity opened up for pioneering animators to explore the possibilities of the ever-growing medium of television. However, Yokoyama had already taken his animation experiment as far as he desired, and did not expand his capacities beyond those required to make *Otogi Manga Calendar*.

At some point in 1958 or 1959, Otogi Pro had a visit from a young artist who had already achieved a degree of fame. He had been working as a storyboarder at Tōei Dōga on a film based on one of his own manga, and had been inspired by the experience to consider setting up his own studio, producing works in the style of Otogi Pro for the lucrative new television market. Yokoyama suggested to the young artist that his interest was misplaced, and that animation would never be a real money-spinner. He advised him not to get involved in the industry, as it would only cause him heartbreak, telling him so repeatedly 'until his mouth was sour' (*kuchi o suppaku shite*), as one observer put it (Oguro 2004a: 4; Minakawa 2009a: 89–90). The young artist's name was Tezuka Osamu.

CONCLUSION

In the immediate post-war period, the sudden loss of military sponsors, the scramble for subsistence and fierce competition over jobs in a shrunken film industry meant animation was sidelined for a decade. By the beginning of the 1960s, Yamamoto Eiichi (1989: 28) estimated the size of the Japanese animation 'industry' at roughly 500 people – 300 working for the former Nichidō, twenty to thirty working for Otogi Pro, and the rest spread out among small operations mainly in advertising, with an average staff size of two or three people.

In the mid- to late 1950s, Japanese animation was transformed again, by the relationship of Nichidō to its patron and eventual owner, Tōei, and by the increased competition among many smaller operations.

Tezuka Osamu, however, would embark on an enterprise that would double the level of personnel by 1967, and double it again before the decade was out. His personal venture, the new studio Mushi Production, would poach Otogi Pro's leading staff, as well as staff from the Tōei studio and would come to be seen as a training venue for much of the rest of Japan's animation industry. Tezuka's leap into television would transform the anime industry and quadruple its size. The development and implementation of this 'revolution' forms the subject of the next two chapters.

NOTES

1. Hu (2010: 81) claims it was pirated abroad under the title *Haru no Gensō* (*Spring Phantasia*) although she offers no clue as to where.
2. JCD 3933.
3. JCD 3889.
4. JCD 3999.
5. Michael Barrier, in *The Animated Man: A Life of Walt Disney* (2007), notes very similar tensions at Disney, where strikers were largely concerned simply with conditions, whereas their boss accused them of Communist sympathies.
6. See also Clements and Tamamuro (2003: xv–xvi) for an account of how Japanese television dealt with the issue in 1958, presenting the mock trial of a man who discovers that he is a C-grade war criminal because he carried out orders when disobedience would have been punished by death.
7. Gerteis (2009: 44) doubts the veracity of the broken-glass story, suggesting it was the result of false reports from military intelligence.
8. The precise origin of 'Everything came but the battleships' (*konakatta no wa gunkan dake*) is unclear. Hirano (1992: 312) notes several occurrences of the phrase in contemporary reportage, although Kurosawa (1983: 167) claims that the phrase was spoken by Watanabe Tetsuzō himself, presumably cackling over his advancing minions like a sci-fi overlord. Kurosawa does not explain how he managed to hear this from several hundred feet away, amid several hundred chanting strikers and the grinding approach of tanks and bulldozers.
9. According to Ushio (2007: 221): 'About a dozen remaining animators, including Ichino Shōji, Niiro Saburō, Sasamori Kei and Ishikawa Komei joined up with [Nichidō] staff including Yamamoto Sanae … Daikuhara Akira and Mori Yasuji. With Yuhara Hajime, Iseki Mitsuo and Yabushita Taiji (formerly of the Ministry of Education film department) as supporters, they rented a room at Seijo High School in Shinjuku's Wakamatsu district, and kept producing animation.

10. Neither film is in the JCD, but both can be found in DAW 724.

11. Daiei appears to have taken little interest in producing Japanese animation of its own as a result.

12. An equally good example is Kumagawa Masao's *Mahō no Pen* (1946, *The Magic Pen*). But since this has already been well covered (Hu 2009: 256–60; Tsugata 2012: 42), I chose a different film.

13. See http://www.youtube.com/watch?v=fJDGQGJZvp4&feature=related.

14. See http://www.youtube.com/watch?v=_Zac1fW_34E&feature=related.

15. See http://www.youtube.com/watch?v=sgNMESa-4x0&feature=related.

16. See http://www.youtube.com/watch?v=aDHJgJHlv0M&feature=related.

17. DAW 132.

18. The very name 'dope sheet' reflects archaic 'early 1900s slang' (Wells 2006: 58), in which 'dope' meant 'information'. *The Cassell Dictionary of Slang* (Green 1998: 357) is more specific, citing several close definitions for 'dope', but stating that its meaning as 'an explanation' dates specifically to the 1920s. The nature of the dope sheet seems to draw directly on Henry Gantt's principles of scientific management, particularly the 'Gantt chart', not widely known in the US until 1922 (Sheldrake 1996: 40). In other words, public knowledge of the dope sheet postdates the publication of Lutz's *Animated Cartoons* (1920). However, the existence of dope sheets, or at least the existence of something similar, is implied in numerous photographs and testimonials from Kitayama Eiga. It seems that the dope sheet was in professional use in the Japanese animation industry by the 1930s, but since its value was not documented, it had to be 'rediscovered' at Otogi in the 1950s. Since Maeda was plainly employing dope sheets at Tōhō during the war, it seems reasonable to assume that they never fell out of use at post-war Nichidō, and hence Tōei.

19. According to Shirakawa Daisaku, Tōhō 'distributed' *Fukusuke* by shoving it on a double bill with 'some live-action melodrama'; it is likely that it earned its money through a captive audience rather than its own merits (Oguro 2004a: 4).

5 DREAMS OF EXPORT
Tōei Dōga and MOM Production 1953–67

The 1950s saw several mostly unsuccessful attempts by the Japanese animation industry to participate in the international film business at the level of ownership, and far more enduring, but largely overlooked participation at the level of production during the 1960s and beyond. The failure of such works to show up in histories of 'anime' suggests many errors of historical practice (Megill 2007: 33), but chiefly an aesthetic prejudice against work for hire, and unwillingness to commemorate the achievements of the 'below-the-line' animation industry, among both its animators and their clients.

Anime's transnational quality is not a recent phenomenon. An awareness and reaction to the world outside Japan has been a powerful influence since the earliest days of cinema, when the owners of films first toyed with the idea of revenue from foreign markets. Aaron Gerow (2010: 113) writes of the 'dream of export' as a fundamental element and 'structuring myth' in Japanese film discourse of the early twentieth century. But although Japanese cartoons occasionally appeared in colonial cinemas or foreign film festivals, animation did not truly approach its long-cherished dream of export until the 1950s, when several companies pursued foreign contracts with varying degrees of success.

According to an article in *Shūkan Shinchō* magazine in 1957 (Minakawa 2009a: 109), 'cartoon fever had reached Japan', with local animation companies 'overwhelmed' by a rush of demands from American advertising and television companies and animation studios. The article focused on Ashida Iwao, formerly prominent in the Shadow Staff, now churning out several 'films' for the American market:

Mori no Ongakukai – The Forest Orchestra? (1953)[1]
Mizukko no Tabi – Mizukko's Journey? (1955)
Ippon Ashi no Kirigirisu – The One-Legged Cricket? (1957)[2]

It is difficult to know how seriously to take the supposedly 'overwhelming' nature of American demand, since the three films were all shorts, and spread out over a four-year period. The article claimed that another of Ashida's projects, an unknown twenty-minute work called *Osaru no Ōkoku* (*The Kingdom of the Monkey*) had also been broadcast by CBS, for a rewarding fee of 219,600 yen – a 'cheering condition for the creator' (Minakawa 2009a: 109).[3]

Ashida's place in history is vulnerable. Starting as a teenage apprentice under Ōishi Ikuo before the war, he went independent under his real name, Suzuki Hiromasa around 1936, in a small operation run out of his house, with a staff comprising only his wife. The company was variously credited as Suzuki Cartoons, Sankichi Cartoons or Ashida Cartoons, diluting his artistic heritage by implying that the companies comprised different people (Kanō 2004: 195). He subsequently joined the Shadow Staff, and much of his post-war work seems to be below the line, in advertising. Ashida appeared to recognise the price of his anonymity, advising a young Tezuka Osamu that it was better to assert one's 'name value' by becoming a manga creator rather than a mere cog in the animation industry (Minakawa 2009a: 103).[4] Most of his forty-eight-minute *Baghdad no Hime* (1948, *Princess of Baghdad*) was lost until the twenty-first century, and hence not included in historical discourse on post-war film. In terms of contemporary reception, there is little evidence that many people saw it. The American Film Institute also credits him on the live-action film *Karate, The Hand of Death* (1961), seemingly for title design.[5] His company, Ashida Manga Eiga Seisaku-sho (Ashida Cartoon Film Production Works) enjoyed little to no presence in Japanese cinemas, and is dismissed in industry accounts as one of the minor advertising operations of the 1950s. And yet, when Ōtsuka Yasuo went looking for work as an animator, he only joined Nichidō, traditionally regarded as the custodians of Japanese animation talent, after he had been rejected by Ashida (Ōtsuka 2001: 61). Moreover, while other animation companies of the period are remembered as cottage industries, often operating out of private homes, Ashida Manga Eiga had a new, gleaming office building, set alongside a canal (Minakawa 2009a: 108). In the early 1950s, Ashida was the uncrowned, unseen king of Japanese animation. Within a decade, however, he had vanished; his studio had become a mat shop, and little trace of his activity remained (Minakawa 2009a: 112). As a result, the tradition of Japanese animation commemorates not Ashida, but his colleagues at Nichidō.

NICHIDŌ BECOMES TŌEI DŌGA

Nichidō was the largest surviving group of Japanese animators, formed around the nexus of Masaoka Kenzō, Mori Yasuji and Yabushita Taiji, and initially operating out of a prefab hut in the grounds of a girls' school. Using materials liberated from the old Tōhō studio, the group eked out a precarious existence until 1956, making ten two-reel and one single-reel animated film for various clients. 'They ... took no risks and endured the wintry era, conducting frugal business for eight years, until Nichidō was acquired by Tōei, and Tōei Dōga (Tōei Animation) was set up' (Ushio 2007: 221).

However, the above account, by Ushio Sōji, is framed with the benefit of hindsight, on the understanding that Nichidō would eventually be seen as the continuous entity that linked pre-war animators to post-war animation. Ushio also would have known, as he wrote his commemoration, that Nichidō would survive. Such knowledge, was of course, unavailable to the Nichidō staff at the time, when work was infrequent and staff numbers gradually dwindled, despite many applications from manga artists whose own business was in a recession by 1950, and who mistakenly believed that animation offered better prospects (Mori 1984: 116). Staff accounts of life at Nichidō at the beginning of the 1950s tell a story of increasingly straitened circumstances, such that often the company seemed to exist in name only, while its employees scrabbled for part-time jobs elsewhere, designing restaurant menus and illustrating everything from children's books to beerhall placemats. In Mori Yasuji's case, while 'working' at Nichidō, he also held down a job for a year in the advertising department of the Seibu department store (Mori 1984: 117–18). Meanwhile, on those occasions where an animation job did arrive, the core personnel of key animators suddenly required a swift influx of temporary female labour to paint and trace (Mori 1984: 116). Late in the decade, shortly before Nichidō was officially taken over by the Tōei studio that was by then commissioning most of its work, an excited Mori wrote of the latest luxuries brought about by the commencement of work on *Koneko no Rakugaki* (1957, *Kitten's Graffiti*) – new staff, new desks and (at last!) a flushing toilet (Mori 1984: 121).

At the time of the production of *Kitten's Graffiti*, the Nichidō animators were still unsure of the level of workflow they should be managing. Yabushita Taiji claimed that Disney's animators on Donald Duck cartoons were managing 60–100 frames in an eight-hour day, whereas his underling Ōtsuka Yasuo protested that Disney animators had been drawing the same characters for years, and hence had acquired a sense of artistic standardisation. This conflict was born of a sense of failure among the animators that they had to put in overtime to meet targets assumed to be attainable. It was also the result of grumbling from the freelance lower echelons that they were paid half as much as the full-time staff for the arguably harder job of bringing the full-time staff's work up to acceptable levels of output (Ōtsuka 2001: 28).[6] These tensions would carry over when the Nichidō company was rebranded as a subsidiary of Tōei in 1956 – finally part of a 'big' studio, but inheriting many of the concerns of the earlier years of small-time struggles.

Tōei Dōga (Tōei Animation)[7] was linked to the newly established Tōei film company, itself the heir to a cluster of companies that had once been Tokyo-Yokohama Films, a subsidiary of the Tokyo-Yokohama Railway Company, as well as the troubled film studio Ōizumi Eiga. As the newest of Japan's 'Big Five' film studios, officially formed in 1951, Tōei took on many refugees from Man-Ei, the Manchurian Film Association, most of whom had returned to Japan jobless and homeless after the war (Sharp 2011: 251). It also aimed to exploit new niche audiences, using its modest holdings of thirty cinemas, mainly near railway stations, to appeal to workmen and children. It was with the latter in mind that the newly appointed studio head Ōkawa Hiroshi, began

Despite self-commemoration as a 'cinema' studio, Tōei Dōga also made commercials, such as this 1964 advert for Pentax cameras

to consider an animation studio subsidiary, which he eventually achieved by acquiring Nichidō and relocating it to a purpose-built, air-conditioned building stocked with state-of-the-art equipment.

Tsugata Nobuyuki identifies two major catalysts for the formation of Tōei Dōga. The first is the Japanese release of Disney's *Snow White* in 1950, a colour film that left a deep impression on animators and animation fans (see previous chapter). The other was the commencement of public television broadcasts in February 1953, expanding to two channels by August and four channels by the end of the decade (Tsugata 2004: 122–3; see also Tsugata 2007b: 117). It was not so much the competition posed by television that inspired producers at Tōei, so much as the opportunity for commercials afforded by the new medium. The rhetoric of subsequent accounts of Japanese animation, particularly from the Tezuka camp, has largely articulated Tōei Dōga as a cinema-oriented company, but Tsugata argues that it was a TV-focused entity before it was even officially 'established' by Tōei's acquisition of Nichidō in 1956.

FROM 'DENTSŪ STUDIOS' TO MOM PRODUCTION

Tōei's efforts did not merely extend to the acquisition of Nichidō. Okawa also made an approach, through the director Uchida Tomu, to Uchida's former Man-Ei colleague Mochinaga Tadahito, implying that Mochinaga would benefit in money, materials and facilities if he would only agree to bring his independent stop-motion unit under the umbrella of the Tōei companies (Mochinaga 2006: 244). Mochinaga, whose animation work since returning to Japan had been made with jury-rigged materials, themselves purchased with a 50,000-yen rehabilitation fund loan, reports this approach after the completion of his short film *Go-hiki no Kozaru-tachi* (1956, *Five Little Monkeys*), suggesting that Tōei was on something of a spending spree of investment in animation technology (Mochinaga 2006: 243). Tōei also appears to have made no secret of its interests in the advertising potential of stop-motion puppets, but Mochinaga declined on the grounds that he did not yet wish to be subject to the demands of a studio system.

Already, in Mochinaga's comments of the 1950s, there is a certain artistic reluctance to dive too deeply into the commercial world, and an educator's sensibility that his true obligation lay with the children entertained by his short films, rather than potential commercial clients. As he says:

> Certainly, I needed to make films one after another without a break. Otherwise, we couldn't make a living.
> It was hand-to-mouth, like cycling. Just like a bike will fall down unless you keep pedalling
> (Mochinaga 2006: 244–5).

However, Mochinaga's memory of his 1950s output also indicates a certain willingness to consider market issues. It is unclear whether he really wanted to take Uchida's offer, or if he was holding out for a better one from elsewhere. Certainly, we might speculate that Mochinaga had already realised that Dentsū would have money in hand for more commercials like the recent *Beer through the Ages* and that, if he were on staff at Tōei, he might be essentially allowing the studio to take a cut from work he would expect to be offered anyway.

His decision-making process on his next film, *Chibikuro Sambo no Tora Taiji* (1956, *Little Black Sambo's Tiger Conquest*), certainly seems to be that of a calculating businessman rather than a starry-eyed children's entertainer. Reporting that the original book by Helen Bannerman was popular among Japanese children aged six to ten years, Mochinaga selects it as his next film. However, for once in the hyperbole of the Japanese animation business, 'popular' is an understatement. The 1953 Japanese edition of *Little Black Sambo* had already sold 1.2 million copies, under conditions seemingly copyright-free – it was not only a popular work, it was a bestseller with no apparent intellectual property costs. Moreover, behind Mochinaga's vague claim that he 'thought he would change the system for the third production' (Mochinaga 2006: 245) is a hard-headed production decision to invest more heavily, hiring specialists in design, puppetry and lighting for what seems more intended as a calling card.

Conversely, despite international festival acclaim for *Little Black Sambo*, which won a prize at the first Vancouver International Film Festival in 1958 (Sharp 2011: 174), Mochinaga's memoir of his own output remains one of implied response – a sequel to *Little Black Sambo*, 'because children's letters asked us to make one' (Mochinaga 2006: 248), and five further short films before the death of his producer, Inamura Kiichi, seemed to cause a stall in production.

Mochinaga was not the only puppeteer whose work was sneaking abroad. Shiba Production (founded in 1958 by his protégé Kawamoto Kihachirō) utilised puppets as both the components of animation and stills photography, seemingly developed from Kawamoto's post-war magazine photoshoots of dolls to showcase fashions or 'impersonations' of celebrities (Miyoshi 2007: 15). The company's Japanese output centred on animation, although its works were exported in book form in the late 1950s through to the 1980s, as 'Golden Books' – with text credited to foreign authors, but with the pictures clearly credited to Iizawa Tadashi and Hijikata Shigemi. Called variously 'Living Picture Books' or 'Pre-school Puppet Books', these works formed a subgenre in children's publishing in several languages. Titles available in English included little *Red Riding Hood* (1959) *Thumbelina* (1966), *The Fairy Tale Treasury in Living Colour* (1967), *Rocket Trip to the Moon* (1970), *My ABC Book* (1971), *Fire Engines* (1971), *My First Book of Numbers* (1971) and *The Clock Book* (1972). Iizawa himself seemed to carry on without Shiba Production, at least as far as the transport book *Things That Go* (1984).

However, it was Mochinaga's work that attracted the most solid foreign funding. The late Inamura, it seemed, was the sole agent raising money for Mochinaga's short films, which had been made at the Dentsū facilities in Zōshigaya (sic, not Sōshigaya) under the aegis of its company Ningyō Eiga Seisaku-sho (Puppet Film Production Works, est. 1955). His loss deprived Mochinaga of a revenue stream at a time when his company was already 700,000 yen in arrears (Mochinaga 2006: 249). It is then, and only then, that Mochinaga reports the most enduring effect of *Little Black Sambo*'s Vancouver plaudits – an approach by Videocraft's Arthur Rankin Jr with an offer to make 130 episodes of *The New Adventures of Pinocchio* (1960), for export to the American market.

Rankin's own account of their association makes no mention of Vancouver, but instead credits the introduction to Kawamoto Minoru, a member of a trade delegation in Washington, who arranged introductions to 'Tōei Studios, Mushi [Production] and some small stop-motion studios' where the techniques in operation were pronounced to be 'slightly dated but very unusual' (Goldschmidt 1997: 90).

Rankin's offer seemed ideal – 130 pre-recorded soundtracks and storyboards from America, each to be turned into a five-minute television episode. Mochinaga (2006: 250), however, appears to have been strongly opposed to the idea, seeing that it was sure to occupy the entire labour force of his company, leaving no space on the schedules for any of the advertising clients whose work had largely funded his previous entertainment films. Essentially, the *Pinocchio* contract would occupy Mochinaga and his staff for an entire year, in which time they would be entirely reliant on Videocraft's money.

In terms of the ownership–access chain, Mochinaga was being offered participation only at the production level. He was neither the owner nor author of the finished work. Minakawa Yūka (2009b: 226) calls it 'social dumping', in the sense that labour has been suddenly outsourced to a cheaper production centre on the periphery, in order to maximise profits at the centre. Nor was such labour particularly visible in the American market; the Japanese were never entirely uncredited on the American productions, but their names were far down the list, and usually overshadowed by the aesthetic celebrity of the English-speaking voice actors. Mochinaga took the job with deep reluctance, seemingly after his producers leaned on his wife to persuade him that it was in his interests to work off the debt already incurred by his independent films and start-up costs. He eventually agreed on the mistaken understanding that this would be the only job of such a type that he ever took. Nor does Mochinaga appear to have been all that pleased with the pace of the work, noting only that: 'the shooting in the studio was fierce and punishing (*satsubatsu*) every day' (Mochinaga 2006: 250). In order to handle the Videocraft workload, Mochinaga set up a new company with his wartime associate Ōmura Einosuke and the independent producer Matsumoto Torizō. The initials of their three surnames spelled the name: MOM Production.

As examination of extant episodes of *Pinocchio* soon reveals,[8] the workload could be thinned out. The opening theme song, in which Pinocchio dances in highly accomplished stop-motion on a stage, is forty seconds that have been made once and recycled in the next several dozen episodes.[9] The title for each episode, presented as a still title card over a soundtrack fanfare, occupies ten seconds of screen time with a single image. The 'story so far', comprising recycled footage from earlier episodes, occupies another forty seconds and the closing title accounts for another ten seconds. In other words, 100 seconds – a full third of each episode's 300-second running time, comprises animation that either only needed to be made once, or could be shot in real time. But with 130 episodes to complete in a year, that would still obligate Mochinaga and his staff to complete 2.5 episodes a week, with approximately 750 seconds of new animation every seven days.

Largely unmentioned in the history of Japanese animation,[10] *The New Adventures of Pinocchio* is a true milestone. A Japanese studio successfully made and exported 12.5 minutes of animation every week for a year, three years before the much-discussed 'pioneering' efforts of Tezuka Osamu with *Astro Boy*. It was literally halfway towards the notional twenty-five minutes per week that would be required for a 'half-hour' televised series. Since animators at Tōei were already telling their bosses that such a schedule was 'impossible' (Ōtsuka 2001: 110–11), it is interesting to see that Tōei had already located, and tried to hire, someone who seemed to be able to meet such demands.

The absence of *Pinocchio* from previous accounts seems partly to be a matter of simple aesthesis – as a stop-motion work, it does not fit the usual cel-based paradigm for Japanese animation. Moreover, there is an issue of nescience or memory concerning the credits over the opening and closing titles, as they merely name Videocraft, with a note that the show was 'made at the Dentsu Studios' (sic, without macron). No individuals are credited apart from Arthur Rankin Jr himself, and Carlo Collodi, the original author of *Pinocchio*. A cynic might suggest that Collodi is credited only to remind all viewers that Pinocchio, the character, was not an original Disney creation.

However, merely because Mochinaga met the demands of his client, he did not do so at great benefit to himself. With 'dozens' of episodes left to film, a fire at his studio destroyed the negatives of twenty-eight completed episodes, along with much of the camera equipment, sets, and other materials (Mochinaga 2006: 250). Although the studio was insured, he still had to endure the inevitable delays, as well as a police investigation that forced his animators to wait around, not working, while arson was ruled out. By the time *The New Adventures of Pinocchio* was delivered, after a Herculean two-month overtime push in order to make back the lost material, Mochinaga had driven his company so far back into debt that he would be obliged to take on another American subcontracting job to balance his books (Mochinaga 2006: 251).

FROM *HANUMAN* TO *HAKUJADEN*

While Mochinaga Tadahito struggled below the line on foreign contracts, Ōkawa Hiroshi at Tōei actively pursued foreign co-production. His model for this was Disney, who was propelled into considering feature-length animation as a means of ensuring better returns. Disney had grown impatient with animated shorts forced to sub-sist as part of an evening at the cinema, jostling for attention with the newsreels, serials and coming attractions, and determined that he would only be able to 'extract premium rentals from reluctant exhibitors' if he turned his cartoons into the main attraction. This would require a feature-length movie, which Disney would eventu-ally produce in 1937 with *Snow White and the Seven Dwarfs* (Barrier 1999: 125). Hence, we might characterise the development of feature-length cartoons in the US as a feature of market forces at the exhibition level, as Disney struggled to find a business model that could increase his returns.[11]

Ōkawa, the head of Tōei, and hence the head of Tōei Dōga, was a fish out of water – a railway company accountant and former basketball-team manager, suddenly catapulted into the stewardship of a struggling film studio. In his own memoirs, he describes the Tōei conglomerate as a trio of hapless companies, limping in a three-legged race and weighed down with over a billion yen of debt, some of it to loan sharks (Ōkawa 1963: 287).

Nevertheless, he appears to have embraced his new task with a positive attitude and a mission statement that proclaimed 'we shall progressively produce and give birth to American-Disney's professional standard of ani-mated films' (Hu 2010: 91; see also Minakawa 2009a: 41). Animators' memoirs credit him with a variety of characteristics, as the affable, slightly dotty boss who would bellow a cheery 'Manga gentlemen, good-day!' (Ōtsuka 2001: 29) on the rare occasions he came to the facility, but also as the shrewd internationalist who tells his colleagues that 'pictures are a common global language' (Yamamoto 1989: 62).[12]

> I believe that animation has great international potential. Language is a big problem, one that diminishes our ability to export Japanese films to an international market. In animation, however, language is not essential, and so it has its own potential as a common, international form of expression. I will thus strive to produce animation with an eye to exportation. (Ōkawa, quoted in Miyao 2002: 206)

Mori Yasuji recalls Ōkawa as a distant but fearsome manager, ever ready with an aspirational soundbite for the credulous media, but humourless and sour in private. A hulking man Mori (1984: 124) describes as 'the king hippo', Ōkawa was visibly 'more excited than us' about the prospects for animation. In Mori's account of the first meeting of January 1957, shortly after the inauguration of the new building, it is Ōkawa who tells his dis-believing staff of his intention to eventually maintain an output of 'two feature-length and four short animations a year' (Mori 1984: 125).

He first put his 'manga gentlemen' to work on three projects – two domestic short cartoons, and the bizarre propaganda project *Hanuman no Atarashii Bōken* (1957, *The New Adventures of Hanuman*), an anti-Communist parable in which the Indian monkey-god Hanuman fights off the predations of a bunch of red-faced monkeys. The film was commissioned for the American embassy in Bangkok, and borrowed the skilled services of the Thai artist Payut Ngaokrachang. However, all of these were merely stopgap measures to keep the staff occupied until such time as the major project could begin: a feature-length film, intended for exhibition both in Japan and abroad.

Despite the anti-Japanese feeling that had closed off the former colonial markets of Taiwan and Korea, Ōkawa doggedly pursued both finance and audiences in Asia, securing co-production money from Shaw Brothers in Hong Kong to make the full-colour live-action film *Byaku Fujin no Yōren* (1956, *Madame White Snake*).[13] Using Hong Kong studio space but Japanese actors (including, perhaps unwisely, Shirley Yamaguchi, the forces' sweetheart of old Manchuria), *Madame White Snake* was intended as a vibrant, foreignised export strategy, seemingly with the expectation that once the actors were dubbed into local languages, it would seem entirely 'Chinese', both in Chinese markets and elsewhere in the world.

This release was followed immediately by announcements that Tōei would now produce a fully animated remake – drawing on the same Chinese legend, but with additional animal characters and animated business. This, too, was initially billed as an international co-production, although Hong Kong interests had evaporated by the time of the film's completion, supposedly over script issues (Hu 2010: 87). Hu Tze-yue identifies mul-tiple levels of 'performance' in the animated *Hakujaden*,[14] including not only the basic narrative, but assertions of international friendship, unthreatening Japanese manners and, above all, industrial competence. *Hakujaden*

東 映 株 式 会 社　　　　　総天色然　漫画映画 白蛇伝 はくじゃでん

Hakujaden (1958) was based on a Chinese folktale, in part to drum up investment and distribution deals elsewhere in Asia

was hence not merely intended as an object for export, but as an advertisement for the abilities of Tōei's new animation division, which was essentially using the film to tout for business, not only in the Chinese sector (which turned out to be uninterested), but also 'covertly courting the American market' (Hu 2007: 56).[15]

Hakujaden's long-term artistic heritage is relatively obscure. Arguably, it attains a lot of 'firsts' – usually regarded as the first post-war Japanese animated feature;[16] the first colour Japanese cartoon feature; and the first Japanese animated feature to be screened in the US, as *Panda and the Magic Serpent*. It was also perhaps the first Japanese cartoon to successfully imitate the characteristics of a Disney movie in terms of length, look, sound and style. However, its true impact was much more immediate, located in the performance of its production and its aspirations. The fact that Tōei Dōga was working on a feature-length, rotoscoped, colour cartoon in the Disney model served as a powerful lure to young would-be animators all over Japan, both during the production (when adverts for staff deliberately played up the Disney allure), and after its release. It allowed Tōei to pick and choose among the cream of new aspirants, including recruits such as the young Miyazaki Hayao and Takahata Isao, both drawn to Tōei not only by the performance of the film, but by the performance of the making of the film.

FORMATS, REGISTRATION AND ROTOSCOPING

Hakujaden was made in a standard ratio, but the next animated film, *Shōnen Sarutobi Sasuke* (1959, *Magic Boy*) was made in CinemaScope, which used an anamorphic lens to compress substantially broader frames – a production process which, when unpacked at exhibition, is better known as 'widescreen' (Haraguchi 2000: 44; Telotte 2008: 84–5). This practice was designed to match that of Tōei's contemporary live-action films, which normally advertised the process as 'TōeiScope' in order to associate it solely with the studio. Sugiyama (1999: 106) recalls:

The standard ratio was 1.33:1 but CinemaScope had a ratio of about 2.6:1. That, in turn, meant we had to adopt those dimensions for all materials, from layout papers to cels to backgrounds. In the switchover, making the paper longer meant we had to make it taller, and so our animation sheets become harder to handle. Until then, the key art and animation were drawn without using taps (we used to use the bottom left-hand of the layout sheets as the reference point when we set the position), but it was decided that taps would be introduced into the process. That was the first time the animators were given taps.

Sugiyama Taku's 'taps' are the same 'perf[oration] and peg' set-up common in cel animation for decades – standardised holes punched in every sheet, to ensure that whatever gets traced on each layout paper is precisely matched to the paper above or below it. His comment that it was the 'first time' may well have been the case at Tōei, but certainly was not true in Japan as a whole, since there is extant footage of Ōfuji Noburō using pegs and perforations in *How to Make Colour Cartoons*. It is, however, rather surprising to see that Tōei had supposedly already made a feature-length cartoon without leaning on such a simple labour-saving device – confirmed by UPA's Jimmy Murakami, who was briefly a consultant at Tōei, and cited the use of paper-clips for registration as one reason for the 'jittery' quality of some of Tōei's animation (Osmond 2012a).[17]

Tōei animators may have developed such a cavalier attitude towards registration because of the company's continued use of rotoscoping as a basis for images. As with Disney films of the period, those sequences in Tōei cartoons that focused on human characters were pre-shot as live, in order to give precise registration and fluid images for the animators to work from (Kanō 2004: 189). Hence many scenes of *Hakujaden* (1958) were shot with the actress Sakuma Yoshiko as model, in an early form of motion capture. This method was particularly useful in the mapping of detailed action or fight scenes, such as those in Tōei's later *Arabian Night: Sinbad no Bōken* (1962, *Sinbad the Sailor*), which captured the performance of the young martial artist 'Sonny' Chiba Shinichi, later to become an action star (Kanō 2004: 207).

However, rotoscoping is a thorny theoretical issue. As Donald Crafton suggests (1982: 174), its function is *mimetic* – its value lies in its replication of the reality of movement, rather than the impressionistic deformation or compression of it that is an inevitable feature of much other animation. Arguably, animation that employs rotoscoping (or later in the twentieth century, other forms of live performance capture), is not 'animation' at all, but instead a form of special effect. In terms of the tradition of the animation business, it is the non-rotoscoped accomplishments in early Tōei films that are deemed most worthy of celebration. Sugiyama Taku, for example, notes that it was *Hakujaden* that first established backgrounds as an important and distinct part of the Japanese animation process, recognising that, if the foreground action was largely a matter of tracing real people, it was the scenery behind them that required true artistic achievement (Sugiyama 1999: 105). For others, however this was not enough, and the Tōei process was derided, with hindsight, as 'like making two films, a live-action film and an animated film' (Miyao 2002: 207–8).[18]

THE 'SINGLE-CROP' PROBLEM

The memoirs of Ōtsuka Yasuo, then a young animator at Tōei, recall his work on *Kuma to Kodomotachi* (1960, *The Bear and the Children*), a heavy-handed propaganda film in which a large Russian bear terrorises a group of children, each of whom is conspicuously clad in the national dress of various East Asian countries thought to be vulnerable to the threat of Communism – Thailand, the Philippines, Indonesia and Myanmar. His account of the production, a sequel of sorts to *Hanuman*, paints it as a disaster from end to end, particularly in his descriptions of tense, smoke-filled meetings at the American embassy in Tokyo, where 'Mr Keith' from the cultural exchange office, and an imposing man called 'Mr White', who claimed to be a former Disney animator, sat through the rushes of the film and demanded a huge number of *redraws* (Ōtsuka 2001: 58).

As with the 1954 production of the CIA-funded *Animal Farm* in Britain (Saunders 2000: 294–5), the involvement of propaganda personnel in an entertainment medium caused considerable friction. White's forceful demands spelled financial trouble for Tōei Dōga, not the least because he was allegedly rejecting artwork that he had previously approved (Ōtsuka 2001: 61). He was explicitly ordering not *repaints* of the images or *reshoots* of the cels, but *redraws* that would require a literal return to the drawing board. The changes were likely to double the film's budget. Meanwhile, the left-leaning Ōtsuka, embarrassed to be working on American propaganda in the first place, was obliged to share the meeting with his nemesis Ashida Iwao of Ashida Manga Eiga, who had only recently refused to give Ōtsuka a job on the grounds that he could not draw (Ōtsuka 2001: 61).

Ashida's involvement on the project is odd. Ōtsuka had already noted that a number of the staff at Tōei were practically idle, but alluded to personal contacts between Tōei's Yamamoto Sanae and the eponymous Ashida, who had been wartime colleagues (Ōtsuka 2001: 61). Ōtsuka's claim implies that Ashida's company was getting work on the project as a favour, pointing to tensions behind the scenes over who was getting the work, and how.

However, Ashida's presence at the beginning of the 1960s highlights another issue behind the scenes, which is the relative lack of experienced animators at Tōei. After the success of *Hakujaden*, Tōei proceeded to make a new feature-length animation every year, with its films generally released each spring. Because Tōei Dōga had a large standing staff, and the pipeline of film production had not yet advanced to the stage where several different films were in different stages at once, the 'film' studio was obliged either to take on work that was not 'films', or to find some other way to occupy its staff. Remarkably, some members of the staff were simply left inactive.

> Before animation advanced into TV programmes [i.e. 1963], Tōei Dōga could be said to have had a situation like that of the single crop (*ichi mōsaku*) in agriculture, making only a single feature-length animation per year. And so, between the end of one film and the commencement of another, the key animators, inbetweeners, artists and cameramen, pretty much all the staff had nothing to do for quite a while. The company had to find something to keep them occupied, at a time when the animation marketplace was substantially smaller than it is now. So, apart from the dozen of us working on *The Bear and the Children*, the company ordered the others to form three- and four-man groups and 'make whatever short films you like!!' Looking back, the company was enforcing a real dream. (Ōtsuka 2001: 60)

It is this policy, a stop-gap measure to find work for idle hands that seems to be the origin of Tōei Dōga's place in anime mythology as, at least to some, the ideal working environment. It certainly seems to inform Miyazaki Hayao's later complaints (2009: 32–3) that the arrival of television deprived animators of the chance to spread out, experiment with their storyboards and treat the workplace as some kind of comic drawing club, with occasional animation output.[19]

However, such a view of this 'golden age' only partially obscures the real problem with the 'single-crop' workflow. While waiting for commissions to arrive from television, film and below-the-line foreign contracts, Ōkawa was maintaining a large standing staff with little to do, and hence bleeding money. Sugii Gisaburō, who started as an animator at Tōei in 1958, saw the company's business model as a disaster waiting to happen:

> Mr Ōkawa from Tōei set up Tōei Dōga and entered the market, but as far as I remember, he spent far too much money on production. There was no way he could break even, if he made one or two films a year. I thought that if I left Tōei, ten years later anime would be nothing but a hobby. That is how much anime costs. I believe that Mr Ōkawa himself was unsure if the company could maintain its profitability. When I joined Tōei, Mr Okawa threatened me with the words: 'This building could be turned into a hospital!' (Tsugata 2007b: 195)

Ōkawa's seemingly counterintuitive business plan concealed an intensive industrial training scheme. In conscious imitation of the apprentice programme at Disney (Takahashi 2011b: 254), it was designed to transform complete novices into animators in a matter of months. Employees of the animation industry would later refer to the studio, only half in jest, as 'Tōei Dōga University' in recognition of the immense labour pool it created in the late 1950s (Sugiyama 1999: 119).

Ōkawa's intention, first put into practice on *Hakujaden*, was to put his two best key animators – Mori Yasuji and Daikuhara Akira – in charge of work groups that would learn on the job. Their inbetweening would be corrected and assessed, and eventually, they would learn enough to advance up the ranks. In the films that followed *Hakujaden*, this was replaced with the Second Key Art System (*daini genga seido*), in which each newly trained key animator was put in charge of his own work group comprising three or four novices – notably, the term 'three- or four-man group' is the same as that used by Ōtsuka when remembering being left to their own devices. Mori and Daikuhara would only create rough key art, which was then delegated to the new work groups to clean up and finish (Sugiyama 1999: 109–10).

By the time of Tōei's third and fourth features, the new system had 'reproduced' itself several times, expanding the staff roster of Tōei, and giving the company the capability to take on bigger workloads. However, there was a price to pay.

> Making animation is a very human enterprise, involving the accumulation of much manual labour. The enthusiasm and vitality of the participants show directly on the screen. The more orderly a production system becomes and the firmer the management structure becomes, the lesser the meaning of the people involved, and the organisation starts to take priority over the individual … . As long as the company does not know much about animation and the wills and opinions of the creative staff are respected, such energy is reflected in the work, but as the company establishes its production and management initiatives, such energy starts to show only indirectly and in the end, the light gets lost. (Sugiyama 1999: 108)

According to Sugiyama Taku, the industrialisation of training at Tōei successfully fostered an increase in available animators, although by the time of the 1962 release of *Sinbad the Sailor* there had been a palpable generation loss in quality. Ōtsuka Yasuo notes that, by 1962, training had advanced to the level where it was possible to split the animation staff into teams that could work concurrently on two films, and that a year later, a third group was calved off to work on Tōei's first television series – Ōkawa Hiroshi's promised output levels had been reached within six years (Ōtsuka 2001: 110). While the process had discovered such future greats as Ōtsuka Yasuō and Kusube Daikichirō, it had also dragged the general level of artwork down to a lower common denominator. Furthermore, at the management level, it had created a sense that low-ranking animators were less labourers than they were animators in training, and that there was no need to raise their wages. As a result, disaffected employees had begun to leak from the Tōei training scheme in search of work elsewhere. Sugiyama (1999: 113) uses the term *dappi* (moulting), as if Tōei were shedding a seasonal skin. However, it was this slough of disaffected animators that went on to establish much of the TV anime business of the 1960s. Employees that remained at Tōei would also begin to agitate for better conditions, in a series of complaints that would eventually become Tōei's first labour dispute (Sugiyama 1999: 111–12).

THE KATSUDON PROPOSAL, 'KILLER WEEKS' AND 'ANIME SYNDROME'

From the animators' perspective, Tōei's staffing policy was far from benign. Many saw not a training scheme, but proletarianised labour paid at such low rates that the animators could not even afford a balanced diet. When the probationary animators eventually demanded better pay, one of their conditions plaintively begged for enough money 'to be able to afford *katsudon* (a pork cutlet) from time to time', which became enshrined in industry lore as the Katsudon Proposal (Sugiyama 1999: 112).

The animator Okuyama Reiko, who joined Tōei in 1957, observed the wide-ranging differences in pay scales, not only between men and women, but between university graduates and high-school graduates. With Yamamoto Sanae's '60-frames-a-day' workload understood to be unrealistic, animators were now expected to turn out between fifteen and forty. Okuyama identifies a descending pay scale that implies Tōei ran its animation division as a Japanese conglomerate would run any other manufacturing operation (Kanō 2004: 92; see also Oguro 2009: 29; Whitehill 1991: 205), with 'company' men at the top.

· male university graduates seconded to Tōei Dōga from sister companies
· male university graduates hired directly by Tōei Dōga
· female university graduates

- male high-school graduates
- female high-school graduates
- freelance workers.

The men at the top earned roughly 13,500 yen a month, whereas a female colourist with a high-school diploma, working as a temporary contractor, could only expect to earn 5,000 yen. Although Okuyama does not state this explicitly, it would seem that at least part of the tension lay not in inequities of pay, but in equity of tasks. Since many of the staff were performing similar jobs, there was considerable resentment at the realisation that, say, former management trainees brought over from the parent railway company earned more for counting through stacks of tracing paper than teenage high-school leavers who were, nevertheless, far better artists than their peers.[20]

Okuyama, who seems to have been the most prominent woman in the animation industry in the 1960s, also cites a set of common patriarchal assumptions that kept women from reaching higher echelons (see Wakisaka 1997: 136; Gerteis 2009: 84–5). Certainly, within the idiom of the anime business there is an implicit assumption that only males can perform certain roles, as evidenced by such terms as *conté man* (storyboarder), *genga man* (layouts) or *dōga man* (animator), which persist to this day (Tomino 2002: 226; Takahashi 2011b: 271). A general, industry-wide belief, still extant today, held that women were simply better colourists than men, with sharper instincts for differentiation. Although this may even be true (Guilford and Smith 1959: 500), it also conveniently discouraged bosses from promoting female workers to ranks in animation proper, thereby severely limiting the likely labour pool of future women directors.[21] Okuyama also reports that she was the first woman ever to return to work in the anime industry after getting married and having a baby (Kanō 2004: 99),[22] but that she was urged to return as a freelancer because salaried employment was likely to prove too 'inflexible'. Upon her refusal to accept such conditions, she faced ever-increasing harassment over her alleged job performance (Kanō 2004: 99).

We might, however, read between the lines of Okuyama's testimony to intuit a couple of other issues at play – workloads for all staff, and the impact of workplace relationships. She was married to her fellow animator and nominal boss Kotabe Yōichi, who was accused of favouritism when he allowed her to work more flexible hours in order to take driving lessons, the latter intended to make it easier for her to transport their child to daycare. When Kotabe was disciplined for his decision, he protested that at that point in the animation process, all the animators were on flexible hours, with the implication being that it did no harm to the ongoing production. This was not what management wanted to hear, and Kotabe was dismissed, infamously proclaiming that he was 'happy to leave such an unpleasant company' and gaining work at another studio (Kanō 2004: 99).[23]

The anime industry still favours the young single man, less likely to have attachments or obligations that would interfere with overtime or make other demands. As Ōkawa Hiroshi had already discovered, the boom-and-bust, famine-and-feast workloads of animation favoured flexible staff. Some days might pass with no work at all, during which salaried employees were a drain on the company and freelance workers went unpaid. Other periods, particularly after the advent of television (which seemed to fill Tōei's hiatuses for good), went far beyond the demands of nine-to-five office work, but turned into massive, periodic overtime allocations, for which the freelancers might expect many more hours, but which the salaried employees were expected to endure without complaint or extra payment. In Japanese animation in the 1960s, the term for such crunch periods was 'killer weeks' (*satsujin shūkan*) (Yamamoto 1989: 54). It was understood that married staff and female employees would be allowed to leave on the last train; single male employees worked through the nights, which not only exerted a greater toll on their health, but arguably established them as the most loyal of employees, and hence the most worthy of promotion. Mori Yasuji notes (1984: 151) that there was eventually a predictable price for such unremitting late nights, irregular diets of junk food and cramped, repetitive labour, which led to occasional but notable lapses of health among the staff. He calls it 'anime syndrome' (*anime shōkōgun*), with its first recorded outbreak on Tōei's film *Saiyūki* (1960, *Journey to the West*; US release as *Alakazam the Great*),[24] the director of which, Yabushita Taiji, was hospitalised for exhaustion at the end of production (Minakawa 2009a: 77). However, Shirakawa Daisaku (Oguro 2004a: 1) claims that Yabushita was actually hospitalised mid-production, and that as Yabushita's assistant, he took over thereafter. Reading between the lines of Japanese occupational-insurance parameters (Whitehill 1991: 185), it is tempting to suggest that this, too, could have a performative component, and that workers might need to be seen to be hospitalised in order to establish the seriousness of their condition. Could anime syndrome sometimes be a performance designed to qualify workers for days off in lieu after prolonged overtime?

TŌEI DISPUTES AND CONSEQUENCES

The same period saw a rise in political activity in Japan, beginning with the Anpo Protests of 1960, in opposition to a renewed US–Japan treaty that permitted the continued stationing of American troops on Japanese soil (Sharp 2011: 21). Animators with contacts with pre-existing film-industry unions agitated for a union of their own at Tōei, in the hope that the staff would then be able to negotiate better conditions. Simple subsistence was one of the chief issues, with staff complaining that they were unable to adequately provision themselves with food, and that directors were often obliged to lend their underlings money for lunch (Oguro 2009: 30). Rintarō recalled the conspirators gathering in a clandestine meeting upstairs at a noodle bar, and likened themselves to the Forty-seven Rōnin, although not so well dressed (Oguro 2009: 30).[25]

Their demands were a list of grievances that allude to the working conditions at Tōei (Minakawa 2009a: 126):

1   Stop ordering overtime without consideration of our personal circumstances.
2   Provide supper during overtime.
3   Show rushes during working hours, not during breaks.
4   Do not restrict our lunchtime activities.
5   Remove pay discrepancies between new graduates and those recruited mid-career.
6   Forbid abuse of authority by section chiefs.

However, it was not until several months later, in September 1961, that negotiations turned hostile. The union demanded an end-of-year bonus of 330 per cent of a normal monthly salary, plus 8,000 yen, amounting to four months' average pay as a bonus, in keeping with the Japanese norm at the time (Whitehill 1991: 179). The studio countered with an offer 5,000 yen lower. With the studio refusing to budge, the animators held three nominal 'two-hour strikes' in early December 1961, and began leafleting passers-by in local shopping streets. The leaflets proclaimed that the harmonious exterior of the animation business belied harsh conditions within, and suggested that the poor pay and harsh hours of the Tōei animators were an infringement of their human rights (Minakawa 2009b: 59).

The leaflets were the work of Nagasawa Makoto, who referred to his document as the 'declaration of humanity' (*ningen sengen*). Provocatively using the same phrase employed by Emperor Hirohito when he renounced his divine status (Dower 1999: 308), Nagasawa went on to make the hyperbolic and unsubstantiated claims that 'one in six' animators had been hospitalised during production, and 'one in seven' could not afford a winter coat (Minakawa 2009b: 60).

Ōkawa Hiroshi was galvanised into action by the leaflets rather than earlier disputes, angrily ordering that the staff be locked out of the studio and all bonuses be cancelled. His directive went into effect at 9 am on 5 December 1961, ironically locking several union animators, who had been working through the night, inside the studio. Unable to get past the security guards at the gate, Tsukioka Sadao scaled the studio walls 'like a monkey' to deliver packed lunches to his union colleagues (Oguro 2009: 30).

The lockout lasted until 9 December, whereupon the combatants reached a compromise. The union was granted its initial six demands, but the studio got to set the size of bonuses. The ones who paid the price were those who had been the most active agitators. As Hayashi Shigeyuki (Rintarō), then a young animator put it to Oguro (2009: 31): 'Once a union was set up, the collective bargaining began. Then, the trade union started cutting the tails off lizards' (*tokage no shippokiri*). He meant that the company used the union itself as the main enforcer of discipline among the most unruly animators, with the understanding that any concessions agreed between management and the union would be an acceptable consensus among all the staff (Oguro 2009: 31).[26]

As a result, several of the most disaffected staff faced pressure from both management and their colleagues to toe the line, leading to the defection of several high-profile animators, including Rintarō himself, who took advantage of a new opportunity that had, entirely coincidentally, started up elsewhere:

> That was how Sugii Gisaburō moved to Mushi Pro, I think. When Tezuka said to me, 'Please come, as I want to set up an animation studio', I decided to move there straight away. It was because I knew I would get fired if I stayed at Tōei. (Oguro 2009: 31)

The most important effect of the dispute was a radical change in staffing policy at Tōei. Where once there had been a large number of salaried animators, Tōei switched its recruitment to a model that mainly favoured free-lances. According to Sugiyama Taku, this is the cause of a new, palpable change in the nature of Tōei products.

Sugiyama (1999: 114) identifies two plateaux in the nature of Tōei's output: he argues that the dilution of talent and training of staff caused a drop in quality from 1962 onwards, and that a second drop was caused by widespread adoption of contracted artists, rather than salaried labour, which is visible from 1966 onwards. According to Sugiyama, the only respite in such a downward spiral came with the release of *Hols no Daibōken* (1968, *Little Norse Prince*), which went into production after another labour dispute, and represented a refo-cusing of talent and a reduction in the number of rookie animators. It was also, memorably, something of a box-office flop – it is rightly commemorated today as an early masterpiece by a young Takahata Isao, although its reception at the time bordered on the disastrous.

The 'Tōei Dōga University' not only trained an entire generation of animators who would move into tele-vision, but provided an identifiable location where they could be found. By the mid-1960s, Ōtsuka Yasuo (2001: 106) described the situation at the company gates as a 'headhunting war' (*hikinuki kassen*), where self-styled television producers would lie in wait for young animators, and attempt to lure them into new start-up companies. Ōtsuka calls such entrepreneurs 'anime racketeers' (*anime goro*), with a phraseology that con-jures images of sleazy talent scouts for low-rent film companies, snapping up impressionable young country girls fresh off the bus (Otsuka 2001: 106).[27]

> This was partly responsible for the decline in animators' *morals* [In English]. Specifically, part-time work became popular; when a new animation company was set up, animators valued their abilities themselves at far too much money, and stayed until they were found out, cheating on their piece-work with every possible trick. (Ōtsuka 2001: 206)

Ōtsuka uses the English term 'moral', but really means work ethic and a sense of company loyalty. He goes on to quote directly from Karl Marx regarding the chaos of new markets, noting that the sudden expansion of television channels, and the widespread anticipation of riches for the eager animator, coupled with the surplus of labour created by Tōei's apprentice scheme, created a sudden, bubble-like expansion in anime studios.

What neither he, nor any other Japanese account of the period mentions is the changing nature of work at Tōei Dōga, where the annual feature-film output continued unbroken. From 1964, this was augmented by ongoing production work on animated television serials, in competition with Mushi Pro (see next chapter). However, from 1966 onwards, and for the rest of the decade, Tōei animators also worked on 'American' cartoon productions, often as uncredited or barely-credited subalterns. The 'Tōei' cartoons *King Kong* (1967) and *001/7 Oyayubi Tom* (1967, *Tom of T.H.U.M.B.*), broadcast as an anthology series on the Japanese channel NET, were originally made in Japan to order, with dialogue tracks from the US studio Rankin/Bass (Animage 1988: 18; Goldschmidt 1997: 96–8).[28] Several later Tōei productions, such as *The Mouse on the Mayflower* (1968), were not screened in Japan at all, but instead functioned as entirely invisible productions, generating revenue for the studio and training for its newer staff, but entirely under the radar of the Japanese audience. However, since neither Tōei nor the animators who worked there have offered much in the way of testimonials regarding these foreign contracts, it is productive instead to return our attention to Mochinaga Tadahito, the first Japanese animator to sign a production deal with Arthur Rankin, and whose own, smaller studio was also providing work for Rankin/Bass throughout the 1960s and beyond.

EXPORTS BELOW THE LINE: RANKIN/BASS

Mochinaga's own account of the hiatus between *The New Adventures of Pinocchio*, and his next job for Rankin/Bass, runs counter to the schedule of his films as actually released. More work was eventually forthcoming from Videocraft (renamed Rankin/Bass), although the commission arrived several months after Mochinaga had expected it, causing him, like Tōei, to waste money keeping many staff on site with no actual work to do. However, it is unclear from Mochinaga's account when this fallow period occurred. According to a history of Japanese animation studios by Miyoshi Hiroshi, the big fire at MOM Production (see above) was in December 1962, surely long after work had been completed on *The New Adventures of Pinocchio*, and indeed, after it had finished its original American broadcast run (Minakawa 2009b: 230). Miyoshi (2007: 15) also notes that MOM Production took almost a year to grind back into action after the fire, intimating that the hiatus between productions was some time later than Mochinaga's memoirs suggest, not in 1960, but in 1963, with production commencing on the next Videocraft project, *Willy McBean and His Magic Machine*, in August 1963, not August 1961 as Mochinaga implies. However, the Rankin/Bass authorised history states that production on *Willy McBean* and *Rudolph the Red-Nosed Reindeer* (1964) ran concurrently (Goldschmidt 1997: 130), and *The Art of Japanese Animation* claims that production on *Rudolph* started in 1961, at least a year before the fire and suggesting, at the very least, that Mochinaga might have been confused about precisely which project's assets were destroyed in the accident (Animage 1988: 20).

Willy McBean was a ninety-two-minute stop-motion theatrical feature, never broadcast in Japan. As a result, the next Mochinaga production to be seen in the US was the fifty-minute Christmas TV special *Rudolph the Red-Nosed Reindeer*. Both were made in the same manner as before, with the soundtracks pre-recorded and sent to Japan for Mochinaga's staff to synchronise with their animation.

Seasonal specials (Christmas, Easter and, in the US, also Thanksgiving) have proved a lucrative strand for animation. Once established as a holiday-season staple, a Christmas-themed animation was virtually assured of a captive, annual, repeat audience. Unlike other shows – which might be shunted around the listings on schedulers' whims – seasonal specials, by their very nature, established themselves as immovable events, sure to be scheduled only in the appropriate period. As Chuck Jones once observed, the expense of animation was a 'sound investment' if repeat broadcasts were assured:

> *How the Grinch Stole Christmas* – which we made independently in 1967 – has run on prime-time
> television each Christmas for fifteen years, for a minimum of $150,000 per run. So you're getting around
> $2 million for something that cost $350,000, and was paid for by the network. (Lewell 1982: 139)

Rudolph the Red-Nosed Reindeer proved similarly profitable in America, where its $500,000 budget was earned back with just two screenings on US television, turning its subsequent annual reappearances over the following four decades into pure profit (Goldschmidt 1997: 2–3). It is less well known in Japan, a country with less of a Christmas tradition, where it was not broadcast until several years later, as *Akahana Tonakai Rudolph Monogatari* (1967, *The Story of Red-Nosed Rudolph the Reindeer*).[29]

Rudolph represented a watershed for Rankin/Bass, a 'breakthrough out of commercials and into the entertainment industry' (Goldschmidt 1997: 2). However, while the Japanese participation in *Rudolph* was never a secret, the many months of MOM Production's work were overshadowed in studio publicity by the aesthetic appeal of the big-name celebrities who supplied the voices and songs. In subsequent studio commemorations, the presence of the Japanese is acknowledged, but semantically buried in an inclusive, first-person plural of 'our' tradition.

> For this special, Rankin/Bass employed 100 people and the total cost of production was $500,000. There
> were 22 room-sized sets built, that took a year to construct. Each 'Animagic' character cost $5000 to make,
> and they all came with various lip and eye-pieces to create the various expressions. The intricate stop-
> motion figures were ball-jointed as well. 'If one elf mouth was out of place, we'd have to re-shoot the entire
> scene,' says Rankin. 'That meant a whole week's work for one droopy mouth.' (Goldschmidt 1997: 4)

Rudolph the Red-Nosed Reindeer (1964) is commemorated as an 'American' work, but was animated in Japan

Rankin's 'we' is an understandable but regrettable distortion. He was indeed occasionally in Japan to witness the filming of his many 'Animagic' specials, but he was never the 'we' of the physical animators. A careful reader can pick between the lines of the Rankin/Bass studio history to ascertain that the '100 people' on the production were Japanese labourers in Tokyo, but it is not made explicit. Instead, the tradition of the Rankin/Bass studio is that 'we' made these American classics, and 'our' efforts at the US end of production, as the owners and originators of the intellectual property, are what 'we' commemorate. Despite taking up many years of labour in Japan, the Rankin/Bass contracts relegate Japanese participation to subaltern status. Nor have the Japanese made much effort to assert the facts of their own participation in such works.

Mochinaga worked on several more jobs for Rankin/Bass before quitting MOM Production in 1967. However, although he mentions them in his memoirs, he dismisses them without much comment as 'the days of hard battle and bitter fights' (*akusen kutō no hibi*) – a potent comment from a man who had lived through World War II! Instead, Mochinaga preferred to reminisce about his occasional, personal projects and his eventual return to China during the Cultural Revolution, where he would work in teaching and news media for many years (Mochinaga 2006: 251–2). As a result, although there is significant nescience as to the involvement of the Japanese on such foreign productions as the Rankin/Bass films, this gap in the historical record has, at least in part, been fostered by the Japanese themselves. Mochinaga, or rather Mochinaga's widow Ayako, is the custodian of much of his memory. It was she who steered her late husband's memoirs into print in 2006, seven years after his death, working only with those parts of his own self-commemoration that he had completed, and doubtless leaving several areas where Mochinaga himself might have clarified or rewritten his manuscript had he lived longer.

Although Mochinaga's involvement in Rankin/Bass productions is not a secret in the American market, the studio's own brand identity usually takes prominence in any coverage of its works – for the real identity of the actual staff on Rankin/Bass productions, and confirmation of whether a particular 'American' film or TV special was made in Japan (or Canada or somewhere else), one must often squint at the credits themselves. Mochinaga's own relative lack of interest in chronicling what was clearly a difficult time for him has also led to a gap in source material. He writes, for example, of his work on a film he calls *Andersen Monogatari: Mannatsu no Yume* (*Andersen Tales: A Midsummer Dream*), and which he translates into English as *Andersen Fairy Tales*. But one must go to Rankin/Bass's own records to see that he actually means *The Daydreamer* (1966), a Rankin/Bass live-action film, based on the life of Hans Christian Andersen, for which MOM Production animated the stop-motion dream sequences that retold several Andersen stories.

After 1967, Mochinaga left Japan to work back in China. The name of his assistant Komuro Ichirō can be found on the credits of several subsequent Rankin/Bass stop-motion features throughout the 1970s, while other studios such as Mushi Pro took on similar below-the-line work for other Rankin/Bass specials such as *Frosty the Snowman* in 1969.

The extent to which the Japanese contribution to 1960s American animation has been acknowledged is patchy in the extreme. It is a matter of repressed memory and uncaring nescience, as animators focus more on more aesthetically appealing and 'Japanese' works, at the expense of work 'below the line', for which others often took the credit. Even those Japanese names that do make it onto the credits are often mis-spelled, which in turn often exiles them to unseen dead-end pages in online search engines. By the time Arthur Rankin and Jules Bass effectively retired in 1990, the staff and companies involved had changed somewhat – a group of defectors from Mushi and Tōei had transformed first into Top Craft, and then into Pacific Animation Corporation, while Mochinaga Tadahito had walked away from his own company, leaving its legacy in the hands of his former assistants. However, if one lists the Japanese participation in Rankin/Bass productions in chronological order, it soon becomes apparent that a genealogy of contacts, established between Rankin/Bass and representatives of Tōei, Mushi and MOM Production in the late 1950s, endured unbroken for thirty years.

Although Mochinaga remained reticent about his work for foreign companies, he had established a line of revenue, contacts and interaction with America that would sustain many members of the Japanese animation industry into the mid-1980s. At the time of the American 'discovery' of Japanese animation in the late 1980s, Japanese animation had already formed a fundamental part of supposedly 'American' works, and had done so for decades. It also laid the groundwork for anime's 'first' export, to be covered in the next chapter.

Table 5.1 lists all the Rankin/Bass productions using Japanese staff, with the named Japanese supervisors, taken from data in Goldschmidt (1997).

TABLE 5.1: JAPANESE PARTICIPATION IN RANKIN/BASS PRODUCTIONS 1960–87

YEAR	TITLE	TV/MOVIE	SUPERVISOR(S)
1960	*New Adventures of Pinocchio*	TV series	**Mochinaga Tadahito**
1964	*Rudolph the Red-Nosed Reindeer*	TVm	Mochinaga Tadahito
1965	*Willy McBean and His Magic Machine*	m	Mochinaga Tadahito
1966	*The Ballad of Smokey the Bear*	TVm	Mochinaga Tadahito
	The King Kong Show	TV series	Hara Tōru (**Tōei Dōga**)
	The Daydreamer (segments)	m	Mochinaga Tadahito
	The Wacky World of Mother Goose	m	Nagashima Kizo
1967	*Mad Monster Party*	m	Mochinaga Tadahito, Nagashima Kizo
	(Mochinaga leaves for China; his assistants take over)		
1968	*The Mouse on the Mayflower*	TVm	Tōei Dōga
	The Little Drummer Boy	TVm	Nakamura Takeo
1969	*The Smokey Bear Show*	TV series	Tōei Dōga
	Frosty the Snowman	TVm	**Mushi Pro**, Steve Nakagawa
1970	*Santa Claus Is Comin' to Town*	TVm	Nagashima Kizo
	The Reluctant Dragon and Mr Toad Show	TV series	Mushi Pro
1971	*Here Comes Peter Cottontail*	TVm	Nagashima Kizo, Steve Nakagawa
1972	*The Emperor's New Clothes* (segment)	TVm	Kono Akikazu
	Mad, Mad, Mad Monsters	TVm	Mushi Pro, Steve Nakagawa
	(Top Craft formed by Hara Tōru)		
	Kid Power	TV series	Hara Tōru (**Top Craft**)
	Festival of Family Classics	TV series	Mushi Pro

YEAR	TITLE	TV/MOVIE	SUPERVISOR(S)
1973	(Mushi Pro declares bankruptcy)		
	Marco (segment)	m	Komuro Ichirō?
1974	*'Twas the Night before Christmas*	TVm	Hara Tōru (Top Craft)
	The Year without a Santa Claus	TVm	Kono Akikazu, Komuro Ichirō
1975	*The First Christmas*	TVm	Kono Akikazu, Komuro Ichirō
1976	*The First Easter Rabbit*	TVm	Hara Tōru, Kubo Tsuguyuki (Top Craft)
	Frosty's Winter Wonderland	TVm	Hara Tōru, Kubo Tsuguyuki (Top Craft)
	Rudolph's Shiny New Year	TVm	Kono Akikazu, Komuro Ichirō
	The Little Drummer Boy Book II	TVm	Kono Akikazu, Fujino Satoshi
1977	*The Easter Bunny Is Comin' to Town*	TVm	Kono Akikazu
	The Hobbit	TVm	Hara Tōru, Kubo Tsuguyuki (Top Craft)
	Nestor the Long-eared Christmas Donkey	TVm	Kono/Fujino
1978	*The Stingiest Man in Town*	TVm	Hara Tōru, Kubo Tsuguyuki (Top Craft)
1979	*Jack Frost*	TVm	Kono Akikazu, Komuro Ichirō
	Rudolph and Frosty's Christmas in July	m	Kono Akikazu
1980	*The Return of the King*	TVm	Hara Tōru, Kubo Tsuguyuki (Top Craft)
	Pinocchio's Christmas	TVm	Kono Akikazu, Komuro Ichirō
1981	*The Leprechaun's Christmas Gold*	TVm	Kono Akikazu, Komuro Ichirō
1982	*The Last Unicorn*	m	Hara Tōru, Kubo Tsuguyuki (Top Craft)
	The Flight of Dragons	TVm	Yamada Katsuhisa (Top Craft)
1983	*The Coneheads*	(30-minute pilot)	'Tsugo Kubo' (Top Craft)
1984	(Former Top Craft staff split between PAC and Studio Ghibli)		
1985	*The Life and Adventures of Santa Claus*	TVm	**Pacific Animation Corp.**
	ThunderCats	TV series	PAC
1986	*SilverHawks*	TV series	PAC
1987	*The Comic Strip*	TV series	PAC
1988	(PAC bought out and renamed Walt Disney Animation Japan)		

NOTES

1. See http://www.jmdb.ne.jp/1955/ce001270.htm, also DAW 803 and Animage (1989: 33). The same title is used in Japanese for Disney's Silly Symphony *The Woodland Café* (1937).

2. See http://www.jmdb.ne.jp/1955/ce001270.htm.

3. I suspect, pending any evidence to the contrary, that *The Kingdom of the Monkey* is actually a garbled reference to *The New Adventures of Hanuman*, on which Ashida would have been working at the time the interview was conducted. He also alludes in the interview to the possibility of a colour 'film' work in cooperation with Shamus Culhane Productions, but nothing appears to have come of this.

4. The term 'name value' is in English in the original. The young Tezuka had also attempted to get work with Ashida's studio. See Tsugata (2007b: 32).

5. F6.2571 in the American Film Institute's catalogue. The credits, however, are not animated, but drawn on several wooden planks, each of which is smashed by a live-action martial artist.

6. Or to put it in Marxist terms, Tōei animators were still unsure of the 'socially necessary' quantity of labour required to produce an animated commodity, and they were unable to determine the 'average condition of labour productivity' (Mandel 1973: 18). The American norm had been defined by an entirely different history and labour pool – Ōtsuka argues that they were comparing apples and oranges.

7. 'Tōei Animation' is both a translation of the original studio name in 1956, and the new, English-language title by which Tōei Dōga was formally known after 1998.

8. See, for example, http://www.youtube.com/watch?v=-sky4JISh-k. Goldschmidt (1997: 91–2) notes that the last five episodes of *Pinocchio* featured stories of the new character 'Willy Nilly', and effectively functioned as test footage for *Willy McBean and His Magic Machine*.

9. At least in theory, although as Goldschmidt (1997: 92) notes, a second theme song was introduced later in the run, so the recycled footage was only half as effective.

10. Even though some episodes were eventually broadcast on Japanese television, they were buried within another puppet show, *Ciscon Ōji* (1963–4, *Prince Ciscon*), and only mentioned as a footnote in Animage (1988: 6).

11. The Wan brothers in Shanghai came to a similar realisation, which was why they put their resources into the feature-length *Princess Iron Fan* instead of a dozen ephemeral shorts (Hu 2010: 169).

12. *Sekai no kyōtsūgo*.

13. The live-action *Madame White Snake* still required a number of special-effects shots, particularly matte work, but these were done by Tōhō's Tsuburaya Eiji rather than any of the Nichidō animators. Note that both films are called 白蛇伝 ('White-Snake-Legend') in Chinese, a fact that has led scholars relying on Chinese sources to misname the live-action version. The Japanese title of the live-action film literally means 'Phantom Desire of Lady Bai/White'.

14. JCD 7226.

15. Hu identifies (2010: 91–2) one other level of 'performance' in *Hakujaden* and its successor films, which is to say the desire among many of the young animation recruits to re-live, or more accurately, *live* a childhood denied them by the Fifteen Years War. Normally, I would discount such a comment as impressionistic whimsy, but Hu clearly states that it was a recurring feature in her interviews with veteran Tōei staff.

16. Ashida Iwao's *Princess of Baghdad* may have reached feature length in one of its lost variants, possibly in 1950.

17. Nagasawa Makoto (Oguro 2004b: 2) claims that he first began using 'taps' at Tōei in the latter half of production on *Hakujaden*. Seemingly, some workgroups were using them and some were not. This is particularly odd, since 'registering pegs' are specifically included in animation table specifications in Lutz (1920: 61–3, 73) – something that the industry had to 'rediscover' after the war, like the dope sheet at Otogi Pro.

18. It was, it should be noted, derided for political reasons to do with the rise of limited animation. Miyazaki (2009: 195–6) pointedly notes that Tezuka was all too ready to denigrate Tōei's rotoscoped footage when he was pushing his own limited animation process, but that Tezuka eventually relented and bought a rotoscope for himself, and 'we all wound up laughing at him'.

19. Compare this, however, to Jimmy Murakami's assessment of Tōei Dōga at roughly the same time:

> It was very big and very new … . They had hundreds of people there. There were no computers, everything was done by hand, on cels and paper. I'd probably call it a factory, about as big as the Disney studio. They were working on two or three feature films a year, a huge volume of work … . if you were tired in Japan in those days, you wouldn't be working! Sheer hard work, get your head down … . They're not sitting there joking around like [the American studio] UPA did! They're very intensive, very serious. In Japan they worked that way, no matter what business they were in. No-one looked up, they were just working intensely.
> (Osmond 2012a)

20. Barrier (1999: 506) notes similar tensions at Disney in the 1940s. Mandel (1973: 19) observes that an assumption of equivalence between a skilled and unskilled labourer would 'destroy the social equilibrium'. Tōei's eventual solution to this was to move entirely onto a piecework system that, at least in theory, rewarded the more productive labourer with greater wages.

21. Satō Yumi (Brains Base, quoted in Clements (2011e: 36)) relates:

> They say that women were better at distinguishing between subtler shades, and pay greater attention to detail. Most of the really good colourists of the cel days were female, although now that computer colouring is the norm, more men are getting involved.

22. Okuyama's 'first' is subjective, and ignores many spouses and pieceworkers from previous decades who were already mothers, not least the spousal assistants of Masaoka Kenzō, Mochinaga Tadahito and Yokoyama Ryūichi. However, in terms of animation as an industry, she may well have been the first labourer in the studio system to test the practice of maternity leave.

23. Okuyama's testimony claims that Kotabe, her husband, left Tōei for Mushi Pro, implying that the events she described took place in 1961, at the time of the first Tōei dispute. However, as noted in his own resumé (Kanō 2004: 232), Kotabe did not quit Tōei until 1971, when he left with Miyazaki to work at A-Pro. There is an error here, either in Okuyama's memory, or more likely in Kanō's transcription of it. Possibly he has attempted to clarify her comments by filling in the names of unnamed studios, but inadvertently named the wrong ones. I leave the discussion here, although it could equally be placed in later chapters that discuss the situation in the 1970s rather than the 1960s.

24. This film will be referred to by its Japanese title, which is better known.

25. As with Okuyama Reiko's testimony above, Rintarō's account of the 1961 dispute contains several elements that seem more appropriate to the 1971 lockout. It doesn't help that protests over the Anpo Treaty, which he mentions to place his account in a historical context, broke out again ten years after the original protests, when the treaty was renewed. However, he very clearly places his reminiscences not only in relation to the protests, but to the production of *Saiyūki*, which was indisputably in 1960.

26. Mandel (1973: 78) sees this as the likely fate of any union organisations that embrace neo-capitalism, transforming them into 'gendarmes for the maintenance of social peace …'.

27. The term *hikinuki*, translated here as 'headhunting', is well established in the Japanese film business. High (2003: 154) uses the same term in reference to the 'star-stealing' of the 1930s, when celebrities were poached by rival studios, particularly after the incorporation of Tōhō in 1937.

28. In a 2004 interview, Shirakawa Daisaku noted that Hara Tōru, later the boss of Top Craft, was the producer at Tōei in charge of the co-productions of *King Kong* and *Tom Thumb*. See http://www.style.fm/log/02_topics/top041220.html (Oguro 2004a: 7).

29. Animage (1988: 20). DAW 16 mentions a TV movie with the same title, but that is the 1977 Japanese broadcast of the Rankin/Bass sequel *Rudolph's Shiny New Year* (1976), made by Mochinaga's former associate Komuro Ichirō.

6 WARRIOR BUSINESS
Tezuka's anime revolution in context 1961–72

Japanese animation was transformed once again, as the new exhibition medium of television tempted animators to alter previous methods of production. This, in turn, led to deep changes at the level of ownership, as this new strand of animation came to rely on investment from multiple sources. In terms of Megill's errors of practice (2007: 33), sources are often skewed by a desire to commemorate the achievements of Tezuka Osamu, even though Tezuka's own testimonials would sometimes contradict his earlier accounts of the period.

In hindsight, it was the production of Tōei Dōga's third feature-length animated film that was to transform the Japanese animation industry. The film itself, *Saiyūki*[1] amounted to a retread of the old story of the Monkey King, as enjoyed by Japanese audiences a generation earlier in the form of *Princess Iron Fan* – indeed, its author had been in the audience for that film as a boy. What set *Saiyūki* apart was not its reception or even production, but the opportunity it provided for one of its participants to break away and found his own animation company. This, in turn, would create new outlets for Tōei's newly trained animators, and inadvertently lead to what was termed the 'era of abridged animation' (*shōryaku anime no jidai*) by Ōtsuka Yasuo (2001: 104).

Saiyūki was originally intended as a return to the Chinese themes of *Hakujaden*, but transformed in pre-production into a movie adaptation of a pre-existing manga on the same theme (Oguro 2004a: 2). *Boku no Son Gokū* (*My Sun Wukong*) had been running in the children's magazine *Manga-Ō* since 1952, and came to an end in 1959, partway through production on the animated film adaptation. The artist, Tezuka Osamu, was already a celebrity in the manga world, and appears to have ignored earlier warnings that an animation production represented a severe, punishing schedule. *Saiyūki* became the first of three Tōei productions that would include Tezuka's involvement – the other two would be *Sinbad the Sailor*[2] and *Wanwan Chūshingura* (1963, *Doggie March*).[3]

STORYBOARDING *SAIYŪKI*

The credits of *Saiyūki* implied that Tezuka was directing it, although the real work appears to have been done by Tōei's Yabushita Taiji. Like Yokoyama Ryūichi in the generation before him, Tezuka the manga artist proved to be hard to motivate to produce work in an industrial animation context, despite his own avowed love of the medium (Ōtsuka 2001: 70). Instead, he was assigned a task that would ensure his intimate involvement with the look of the production, without actually animating it. In accordance with Ōkawa Hiroshi's desire to follow a 'Disney' mode of production, Tezuka was put to work drawing a complete storyboard for the film, condensing eight years of manga into a pertinent, feature-length storyline. The 'script', credited to Uekusa Keinosuke was presumably assembled afterwards, and reflected Tezuka's visual narrative (Animage 1989: 41).

Tezuka did not complete his storyboard until the autumn of 1959. In a semi-contrite article for his fan-club newsletter several years later, he boasted that he had not taken Tōei's initial deadlines seriously, assuming that they would be flexible about delivery times, as manga magazines continued to be (Minakawa 2009a: 61). Of course, in an environment of 'single-crop' animation production, the late arrival of assets from Tezuka meant

In bringing in Tezuka Osamu to storyboard *Saiyūki* (1960), the Tōei studio inadvertently encouraged a powerful rival

no work for Tōei's animators, and he eventually delivered his 500-page storyboard after a year of work and, it is implied, many weeks of threats from the producers (Minakawa 2009a: 61).

Ōtsuka Yasuo (2001: 71) recalls that Tezuka repeatedly visited the Tōei Dōga building, often accompanied by an entourage comprising his assistants Ishinomori Shōtarō and Tsukioka Sadao, the latter of whom would eventually join Tōei. However, Tezuka's storyboard was problematic for Tōei's animators, who found it lacking in practical pacing, often muddled and frustratingly picaresque. Ōtsuka (2001: 109–10) notes that Tezuka drew on a vast reservoir of innovative in-jokes, anachronisms, stylistic flourishes and ideas, which came pouring out onto the pages of his comics. The animators called it the 'supermarket method' (*supermarket hōshiki*), implying that this unwelcome superabundance of ideas only served to crowd the frame. Tezuka seemed to be more interested in long, ongoing stories and jumbles of scenes, as might befit an open-ended comic series generated on a weekly basis. This ran counter to Tōei policy, which, common to many film studios, advocated a 'climax method' (*yamaba moriage hōshiki*) in which the budget and narrative force of a film would favour its final reel, in order to ensure that audiences always left the cinema remembering a cathartic big finish – a spectacular swordfight or a daring chase sequence (Ōtsuka 2001: 110).

Tezuka plainly did not enjoy the lack of control over 'his' story, particularly the ending, into which he had hoped to inject a note of sudden pathos and bereavement. Moreover, although he had been hired because of his imagination and art style, his creativity was reined in by the demands of mass-produced animation. He would eventually comment that although *Saiyūki* capitalised on his celebrity name, only 50 per cent of its aesthetic appeal was down to him (Sugiyama 1999: 107).

What I learnt at Tōei was that human relationships were more important than work itself in the animation business. There is no other job that requires specialists in each sector to work together like the cogs of a clock, to the extent required in animation. It will brook no lone-wolf gestures or elitist attitudes. Moreover, I realised that there was a danger that the more brains and technique required by animation, the more individuality was lost. (Tezuka 1999: 232–3)

However, Tezuka also surprised his colleagues. Ōtsuka Yasuo notes that, as one of the animators, he was given a stack of Tezuka's storyboards to animate, which initially seemed literally unworkable.

I had to do more than two hundred shots in about seven months, which meant twenty-nine shots a month, or one per day. At first, I thought it was impossible, but once I started, the process was much quicker than I'd thought, and I could finish one after another. The reason was Tezuka's characters. Unlike Sasuke [*Magic Boy*], with his top-knotted hair, patterned kimono and sandals, Tezuka's drawings were *modern* to start with, and Daikuhara Akira and Mori Yasuji had simplified them so that they were easy to animate. Inbetweening was just as quick. (Ōtsuka 2001: 71)

Despite setting a new record at Tōei, with over 100,000 frames of animation, *Saiyūki* proved less intricate in animation terms than some of its predecessors. Ōtsuka's use of the English term *modern* points to a sense of graphic shorthand in Tezuka's figures, born in part from his own breakneck schedules of year upon year of weekly manga production. Although not articulated at the time as an example of 'limited' animation, his 'modernist' economy of line was seen to be a labour-saving stylistic device. However, even if this were noticed at the time, it did not immediately affect Tōei policy, which barrelled onwards to the Japanese stylistic complexities of its next animated feature *Anju to Zushiō-maru* (1961, *The Littlest Warrior*).

Tezuka's time at Tōei, working on *Saiyūki*, is an event of powerful hybridity, and a turning point in many anime histories. It introduced Tsukioka Sadao to the studio, inadvertently supplying Tōei with the man who would eventually run its first television series. It also introduced Tezuka to the core animators who would eventually defect to join his own company (Misono 1999: 337). In terms of Tezuka's own impressions of the experience, it is difficult to articulate cause and effect, particularly since his own testimonials often transpose motivations and reactions. One certainly gets a sense from Tezuka's own writings that he had cherished an ambition to become an animator since his teens, even to the extent that his career in manga could be regarded as a stopgap measure in his ongoing dream to emulate his beloved Disney (Tsugata 2007b: 45). It is also implied that Tezuka left Tōei with a desire to set up his own animation company, where there would be no producers above him to compromise his vision and veto his decisions. The question, then, is to what extent Tezuka arrived at Tōei with that aim already in place? He appears to have already been somewhat envious of the attention Yokoyama Ryūichi had received since the 'premiere' of *Piggyback Ghost* in 1955, and had told Yokoyama of his intention to try something similar (Tsugata 2007b: 56). When Shirakawa Daisaku first visited Tezuka to propose the *Saiyūki* project in late 1958, Tezuka openly avowed that he had been considering something along similar lines, but that 'collaborators' (*kyōryoku*) were not available to him (Oguro 2004a: 2). In Tezuka's account of the premiere of *Hakujaden* in 1958, there is a distinct sense of jealousy that Ōkawa Hiroshi was able to lay claim to the status of the 'Japanese Disney' (Tezuka 1999: 204). Meanwhile, in 1960, three animators from the advertising world first screened their independently made 8mm shorts as the Sannin no Kai (Group of Three); this only seems to have fired Tezuka up even more, along with other manga artists including Tagawa Suihō, with the realisation that significantly less wealthy solo practitioners were already making animation (Tezuka 1999: 231). Minakawa Yūka (2009a: 166) notes that only 600 people came to see the works of the Group of Three. However, these animators swiftly began winning prizes for their work, achieving an artistic heritage far in excess of their limited reception.

Hence, it seems far more likely that Tezuka regarded his association with Tōei as a paid internship at the 'Tōei Dōga University' and that, while he seems to have been genuinely thrown by the feeling of being just another cog in the machine, he took the storyboarding job at least partly to examine that machine from the inside, so he could leave and build his own (Yamaguchi and Watanabe 1977: 71).

MUSHI PRODUCTION AND *TALES FROM A CERTAIN STREET CORNER*

Tezuka's move into production began with the establishment of an 'animation division' to his pre-existing comics company, which was soon rebranded as the dedicated animation studio Mushi Production (Mushi Pro for short). Tezuka started with just five people, but soon expanded to twenty or thirty by 1961 – a tenth of the staff roster of Tōei, quite literally. As one animator put it: 'at times it seemed as if a part of Tōei had simply upped and moved to Mushi' (Sugiyama 1999: 116).[4] Tōei animators, annoyed at their pay prospects or pushed out by union pressures, found at Mushi Pro an eccentric boss whose bullish insistence on getting his own way extended to ignoring many of the precedents of Tōei's troubled salary issues.

> I was earning an 8,000 yen salary at Tōei, but when I came over to Mr Tezuka's place, I was on 21,000. That's massive! From the start, Tezuka was saying: 'How much do you want?', and I was saying: 'Er … I … um …' until he said, 'All right, how does 21,000 sound?' I was speechless …. That's what Mr Tezuka was like. And, I guess, it's stuff like that that added to his massive debts! (Rintarō, quoted in Oguro 2009: 32–3)

Tezuka would also pay for food, in what seems to have been an effort to demonstrate that he was a better bet than Tōei – doling out a 100-yen/person daily lunch budget that came to be referred to as the 'treasure' (Minakawa 2009b: 75). The implication, or perhaps even 'performance', was that staff at Mushi Pro did not have to strike for the right to have the occasional *katsudon*. Yamamoto Eiichi (1989: 33) notes that his starting salary at Mushi Pro was double his pay at Otogi Pro.

Aru Machikado no Monogatari (1962, *Tales from a Certain Street Corner*)[5] was Tezuka's calling card, an experimental film designed from the outset as an 'anti-Disney' exercise in dialogue-free, modernist animation (Tsugata 2007b: 75). Graphic art was both its content and its form, drawing on the skills of several of its staff, notably Sakamoto Yūsaku (ex-Tōei), Watanabe Chizuko (formerly of an advertising company) and Yamamoto Eiichi (ex-Otogi). Openly described as a 'warming-up' exercise (Tsugata 2007b: 79), its production history ironically contains a miniature foreshadowing of every element that would trouble later productions at Mushi Pro. Tezuka steered the production, but often lagged behind the schedule that he had set himself, forcing his staff to take up the shortfall on creative decisions for which Tezuka would ultimately take the credit (Yamamoto 1989: 41).

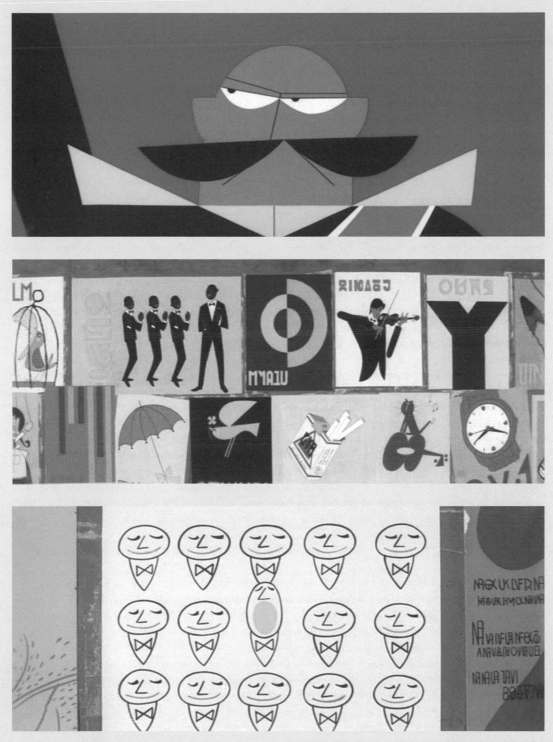

Tales from a Certain Street Corner (1962) was a cinema event from Tezuka that nonetheless relied on limited animation

Thanks largely to 'killer weeks' no less punishing than those its staff had hoped to leave behind at Tōei, it was finished on time, although it cost far more than expected and suffered from the secondment of two of its animators to ongoing work on the pilot of *Astro Boy*, itself already suffering from a lack of direct involvement from its alleged creator (Yamamoto 1989: 88).

Tales from a Certain Street Corner's performative action, of advertising billboards coming to life and interacting with one another, is almost as old as cinema itself, dating back to Georges Méliès' *Les Affiches en goguette* (1906, *The Hilarious Posters*). In a typical histrionic Tezuka touch, the titular street is itself in a country struggling under a military dictatorship, which brings disaster upon all inhabitants, and ultimately engulfs the street itself in flames. However, the film's representative event was far more important – presenting thirty-eight minutes of colourful, dynamic animation, mixing a variety of styles, but chiefly reiterating the fact that the stripped-down, stylistic shorthand of commercial art, as popularised by UPA and Hanna-Barbera in the West, was well within the grasp of Tezuka's team.

Perhaps most crucially, *Tales from a Certain Street Corner* was a hit-and-run performance event like Yokoyama Ryūichi's earlier *Piggyback Ghost* – worth much more to Tezuka through discussion of the fact of its existence, and the sight of colour stills from its scenes, than from the experience of actually having to sit through it. Watching it today, it seems twee and leadenly repetitive, with Takai Tatsuo's music forming an irritating, ceaseless loop. The antiwar message seems ham-fisted, lachrymose and manipulative ('I was so disgusted that chills ran down my spine' – Miyazaki 2009: 195), and the animation is clearly, patently limited (Tsugata 2007b: 84). *Tales from a Certain Street Corner* runs single frames for seconds at a time, and repeats loops of 'dancing' characters that simply flip from one direction to another. Although Tezuka proclaimed that he intended to diverge Mushi Pro's operations into a TV division and a film division, he stated from the outset that the film division would be set to work on creating works in the style of *Tales from a Certain Street Corner*. Whatever the hype, whatever the twists in memory that would later jumble elements of the story, Mushi Pro began as it meant to go on, with limited animation.

Tales from a Certain Street Corner was not subject to general critical scrutiny or mass audience reception until many decades after Tezuka's death. It was designed, instead, to test the animation capabilities of Tezuka's newly created team, and to function, like *Onbu Obake* before it, as an event whose artistic heritage was perpetuated not by people who were there, but people who had merely heard or read about it. Although *Tales from a Certain Street Corner* was 'exhibited' to a Japanese audience, it was not distributed to the Japanese public and would remain largely unseen until its eventual release on a twenty-first-century DVD compilation. Instead, it was shown at a specially arranged 'Mushi Pro Showcase' event, along with the three-minute short *Osu* (1962, *Push*) and the pilot episode of Tezuka's first animated television series (Animage 1989: 152–3).

ASTRO BOY

Tezuka Osamu's *Astro Boy* was first seen eight weeks before its official broadcast date, at the same Mushi Pro Showcase at the Yamaha Hall, Ginza, Tokyo on 5/6 November 1962 (Animage 1989: 153). This fact is not widely known, perhaps because the Yamaha Hall event seems to have been somewhat shambolic. Tezuka's staff had to drop their initial plans to screen the first two episodes of *Astro Boy*, when recording the audio turned out to be more difficult than expected. As it was, the sound was not properly mixed, and had to be played on a separate tape recorder, which ran at a different speed to the film it was supposed to be accompanying (Yamamoto 1989: 92). It cannot have been all that impressive. Although we know that some experienced animators would be left aghast at the sight of Tezuka's limited animation on broadcast, that is no reason to assume that they were present at the Yamaha Hall to be appalled, and even if they were, simple etiquette would have precluded anything but acclamation. Tezuka packed the hall with his friends (Ushio 2007: 227, 279), presumably in the hope that a positive audience reaction was assured.

The hype was already set in motion. The broadcast of *Astro Boy* on New Year's Day 1963, is generally taken to mark the beginning of a new age in Japanese animation. There are, however, some dissenters, who argue that Tezuka could never have created his animation company so swiftly were it not for the labour pool available to him from his rivals at Tōei (Sugiyama 1999: 115–16), or even that, had Tezuka not made *Astro Boy*, some-one else would surely have produced something similar by the mid-1960s (Miyazaki 2009: 196).

Tsugata Nobuyuki sees Tezuka as one of the polar opposites of the anime medium, set against Miyazaki Hayao. Although there is little evidence of what Tezuka thought of Miyazaki,[6] Miyazaki has given us ample indi-cation of what he thinks of Tezuka, most notably in a 1989 article that derides the creator of *Astro Boy* for his 'bankrupt vanity' and which observes 'everything that Mr Tezuka talked about or emphasised was wrong' (Miyazaki 2009: 193–7).

If the only source we had for Tezuka were Miyazaki Hayao's hatchet job, we might think that Tezuka was an insecure hack, weighed down by 'cheap pessimism' and lifelong envy for Disney. But we might also note that Miyazaki is a lifelong left-winger and former studio union representative, unlikely to subscribe to the con-servative idea that history requires 'Great Men' to move it. In Miyazaki's writings on anime, we might even perceive the shadows of Marxist structuralism, lamenting the passing of the primitive Communism of the good old days when animators supposedly made animation for animation's sake, decrying the proletarianisation of labour in the animation business, and silently anticipating the end of anime prehistory, when animators alien-ated from the products of their labour are liberated through the arrival of new technologies, and the destruction of old ownerships of the means of production, distribution and exchange.

Moreover, Miyazaki wrote his piece immediately after Tezuka's death, in the full knowledge that Tezuka would be eulogised all over Japan in countless obituaries. It would, in this case, not be an arrogant assumption for Miyazaki to believe that many journalists were sure to cite him as an inheritor of Tezuka's tradition if he did not get in first with a pre-emptive strike. His own piece is ungracious but not necessarily unfair comment, but also a bold assertion of Miyazaki's own tradition. In the guise of an opinion piece about Tezuka, Miyazaki notes all the things about himself that Tezuka was not. In effect, he makes a statement about his own personal tradition, and categorically denies that it is related to Tezuka's. Miyazaki tells us he was not inspired by Tezuka; in fact, he names other artists who had a greater effect on him. Miyazaki did not admire Tezuka's works; in fact, he recounts his burning of drawings that seemed too much like Tezuka's. Miyazaki does not even regard Tezuka as a pioneer; In fact, he bluntly states that, if Tezuka had not instigated his anime revolution, someone else would surely have done so. Taken out of context, Miyazaki's anti-commemoration is a bilious attack, but we might also consider its value to Miyazaki as a statement of his own position. Miyazaki did not want to be seen as an inheritor of Tezuka, any more than he wanted to be seen as a representative of the television anime medium for which Tezuka took the credit. However, as Sugii Gisaburō has suggested, the glory days that Miyazaki posits at Tōei Dōga were nothing of the sort, and the business model at Tōei was untenable: 'It was *Astro Boy* that changed such a situation, turning anime into a proper business. Therefore, in an extreme sense, it is thanks to *Astro Boy* that Miyazaki Hayao, a critic of Tezuka, is still in business' (Tsugata 2007b: 195).

In fact, it is even arguable that Tōei had already realised that its own business model did not work, which is why it was already drifting into a piecework, contract-based system by the mid-1960s. The animators who stormed out of Tōei, to find work at Mushi Pro and other start-ups, consciously or unconsciously exploited the fact that those same start-ups had yet to learn the harsh realities of running large-scale animation projects. The period 1963–72 is something of a false dawn, as Tōei's talent expanded out into the marketplace, but without adequate controls. This market chaos was brought to a halt in the 1970s recession, when a new set of studios, such as Sunrise, learned from Mushi's mistakes, and adopted a system redolent of that in place at Tōei since 1966.

To a certain extent, the *Astro Boy* animated series was born not at Mushi, but at Tōei, as a result of a con-fluence of opportunities, contacts and discussions in the late 1950s. The Tōei studio certainly provided an inspiration and an impetus for Tezuka, as it was there in the 1950s that the subject of *Astro Boy* on television was first debated, during Tezuka's time at Tōei storyboarding *Saiyūki*. During a post-Sputnik fad for futurism (Minakawa 2009b: 280), animators mooted the possibility of a short theatrical film, or perhaps a TV series, but any discussion of television soon favoured a look inspired by *kamishibai* – in other words, a story read out over still images with minimal zooms and pans, in the manner of the later British children's series *Jackanory* (1965–96). The director Shirakawa Daisaku recalled a discussion about the possibility of a truly animated series, ridiculed by Tōei's veteran animator Yamamoto Sanae as an absurd idea, impossible even with the manpower of the entire animation industry (Tsugata 2007b: 110–11). The idea was dropped, and *Astro Boy* appeared on TV instead in a live-action series, running for sixty-five episodes from March 1959–May 1960 (Clements and Tamamuro 2003: 14). Notably, however, the 'live-action' series featured an animated credit sequence, clearly prefiguring the look of the later anime. The production company Matsuzaki Films subcontracted the animation work to the Murata Eiga Seisaku-sho (Murata Film Production Works), a film company established by Murata Yasuji after the collapse of the Nihon Manga Eiga-sha in the 1940s (Minakawa 2009a: 60).

Tezuka was unable to resist the temptation to become an animation producer in his own right – an ambition to which he had often alluded (Tsugata 2007b: 42–7). However, the production issues seemed insurmountable. Assuming a weekly output of thirty minutes of Tōei-quality animation, Tezuka's assistant Yamamoto Eiichi calculated an improbably huge staff requirement of 3,000 employees, and a budget of between 60 and 70 million yen. Moreover, the entire population of animators then working in Japan would only account for 20 per cent of the necessary labour allocation and, once the show was completed, it would still be too expensive for any TV channel to afford. Limited animation was considered to be the only option, although the general sense among Japanese animators in 1962 was that Hanna-Barbera's limited animation was of poor quality, and had been poorly received critically (Yamamoto 1989: 64). It was imperative that Mushi Pro cut corners, in order to bring the unit cost of its show down.

However, these assumptions were often facetious. 'Tōei-quality animation' output at that rate might have required such vast numbers, but Mochinaga Tadahito had already successfully produced animation for half the required running-time on his 1960 *New Adventures of Pinocchio* with only a few dozen staff. Tezuka would need to find similar means of industrialising his animation, and indeed, was already halfway there with production on *Tales from a Certain Street Corner*. Tezuka slashed costs on *Astro Boy* to a mere 2.5 million yen per episode, through a number of drastic measures, telling his staff that this amounted not to 'full' animation, but 'limited anime' – the contraction, here, seemingly intended to reflect the truncated nature of the form. At no point, however, did Tezuka define what this notional 'anime' actually was. His staff came to regard it as a style, born from the cost-cutting measures and perceived as an opposite to what was now regarded as the 'realistic' style of the Tōei studio. Posterity has recorded a series of elements, much cited among anime scholars, and first found in the semi-fictionalised autobiography of one of Mushi Pro's founding staff, Yamamoto Eiichi (1989: 105–6).[7]

- *San-koma tōri* – shooting on threes. Aiming to use only eight images per second of film, instead of the available twenty-four. NB: 'full' animation generally uses twelve images per second, or 'shooting on twos'.
- *Tome[-e]* – stop-[images]. Using a single still frame for sequences where animation is not really required, such as reaction shots, establishing shots, crowd scenes, gasps or close-ups on the eyes while a character is speaking.
- *Hiki-cel* – pull-cels. Pulling a single background behind a foreground image in order to give the impression of movement. Particularly useful in scenes of vehicles or flying characters in motion.
- *Kurikaeshi* – repetition. Using a simple loop of animation, sometimes in conjunction with a sliding background for walking scenes. With this technique, combined with pull-cels, a mere dozen cels can be reused to create scenes far exceeding the initial effort required to draw them.
- *Bubun* – sectioning. The face or body remains still, while only the essential part – a raised arm, a kicking leg, etc. – is animated. Prime examples include *kuchi-paku* [mouth flaps], in which the mouth is animated separately from the face, allowing for a limited set of three or four mouth positions to be cycled in place, thus creating the illusion that the character is speaking.
- *Kenyō* – combined use. Today more commonly termed a *cel bank* or *image bank* or, as Tezuka preferred, a *bank system*, this refers to an archive of cels from previous episodes, such as cityscapes, backgrounds and characters in certain positions. These images are not discarded or destroyed, but filed away for reuse. An image, for example, of Astro Boy in flight might recur every episode, but only needs to be drawn once and swapped into different backgrounds.
- *Short cut* – short shots. Since longer shots require longer animation, a sequence of shorter shots is more likely to get away with single frames, pull-cels, repetition and other cost-cutting measures.

Tobio's car crash in *Astro Boy* (1963) uses fewer than twenty images, but covers more than 200 frames

Tezuka used these cost-cutting measures to meet *Astro Boy*'s weekly schedule, but he was certainly not their inventor. Nor was this fact generally unknown, even in the year of *Astro Boy*'s release. In June 1963, an article in the *Asahi Shinbun* by Tada Michitarō noted not only the pre-war precedents for still images in 'animation', but also the stylistic similarities of such stop-images and pull-cels to the live performance of *kamishibai* street theatre (Minakawa 2009b: 51–2). Tezuka himself would push for a slightly different interpretation, arguing that his inspiration had less to do with kamishibai itself, and more to do with his childhood memories of the similar effect produced by the jerky and inconsistent speed of *Felix the Cat* (1959), as viewed on his father's malfunctioning home movie projector (Minakawa 2009b: 52). He also asserted that comparing his animation directly to kamishibai was a reduction to the absurd, as a strict kamishibai interpretation of his work would require only 300 images to accomplish that which took 900 images in *Astro Boy* (Tezuka 1997: 120).

However, as Yamamoto and Katō have persuasively demonstrated with a frame-by-frame analysis of *Astro Boy*, even Tezuka's claim to animate 'on threes' was merely a broad statement of intent, while actual production often reduced the cel count still further. Moreover, with the average cel count per episode of *Astro Boy* at a mere 2,500, we might even argue that the production averaged only 1.89 cels per second (Yamamoto and Katō 2009: 286–8; Yamamoto 1989: 173). Tezuka himself claimed to have reduced the cel count on *Astro Boy* down to the bare bones of 1,200 cels per episode, suggesting that Yamamoto Eiichi's count of 2,500 included repeated or sectioned cels from earlier episodes such as generic body parts, mouth flaps and cityscapes (Tezuka 1997: 117). According to industry rumour, one episode of *Astro Boy* was even completed with a cel count of only 1,000, a mean rate of 1.44 cels per second. However, presumably this refers to 1,000 *new* cels, added to material from the pre-existing image bank (Ishiguro and Ohara 1980: 51).[8]

None of the corner-cutting measures could reasonably be said to have been invented by Tezuka or Mushi Pro, and many had been features of animation since its earliest days.[9] The tricks were developed and refined not by Tezuka personally, but by staffers under his command such as Sugii Gisaburō, who had initially complained that what they were doing barely warranted the term 'animation' at all (Oguro 2009: 34; Minakawa 2009a: 207, 298–9). We need only look at *Tales from a Certain Street Corner* to see that Tezuka was already working with clearly 'limited' animation over a year before he was supposedly compelled to do so by the strictures of the *Astro Boy* production (Tsugata 2007b: 84).

Another of the Mushi Pro staff, Takahashi Ryōsuke, prefers to define Tezuka's decisions in slightly different terms. While both Yamamoto and Takahashi report on Tezuka's 'revolution' long after it was over, their approaches are distinctively different. Both look back from later points in time (these are memoirs, not testimonials), but Yamamoto writes semantically and narratively in the present-tense chaos of Mushi Pro in 1963, discussing the tricks and fixes of hard-pressed labourers, with no discussion of the implications, replicating the effect of a synchronic testimonial. Meanwhile, Takahashi (2011a: 50–4) embraces the memorial quality of writing forty years later, with a rhetoric of diachronic hindsight, working backwards from what anime has become in 2011, in an attempt to trace roots for it in 1963:

· *Bank system*, as above.[10]
· *E-conté no jūshi* – emphasis on storyboards. Takahashi regards a storyboard as vastly more useful than a script in unifying the disparate parts of a production, since it contains 'direction to the art unit, colour settings and backgrounds, specific camera work for shooting and calls for sound effects'. He regards this as vital in an industry where outsourcing is the norm, as it allows better communication with workgroups absent from the main studio, in scattered subcontracting ateliers and foreign studios.
· *Tome-e no senren* – refinement of the still image. As above, although with somewhat different implications. Takahashi does not see 'stop-images' as mere corner-cutting measures, but as defining elements of the style and pace of anime. Accepting that still images are a 'necessary evil', Takahashi notes that successive animators have embraced them as a stylistic device, and hence made a virtue out of necessity.
· *Kigōka no sokushin* – promotion of encoding. Takahashi believes that limited animation swiftly developed a series of visual cues, shorthands and tropes, transcending the work of a single creator, genre or story. He argues that sheer volume of output in the early days of television ensured that Tezuka's

particular style overwhelmed that of many of his competitors, establishing consensual norms that have endured ever since, encoded in the very nature of Japanese animation. Audiences collaborate in the dissemination of these codes, by learning as children how to read anime texts.

- *Dokutoku no onsei enshutsu* – distinctive sound production, claimed by Takahashi to occupy a broader and more distinctive proportion of the work than in other visual media.
- *Manga to eiga to anime no triangle* – comics, films and cartoons triangle. Takahashi here notes an oscillation of inspiration between three media, in which manga creators funnelled their frustrated ambitions to be movie-makers into their comics, and animators in turn funnelled their frustrated ambitions to be manga creators into their cartoons. Modern films, in turn, draw inspiration from cartoons.

Yamamoto's points are empirically testable, and indeed *have* been tested, by researchers counting the pull-cels, stills and recycled frames in an episode of *Astro Boy* (Kuwahara 2008; Yamamoto and Katō 2009). Takahashi's claims are far more impressionistic and unsupported, except in the sense that they are the memoir of a man who was undoubtedly present when the stylistics of television anime took shape.

His emphasis on the importance of storyboards is an interesting assertion, although this, too, was not unique to Tezuka. In fact, several years earlier, the Tōei studio had made the deliberate decision to storyboard *Saiyūki* before the script was written. There is no way Tezuka, who drew the storyboard himself, could not have known this, or indeed that the storyboard-first style of production was referred to by the Tōei staff as the 'Disney Method' (Minakawa 2009a: 25) – the biggest clue of all that it could not possibly have been Tezuka's idea.

Takahashi's comments on 'distinctive sound production' are confirmed by Sugii Gisaburō, one of the original dissenters at Mushi Pro, who was forced to admit that, while it pained him to see a single frame stretched across three whole seconds, the apparent cheapness was often reduced once sound was added (Tsugata 2007b: 105). Notably, however, when *Astro Boy* was exported, sound production was one of the points that the American localisers sought to improve even further. Fred Ladd found the soundscape on *Astro Boy* to be uninspiring enough to warrant radical interference in the English-language dub, which he spiced up with Foley and clamorous crowd noises. Such audio additions were relatively cheap and simple to introduce, and intended to distract viewers even further from the spartan quality of the visuals.

> Coming from a radio background, I knew we could 'sweeten' the soundtracks to make viewers think they were seeing more than they actually were. For instance, we added traffic sounds (cars whizzing by, horns honking, etc.) to visually static street scenes to 'bring them to life'; similarly we might add the sound of a dog barking or the lonely howl of a faraway train to a night scene. And, where feasible, we added off-screen 'dialogue', usually grunts and other sounds of assent, to fill voids in otherwise still shots. All these touches helped add a sense of life, briskness, energy and 'drive' to the action (Ladd with Deneroff 2009: 23).

There is more, however, to 'distinctive sound production' than realism. By the late 1960s, animators were adding impressionistic sounds in order to distract audiences from the absence of emotion or drama in the images themselves. Tsuji Masaki (1996: 151), for example, notes the introduction of a chiming sound effect, the ringing of metal on metal, every time a volleyball player blinks in *Attack No.1* (1969), emphasising that *this* stare, *this* moment, shows the character concentrating. The same year, Sugii Gisaburō (Oguro 2009: 169) recalls the director Rintarō literally articulating each still in a combat storyboard as little more than a sound effect, pointing at samurai in poses and simply shouting '*Shaan!*', '*Kakeen!*' in lieu of any other description.

Takahashi's comments on 'encoding' are far more provocative, and seem to draw on the vocabulary of semiotics as the basis for a panoply of signs and signifiers in anime – actions, reflexes, dialogue, art styles and even particular shot compositions that are expected to impart general meaning to all anime viewers. Takahashi suggests that whatever visual or textual elements we might isolate as anime tropes, such memes have replicated in part because they are an aid to highly compressed storytelling using severely limited animation. Or to distil his argument even further – anime looks the way it does because of Tezuka.

But Takahashi only gives a single example, and it is Tezuka's 'star system', which is to say, his habit of recycling characters from one story to the next: 'The same character has the same role, mannerisms and expression, regardless of the work itself; this is what we call encoding' (Takahashi 2011: 53; see also Power 2009: 66–88). It is not clear how far Takahashi expects this to apply across the medium as a whole. Does he mean that stereotypes should become archetypes, in which case surely other cultures' cartoons can similarly gravitate towards such obvious tropes as, 'speciesism', the smart kid with the spectacles or the hulking bully? One might argue that such shortcuts and shorthands did develop, but over several years, not with *Astro Boy* alone, but as general 'trended change' across the Japanese television animation industry as a whole – the next chapter will return to this issue.

UNDERVALUATION

The immediate impact of *Astro Boy* had little to do with the way it looked. Far more important to the history of animation in Japan was the way it was sold (i.e. the distribution stage). Tezuka secured the interest of Mannen-sha, an advertising company that, like Dentsū, was in the habit of buying airtime on television in order to ensure advertising slots for its clients. The time-slot eventually assigned to *Astro Boy* could be purchased by Mannen-sha for a cost of 20 million yen a week – a cost to be recouped through the sale to third parties of advertising slots within the programme. Mannen-sha would commit to the 0.5 billion yen a year required to secure the airtime, but was reluctant to pay much for the programme itself. Upon seeing the *Astro Boy* pilot film late in 1962, Mannen-sha was only prepared to offer Tezuka 300,000 yen for each episode (Minakawa 2009a: 248–9). Spread across 'thirty minutes' of television time, this amounted to barely 10,000 yen per minute – an impossibly low price that reportedly left Tezuka crestfallen. The low price estimate was based on Mannen-sha's understanding of the price of imported American cartoons. Since they had already recouped their production costs in the home market, cartoons such as *The Flintstones* (1960–6) and *Popeye* (1960–3) were sold to export markets such as Japan at a cost that made it impossible for local productions to compete.[11] Moreover, a live-action children's show in 1962 would have an average production cost of 600,000 yen; Mannen-sha was working on the assumption that animation could or should work out to half the cost of live-action production.[12]

However, the assistant director of Mannen-sha's Tokyo branch, Komura Ichirō, explained to Tezuka that Mannen-sha's assessment of the value of *Astro Boy* did not preclude attracting other investors to increase its revenue (Minakawa 2009a: 248–9). Mannen-sha's account executive, Anami Kaoru, took the decision to solicit the interest of confectionery companies in sponsoring the *Astro Boy* cartoon. Anami was keen to find a new, untried and untested format for a television show, spurred on in part by the arrival of Nielsen ratings in Japan in 1960, and hoping that the shock of the new would be enough to propel a television show into heights of popularity that would justify high costs for advertising space (Minakawa 2009a: 222). Anami approached the market leader, Morinaga Chocolate, with the offer of a sponsorship deal for *Astro Boy*, ready to discuss everything from simple advertising slots to the selling of space for the company's distinctive 'angel mark' logo at the commencement of each programme.

Morinaga Chocolate, however, was reluctant to take the risk:

> We took a pilot film to Morinaga and showed it to their advertising division. They liked the look but wondered whether we could make the same quality of *Astro Boy* on a weekly basis. They adjudged it to be impossible. If a thirty-minute series missed a single broadcast deadline, 'it was all over' (*banji kyūsu*). This was understandable. The project was said to be a pioneering challenge in uncharted territory. The risk was so great that no one wanted to touch it in the TV world.[13] (Ushio 2007: 230)

Although not stated outright, Morinaga's lack of interest may have been compounded by the fact that Astro Boy was an untested character – the company's pre-existing confectionery was branded with Disney images.

Undeterred, Anami took the idea to Morinaga's biggest rivals, Meiji Seika, inadvertently stepping into the middle of an ongoing conflict over confectionery market share, referred to in the Japanese press as 'the chocolate wars' (Minakawa 2009a: 352).[14] Executives at Meiji Seika were intrigued by the idea of being on board with

Song of Spring (1931) was monochrome but dyed a vibrant pink in its original release, hence placing it within a tradition of 'colour' films. Tinting died out with the advent of sound, as the all-over dyes could corrupt the audio track on a film strip

Magic Boy (1959) used widescreen cels, finally
forcing all the work-groups at Tōei to use their
registration pegs on each frame

One of the critical successes of the turn of the twenty-first century, Satoshi Kon's *Perfect Blue* (1998) lampooned the obsessions of the otaku audience, even as it pandered to many of their interests

Jin-roh: The Wolf Brigade was premiered abroad in 1999 to drum up critical coverage, although its marketers later insisted it was released in the year 2000, in order to make it appear more 'modern' on sales sheets

Despite Miyazaki Hayao's public and frequent refusals to site his work within a limited, TV-focused tradition of 'anime', the global acclaim for his *Spirited Away* (2001) made him a reluctant representative of the medium. Its success led to many false equivalences in the film business, with some rights buyers assuming that its earning potential would be duplicated everywhere from late-night TV to video erotica

Afro Samurai (2007) was conceived at the height of foreign investment in the anime business, but repeated many paradigms of 1960s work-for-hire. Although the original work was already Japanese, the staff were induced to work in an aesthetic style that met the expectations of an *American* audience as to what 'anime' should be

In a globalised anime economy, *Hellsing*
(2006) benefited from a European setting, but
also existed in two incarnations – one for TV
and a later video variant, thought to be closer
in tone and plot to the original manga

Although foreign advertising highlighted the science-fictional content of *The Girl Who Leapt through Time* (2006), its Japanese reception relied upon tradition, as a new adaptation of a well-known 1960s story, and an elegy to the beauty of mundane modern life

Mamoru Hosoda's *Summer Wars* (2009) allegorised life in modern Japan, with traditional family structures under threat from permeable global communication, bringing distant threats into immediate proximity. Artistically, it contrasted realist depictions of the Japanese countryside with hyperreal combat between avatars in cyberspace

Illustrative of the problematic handover of power between the elders of anime and their successors, the poster for *Tales from Earthsea* (2007) highlights it as the work of the studio behind '*Spirited Away* and *Howl's Moving Castle*', skirting around the issue that it was the directorial debut of Miyazaki Hayao's son

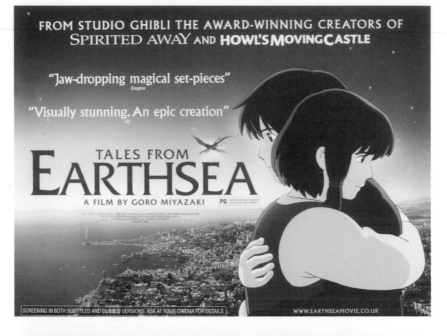

Put into production eight years after the original *Last Exile*, its sequel *Fam the Silver Wing* (2011) demonstrates a continued faith in the strength of the overseas market for anime, despite the doldrums of the first decade of the twenty-first century

Japan's first half-hour animated series and, unknown to Anami, had already been considering buying a half-hour Tuesday-night slot on Fuji TV in order to promote Kinkei Curry (Ushio 2007: 232).

There was an additional, personal connection unmentioned in most sources – Tezuka's colleague Shirakawa Daisaku had a brother working at Fuji TV (Oguro 2004a: 7).[15] It was this connection that smoothed the passage for several early anime productions at Fuji TV and created a committee of Meiji Seika, Fuji TV, Mannen-sha the advertising company and Tezuka's Mushi Pro. It was then that Tezuka, keen to be an animator whatever the cost, made a fateful decision on costs. Testimonies concerning the moment offer widely varying numbers, with the same respondent often changing his figure in several different interviews. But a consensus among the differing sources, including varying accounts by Tezuka himself, suggests that Mannen-sha eventually agreed on a production fee of 550,000 yen, in order for *Astro Boy*'s costs to compare favourably with live-action children's programming, and to undercut potential rivals by setting a price too low for any competitor to match (Minakawa 2009a: 261).[16]

The decision was a watershed moment in the history of Japanese animation, and made Tezuka many enemies in the industry. A story soon ran in the press claiming that Mushi Pro had already spent so much of its budget on the pilot that no money remained to make further episodes (Tezuka 1999: 242–3). This was not too far from the truth, although Tezuka had tried to hide the costs as much as possible by not charging for his own intellectual property – production costs were inevitable, but Tezuka added no additional fee for his role as author.

UNDERSTAFFING AND OUTSOURCING

Tezuka also faced a permanent issue of understaffing. He was able to stem some of the labour issues by outsourcing much of the work to other studios. This did not so much solve the problem as turn it into someone else's, as smaller start-ups such as P Pro and Ōnishi Pro took on piecework in layouts, inbetweening or backgrounds. However, these studios in turn often overestimated their capabilities, and found themselves shunting work on to third or fourth parties. Ishiguro Noboru, for example, who avoided working for Tezuka only to find himself working on *Astro Boy* anyway as a subcontractor at Ōnishi Pro, reported a rash promise to turn an episode around in thirty days, despite a labour requirement of six person-months, causing Ōnishi Pro to outsource the work too (Ishiguro and Ohara 1980: 96). Before long, animators began referring to the show as *Tetsu-ya* (*Up All Night*) *Atom* (Minakawa 2009b: 50).

Nor did the outsourcing solve the central issue of the dearth of available animators. Instead, the 'outsourcing' often involved overtime by staff members who already had day jobs in the industry. Many animators would return to their apartments each evening, only to continue working as freelances on storyboards, key art or layouts for other companies – Ishiguro Noboru claimed to have spent the latter half of the 1960s living a life of such '*animator arbeit*', and that it not only gave the misleading impression that the anime business was coping with the workload, but also pressured some animators into cutting corners on their day jobs in order to cope with their moonlighting (Ishiguro and Ohara 1980: 84).[17]

Crucially for Tezuka, he received the foreign investment for which he had been hoping, with a commitment from the US to order fifty-two episodes of *Astro Boy* (Ladd with Deneroff 2009: 12). Tezuka was waved off to America by his staff at an exuberant send-off, with everyone under the impression that he had sold *Astro Boy* to NBC, one of the three major American television networks at the time (Yamamoto 1989: 119). However, *Astro Boy* was never sold to the NBC network. It was sold to NBC Enterprises, a subsidiary that traded lesser imports to smaller, local markets in syndication (Ladd with Deneroff 2009: 6). It is easy to see why observers might have been confused; NBC Enterprises seems to have been deliberately named to imply a direct affiliation with the NBC network, which probably helped open doors for its representatives all over the world. If such was the intention, then it worked remarkably well, and the incorrect assertion, that *Astro Boy* was broadcast all over America on the NBC network, is common to Japanese accounts (e.g. Misono 1999: 129; Masuda 2011: 47) and is even repeated in the Association of Japanese Animations' own history of anime (AJA 2008 I: 41). NBC Enterprises' promise created a vital financial cushion for the production process; at the time of the broadcast of the inaugural episode, Mushi Production had only four other episodes of *Astro Boy* banked, and only enough money to make another single episode.

However, American involvement also brought requests that diluted Tezuka's original vision, with the animators exhorted to avoid adult themes, nudity and ongoing storylines (Yamamoto 1989: 120). These demands arrived at a greatly dispiriting moment, when Mushi Pro had delivered the first twelve episodes to NBC Enterprises, only to discover that the company's Standards and Practices scrutineers had rejected six of them. Although Fred Ladd, the American localiser, salvaged three of the shows with judicious editing, three could not be broadcast – one on account of scenes of animal vivisection, one for backgrounds containing nude images of women and one for a plot device involving a message scratched into the eyeball of a statue of Christ (Ladd with Deneroff 2009: 35; Minakawa 2009b: 256).[18]

NBC Enterprises never supplied *Astro Boy* to its parent company; instead, it sold it in syndication to independent channels dotted across the US. As a loss leader to generate high ratings, *Astro Boy*'s early episodes were sold at a knockdown price to a New York independent broadcaster WNEW-TV, in order to generate impressive ratings figures in the prestigious New York market (Ladd with Deneroff 2009: 22). This apparent 'popularity' was then enlisted to sell *Astro Boy* into other markets across the US, with its Japanese origin kept discreetly obscure. According to Jim Dodd of NBC Enterprises:

> We don't plan to advertise the fact that the series is being animated in Japan. We're not going to deny it, if anybody asks, but we're not going to publicize it, either. First of all, there are probably some buyers at stations out there who haven't gotten over the fact that Japan was our enemy in World War Two. Second, if a buyer hears that the show is of a Japanese origin, he's going to think it must be cheap … . (Ladd with Deneroff 2009: 21)

Tezuka was encouraged in this himself by the Americans, and soon agreed to feature English-language street signs, even in Tokyo scenes, to ease the transition during the localisation process. He summarised the appeal as 'denationalised' (*mukokuseiteki*), suggesting that its sci-fi setting and sparsely furnished future allowed for an easier transition into foreign markets (Chun 2007: 279). Referred to elsewhere as 'placelessness' (*mukokuseki*), this concept came to form an important element in the articulation of many later anime, with the recognition that the removal of openly 'Japanese' elements, either through setting in exotic foreign locations or characters who appeared Caucasian, would similarly ease the process and encourage foreign sales (Minakawa 2009b: 199–200; Clements 2011a: 312).

There appears to have been a misunderstanding over the nature of the order from NBC Enterprises. Its investment ensured that *Astro Boy* brought in $10,000 per episode, adding roughly 300,000 yen per week to Tezuka's revenue (Ushio 2007: 294). The fifty-two-episode (i.e. year-long) order guaranteed revenue of 54.6 million yen from Japanese and American TV rights, but would only pay for roughly six months of completed episodes. Tezuka assumed that fifty-two episodes was merely the first tranche of an ongoing order, whereas NBC Enterprises saw no need to go beyond the initial order of fifty-two episodes, believed to be more than enough to repeat indefinitely. As a result, Mushi Pro's sales agent arrived in the US to negotiate on the next year's order, only to find that NBC Enterprises had no intention of buying it. Fred Ladd claimed Mushi Pro was now so dependent on the revenue from America that it threatened to sell the next fifty-two episodes of *Astro Boy* to a rival, forcing a compromise in which NBC Enterprises agreed to fifty-two more episodes. Future deals *specified* fifty-two episodes in the original contract, limiting the commitment from NBC Enterprises to a single year (Ladd with Deneroff 2009: 39)

Little of these issues made it back to Japanese personnel, who only heard of American success and continued sales, with the implication that Japanese animation was taking the world by storm.

RATINGS AND REVENUE

In Japan, the first episode of *Astro Boy* was a success, with a rating of 27.4 per cent (Yamamoto 1989: 113).[19] However, nobody in the Japanese animation industry seems to have really understood what this actually meant, and subsequent definitions of 'success' fluctuated wildly between ratings as high as 40 per cent and as low as 15 per cent, depending on how one was counting (Yamamoto 1989: 113, 117–18; compare to Yamazaki 2005: 49;

Tsugata 2012: 75). Success and, indeed, failure was often in the eye of the beholder, as demonstrated by Yamamoto Eiichi, who diligently supplies figures and then misinterprets his own evidence in order to substantiate a consensual pessimism among the Mushi Pro staff. By mid-1966, Yamamoto writes 'the popularity of *Astro Boy* had begun to decline after three and a half years; where once its ratings had peaked at more than 40 per cent, they had now fallen to 27 per cent' (Yamamoto 1989: 205). In making this claim, Yamamoto neglects to qualify his figures, and, like many authorities, conveniently forgets that *Astro Boy*'s remarkable peak rating of 40.3 per cent was generated by a one-off colour test broadcast on 25 January 1964 (Yamamoto 1989: 137; AJA 2008 I: 37). In fact, using Yamamoto's own statistics, we can see that the supposed 'decline' in popularity of *Astro Boy* was a deeply subjective assessment. *Astro Boy* remained about as popular with viewers in 1966 as it had been on the day of its first broadcast, and was merely declining in the affections of its makers, since it was still being produced in the increasingly outdated monochrome format, at a time after the Tokyo Olympics when colour television ownership in Japan had risen sharply. Tezuka even said as much in 1965, when subcontracting *Astro Boy* out to another studio, in order to allow him to concentrate more fully on colour work (Ushio 2007: 250). In fact, by 1965, Tezuka was already being pressured to switch all production over to colour, in order to meet the demands of his American clients (Ladd with Deneroff 2009: 50). Moreover, it is somewhat disingenuous for Yamamoto to claim that ratings were falling in mid-1966, considering not only that ratings always fell during the summer as children spent more time outdoors, but that *Astro Boy* had been killed off in manga form in March of that year, surely likely to lead to a drop in interest (Schodt 2007: 145).

Tezuka also faced far more disappointing results for advertising revenue – a fact that was not immediately apparent, but which slowly became obvious as the 1960s progressed. Tezuka began broadcasting at the pinnacle of post-war growth in Japanese advertising revenues, after which the likely income from commercials largely flattened or declined. Because of the proliferation of new channels and swift rises in TV ownership, Japanese advertising revenue had quadrupled between the years 1958 and 1963. There were even early indicators that his spending spree was paying off with spin-off commissions, such as the offer of an advertising contract using the image of *Astro Boy*. Advertisers were accustomed to notably higher fees, and paid 1 million yen, the cost of two complete episodes of the TV series, for less than a minute of animation (Tsugata 2007b: 133). Between 1963 and 1965, however, the previously stellar growth stagnated. Within six months of the broadcast of *Astro Boy*'s first episode, only pharmaceuticals and food continued to generate increasing revenues, and even then only at a vastly reduced rate compared to the previous rise. Anime benefited in the short term from its association with confectionery, which remained one of the sturdiest areas in advertising. However, the implications of the slump cannot be ignored: Tezuka had bet on a continued bubble market in advertising, only to discover that he was stuck with what he already had (Uchikawa 1980: 243).

RIVALRY AND REACTION

Other companies were soon scrambling to imitate Tezuka's achievement. By September 1963, Fuji TV had broadened its animation remit with a late-night 'adult' show *Village of the Immortals*.[20] Both it and *Tetsujin 28* (1964), also broadcast on Fuji TV, were made by TCJ, a company with a previous output in commercials. Over at Tōei, half a dozen animators were seconded from the ongoing feature-film production of *Gulliver's Space Travels*, and put to work on a TV animation project of their own, *Ōkami Shōnen Ken* (1963, *Wolf Boy Ken*). They were placed under the command of Tsukioka Sadao, a twenty-four-year-old animator, and former associate of Tezuka, who ironically appeared to get the job because he had no experience of working with Tōei's usual production methods. Several older animators were offered the job first, but had claimed it was not possible (Ōtsuka 2001: 112–13).

Astro Boy's reign was seriously challenged in the autumn 1963 TV season, with *Tetsujin 28* (Fuji TV)[21] commencing broadcast on 20 October, *Wolf Boy Ken* on 5 November (NET/Asahi) and *Eightman* (TBS) on 7 November. Moreover, the rival shows swiftly seized a new market in cinemas in the following spring, when selected episodes were shown on a single bill under the umbrella title of the *Ōkami Shōnen Ken Manga Daikōshin* (1964, *Wolf Boy Ken Great Manga Parade*). Meanwhile, since *Wolf Boy Ken* was made by Tōei Dōga, it made its way into cinemas in December 1963, when an episode played on the same bill as Tōei's new

Tezuka had hoped that his austere production would thwart competitors, but *Tetsujin 28* (1963) soon ran against him in the schedules, made by the former advertising company TCJ

animated feature, *Doggie March* – ironically, a feature film that carried Tezuka's name in the credits, as the third and final Tōei production in his original deal.

But Tezuka already had a plan, and instructed his animators that episode #56 of *Astro Boy* would be a backdoor experimental pilot, made in colour. He was nudged in this direction by both his American and Japanese clients, who had made it plain that they would require colour products in future (Ladd with Deneroff 2009: 40).

The episode featured *Astro Boy* travelling to the Moon and helping a squad of Earth Defenders protect the solar system from aliens. The supporting cast were all characters from another Tezuka story, *Number 7*, which was one of the likely candidates for a full-length colour series. The episode was broadcast on 25 January 1964, and *Astro Boy*'s oft-cited peak rating that year, 40.3 per cent, was the result of this gimmick. The colour episode served another purpose in the summer, when it was edited together with the monochrome episodes #46 and #71 to form the first *Astro Boy* 'feature film', *Tetsuwan Atomu: Uchū no Yūsha* (1964, *Astro Boy: Hero of Space*).[22] This not only beat the opposition by being a true feature-length film, but in being partly made in colour, it re-established Tezuka as an innovator in the market (Animage 1989: 43–4).[23]

However, there were still issues. Some exhibitors were reluctant to push *Hero of Space* as a 'real' animated feature, noting that, whether it was in colour or not, it was still little more than three TV episodes cut together. Aside from the issue of managing audience expectations for something that did not match the quality of a Tōei animated feature, *Hero of Space* was carried in the Nikkatsu cinema chain in the summer, discreetly out of competition with Tōei's *Gulliver's Space Travels* in the spring, and instead running against a more properly matched opponent, the second *Wolf Boy Ken Great Parade* (1964) compilation programme (Yamamoto 1989: 139; Animage 1989: 43–4).

The colour experiment was successful. In 1964, Tezuka revealed to his staff that he had secured a commitment from NBC Enterprises to invest in a full-colour animation series, based on his manga *Jungle Emperor*, which had run from 1950–2 in the magazine *Manga Shōnen*. Hence, all other colour TV anime prototypes were suspended, and even *Astro Boy* would be wound down to meet this foreign deal. The story of a lion cub that endures hardships to become the king of the jungle, it had all the quest narrative, pathos and adventure that Tezuka thought necessary for an ongoing success, coupled with an exotic African setting. Referring to the epic, year-long live-action NHK TV serials that were the talk of contemporary broadcasting, Tezuka referred to it as a *taiga dorama manga* (Yamamoto 1989: 151; for *taiga* see Clements and Tamamuro 2003: xviii–xix).

However, there was a price. Determined to avoid the localisation and continuity issues that had troubled some episodes of *Astro Boy*, NBC Enterprises sent a pre-emptive list of directives for Tezuka to follow. These included a request that there be no ongoing story; instead, every episode should have a distinct

Foreign investment in *Jungle Emperor* (1965, *Kimba the White Lion*) compromised Tezuka's plans for the storyline ending, with no episode carrying over into cliffhangers or developing storylines. As a sop to civil- and animal-rights movements, Tezuka was also instructed to avoid any cartoon portrayals of blacks, and not to show any scenes of humans being cruel to animals: this in a drama series involving big-game hunters in Africa (Yamamoto 1989: 153–4). Some, although not all, of these directives were later challenged by the writers of the show, who forced concessions from the producer Yamamoto Eiichi – that animals were permitted to be 'naked' in natural settings, and that the depiction of black characters was permissible, as long as they were presented as 'civilised'; evil characters could still only be white (Tsuji 1996: 79–80). Amid concerns from his staff that the story was already a decade old, and hence possibly out of touch with modern audiences, Tezuka agreed that the first year would concentrate on Leo (Kimba in America) the lion as a cub, in order to avoid continuity issues. A later series, with a separate name, would cover Leo's adulthood.[24]

CRISIS AND MANAGEMENT

In 1964, only a year after *Astro Boy*'s TV debut, Tezuka was already privately admitting that Mushi was following a 'dangerous business model', forced to invest vast amounts in advance for a product that was only sold piecemeal – the broadcaster generally paid for each *completed* episode, rather than the dozen that would already be in various stages of production as each was finished. He had already had to sink his own money into Mushi Pro, as banks were reluctant to invest in the production of a commodity with a variable and unpredictable value. Moreover, since money was not forthcoming for a project at the moment of its inception, Tezuka was already obliged to spend money from another in order to keep the studio running. He therefore attempted some semblance of financial control, budgeting 130 million yen for *Jungle Emperor*, with an estimated cost per episode of 2.5 million yen (Yamamoto 1989: 156).

The pessimist perspective on such brinkmanship is a story of inevitable decline, with Tezuka's undervaluation of his own property instigating a vicious circle of declining returns and budgetary cuts, bolstered only by random injections of revenue from merchandising and foreign sales. This awful flaw was obscured in the early days of TV by the meteoric success surrounding the new shows of the early and mid-1960s. The shock of the new propelled the monochrome *Astro Boy*, and then the colour *Jungle Emperor* into ratings successes, although competitors soon diluted their achievements. There are, after all, only a finite number of children, which means only a finite number of lunchboxes, dolls and toys to sell each year. As more serials competed for attention, Tezuka's market share was eroded, and he was obliged to fund the production of one show's deficit with the

Tezuka's *1001 Nights* (1969) was an unsuccessful attempt to pay off debts by appealing to the adult market

advance money from the next. Meanwhile, from the very outset, his serials were unable to profit solely on sponsorship and broadcast. They demanded merchandising and foreign sales in order to survive, and it only took a single disappointment to expose the dangerous financial model followed at Mushi Pro.

By the end of the 1960s, Tezuka was turning his back on television, investing his hopes in the world of films for grown-ups, on the understanding that the cinema market in general was still bigger for adults than it was for children. When *Sen'ya Ichiya Monogatari* (1969, *1001 Nights*)[25] failed to recoup its production costs, Mushi Pro was spiralling into danger, and was so fragile that the economic downturn in the early 1970s destroyed it. However, Mushi Pro was not the only corporation affected by such issues; even Tōei Dōga was laying off staff in the early 1970s (Funamoto 1998: 32). Advertising and sponsorship, too, were diluted across multiple channels and properties, and would never repeat the rapid revenue rise of the early years 1958–63.

When the release of *1001 Nights* failed to turn into the hoped-for international success, the net shortfall on Tezuka's budget receipts was 9.1 million yen. He was forced to amortise this loss onto his next film, *Cleopatra* (1970, *Cleopatra: Queen of Sex*),[26] squeezing an already tight budget, disenchanting an already overworked staff[27] and creating an even less realistic sales target for the production to break even (Yamamoto 1989: 268). But, as with discussions of TV ratings, things look different when appraised with the eyes of industry accountants. The budget shortfall on *1001 Nights* is minimal by early twenty-first-century standards, to the extent that a modern big-name anime feature can easily make such amounts back from a minimum guarantee for a single foreign territory's video rights. Was Tezuka really wrong, or was he merely tragically ahead of his time? Ten years after the collapse of Mushi Pro with debts of 220 million yen, the shape of the film industry would be transmuted forever by the new markets of video and cable, rendering a completed property such as *1001 Nights* an asset, rather than a liability (Vogel 2007: 92, fig 3.9).

AHEAD OF HIS TIME?

There is remarkably little published about the actual collapse of Mushi Production. Even Minakawa Yūka's modern two-volume account of the studio, which has the uncompromising subtitle 'The rise and fall of Japanese animation', concerns itself almost entirely with the rise, and barely alludes to the fall in its closing pages (Minakawa 2009b). Animator memoirs concern themselves largely with the boom time, and not with the departures of staff and contraction of capabilities of the late 1960s and early 1970s. Only Yamamoto Eiichi is truly, bluntly honest about Mushi's doldrums, but even he brings his narrative to a close before the hard times of the early 1970s. Narratives of or by Tezuka Osamu tend to gloss over the period, not the least because Tezuka himself remained active – Mushi Pro might have failed, but his new company Tezuka Productions continued to trade, making anime TV specials throughout the 1970s, and presumably had the power to withhold work from those who embarked upon negative commemorations.

The early 1970s, it seems, were such unpleasant times for Japanese animators that few had the time or inclination to chronicle them in detail. Most accounts of the period draw a veil over the last days of Mushi Pro, partly for aesthetic reasons, as there is little of lasting value to discuss except, perhaps, for the cash-strapped production of Yamamoto Eiichi's *Kanashimi no Belladonna* (1973, *Tragedy of Belladonna*), so limited in its budget as to be described by its own director as a 'patchwork film' (Yamamoto 1989: 323) and by Tsugata Nobuyuki (2007b: 160) as 'inanimate animation' (*udokanai animation*). As Sugii Gisaburō put it:

> That was the fall in a real sense. *Belladonna* was the last piece that Mushi Pro made with its art-orientation. Originally, [making something arty in commercial films] was what Mushi Pro was and what Mr Tezuka wanted. (Tsugata 2007b: 235)

Partly, it is for reasons of nescience – there were few direct witnesses to the meetings and arguments that must have characterised Mushi's slide into bankruptcy, and those witnesses who have gone on the record about the period were only bystanders – Ishiguro Noboru, for example, who was working at another studio, or Takahashi Ryōsuke, who was conveniently abroad for the worst of it. Partly, one suspects, it is for a subset of reluctant memory, which is to say that the period saw several incidences of sleight-of-hand and legal skulduggery, by notoriously litigious figures, whose continued presence suppressed further testimonies (Clements 2010b).

Ushio Sōji, the founder of P Pro, who entered Japanese TV animation in imitation of Tezuka and soon discovered the flaws in his business model, articulates Tezuka's failure as a combination of arrogance, ignorance and naiveté, beginning with his wilful undervaluation of his product.

> Tezuka Osamu's words set the standard for anime pricing within the Japanese television business, and Tezuka himself suffered from it. He had to face a deficit of one and a half million yen per episode … 6.45 million yen a month. Mushi Pro did what we call 'a warrior's business' (*buke no shōhō*). (Ushio 2007: 236)

Contrary to many expectations, in a post-modern era that valorises the Japanese work ethic and samurai management, the term 'warrior business' is far from complimentary. It is a phrase from nineteenth-century Japanese slang, alluding to the many impoverished samurai who turned, too little and too late, to commoner commerce, only to discover that their brash self-confidence was of no use in a business environment.

Tomino Yoshiyuki claims (2002: 172) that, as a young production assistant at Mushi Pro, he would pointedly address Tezuka as *shachō* (boss) rather than *sensei* (an honorific for artists), in an unsuccessful attempt to instil some managerial sense in his employer. He also suggests (2002: 164) that the business manager Anami Kaoru, the broker of *Astro Boy*'s groundbreaking distribution deal, was well aware of Tezuka's shortcomings, and plotting to edge him out of operations – a scheme aborted by Anami's sudden death in December 1966. In Tomino's version of events, it was Anami's level head that calmed a labour dispute in Mushi's Number Three studio (the cash-strapped tail-end of the unloved *Astro Boy* production); Anami who planned to diversify into a theme park; and Anami who hoped to increase the company's revenue by taking on non-Tezuka work. At least as far as Tomino is concerned, Anami's death was the beginning of the end, in that it deprived Tezuka of the one man who might have steered him through the coming crises.

Popular myth holds that Tezuka Osamu was a creative genius, but not a businessman, although there is some evidence that he was notably ahead of his competitors in terms of crisis management. After all, *Snow White and the Seven Dwarfs* had been a leap of faith on the part of Disney, and one with a cost of almost $1.5 million dollars in 1937 (Barrier 1999: 229). Once ridiculed in Hollywood as 'Disney's Folly', it would have bankrupted its creator if it had failed at the box office. Tezuka's gamble with Mushi Pro, when set against Disney's with *Snow White*, seems almost conservative by comparison. He was simply not as lucky. Moreover, Tezuka himself claimed to be fully aware of the financial pressures and risks that Disney had faced. In his own memoirs, written in the 1980s and published posthumously, so possibly only wise in hindsight, he wrote: 'Disney was said to be rich, but he rarely had any cash. He borrowed from banks; he borrowed from people; he mortgaged his land and house to get money' (Tezuka 1997: 114). Tezuka the profligate spender, who essentially bought a talent base off the shelf by poaching employees from Tōei, is a world away from Tezuka the penny-pinching businessman, reduced to dropping an outsourcing studio because another company was just five yen per cel cheaper (Shibayama and Kobayashi 2009: 106).

If Tezuka was misled by *Astro Boy*'s early success into investing too much in a flawed business model, then he was not alone in the Japanese animation industry. In fact, it was Tezuka who seems to have first appreciated the limited shelf life of monochrome animation, and who was first with a colour TV pilot – the experimental episode #56 of *Astro Boy*, which helped secure his swift deal from NBC Enterprises for a year's worth of *Jungle Emperor*. If one regards the collapse of Mushi Pro in 1973 as part of a larger, recessional malaise, can Tezuka really be held responsible for the company's demise? Instead of standing, baffled, at the helm of his sinking ship, he made careful efforts to separate it into discrete corporate entities as early as 1966 – the same year as Tōei's contractual restructuring. As production began on *Ribon no Kishi* (1967, *Princess Knight*), Tezuka noted that all the company's successes since *Astro Boy* relied on merchandising and foreign deals to take the company out of deficit and into profit. Accordingly, he restructured so that a new company, Mushi Pro Shōji (Mushi Pro Commercial Affairs), based in a rented office building near Ikebukuro, collected payments and then hired separate corporate entities, including Mushi Production, to produce the work (Yamamoto 1989:

212). A similar satellite entity was the manga company Tezuka Productions (Tezuka Pro), incorporated in 1968, which would be the eventual inheritor of Tezuka's estate. Tezuka stood down as Mushi's company president in 1971, severing the direct relationship that had led Mushi to adapt many of his works in earlier years, but also freeing Mushi to adapt works by other creators, such as *The Moomins* and *Tomorrow's Joe* (Yamamoto 1989: 270).[28]

Tezuka's move into adult-oriented films in 1968–70 might appear with hindsight to be a deluded, doomed venture, but it represented no greater risk than his initial gamble on *Astro Boy*, and prefigured that of Ralph Bakshi in America, whose *Fritz the Cat* (1972) would make a fortune. Unlike many fellow producers, Tezuka was at least eagerly searching for a new source of revenue, and hoped to find it in foreign markets for *1001 Nights* and *Cleopatra*. His pursuit of adult themes mirrored that of the contemporary softcore erotic films, the *pink eiga*, which would form one of the few lucrative areas in live-action Japanese cinema in the 1970s. His decision to under-value his own product forced him and all his successors to approach television animation ever after as a medium that demanded direct and invasive contacts with merchandise and marketing. He deliberately chose foreign stories and settings in order to create a commodity whose Japanese origins could be occluded with the replacement of its original language track – the very basis of many 1970s coproductions. He similarly stated that animation, by its very 'placeless' nature, could carry Japanese artistic works abroad in a manner that would be forever closed to live-action entertainments – a fundamental part of anime's foreign success in the 1980s. Moreover, he sought foreign sales as the core of his revenue (Yamamoto 1989: 233) – the basis of anime's booms and busts in the 1990s and 2000s.

Hence, it is no wonder that Tezuka is often credited as the creator of 'anime', as distinct from 'Japanese animation'. As noted by Tsugata Nobuyuki (2011b: 30), Tezuka's arrival in the industry created a series of structures, assumptions and expectations that Japanese TV animation in particular would never shake off. There are suggestions in other animators' testimonies that Tezuka's cost-cutting measures were largely based on common sense, and merely refined several production practices common since the 1930s, and that several other producers, such as Tsukioka Sadao at Tōei and Ushio Sōji at P Pro, could and did independently reach similar conclusions (Ōtsuka 2001: 112–13; Ushio 2007: 236). However, they did so in reaction to Tezuka's invasion of the marketplace, and in reaction to the most revolutionary of all his decisions: setting the notional value of anime as a fraction of its actual production cost. This radical decision, damning television anime even as it made it feasible, marked a permanent revolution in the Japanese animation industry that still reverberates today.[29]

Despite cavils from some quarters that Tezuka merely put his name to changes that would surely have happened anyway, his production of *Astro Boy* flung open the doors to an entirely new market for Japanese animation. Television dominated the medium for the next twenty years, although disruptions to the industry and new developments in technology would refine the initial look of Mushi Pro's 'limited' animation, augmenting it with new tropes and flourishes that arguably created the basis of an 'anime style'. It is these developments that form the basis of the next chapter.

NOTES

1. JCD 8182.
2. JCD 9091. A second entry for the same film, JCD 10788, suggests that it was re-released in 1968.
3. JCD 9601.
4. Serikawa Yūgo, an animator at Tōei, turns traditional assumptions on their head by suggesting that the revolution did not 'begin' with *Astro Boy*, so much as a previous paradigm 'ended' with the production of Tōei's *Wanpaku Ōji no Orochi Taiji* (1963, *Little Prince and the Eight-headed Dragon*), which Serikawa directed himself. He thus articulates Tezuka's sudden rise as the filling of a vacuum created by the absence of Tōei, rather than any particular innovation on the part of Tezuka (Oguro 2004c: 2). *Little Prince* had a distinctly angular, 'modern' style, and was in production at the same time as the first episodes of *Astro Boy*.

5. DAW 47.

6. Tsugata Nobuyuki suggests that if Tezuka and Miyazaki were ever left in a room together, the feeling would have been mutual. He attempts to back this up with suggestions of how Tezuka *might* have criticised Miyazaki in return, citing as evidence some nebulous comments made in the early 1980s, and the plausible speculation by one of Tezuka's assistants that, although he said very little about Miyazaki, he seemed somewhat jealous of all the attention received by Miyazaki's *Nausicaä* (1984) (Tsugata 2004: 36–8, 45).

7. Steinberg (2006: 198–9) includes mouth flaps as a subset of sectioning, not as a separate development as listed in Yamamoto. As other examples of sectioning, eye blinks (*me-pachi*), might also be included, as they are cited elsewhere as another of Tezuka's cost-cutting measures (Kanō 2004: 223). Tsuji Masaki (1996: 18) adds *ashi-teke* or foot blurs as yet another example.

8. This would be nothing unusual in modern anime, especially considering that many contemporary shows have a seasonal 'recap' episode that similarly recycles footage and adds little that is new. Notably, such corner cutting was easier on *Astro Boy*, with its robot hero and its minimalist sci-fi furnishings, than it was on some later cartoons. When Mushi Pro branched into colour television with *Jungle Emperor*, a cast of four-legged talking animals proved significantly harder to animate economically (Yamamoto 1989: 173). A similar realisation in 1912 convinced John Randolph Bray that it was futile for him to attempt to adapt his comic strip, *The Teddy Bears*, into animation because of the sheer number of main characters. His attempt to get around the problem, however, was instrumental in his invention of the cel animation process (Crafton 1982: 143).

9. Combined use, for example, is implicit in the use of animation on cels since the 1930s. An early form of sectioning was a primary feature of J. Stuart Blackton's *Humorous Phases of Funny Faces*, which added a cardboard arm to its blackboard depiction of a man raising his hat, that 'relieved Blackton of having to redraw the arm for each exposure' and also of Raoul Barré's 1912 'slash system' (Crafton 1982: 23, 194). In fact, very little of Tezuka's supposed innovation is absent from Lutz's *Animated Cartoons* (1920), and hence would have been known, if not actively employed, by Kitayama Seitarō and his disciples since the mid- to late 1920s.

10. Takahashi employs the same English-loanword term used by Tezuka in contemporary interviews. Tezuka's insistence on the term 'bank system', and the context in which he used it, seemed deliberate, as if he were reinforcing the notion with his colleagues and financiers that every image saved was literally 'banked' for future use, and hence constituted a concrete investment (Minakawa 2009a: 312).

11. Minakawa notes that the cost of producing the *Astro Boy* pilot appears to have been 1.2 million yen. The cost of producing finished episodes of *Astro Boy* was estimated at 2.5 million yen. Since the 'pilot' was reportedly shown to Mannen-sha in September, some time before the first episode was officially completed, it seems likely that the pilot only comprised half an episode's footage in September 1962.

12. In comparison, Misono (1999: 13) puts the cost of an episode of the live-action superhero show *Gekkō Kamen* (1958, *Moonlight Mask*) at half a million yen.

13. Morinaga's lack of faith in Japanese capabilities was shortlived. The company swiftly changed its tune and invested in the next property offered to it: Tōei's *Wolf Boy Ken* (Yamazaki 2005: 86).

14. Tezuka (1999: 241) coyly does not name Morinaga in his memoirs, instead referring to it as 'M' – as if it were not immediately obvious which chocolate company he meant.

15. At the time, Shirakawa was working for Tōei. His wife was working for Mushi Pro (Oguro 2004a: 4).

16. Minakawa (2009a: 259) notes that Mannen-sha was prepared to offer Tezuka 1.2 million yen per episode, but that Tezuka shocked everyone by naming his own price of 550,000 yen, deliberately calculated to undercut the cost of the average live-action children's show by 50,000 yen per episode. However, there is some confusion over the 1.2 million yen amount, as this was also the amount that Meiji Seika paid to Mannen-sha, and was thought to include the cost of production, and broadcast fees and the 20 per cent rake-off that Mannen-sha put on top (Minakawa 2009a: 264). Yamamoto (1989: 94) and Misono (1999: 14) claim that Tezuka may have charged a more substantial, but still unprofitable, 750,000 yen. Tsugata (2007b: 124) notes the discrepancy between Tezuka's figures and Yamamoto's, but also another testimonial that suggests an actual fee of 1.55 million yen, the existence of which was supposedly kept secret from Tezuka (by Anami Kaoru and Imai Yoshiaki) in order to let him believe that he was charging only a third of that amount. Tsugata himself remarks that this seems not only unlikely but potentially corrupt.

17. The German *arbeit,* transliterated as *arubaito,* is used in Japanese to mean part-time work. The problem was not limited to the art, either. Tsuji Masaki (1996: 24) had to use pseudonyms on several of his anime scripts to avoid potential conflicts of interest with rival licensors.

18. The total number of rejected episodes from *Astro Boy*'s first year was eventually five (Minakawa 2009b: 258). For a comparison with the way standards and practices affected other animators, see Cohen (1997: 135).

19. A cynic might argue that, since there were five television channels in operation at the time, a rating that suggested *Astro Boy* garnered little more than a quarter of all viewers in its time-slot was far from impressive, and in fact only marginally better than average. In 1963, a year in which foreign television still dominated the Japanese airwaves, Lucille Ball in *The Lucy Show* (1962–8) was still able to gain a rating of 31.0 per cent on the rival channel TBS, and the Hanna-Barbera cartoon show *The Jetsons* (1962–88) pulled 29.1 per cent on NHK later in the year. In the year of *Astro Boy*'s supposed meteoric success, the American medical drama series *Ben Casey* (1961–6) still commanded 50 per cent and local professional wrestling 45.8 per cent (Inui 1988: 82; NHK Hōsō Bunka Kenkyūsho 2003: 299).

20. *Village of the Immortals* was the first of the 'late-night anime', a subset of broadcast animation that would not achieve true prominence until the late 1990s. Sagisu Tadayasu (Misono 1999: 338–9) asserts that, far from being made in reaction to *Astro Boy*, *Village of the Immortals* was already in production at the time that work began on *Astro Boy*, and that Tezuka even visited TCJ to see how the work was going. However, it seems unlikely because, if that were the case, episodes of *Village of the Immortals* would have sat around on the shelf, unbroadcast, for nine months. Since it was an 'adult' animation, it had difficulty attracting sponsors, pushing subsequent animation producers back into the children's market.

21. Minakawa (2009b: 305) reports a rumour that *Tetsujin 28* only went into production in the first place as insurance in case a fire at Mushi Pro shut down the production of episodes on *Astro Boy* and created a gap in the television schedules.

22. JCD 9783. There is another version of this story that rearranges cause and effect, suggesting that Tezuka originally *planned* a full-length colour feature, but abandoned it partway and repurposed the partially complete footage as the colour 'test' episode of *Astro Boy*.

23. The film remains tantalisingly obscure, although in 1964 it travelled as far as the Yugoslavian Children's Film Festival. It has never been released in translation, although it was shown at London's Barbican Cinema in September 2009, with a live translation performed by Jonathan Clements.

24. Tezuka's original *Jungle Emperor* business proposal to NBC Enterprises is reprinted in Ladd with Deneroff (2009: 53–62).

25. JCD 11113.

26. JCD 11434.

27. Sasakado Nobuyoshi recalls that as a young animator on the ill-fated Mushi movies, he was reduced to less than three hours' sleep a night, and obliged to draw 200 cels a day by the time the studio shut down (AJA 2008 I: 76).

28. In fact, as noted in Chapter 5, Mushi had already been taking foreign money for below-the-line work on other properties, such as the Rankin/Bass Christmas special *Frosty the Snowman*.

29. Steinberg (2012: 40) calls it 'Tezuka's curse'. Masuda (2007: 147) suggests that, if Tezuka had had all the facts in 1963, he would have waited ten years to enter the anime business, at a point when his ownership of the intellectual property would have made him truly unassailable.

7 THE BROWN SCREEN
Trended change in Japanese animation 1966–83

The 1970s brought changes to the Japanese animation industry at the levels of ownership (sponsors and advertisers), production (animation technology) and access (audiences). Anime became considerably more diverse in the early 1970s, even as a general recession led all studios to cut back. Mushi Pro filed for bankruptcy, scattering its animators to new studios such as Office Academy, Sunrise and Madhouse. Similar start-ups offered refuge for victims of a new round of putsches at Tōei Dōga, as the studio tried to thin its full-time staff even further, replacing many tiers of the process with subcontractors (Funamoto 1998: 32).

Tōei's actions were entirely in keeping with the Japanese management tradition of 'shoulder-tapping' (*kata-takaki*), whereby employees would be quietly asked to leave in order to reduce the expense to a troubled company (Whitehill 1991: 133). Okuyama Reiko, who was a victim of one such purge, noted (Kanō 2004:107) that at least part of the problem was continued union agitation, and the fact that full-time staff were still paid a flat rate, regardless of how many frames they produced. With some workers on a go-slow, only producing a few cels a day, the company was bleeding money.

According to Okuyama, the shop steward Miyazaki Hayao had raised this issue with management, only to be accused of being elitist by his own union for suggesting that people should only be paid for what they achieved (Kano 2004: 107).[1] Miyazaki and Kotabe, Okuyama's husband, quit the company. Others were asked to leave, and ninety animators were laid off. This chapter charts the fortunes of the members of this last diaspora from Tōei and their contemporaries, as they struggled to compete in a marketplace in which art was entirely subordinate to commerce. It does so with special consideration of the narrative of a new 'chronology', formed by the occasions on which animated works were featured on the cover of the Japanese edition of the *TV Guide*. It also considers the development of 'anime style' in the light of the concept of 'trended change', as delineated by Leonard B. Meyer (1996: 102), as the result of an ongoing discourse between historical contexts and individual creatives, technological innovations and financial necessities. Meyer (1996: 69) notes: '[A] chronological arrangement of style traits will not give rise to a history of style unless hypotheses relate the traits not only to one another, but also to the reasons why the traits were chosen.'

There was, assuredly, no secret midnight meeting between members of the animation industry, in which shadowy figures voted and agreed on how 'anime' was going to look. Despite occasional assertions to the contrary, there was no single eureka moment, when a single figure suddenly hit upon all the tropes that make 'anime' what it is. Nobody can even agree, even today, exactly what 'anime' is, although there is some consensus (Tsugata 2004: 78; Steinberg 2012: 108–9) that its most distinctive elements reached their tipping point between the mid-1960s and mid-1970s.

CONTINUITY OF STRUCTURES

Despite such upheavals at the production level, several mainstays of production, distribution and exhibition continued untroubled in the 1970s, maintaining an equilibrium of their own while newer companies struggled over peripheral areas. Several studios, for example, maintained contacts abroad that kept them in below-the-line production work (see Chapter 5). Tōei Dōga, meanwhile, continued to release animated films, as it had done since the 1960s, foregoing large-scale features in favour of anthology cinema 'events' such as the Tōei Cartoon Festival (1964–90, *manga matsuri*), a children's vacation special, usually in the spring and summer, combining a short original film with several repurposed episodes or spin-offs from pre-existing television serials. Tōei's Cartoon Festivals ran in competition with Tōhō's similar Champion Festivals (1968–78, *champion matsuri*), quarterly anthology events in cinemas, timed to coincide with school vacations, and often mixing animated content with live-action material such as *Godzilla* films.[2]

Panda Go Panda (1971) is remembered today because of its creators' later fame, and the existence of a sequel that augmented it to feature length on video

In both cases, we can see structures, established in the 1950s and 1960s, continuing without disruption. Relationships between the two companies and the exhibition sector allowed them to continue to exploit their properties, and to create programmes that treated cinemas as a kids' club or television away from home. However, the *matsuri* often fall through the cracks in methodology. Many were strongly tied to the continuity of the TV shows of the day, and hence have limited aesthetic appeal outside that context. Since many were not exclusively animated events, they may also escape the notice of researchers who cling to a methodology that concentrates solely on the tradition of animation. Since many of the new works were below a standard feature length, many went unreleased on VHS, and hence disappeared beneath the nescience of the video era – Tōei did not begin re-releasing *manga matsuri* programmes on DVD until August 2012. One notable exception is *Panda Go Panda* (1971, 1973), which has survived partly because its two instalments could be combined into a substantial length for video, but largely because of the industry's subsequent desire to commemorate and exploit the reputations of its makers, Takahata Isao and Miyazaki Hayao.

A similar equilibrium was maintained on primetime television by Eiken, the animation division of TCJ, which achieved blue-chip status with the broadcast of the inaugural episode of *Sazae-san* (1969), an animated comedy series that continues to run to this day. Aesthetically, *Sazae-san*'s humour and parochial perspective has made it unsuitable for foreign broadcast – it seems unfair to call it bland, although its very mildness is surely one of the factors that allows it to remain part of the televisual wallpaper more than forty years after its first broadcast.

Where science-fiction anime might remain 'placeless', *Sazae-san* was deliberately 'timeless', with its writers urged to ensure that it made no reference to negative news items, and featured no modern slang, no bad language or electronic devices (Tsuji 1996: 292). Although its imagery seemed simple on the surface, the scripts were often three or four times longer than equivalent time-frames in other shows, owing to the amount of incident packed in (Tsuji 1996: 295). Notably, *Sazae-san* has been running on Japanese TV for half a century, but only generated a handful of video spin-offs (Takahashi and Nunokawa 2011: 309). It is a permanent feature of Japanese life, screened in primetime, watched by a multigenerational audience, and with a peak rating of 39.4 per cent (Hiramatsu 2000: 446). Despite the attempt to establish its 'timelessness', it has been running so long that its basic form is out of step with modernity – *Sazae-san*'s family is significantly larger than the modern norm. Although Eiken was involved in several dozen other productions in the intervening years, *Sazae-san*'s ongoing status allowed the company to largely cease its quest for new markets or indeed new technology – by 2007, *Sazae-san* was reportedly the very last Japanese animation series still made with old-fashioned cels instead of digital animation (Asahi Shinbun 2007).

However, in the cases of continued below-the-line work for Rankin/Bass, Tōei's events in cinemas or *Sazae-san* on TV, there is little 'development' to discuss. In business terms, such works had an enduring, blue-chip value, and needed no innovation. In the period under study, such mainstream events were examples of Japanese animation in a state of equilibrium, in possession of a relatively safe revenue stream or venue of exhibition. It is elsewhere in the Japanese animation industry, amid the fervid competition of commercial channels and the untapped potential of 'context-integrated' broadcasting, that the period's true innovation and evolution can be found.

DISCONTINUITIES AND DISSONANCES

In the final episode of *Flanders no Inu* (1975, *Dog of Flanders*), the protagonist Nello stumbles into Antwerp Cathedral and gazes in wonder at Rubens's triptych of *The Elevation of the Cross*. This seems to have been an aesthetic issue that troubled the production staff, as seeing the paintings is supposed to represent the pinnacle of Nello's life and yearnings – the episode itself is called 'Tenshi-tachi no E' (Pictures of Angels), denoting both the Rubens paintings and the fact that Nello will only gaze upon them at the moment of his own death. The staff, under director Kuroda Masao, chose to use photographic representations of Rubens's actual paintings, confronting the flat-coloured, simply drawn cartoon images of Nello and his dog with the intricate Baroque style of the originals. It is unsurprisingly jarring in a cartoon, accentuating the rough, simple, 'limited' quality of the animation, and presenting it in cruel contrast to the triptych – a single 'background' image, on which Rubens worked for a year, set off against images drawn at a rate of dozens a day by the animators.

There had been other juxtapositions of 'live' imagery with cel animation. *Star of the Giants*, for example, had once famously set an animated foreground against a background composed from World War II archive footage. A later sequence showed a photograph of a genuine 'red paper' call-up slip, similarly imparting realism to flashback scenes (Tsuji 1996: 151). But such gimmicks could not hide – in fact, were more likely to emphasise – the fact that anime's general style was now well established as a sideways turn away from reality. Limited animation and developments in technology and production practice had turned Japanese television animation into a medium of its own, with its own rules and traditions.

In the finale of *Dog of Flanders* (1975), the hero is confronted with a Rubens painting, depicted in the anime with photographs of the original

TABLE 7.1: CARTOONS ON THE COVER OF JAPAN'S *TV GUIDE* 1963–84

DATE	COVER CARTOON
7 June 1963	*Astro Boy*
4 October 1963	*The Jetsons* (*Uchū Kaizoku Jetson* – US)
5 February 1965	*Tom and Jerry* (US)
5 March 1965	*Astro Boy*
13 August 1965	*Wonder Three*
12 November 1965	*Jungle Emperor*
4 February 1966	*Qtaro the Ghost*
11 February 1966	*Jungle Emperor*
18 February 1966	*Wonder 3*
25 February 1966	*Astro Boy*
24 March 1967	*Songoku no Daibōken* (*Sun Wukong's Great Adventure*)
10 May 1968	*Star of the Giants* – baseball
2/9 May 1969	*Star of the Giants* (double issue)
8 August 1969	*Star of the Giants*
12 December 1969	*Tiger Mask* (pro wrestling)
6 February 1970	*Attack No. 1* (girls' volleyball)
27 February 1970	*Tiger Mask*
20 March 1970	*Mōretsu Ataro* (*Exaggerator Ataro* – comedy)
3 April 1970	*Star of the Giants*
22 May 1970	*Akikichi no Eleven* (*Hot-blooded Eleven* – soccer)
16 April 1971	*Star of the Giants**
22 December 1972	*Moomin*
9 March 1973	*Sazae-san*
21 December 1973	*Kagaku Ninjatai Gatchaman* (*Battle of the Planets*)
1 February 1974	*Mazinger Z*
8 February 1974	*Alps no Shōjo Heidi* (*Heidi, the Girl of the Alps*)
1 March 1974	*Miracle Shōjo Limit-chan* (*Limit the Miracle Girl*)
19 August 1977	*Manga Mukashibanashi* (*Cartoon Fairy Tales*)
27 October 1978	*Uchū Senkan Yamato* (*Space Cruiser Yamato*)
26 January 1979	*Akage no Anne* (*Anne of Green Gables*)
11 May 1979	*Shin Kyojin no Hoshi* (*New Star of the Giants*)
28 September 1979	*Anne Frank Monogatari* (*Story of Anne Frank*)
7 March 1980	*Kagaku Ninjatai Gatchaman, Doraemon* and *Koguma no Mischa* (*Mischa the Bear Cub*)
1 August 1980	*Uchū Senkan Yamato* (*Space Cruiser Yamato*)
24 September 1982	*Mobile Suit Gundam*
30 March 1984	*Lupin III*

Note: *with Shimamoto Kōhei from the Nankai Hawks.
Source: (Hiramatsu 2000: 16–26, 122–36, 218–32)

CONTENT AND THEMES: A MULTIPLICATION OF GENRES

Cartoon imagery appeared on the cover of Japan's *TV Guide* on three dozen occasions between 1963 and 1984, before a change in cover policy favoured only live-action images – see Table 7.1.

The simple list of cover subjects offers a new perspective on the landmark shows of the period, and the same sort of 'implied editorialisation' discerned by Hayden White (1987: 6–7) in all such chronicles.

The apparent narrative revealed by *TV Guide* cover imagery breaks down into several distinct periods: first of American imports giving way to science-fiction and fantasy products from Tezuka's Mushi Pro (1963–5), then of Mushi Pro's continued dominance, challenged by Tokyo Movie (1965–7). There is a sudden switch in interest (1968–71), with SF shows dumped in favour of a rush of sporting anime, including baseball, wrestling, volleyball and soccer. An interregnum from spring 1971 to the very end of 1972 sees no anime at all, and then a patchy period of shows without a particular unifying theme. However, the final period (1973–84) sees a multiplication of shows, seemingly split between merchandise-oriented action shows aimed at boys, and gentler pastorals aimed at girls. The last show to appear is the criminal caper *Lupin III*, before animation disappears from the cover of the *TV Guide* thereafter.

We must be cautious with this narrative. In general, the appearance of an anime show on the cover of *TV Guide* is an indication of its popularity, made partway through its run or even towards its finale, and usually in reflection of a TV rating above 30 per cent (Hiramatsu 2000: 446). *TV Guide* is not a magazine dedicated to Japanese animation, but a mainstream, middlebrow publication that generally featured a cartoon only once a year. Hence, the cover of *TV Guide* is perhaps regarded as an exclusive club, admission to which requires a Japanese cartoon to obtain ratings twice as high as the period average – an achievement itself implying an extraordinary viewership far from the norm. Moreover, an anime must also be in the right place at the right time; *TV Guide*'s adult readership mainly favours live action, and the magazine is under no obligation to commemorate every successful anime, so several similarly highly rated shows from the period, such as *Dokonjō Gaeru* (1979, *The Gutsy Frog*) and *Doctor Slump* (1981) do not appear on the cover at all. *TV Guide* presents a snapshot of how Japanese animation looked to an 'audience' that for the most part ignored it and, while it offers glimpses of changes during the period, it would be a gross error of practice to rely solely on *TV Guide* for an appraisal of TV animation.

Initial TV serials in the wake of *Astro Boy* imitated its general themes of boys' adventure and science fiction or fantasy. Misono (1999: 18) suggests that this initial content began to broaden in 1966, with the arrival of the comedy *Osomatsu-kun* (1966) and serials aimed at a female audience such as *Mahō Tsukai Sally* (1966, *Little Witch Sally*). However, some clarification is required lest Misono's choice of date seem arbitrary. There were, of course, funny moments in television cartoons before 1966. There were, of course, female viewers before 1966. Misono's choice of *Osomatsu-kun*, the story of mischievous sextuplets, reflects less the presence of gags than the absence of fantasy or science-fictional components. Unlike the talking animals of *Hustle Punch* (1965), or the ghostly protagonist of *Obake no Qtarō* (1965, *Qtarō the Ghost*), *Osomatsu-kun*'s situations, however far-fetched, were firmly grounded in the real world. It is, perhaps, the very danger that this presented for imitation among its viewers that led to parent–teacher associations (PTAs) across Japan criticising it as 'the worst of programmes' (Animage 1988: 12).[3] Episodes of *Osomatsu-kun* present children, typically lacking adult supervision, playing with fire, attempting to cook, larking about on rooftops and raiding knife-drawers. As in other countries, there was a concern that such 'imitable' situations, presented in cartoon form without real-world consequences, constituted a dangerous precedent (Cohen 1997: 133–4). *Little Witch Sally*, it seems, got off more lightly, spared the accusations of satanism and witchcraft that hounded similar programmes in Christian America (Cohen 1997: 133). *Little Witch Sally* opened a new discourse in Japanese animation, with the first steps in bifurcating what had previously been regarded as a '*children's*' market into separate thematic strands for boys and girls.

More crucially, 1966 saw an anime heralded in some sources, although by no means all, as the first appearance of sports as a TV anime theme. *Harris no Kaze* (1966, *Harris's Wind*) was a school drama in which a troubled, energetic boy channels his anger and frustration into a number of sporting activities, eventually benefiting both himself and the school by becoming an accomplished athlete (Clements and McCarthy 2006: 271). However, it was arguably still a school drama that simply featured a lot of sports. Misono (1999: 19) follows

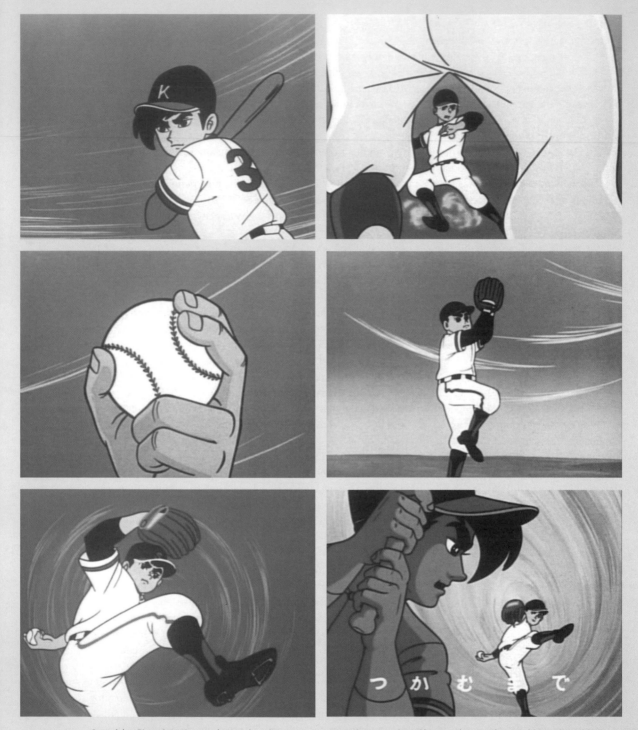

Star of the Giants (1968) not only introduced sports to TV anime, but a number of hyperreal tropes that would be adopted in many other anime genres

wider opinion in Japan by instead suggesting that the first true sports anime was *Star of the Giants*, a manga-based tale of a baseball pitcher haunted by his father's stalled career. One of its producers, Yamazaki Keishi (2005: 92), described it as a specific kind of sports anime, which valorised the pursuit of training and dedication in quasi-martial terms, which he calls the Fervent Spirit Route (*nekketsu konjō rosen*). According to Yamazaki, *Star of the Giants* was the first in this subgenre,[4] with a structure that was co-opted for many later shows, including the tennis story *Ace o Nerae* (1972, *Aim for the Ace*) and the live-action *Sign wa V* (1969, *The Sign Is V*). It is worth noting, however, that such an influence may owe only a partial debt to the artistic heritage of the *Star of the Giants* anime – sport in general became a major theme in Japanese popular culture as a result of the 1964 Tokyo Olympics, and all the shows mentioned began their lives in manga incarnations substantially before their emergence as anime. However, regardless of the actual origins of the Fervent Spirit Route, it is not a concept imposed retroactively in someone's memoir, but a topic discussed at the time of *Star of the Giants*, with a group of producers immediately replicating it in the late 1960s (Yamazaki 2005: 113).

Star of the Giants is a landmark show for a number of other reasons, not least the attempt it represents to expand anime beyond the children's ghetto – which is to say, a growing awareness on the part of producers that there were 'implied viewers' and potential viewers of their work beyond the audience of under-twelves previously assumed. Miyazaki Hayao (2009: 79) delivers a backhanded compliment when he writes of its appeal to 1960s audiences, suggesting that older Japanese viewers 'over-identified' with the story as a metaphor for the hardships of Japan's post-war reindustrialisation, investing substantially more meaning in the text than was really there. Whatever the audience's reasons for watching *Star of the Giants*, the high ratings generated by such attention guaranteed that there would be later attempts to copy it.

Its commissioning was an early example of vertical integration, with a storyline revolving around a fictionalised version of the real-life baseball team, the Yomiuri Giants, pushed in manga form in Yomiuri group publications and broadcast on a channel owned by the same Yomiuri conglomerate. Moreover, although many other anime were sponsored indirectly by pharmaceutical companies, through a subdivision that made confectionery, *Star of the Giants* was sponsored directly by Ōtsuka Chemical Holdings, which did not use it to advertise candy, but instead to push the energy drink Oronamin C (Yamazaki 2005: 87). Hence, implicit from the beginning of production on *Star of the Giants*, there was an understanding among its makers that it, or at least the adverts that it encompassed, would need to be seen by adults.

Yamazaki Keishi (2005: 13) goes so far as to describe *Star of the Giants* as 'entirely different from animation for children', terming it the first *gekiga* anime, using a 1960s term for 'dramatic pictures' commonly attributed to comics with adult sensibilities. But *Star of the Giants* was not, of course, the first 'adult' anime. As previous chapters have noted, anime intended for an adult audience, be it instructional or erotic, had been around for decades previously. Nor was it the first 'adult' animation on television, since 1950s whisky commercials cannot, logically, have been aimed at children. Its 7pm time-slot was valuable primetime territory, but no different from that occupied by *Astro Boy*. Nor were its themes a radical departure from established styles – Hikawa Ryūsuke (1999: 187) locates the origin of adult nuances and sensibilities, particularly in terms of character motivations, five years earlier in *Eightman*. Regardless of the intended audience of *Star of the Giants*, its ratings averaged 30 per cent across three years, and peaked at 36.9 per cent when other anime were settling at half that number (Hiramatsu 2000: 446), suggesting that it was being regularly consumed by adults and children alike.

FROM THE HITOMI-ZA TO TOKYO MOVIE

Star of the Giants was made by Tokyo Movie, a company founded in 1964 in an attempt to cash in on the sudden interest in animation engendered by the broadcast of *Astro Boy* (Tada 2002: 55). However, Tokyo Movie's roots extended far further back, and amount to an alternate strand in the 'seeds of anime'. In effect, they represent an entirely different set of artistic concerns, suddenly repurposed for animation after sixteen years in another medium.

The company founder, Fujioka Yutaka, had spent the war years at Kyoto University's Department of Agriculture in order to avoid the military draft. Dropping out as soon as the war was over, he found a job at the Daimaru department store while training to be a puppeteer under Kiyomizu Kyōji. In 1948, he founded the Hitomi-za puppet troupe. In the hiatus between the end of the war and the commencement of TV broadcasting in 1953, the Hitomi-za attracted a number of talents who would eventually transfer to broadcast or recorded visual media. Unafraid to feature adult material alongside its children's entertainment, the Hitomi-za established an early penchant for adaptations of Shakespeare plays into puppet performances. It was, according to Ōtsuka Yasuo, Fujioka himself who was mainly responsible for the success of an 'epoch-making' puppet performance of *Macbeth* in 1961, in charge of a squad of puppeteers later known as the 'Fujioka Soldiers' (Ōtsuka 2004: 21; Katō 2007: 144). It was this group of designers and puppeteers who worked for the TV channel TBS on a year-long puppet adaptation of Yokoyama Mitsuteru's 1961 manga series *Iga no Kagemaru* (1963–4, *Kagemaru of the Iga Ninja*), for which Fujioka would establish the Shinkaisha Tōkyō Ningyō Cinema (New Tokyo Puppet Cinema Corporation), regarded by Ōtsuka as a crucial step in the development of the institutions that would later be repurposed into anime companies.

New industries often attract a mixture of labourers from the closest pre-existing analogue, such as the former radio and cinema workers who contended to establish the basic norms of television broadcasting in Japan (Clements and Tamamuro 2003: xiii). Animation was already established as a discipline since the first experiments in 1917, but animation for television, on a weekly schedule, remained tantalisingly unbroken ground. With television workers occupied on 'real' programming such as news and drama, children's programming attracted a new wave of pioneers, drawn from cinema animation, comics and the puppet theatre.

With the release of *Astro Boy* and its legendary success, Kiyomizu exhorted his staff to adapt to the changing times, noting that 'we are sure to be seeing many more short animations like the works by the American Fleischers' (Ōtsuka 2004: 21). Interestingly, the puppeteers seem to have regarded the 7 pm primetime slot (or 'golden time') as their territory; *Kagemaru of the Iga Ninja* dominated its time-slot until 4 January 1964, the date when Fuji TV cunningly moved *Astro Boy* forty-five minutes later, putting the shows into direct competition. Forced to choose between *Kagemaru* or *Astro Boy*, viewers overwhelmingly selected the latter, wiping out much of the puppet show's reception and artistic heritage (Yamazaki 2005: 36; Animage 1988: 4). The puppet-makers Kawamoto Kihachirō and Okamoto Tadanari were reluctant to leave their chosen field, but Fujioka soon formed Shin Studio Tōkyō Movie (New Studio Tokyo Movie, later Tokyo Movie) in order to produce the animated cartoon series *Big X* (1964), based on a manga by Tezuka Osamu. Former puppeteers who switched careers with Fujioka included Nagahama Tadao, Ōsumi Masaaki and Imaizumi Atsushi, all destined to become anime directors. Ōtsuka (2004: 20) regards their time in the puppet theatre as vital to the development of their skills as animators, in terms of their understanding of the necessary compartmentalisation of shooting schedules, managing of artistic assets and basic craft techniques for assessing timing and poses.

By most definitions, a puppet show is not animated. Such works often slip through the cracks in research methodology and are generally not included in accounts of the Japanese animation world except as a prelude to discussions of stop-motion work (Clements and McCarthy 2006: 513–14). But if Ōtsuka's contention is correct, and there is no reason why it should not be, we might point to puppet shows in the late 1950s and early 1960s as forgotten prototypes for the sudden boom in TV anime from 1963 onwards. The most obvious candidate is the Takeda Ningyō-za's (Takeda Puppet Theatre) *Uchūsen Silica* (1960, *Spaceship Silica*), which ran weekdays on NHK for three years and 227 episodes before the arrival of *Astro Boy*.

Notably, with *Astro Boy* turning cel-based animation into the new growth medium, the Takeda Puppet Theatre's next puppet series *Ginga Shōnentai* (1963, *Space Patrol*) leaned on animation from Tezuka's own studio to sell itself. Although the show itself remained puppet-based, Mushi Production animated the opening credit sequence; moreover, the show was based on an idea by Tezuka himself, and seemed to suggest that his success with *Astro Boy* had already pushed his puppeteer predecessors into a subordinate position (Ikeda and Itō 2003: 22–5). In particular, it is interesting to observe on a surviving episode that much of the special-effects work and exterior shots were accomplished with cel animation, not puppets at all.

However, the primacy of animation in this period is assumed mainly because, at the risk of stating the obvious, animation historians are telling the story of the history of animation. Meanwhile, very few of these multipart puppet shows survive, with even a modern Japanese DVD of *Space Patrol* having to be pieced together from a few scattered remnants broadcast in French-speaking territories. In terms of the 'aesthesis of history' (Megill

2007: 33), such obscurities are inconvenient, incomplete fragments, difficult to show in festival restrospectives or include in general discussions of animation history. But we should at the very least acknowledge the presence of animation on 1960s television that has grown out of the puppet field, and somehow fallen into the shadows. For example, while Tezuka's *Astro Boy* dominated Saturday-night cartoons a year after its initial broadcast, it appeared only once a week, whereas Kuri Yōji's sixty-second cel-animated opening sequence for the puppet show *Hyokkori Hyōtanjima* (1964, *Madcap Island*) appeared every weekday, and continued to do so for the following five years. Neither Kuri nor *Madcap Island* appear in histories of television animation – he is usually an 'art-house' animator, and it is a 'puppet' show – but Kuri's animated sequence for the show endured on television for six times as many appearances as *Astro Boy* (Ikeda and Itō 2003: 26).

Moreover, the primacy of former puppeteers at Tokyo Movie has been at least partly obscured by the co-option of yet another group of defectors from Tōei. The studio A Pro, set up in 1965 by Kusube Daikichirō, mainly comprised colleagues from Tōei who had worked with him on *Shōnen Ninja Kaze no Fujimaru* (1964, *Fujimaru the Wind Ninja*), and chiefly worked for Tokyo Movie as a subcontractor, beginning with *Qtarō the Ghost* in 1965.

STAR OF THE GIANTS AND THE IMPLIED VIEWER

Hikawa Ryūsuke (1999: 188) places the production of *Star of the Giants* at the nexus of a series of contextual and industrial concerns, not merely as part of the search for a new theme that did not rehash other anime, but in competition with the rising popularity of live-action superhero shows. Tsuburaya Eiji's special effects-laden *Ultra Q* (1966), and its more famous successor *Ultraman* (1966) had transformed live-action children's television, and led to an ebb in the popularity of animation, against which *Star of the Giants* contended.

In *Audience Studies: A Japanese Perspective*, Takahashi Toshie notes that today's average Japanese home has two television sets, which are switched on for an average of eight hours a day (Takahashi 2010: 5). But we should not assume that the viewer is affording 100 per cent of his or her attention to the TV. From the earliest days of Japanese TV, broadcasters have understood that a busy housewife might only have half an eye on a drama series, and played to this method of consumption with explicatory voiceovers and even an on-screen clock so that viewers were kept apprised of the imminent disruption of their leisure by returning family members (Clements and Tamamuro 2003: xviii).

Moreover, we might consider that the home is not the only place in Japan that has a television set. I have spent many an evening at a Japanese bar or café, with a large TV burbling away to itself in a corner, almost entirely ignored by the clientele. In other words, much as TV spectatorship has been characterised in the West as a casual glance rather than a cinematic gaze (Fiske 2011: 58), the default setting for Japanese TV consumption might similarly be one of watching 'with one eye'. Such a mode of access might help explain the proliferation of broad melodrama and overacting, easier to follow for a distracted audience. If advertising is still delivered to the viewers, what does it matter if many are only the most casual of observers? Moreover, such advertising might even reach family members who are not present at the hypothetical primetime viewing experience. If the stereotypical salaryman, more beholden to his workplace than to his spousally dominated home environment, is out drinking with colleagues during primetime, then perhaps the advertising and the message of such shows could be said to be directed at him. There is certainly a recurring message in anime shows that must surely have a subliminal meaning for a returning office worker hoping to buy his child's love: *my father gave me a robot, my father gave me a robot, my father gave me a robot*. Moreover, Tada Makoto notes (2002: 99–100) that, even if a hypothetical salaryman is still at work, and hence misses the commercials for Toyota that form part of the company's sponsorship deal on *Boy Detective Conan* (1996), these may still influence the rest of the family, who will pass on their message indirectly when the household next buys a car.

Anime watchers are not necessarily 'viewers' – they might be better described as 'participants' in a fairy-tale ritual of good versus evil, as 'creators' of a subjective play experience for which an anime forms only part of the narrative (a 'media ecology', for which see Steinberg 2012: 18–19) or as 'consumers' of an extended advertising message (Takahashi 2010: 4, 13). As Takahashi (2010: 32–3) herself notes, consumption is sometimes conducted while multitasking – surfing the Internet, cooking or talking, and cites (2010: 92) cross-cultural empirical research, suggesting that in Japan, oddly, it is the children who are more likely to control TV access at prime-time. In other words, a primetime programme appealing to children is more likely in Japan to contain advertising messages intended for adults. Yamazaki Keishi (2005: 124) recalls that the late 1960s saw several attempts by animation producers to target this 'adult' audience directly.

The implied viewer of a children's show is, of course, a child, but the aim of such a show is to sell toys to the children and, while it is within the 'pester power' of children to demand them, it is adults who hold the purse-strings for those toys. Considering the primetime broadcast slot of many TV shows, we might assume that the family is eating, or the consumption of the programme takes place at two levels. The children might be close to the TV set, actually watching the show. The parents might be entirely removed from the viewing experience, aware only that the TV is on and that their offspring are momentarily silenced at the sight of a particular show. Most importantly for the advertisers, a show should advertise its product. It does this not only through push-ing its characters, but through pushing the impression to the adults at the sidelines that it is this show, these characters, these toys that most occupy their children's interests.

This suggests, in turn, that there is a subsidiary implied viewer for children's animation. As the title of the show *Okaasan to Issho* (1959, *Watch with Mother*) readily acknowledges, up to 50 per cent of the viewership for some 'children's' shows might comprise adult parents. Moreover, televisions outside the home, even if the sound is unintelligible or muted, continue to deliver their images, not only of advertising, but of an implied viewer elsewhere – that, while a hypothetical salaryman is in a bar across town, his children might be watching that same show at home. It does not matter to the advertisers if salaryman father watches their show; it matters to them that he thinks his children do, and that he might be able to win their affections by purchasing some of the products advertised on the way home. Similarly, early twenty-first-century programmers also identified the subversive potential of the 'Odagiri Effect', named for the *Kamen Rider Cougar* (2000) actor Odagiri Jō, in which audiences for children's programming might be swelled by lonely mothers who enjoyed the sight of handsome young male heroes (Clements and Tamamuro 2003: 182). Hence the message of advertising can have a notional audience beyond infant viewers, and advertising itself should be designed to impart its message to a viewership that is not really paying attention. As the advertising guru David Ogilvy (2004: 160) once said: 'Try running your commercial without sound. If it doesn't sell without sound, it is useless.'

We might consider the rise of primetime sports anime in such a context – of disinterested parents who watch with one eye – as a basic viewing experience that can, at least in theory, be readily intelligible to any viewer. Regardless of the behind-the-scenes machinations, intrigues and conflicts of *Star of the Giants*, many of its episodes invariably boil down to a game of baseball, complete with cutaways to the scoreboard. There is none of the arcane taxonomy of *Pokémon* here, nor the Byzantine politics of *Ginga eiyū densetsu* (1988, *Legend of the Galactic Heroes*). A hypothetical adult, blundering in through the door after dinner, or home from work or back from the shops, can usually tell, at the merest glance who is winning and who is losing. The basic, for-mulaic performance of any team sport hence lends itself superbly to anime, not for its escapism or fantasy quality, but because of its mundane, banal, everyday quality. If you are the sort of person who likes sport, then you might conceivably be the sort of person who likes, or would at least tolerate, sports anime, devoid of the fantasy or science-fiction stigma of many other shows. However, such an assumption ignores the fantasti-cal uses to which animation was put in the telling of a supposedly mundane story.

XEROGRAPHY AND DEFORMATION

The Disney animator Ub Iwerks first modified a Xerox camera in 1959, adapting it so that it could photograph and then print an animator's pencil lines directly onto a cel, automating the tracing process, and allowing for much more of the original detail to be preserved. Although this greatly sped up the process of moving from pen-cils to inked cels, it also preserved many of the imperfections in a pencil image – the 'clean-up' stage of animation was normally undertaken as part of the process of tracing to the cel, but was now sometimes ignored. Xerox photography, often shortened to xerography, also allowed for images to be rapidly reduced or enlarged, making several previously time-consuming tasks significantly easier. As Chuck Jones explains:

For example, in *One Hundred and One Dalmatians* (1961), they had a hundred and one dogs, and in a couple of shots there were acres and acres of puppies. There the Xerox helped them tremendously, because they animated eight or nine cycles of action, of dogs running in different ways, then made them larger or smaller, using Xerox, knowing that if there are a hundred and one dogs, and if there are eight or nine distinct cycles, and they're placed at random in this rabble of dogs, no one will know that they all haven't been animated individually. (Barrier and Spicer 1971)

The same film, released in Japanese in 1962 as *Hyakuippiki Wan-chan* (*101 Doggies*) was the first encounter for Japanese audiences with what the anime industry would term, in English, 'machine tracing' (Oguro *et al.* 2008: 38). The technology was in place in the Japanese animation industry by the time production began on *Star of the Giants*, making it, perhaps inadvertently, the first show to make use of the process.

Xerography had a powerful impact behind the scenes, devaluing the labour of the women who had become experts at tracing cels, and allowing key animators' lines to be replicated with a greater degree of precision (Tomino 2002: 62). Japanese testimonials make no mention of the use of machine tracing for replicating armies of similar characters or altering the size of pre-existing images. However, its value was immediately noted in replicating the scratchy, complex *gekiga* art style of Kawasaki Noboru in the original manga. Hence, *Star of the Giants* did not merely introduce more complex themes to Japanese animation, but also an art style that was a world removed from the simple, curving lines and sparse backgrounds of the previous five years.

The introduction of *trace machines*, which enabled animators' lines to be copied directly on cels, changed the attitude of those animators. Until then, key artists attempted to use simple movements and simplified characters, and refined their technique in order to express themselves with such means. However, now on a frame-by-frame basis, and in movement, they seemed to demand art or motion as dense as that in *gekiga*. Using dark, soft 2B and 4B pencils, they drew rough, flat lines. (Hikawa 1999: 189–90)

Hikawa Ryūsuke claims that xerography, and the potential it offered for transferring dynamism and deformation directly from an artist's pencil to a finished cel, led to a sea-change in the appearance of Japanese television animation, with the rounded, simple lines of early works like *Astro Boy* cast aside in favour of more complex imagery, and scrappier, rougher line-work that allowed adult sensibilities to transfer across from manga along with the artwork. He suggests that the apotheosis of xerography experimentation was an episode of *Star of the Giants* in which director Nagahama Tadao exploited numerous innovative perspectives and ideas:

When the pitcher winds up ready to throw a ball, the movements of hands and legs are slowly stretched as though time has slowed down. When the pitcher's body strobes (a technique that flickers between black and white drawings of the same image), the baseball stadium switches into an eerie red and black colour as if it is in an alternate dimensional space. The thrown ball is rotated and flattened, approaching the batter at high speed. (Hikawa 1999: 189)

This drift into hyperreality has been cited by many critics, most notably the disapproving Miyazaki Hayao (2009: 79) as another turning point in the construction of television anime. But Nagahama was not solely responsible for the storyboards that established the visual look of the series from which the key animators then worked – in fact, several future anime celebrities are credited with the storyboarding on *Star of the Giants*, not least Tomino Yoshiyuki (Tomino 2002: 224–5), who would go on to author the industry's leading textbook on storyboarding technique. Moreover, Hikawa's animator- and technology-led account of the adoption of this anime style is at odds with that of Yamazaki Keishi, the producer at Tokyo Movie who was intimately involved with the production of the series.

While Yamazaki does not deny the immense visual and stylistic impact of Nagahama's direction in *Star of the Giants*, he suggests (2005: 13–14) that Nagahama was merely adopting such techniques in order to tell a story that already existed on the pages of the script. In other words, Yamazaki places the change in the pacing and style of *Star of the Giants*, not in the storyboards, or the application of the trace machine, but in the original story conferences that led to the screenplay.

In Yamazaki's account, Nagahama Tadao is still instrumental in the process, convening an emergency meeting when he realises that the weekly schedule of the *Star of the Giants* anime is so swift that it risks catching up with the manga from which it draws its story (Yamazaki 2005: 13–14). Yamazaki's term is 'devouring the original work' (*gensatsu o kuu*) – a common phenomenon today, that had seemingly not troubled anime productions before *Star of the Giants*, since they had all drawn on long-established manga titles, or open-ended franchises. Yamazaki was having problems of his own with his main writers, who were increasingly resistant to demands that they not only adapt a set spread of pages from the manga each week, but also inject a three-act structure into whatever situation was contained therein.

Yamazaki (2005: 64–6) coyly identifies the offending writers only by their initials, although it is clear from extant staff listings that the troublesome 'Mr M' and 'Mr S' must have been Matsuoka Seiji and Sasaki Mamoru (Tokyo Movie Shinsha 1999: 158). The producer took on another writer hungrier for the work, Yamazaki Haruya, who would transform *Star of the Giants* by writing an infamous episode in which the passage of a single ball, from pitcher's hand, to batter, to outfield, to plate was somehow stretched into an entire episode (Yamazaki 2005: 100–1).

Yamazaki Haruya's script builds the tension on the pitcher's mound, as the pitcher draws back his arm and throws the ball. Exploiting the potentially infinite camera positions available to animators, the script zooms in and out of multiple perspectives – the inner monologue of the pitcher himself and the calculating thoughts of the batter he faces; the commentary of the excitable journalists in the outside-broadcast booth; viewers at home yelling at the television; fans in the bleachers; team members on both sides; the pitcher's father and dewy-eyed love interest. Coupled with shots of the arena and sudden zooms and splitscreen effects, flashbacks and voiceovers, the sequence occupies the entire first half of the episode, cutting to the commercial break just as the ball leaves the pitcher's hand. After the commercials, the episode continues with a similar hyperreal deformation of time, pursuing the ball's trajectory towards the batter, the bat's connection with the ball and the frenzy of action among both teams as the batter hits a home run.

Undeniably, Nagahama Tadao and his animators put new technology to good use, with extensive recourse to xerography to transfer foreshortening, deformation, impressionistic speed lines and other artistic effects directly to their cels. They also drew on the toolkit of tricks and tropes already popularised by Mushi Pro. But as Yamazaki Keishi's account makes clear, the development of this new anime 'look' was not the decision of a single creative, but the convergence of a series of influences and requirements, including the plot of the original manga, a need to eke out diminishing source material, and Yamazaki Haruya's decision to expand a mere couple of pages into an entire episode.

ANIMATION TRAINING AND OUTSOURCING

Sugiyama Taku (1999: 133) notes that technical, or to be more precise, labour and training concerns, also steered the nature of anime, with producers instructing scriptwriters to avoid depictions of four-legged animals and scenes on a seashore, both of which were considered to present difficulties for unskilled animators. As Tezuka had already discovered at Mushi Pro on *Jungle Emperor*, four-legged animals were at least twice as much work to animate (Yamamoto 1989: 173). It is, then, no surprise that so many early television anime kept to subjects that might more easily lend themselves to limited animation – flying superheroes or heavily stylised comedies.

Staffing also played a part in the anime that went into production. Tezuka's high spending on wages leeched many animators from Tōei Dōga, capitalising on Tōei's preceding half-decade of investment in training. Essentially, Tezuka threw money at his problem, allowing Mushi Pro to attract the best start-up talent – even the screenwriters were paid substantially more than offered by other studios in the 1960s (Tsugata 2007b: 132). As competition over animators heated up, Tezuka was determined to hang onto the staff he had poached and trained for *Astro Boy*. With 239 staff at Mushi Pro in 1965, of which ninety stayed on *Astro Boy* and another 115 began work on *Jungle Emperor*, Tezuka found himself with two dozen 'spare' staff. Unwilling to leave them fallow or send them home as would have happened in Tōei in the 1950s, he instead put them to work on an all-new TV series, *W3* (1965, *Wonder Three*), a low-rent operation run out of an apartment near the Mushi building (Yamamoto 1989: 169), in spite of the fact that all three productions still had to outsource part of their work elsewhere. Mushi Pro had obtained a nickname from somewhere that referred to it as the 'talent ranch' (*jinsai bokujo*), although we might consider the implied difference in quality between the herd animals of a farm and the 'graduates' of the 'Tōei Dōga University' (Minakawa 2009a: 273).

Outsourcing remained a constant feature of the Japanese animation business, meaning that each studio's ongoing labour issues were passed on to other corporate entities. Ishiguro Noboru at Ōnishi Pro was told that the company had committed to supply outsourced episodes of *Astro Boy* at a rate of one episode a month. His initial resources amounted to six empty desks, and a directive to advertise for 'animators' to sit at them, whom he was expected to train himself. Although he hired the required recruits, it was understood that it would take six months to get them up to a professional standard, forcing Ōnishi Pro itself to outsource the first six months of its work while he trained them (Ishiguro and Ohara 1980: 97).

This outsourcing chain reached offshore for the first time in 1966. Although the script, storyboards and key art for TCJ's *Ōgon Bat* (1966, *Golden Bat*) were produced in Japan, the inbetweening and other elements were done in South Korea by the Tongyang studio (Animage 1988: 16). This development went unremarked in the Japanese industry, so far beneath the notice of many that several later producers would claim to be the 'first' to hire foreign labour, but it marked a watershed moment in Japanese animation history. Even as Japanese studios continued to work 'below the line' on American projects (see Chapter 5), the advent of television had created a new subaltern class, of foreign animators working below the line on 'Japanese' animation. Japan, previously at the periphery of an American core, now had a periphery of its own in Korea. Such outsourcing could also have a political dimension. *Yōkai Ningen Bem* (1968, *Monster Man Bem*) is described as the first Korean 'co-production' in Japanese sources, although in South Korea it was broadcast as *Yogwe Ingan* (1968, *Monster Man*), as a 'local' production, and not a foreign show subject to import restrictions (Animage 1988: 24; Yu 1999: 74–5).

That same year, Fred Ladd put a second group of Korean artists to work in Seoul, colourising monochrome cartoons. It had been Ladd's intention to employ the newly established Kaemi Production to colourise *Tetsujin 28* (*Gigantor*), and an episode of the Japanese show indeed served as their test project. However, when the colouring process proved viable, Kaemi was put to work on American cartoons, rather than the Japanese productions originally intended (Ladd with Deneroff 2009: 85–7).[5]

Korean subcontractors would remain a periodic presence in the 'Japanese' industry thereafter, although the logistics of both sending production objects abroad and communicating across international borders would often prove counterproductive in the pre-Internet era. Some studios resorted to sending agents to personally carry cels and storyboards to and from Seoul as hand luggage on planes (Ishiguro and Ohara 1980: 222), but this itself incurred additional costs and risks. As a result, the Japanese animation industry still clung to domestic labour wherever possible, despite the apparent absence of suitable candidates. As Ishiguro Noboru observed:

> It is so easy to create a subcontracted TV anime production company. It is because 90 per cent of the cost is labour and hardly any investment is required. As long as you have money to rent a studio and to buy desks for animators, all you need is people. You could start an animation production company tomorrow. But they also go bust quickly, too – just like bars. Because the production cost is cheap, subcontractors never make a big profit. You are lucky if you are not making a loss. As soon as you start doing a different job and the efficiency level drops, or an animator quits, the business goes downhill. (Ishiguro and Ohara 1980: 162–3)

Similar problems troubled even the established studios, although 'established' is something of a misnomer when 'veteran' animators were still in their twenties (Yamamoto 1989: 36). The former puppeteers running Tokyo Movie, unaware of the ways in which animation piecework might be manipulated to create more revenue, were swindled by some of their animators on *Qtarō the Ghost*:

Such an instant organisation, lacking production management, could create unexpected side effects. The animators ran scams to rake in more money paid per animated frame, such as drawing Qtaro's torso, eyes, legs, hands and mouth on separate sheets, and counting the whole as five still images, which the inexperienced management section failed to check. Contemporary common sense held that a 30-minute timeframe (more like 22 minutes) of television animation would utilise five to six thousand cels of animation, but [*Qtarō*] was charging for over ten thousand frames every episode. This is unimaginable today. (Ōtsuka 2004: 22)

Some staff were also caught prioritising the easiest sequences, which were invariably the ones with the least animation, or still images requiring no animation at all. They then demanded overtime to complete the harder sections as deadlines approached. Miyazaki Hayao (2009: 78) directly equates such labour issues with a further decline in the quality of television animation during the 1960s and 1970s, but also as a structuring impetus towards an increasingly impressionistic mode of storytelling, favouring the 'flashy or cool' moments of still poses or flaming firepower, and largely dumping the earlier concerns of realistic movement or subtle human emotion.

FROM *KETSUDAN* TO *GATCHAMAN*

Another of the start-up studios that competed in the 1960s television market was Tatsunoko Pro, founded in October 1962 by the manga artist Yoshida Tatsuo and his two brothers. The precise dating, a fortnight before the Yamaha Hall premiere of *Astro Boy*, is notable, as it suggests Yoshida was directly aping the public aspirations of his rival Tezuka Osamu (Ladd with Deneroff 2009: 106; Tsugata 2004: 153). The Yoshida brothers had already worked as subcontractors to the television world, adapting the live-action show *Allah no Shisha* (1960, *Envoy of Allah*)[6] into manga form, and had seen their manga *Shōnen Ninja Butai Gekkō* (*Boy Ninja Platoon Moonlight*)[7] adapted into live-action television (Misono 1999: 146–7). Yoshida Tatsuo saw the potential for producing his own adaptations in animated form, vertically integrating his manga work with TV spin-offs, or vice versa. He had first planned to work in coproduction with Tōei Dōga over a TV adaptation of his manga *Uchū Ace* (*Space Ace*), seemingly intended by both as an imitation of Tezuka's *Astro Boy*. However, Yoshida disputed the larger studio's attempt to assign copyright ownership to itself, and cancelled the deal. As a result, Tōei instead made the TV series *Uchū Patrol Hoppa* (1965, *Space Patrol Hoppa*), while Tatsunoko wandered into production on its own on *Space Ace* that same year. Tsugata Nobuyuki (2011b: 28) describes Tatsunoko specifically as a company with roots in manga rather than advertising, like TCJ, or in animation itself, like Tōei Dōga. It should, then, not be surprising that the Tatsunoko animators would have mastered all the processes of taking a story from idea to storyboard and key frames, but be predisposed to cutting corners at the stage of animation itself.

However, while this certainly favoured Tatsunoko's adoption of the policies of image bank and limited animation as already in use at Mushi Pro, it also led the Tatsunoko animators to tinker with new technologies.[8] Unlike Mushi Pro, which was beholden to the spare, rounded style of Tezuka, Tatsunoko was immediately able to embrace new developments to create its own shows, the most famous of which in the US was *Mach Go Go Go* (1967, *Speed Racer*).

Ketsudan (1971, *Decision*)[9] was an experimental show from Tatsunoko Pro, combining the media of animation and documentary, published in tandem with a print magazine on the same topic, and leading to its description as an 'animentary' (Animage 1988: 37). The series dramatised the battles of the Pacific War, beginning with Pearl Harbor and extending to Japan's surrender. With xerography now facilitating the process of transferring images to cels, the Tatsunoko animators under director Kurokawa Fumio devoted a *documentary* level of detail to the replication of machinery – in a historical series about such a contentious and sensitive subject, an emphasis on the workings of the planes, tanks and battleships would allow animators to avoid more political issues, fill up screentime, and appeal to an implied audience of model-makers and military enthusiasts. Hikawa (1999: 196) also notes that a 7.30 pm Saturday primetime show about the war was sure to reach an implied audience of middle-aged Japanese with direct experience of the technology on display, necessitating a greater attention to detail. As a result, *Ketsudan* was the first animation series in which the English-language job title of '*mechanic*

Born from the discourse between cartoons and live-action *sentai* shows, *Science Ninja Team Gatchaman* (1972) was repurposed abroad post-*Star Wars* as *Battle of the Planets*

design' appears among the staff credits, denoting a group of artists and draftsmen whose responsibility was not for the look of characters, but of machine objects.

The Tatsunoko studio's penchant for experimentation is also evident in other innovations – or rather, in rediscoveries and repurposing of formerly neglected animation processes. Textures were added to cels of deck scenes in order to create an illusory solidity to images of metal bulkheads or floors. To give the impression of the presence of bullets in the air, the *Ketsudan* animators used transmitted light photography (*tōkakō*), a back-lighting process that allowed light to shine through the film from behind the image. When the luminosity was carefully controlled, transmitted light made bullet traces show up as barely perceptible 'speed' lines that cut across the image in a moment of visual absence. Hikawa (1999: 196) reports this as if it were an all-new innovation, although Mochinaga Tadahito (2006: 89) describes using a similar process several decades earlier for creating a moon-light effect in *Ari-chan*. Colour television, however, made backlighting effects far more versatile, as the colour of the light could be altered. When the luminosity was taken to higher levels, transmitted light could create a flare effect in which light bled into other areas of the image, useful for imparting flame or explosion effects, rocket trails or a solid quality to images of headlights or spotlights. Explosions became a particular fetish for the Tatsunoko animators, combining xerography, transmitted light and additional airbrush effects added to the cel.

This knowledge converged in 1972 in a Sunday evening show designed to compete in the children's market against the rising popularity of the live-action 'rubber-monster' shows such as *Ultraman* and *Kamen Rider* (Clements and Tamamuro 2003: 179, 334). Hikawa (1999: 195) regards the beginning of the 1970s as an era of intense competition for the attention of children, not only on screen, but in toy stores, with the live-action shows offering a combination of 'transformation (*henshin*) and monsters (*kaijū*)'. Tatsunoko's answer to this was the reverse-engineering of the live-action paradigm to create 'SF + transformation + monsters + a group of heroes' in the form of *Kagaku Ninjatai Gatchaman* (1972, *Science Ninja Team Gatchaman*, released in the US as *Battle of the Planets*).

Gatchaman's characters adopted many tropes from the live-action shows – a five-person team, each with his or her own vehicle and the inevitable toy tie-in; a mechanical monster of the week, which would only be defeated by group effort; and a series of transformations that both ritualised each episode and permitted regular recycling of certain animation sequences.

ALTERNATIVE ANIME BOOMS
Tsugata Nobuyuki (2011a: 7) argues that the formation of a consensus on what 'anime' truly was can be dated to the early to mid-1970s, as the strands of limited animation, context-integrated merchandise and active fandom began to coalesce around the works then shown on television. However, he also offers a negative dialectic for this discourse, suggesting that, while anime may have been articulated in such terms among its fans by the beginning of the 1980s, other communities were more likely to define anime through a set of criticisms and complaints.

'Anime', to the mainstream, comprised those cartoons on television that were deemed gratuitously violent – a reaction, here, to the surfeit of explosions and effects, and the more mature themes sneaking in after *Zambot 3* (1977 – see below). 'Anime' was hence a pejorative flung at the limited animation and corner-cutting prevalent in the industry, particularly since the early 1970s recession. 'Anime' was also a term applied (Tsugata 2011a: 8) within the broader animation community, in reaction to the resurgence of art-house animation at the first Hiroshima International Animation Festival in 1985. In other words, just as the Group of Three once differentiated between the adverts they made for money, and the short films they made for art, the animation community now distinguished between the experimental films and apprentice pieces that could be seen at film festivals, and the junk that was on television. Notably, the first Grand Prize at Hiroshima was awarded to Tezuka Osamu's experimental *Onboro Film* (1985, *Broken-down Film*), and was not given to a Japanese work again until Yamamura Kōji's *Mt Head* (2004). As Tsugata (2011a: 8) notes, it is as if the artistic animation community wished to establish that there was an 'original' (*honrai*) notion of what animation should be, still maintained by foreign creators, but that the Japanese creators had lost their way.[10]

There was, however, yet another implied viewer – a palpable sense in the mid-1970s that the generation born in 1960 and reared on the maturing late 1960s anime TV shows, had developed a sense of connoisseurship towards them. Ishiguro Noboru noted (Ishiguro and Ohara 1980: 213–14), with a degree of bafflement, that teenage fans had started turning up at his Artland studio while production was ongoing on *Uchū senkan Yamato* (1974, *Space Cruiser Yamato*):

> Two or three months after the broadcast started [i.e. around the beginning of 1975 – JC], middle- and high-school fans began to make frequent appearances at the studio, full of curiosity and amazement. We didn't know it, but it was an early sign of the coming anime boom. They included enthusiastic girls who came by plane from Kyūshū and we gave them several cels and background paintings as souvenirs because they had taken such great pains. Those cels now have the same street value as drugs, but in those days they were just a waste of space.

Ishiguro's comments point to a phenomenon widely testified to in subsequent narratives of anime history (e.g. Tsugata 2011b: 30), which is to say that *Space Cruiser Yamato* was a key work in an 'anime boom' that spanned the 1970s. However, such a bias towards *Space Cruiser Yamato* relies, at least partly, on the discovery later in the decade that the new growth medium for *all* media was science fiction. In the wake of George Lucas's *Star Wars* (1977), both *Space Cruiser Yamato* and the earlier *Science Ninja Team Gatchaman* were repurposed for the American market as *Star Blazers* and *Battle of the Planets*. Arguably, both shows also enjoyed a longer lease of life, renewed and remade throughout the decade, at least in part because their themes were thought in some way to match those of the Hollywood blockbuster.

The narrative of anime history, particularly as set down during the 1980s and 1990s, seems to have been recorded largely by male observers, who chose to commemorate science-fiction works at the expense of other genres. Tomino Yoshiyuki (Schodt 1988: 89) suggests a theory of negotiated consumption for the initial alleged success of the male-oriented stories, claiming that 'few people watch the whole shows', but that men only paid attention during the battle scenes, while women stayed for the drama, but wandered elsewhere during the fights. When a true alternative became available on another channel, the females flocked to it. As Ishiguro noted (Ishiguro and Ohara 1980: 208), the girls who visited his studio sheepishly confessed that, although they had seen *Space Cruiser Yamato*, they much preferred the Zuiyō Eizō studio's *Heidi, the Girl of the Alps*, a Swiss pastoral running on a rival channel. Ishiguro's observation suggests, while science fiction might have formed the most noticeable form of reception and consumption during the period, there were alternative forms with a stronger appeal to a female audience. 'Magical Girl' (*majokko*) shows drew on earlier tropes established by the manga artist Yokoyama Mitsuteru and, to some extent, Tezuka, and featured young female protagonists with magical powers (Takemura 2009: 4–5). Beginning with *Little Witch Sally*, these shows ran throughout the period, rarely for less than a year, adapting the male-oriented, superhero-derived themes of transformation for a female audience that favoured magic, fashion and family. Merchandise for this girls' audience was no less integrated than toys for the boys, and included tiaras, wands, school equipment, branded clothes, make-up sets, sewing kits and even a toy nurse's medical kit (Takemura 2009: 105–8). Anne Allison (2004: 39–40) points to a parallel strand of 'cute' merchandise and mascot animals, directed at a female consumer base, and growing during the 1970s.

Heidi (1974) was just as popular in the ratings as *Space Cruiser Yamato*, although the latter is often accorded authority in the light of a sci-fi boom in the late 1970s

Yet another skein of animation also ran throughout the decade, drawing on the success of Zuiyō Eizō studio's *Heidi*, based on the children's books by Johanna Spyri. Zuiyō Eizō (literally 'Auspicious Falcon Images') was founded in 1969 by Takahashi Shigehito, an animator who had left Eiken, the animation division of TCJ. The studio began by taking on outsourced work from both TCJ and Tokyo Movie, before initiating its own productions with *Heidi* in 1974. Zuiyō's triumph also contained the seeds of its own destruction, with animators on *Heidi* investing substantially more effort than was commonly expected in a TV animation. Kotabe Yōichi, one of several former Tōei employees working on the project, reported that despite directives to shoot 'on threes' in the Mushi Pro mode, certain animators on *Heidi* often racked up cel counts of 8,000 per episode (Kanō 2004: 57).

The production of *Heidi* highlights the ever-present tension between art and commerce. As John Ruskin argued in *The Political Economy of Art* (1867: 57), there is often a trade-off between low-cost objects that fulfil an immediate market, and higher-cost items, more expensive to produce but also longer-lasting, whose value might only be appreciated by posterity. Ruskin's example is the speedy, rapid production of watercolour images, which often lack long-term durability, versus the longer potential lifespan of woodcuts or oil paintings. In the blunt, businesslike terms of the post-Mushi television animation industry, *Heidi*'s quality was over-engineered, far in excess of the minimum requirements for it to be fit for purpose. *Heidi*'s animators went on a location-scouting trip to the Swiss Alps, to help them replicate real-world environments. They also conducted painstaking research in order to achieve lasting images. *Heidi*'s opening credits included a sequence in which Heidi and her shepherd boy Peter clasp hands and skip around in a circle. Mori Yasuji ordered his colleagues Kotabe Yōichi and Miyazaki Hayao to shoot reference footage to aid in the placement of arms and bodies, leading the two animators to re-enact the scene in the studio car park (Kanō 2004: 57).

Miyazaki Hayao (2009: 137) has written of his desire to produce quality artwork in *Heidi*, the toll it took and the dangers of setting such standards in the television medium: 'We wanted to create a work for children that wasn't frivolous, and we wanted to break away from the compromised and slapdash television animation shows of that time.' Producing *Heidi* in a 'year-long state of emergency', he reported a sense of relief and achievement among the staff when it generated positive reviews and audience response. The Zuiyo animators' emphasis on quality was less a new development than a vestigial remnant of the attention to detail practised in Tōei's cinema animation. Nor was it necessarily a 'failure', since *Heidi* was well received in Japan, becoming one of the rare animation shows to grace the cover of *TV Guide*, and was also sold on to many foreign-language territories, including Italian, Spanish, Arabic, Chinese and its 'native' German. The staff's efforts, however, ran the studio's finances into the ground, forcing its managers to restructure. Zuiyō Eizō continued as a corporate entity – a distributor in terms of the ownership–access chain – holding the copyright for *Heidi*, along with its debts and the expectation that it would eventually come back into profit through foreign sales. The production elements of the studio, including the animators such as *Heidi*'s director Takahata Isao and lead animator Ashida Toyo'o, were rebranded as the 'new' studio Nippon Animation (Clements and McCarthy 2006: 453). Moreover, as Miyazaki confessed:

It was only then that we came to understand the danger of television. Television repeatedly demands the same thing. Its voraciousness makes everything banal. We realised that television required that our state of emergency become a normal condition … . The only way to have a long-term relationship with television is to lower the level of production quality to one that can be sustained. (Miyazaki 2009: 137–8)

Mazinger Z (1972) introduced the notion of 'mecha' as pilotable war machines rather than remote-controlled robots

Despite the protests of its makers, the success of *Heidi* helped create a new genre of 'masterpiece anime' (*meisaku anime*), based on works of children's literature (Minakawa 2009a: 194). The project gained the sponsorship of the soft-drinks company Calpis, and would eventually be corralled under the umbrella title of World Masterpiece Theatre (*sekai meisaku gekijō*), often retroactively incorporating several works such as *Heidi* that were either not covered by the original Calpis sponsorship or which pre-dated the incorporation of Nippon Animation. Despite the continuity of staff and facilities, the self-commemorating history of Nippon Animation (2001) ignores the work of Zuiyō, and instead cites *Dog of Flanders* as its 'first' production, soon followed by many other adaptations from children's books, including *Little Women*, *Anne of Green Gables* and many others (Clements and McCarthy 2006: 730).

Ishiguro Noboru (Ishiguro and Ohara 1980: 208) has suggested that the bifurcation of 1970s anime into lachrymose romance and classics of children's literature on the one hand, and brash action adventure on the other, reflects a battle behind the scenes epitomised by the scheduling clash between *Heidi* and *Space Cruiser Yamato*. Each gained a rating of 15 per cent, suggesting a combined viewership twice the size of the available juvenile audience. Ishiguro regarded this as an indicator of an invisible audience segment – mothers watching *Heidi* with their daughters, and fathers watching *Space Cruiser Yamato* with their sons. However, later research in audience studies suggests that Ishiguro may have identified the effect rather than the cause. As children in Japanese homes are more likely to be given control of the choice of television channel by indifferent parents (Takahashi 2010: 92), this rather suggests a selection made by male or female children, for which the father or mother stayed to watch if the programme choice matched their gender profile.

TRANSFORMATION AND COMBINATION: MECHA AND MERCHANDISE

However, there was a limit to the number of potential spin-offs that could be generated by a retold children's classic. The most noticeable strand of thematic development in the period was in the boys' market, in the gradual transformation in anime from autonomous robot *characters*, to remote-controlled robot *machines*, to *pilotable* bipedal machines. As part of the ongoing discourse and competition with live-action shows, and the scramble for investment from toy companies, anime for boys increasingly favoured the 'robot', or more precisely *mecha*, which is to say a 'pilotable or remote-operable machine, often bipedal or otherwise humanoid in form' (Clements and Langford 2012).

Frederik L. Schodt (1988: 94–5) cites changes in industrial practice as the major impetus for a change in the nature of Japanese toys, a 'second generation' in manufacture away from the tin toys that once accompanied *Astro Boy*, to articulated diecast models combining metal and plastic parts. He points to 'toy town' (*omocha no machi*) – an industrial sector established in 1965 on the outskirts of Tokyo, where eleven initial companies, and eventually forty-four toy manufacturers pooled certain large-scale facilities, and shared warehouses and company dorms.

In particular, he cites two animated shows based on the work of Nagai Gō as epitomes of the growing convergence between the concerns of toy manufacturers and the production of Japanese animation. *Mazinger Z* (1972, released in the US as *Tranzor Z*) took the machinery in anime beyond simple 'robots' and into the realms of pilotable machinery, with a youthful protagonist who climbed inside his humanoid machine. *Getter Robo* (1974) replaced the pre-existing 'transformation' scene with one of 'combination': in which separate modules would slot together to form a super-robot – not only permitting the recycling of footage of the transformation sequence, but also encouraging sales of not one, but three tie-in toys (Clements and McCarthy 2006: 567).

> Transformation – whether of a toy car that transforms into a spaceship, or a character that transforms from one form to another – has a particularly powerful impact on the 3-through-7 year old. The child below approximately 8 years old does not have the cognitive sophistication of the 8+ year old and this limits his ability to see and discern the beginning, middle and end of a transformation process and hold it in his mind all at once. A transformational event, therefore, appears magical to him and has a great deal of surprise impact.
>
> After approximately the age of 7, the child's brain is developing sufficiently so that he/she can, in a sense, see behind the curtain and know that X has changed to Y but still remains X 'really'. The 7+ year old will still enjoy the transformations but will 'know the trick', so to speak. **He will also demand more and more sophisticated transformations in order to be impressed.** (Acuff with Reiher 1997: 69 – my emphasis in bold)

The same toy company, Bandai, was responsible for both *Mazinger* and *Getter Robo* toys,[11] and had developed a policy for its animation tie-ins that demanded a tripartite design sequence: they must look 'cool', they must look 'strong' and they must have some form of motion or functionality (Schodt 1988: 96). It is this latter variable that can be seen as the impetus towards the ultimate functionality of Japanese toys later in the period: that of modularised toys that could either be reconfigured into supertoys, or transformed through a puzzlelike sequence of twists and turns, to alter from one form to another. This, in turn, reflects an industrial development, as larger, less functional twelve-inch 'dolls' were superseded in the 1970s and into the 1980s by smaller five-inch 'action figures' – easier to store and transport, but requiring some element of functionality to justify the higher price for a smaller object.

These action figures are cited by Tanizaki Akira (1999: 163–80) as the objects that form a new chronology within Japanese animation, from the simple, clunky tin robots of the 1960s, leading to the intricate, dual-purpose 'transforming' toys of *Chōjiku Yōsai Macross* (1982, *Super Dimension Fortress Macross*) and ultimately the vehicle/mecha combinations of *Transformers* (1985).

The studio with the greatest investment in the burgeoning mecha sector was Sunrise, formed in 1972 by refugees from the collapse of Mushi Pro. The Sunrise animators spent the first half of the 1970s working on unassuming TV shows, drifting all the while closer to the mecha toy tie-in genre, which, unlike other genres, had not already been colonised by other studios. Notably, Sunrise also attempted from the outset to run on lines less subject to the flaws that had created tension at Tōei and brought Mushi down. As the Sunrise director Takahashi Ryōsuke put it:

> You ask me what the difference was between Mushi and Sunrise. Largely, it was that Tezuka wasn't there. He had a real faith in artists and animators. The trouble with artists and animators, is that they often don't like to work! Artists weren't salaried at Sunrise. They had to produce work in order to get paid, and that made a big difference. All the companies in the 1970s were set up, to some extent, in reaction to the failure of Mushi, but it was only Sunrise that perfected it. (Takahashi 2012)

Sunrise favoured a producer-led system, moving away from the schmoozing required to drag sponsors to a pre-existing property, to a more businesslike arranged marriage in which a property could be concocted to meet the needs of sponsors. Sunrise found its footing with *Muteki Chōjin Zambot 3* (1977, *Super Machine Zambot 3*), one of several shows in the period which paid lip-service to an 'original work' in manga form in its credits, albeit one written by one of the Sunrise founders (Animage 1988: 75). In other words, the manga was no longer a source for the anime, but a complement to it – an example of what would come to be known as the 'media mix' (Katō 2009: 151). Sunrise achieved lasting notoriety with the show that would represent the perfect opportunity to sell literally millions of robot toys and model kits, *Kidō Senshi Gundam* (1979, *Mobile Suit Gundam*), the sequels, prequels and reimaginings of which continue to this day, in addition to the seasonal alteration of factory moulds and peripherals, which permits the toy industry to maintain the same essential workflow, producing very similar products year to year, but with differences in branding that prove essential, and collectible, to the show's fans.

The segmentation of animation, once a mainstream phenomenon watched by all, into an age- and gender-based ghetto mainly aimed at children, was a function of the way in which the available sponsors were able to justify their market. Where once producers and sponsors alike had been unsure of how ratings monetised into actual sales, it had only taken a few seasons to determine the correlation between viewers and consumers. *Qtarō the Ghost* was an early documented case of the statistical anomalies of perceived 'popularity', versus ratings and toy sales. Initial broadcasts of *Qtarō* showed a TV rating of around 15 per cent, regarded as disappointing by its owners. However, as the merchandise took hold and the theme song gained ground with the public, it rose to a healthy 30 per cent broadcast share (Yamazaki 2005: 46). Producers on the show realised that fighting over audience share became irrelevant in the children's market once the relatively small sector of young viewers was on board. With a finite number of children, only a finite number of toys could be sold.

> In the case of children's programming, including animation, sales of merchandise do not change above an audience rating of 15 per cent. In other words, once the goods are distributed, the audience rating no longer affects revenue. Even though *Obake no Qtarō* was popular, once the merchandise stopped selling, the animation served no purpose. It became more profitable to make a new programme, in order to sell new merchandise. After all, TV cartoons are nothing but advertising. There should not be a cultural value to protect as 'art'. That, at least, was the attitude of advertisers and television companies towards the nascent genre. (Yamazaki 2005: 49)

In other words, if a show was designed to sell commodities, and the value of those commodities had a shelf-life of only six months or a year, it was better to shut a show down after twenty-six or fifty-two episodes, and replace it with something that was similar, but not exactly the same. Steinberg (2012: 158) notes that this has proved an increasingly tantalising prospect to manufacturers, where a fridge or car, even with built-in obsolescence, might last a consumer seven years, but a flavour-of-the-moment TV show, badge or song, was likely to require 'replacement' after a half-life of only eighteen months.

The direct involvement of sponsors in production came to suggest, and then demand, a recurring structure of investment: a TV broadcaster, a record company, a toy company and possibly even other investors – candy manufacturers, perhaps, or book publishers. Such an organisation was already implicit in the confluence of companies that funded *Astro Boy* in 1963, but *Astro Boy* had remained the property of Tezuka Osamu. The potential for merchandising, it seems, took many staff by surprise – Tsuji Masaki (1996: 37–8) reports taking calls in the early 1960s from manufacturers keen to put images from children's shows on cards, records and colouring crayons/pencils, and the realisation at the channel TBS that, because the intellectual property of *Eightman* belonged to the channel, the channel stood to make extra money from the licensing. By the beginning of the 1980s, the ownership of new anime shows was often divided between a patchwork of business interests, each expecting some form of return on its investment – a particular kind of merchandise, for example, or exclusive rights to sell a particular spin-off commodity. Such assemblies of interests became known as production committees (*seisaku iinkai*), and their presence is implicit in the sameness of much anime that followed – not in terms of mere 'product placement', but of 'context integration' that makes the elements of the story itself a prolonged advert for associated merchandise: robots that transform, a multi-member team with a token female, signature vehicles, a cute mascot that can be turned into a plush toy, or a theme song that highlights the new single from a particular company's star.

THE KANADA PERSPECTIVE AND THE ITANO CIRCUS

Miyazaki Hayao wrote in the 1980s of the long-lasting effect of these shows, suggesting that the piling on of vehicles and action and 'context integration' had created an unwelcome superabundance – a hyperactive, hyperreal on-screen chaos of TV shows that were often indistinguishable:

> To help shows recover after slumps in popularity, the creators then went to ever more excessive lengths to compensate. Whereas in the beginning they might have had two *mecha* machines combining together to form one giant robot, they began making three, or five, or ultimately – in a ridiculous extreme – twenty-six elements combine into a robot … . They also started using more and more colors … painting hair in every imaginable wild color in emulation of the latest fashions. (Miyazaki 2009: 79)

Miyazaki notes that this surfeit of busy on-screen action goes hand in hand with the drastic drop in animation quality fostered by Tezuka and his successors. The wild variations in anime hair colour, for example, have less to do with punk fashion and more with methods of finding an easy way to differentiate a large cast that has been cheaply drawn. Character archetypes soon drifted into stereotypes, with a male lead often adopting identifiably 'Japanese characteristics' – black hair and a red/white colour scheme on his uniform or signature vehicle. As in the live-action hero shows, five becomes a recurring number, reflecting the five cardinal colours of the Chinese elements, but also a belief among producers that three was a 'lonely' number and four was unlucky (Gill 1998: 41).

Animation remained 'limited' in the Mushi Pro style, itself pushing storytelling towards conditions that favoured repetition, fast cutting and cutaways to still background vistas. Miyazaki notes (2009: 78–9) that the audience has been 'conditioned by the visual language of manga' into accepting not only the deformation of images, but the absence of movement. Marc Steinberg (2012: 24–5) calls this the 'immobile image', and observes that it has been a feature of Japanese visual storytelling since at least the days of the kamishibai. It was, however, anathema to the very idea of 'animating' as pursued by Tōei Dōga.

The 'mechanic design' of the early 1970s had transformed by 1980 into a 'mecha corrector' (*mecha shūsei*), a post originally ascribed to the animator Kanada Yoshinori, with special responsibility for modifying others' artwork in order to accentuate the accuracy of the machinery, the action of the machinery and, ultimately, the destruction of said machinery, including the explosions involved (Hikawa 1999: 205–6). It is Kanada who is largely credited with certain common images in anime, in part because the imminent arrival of video (see next chapter) would ensure that his particular style was available for close and slow-motion study by younger animators still in education.

> Kanada's unique drawing style featured boldly exaggerated perspective and posing, which earned the popular nickname of 'Kanada Pers' (short for 'Perspective'). Rather than falling back on the stock-standard camera angles of previous anime he expanded the stage by using wide-angle lens and fish-eye distortion in his layouts, which gave them a new sense of depth. This was ideal for mecha anime, and Kanada greatly emphasized the power of giant robots with acrobatic flying and fighting styles. (Eldred 2009)

Kanada also exploited the potential for camera angles even further than had already been attempted in *Star of the Giants*, capitalising on the fact that scenes in space did not require horizons or even a consensus on which way was up.

Other animators soon imitated Kanada's approach, leading to what Hikawa (1999: 206) terms the 'mock Kanada' (*Kanada-modoki*) style of subsequent science-fiction anime – although this rather implies that Kanada instigated much of modern mecha anime's stylistics, whereas other animators can certainly lay claim to influences on such trended change. Itano Ichirō, for example, an early 'mecha director' who specialised in combat machinery after early employment on *Danguard Ace* (1977), and was an animator on both *Gundam* and *Macross*, also worked with fish-eye or wide-angle effects, but experimented with furious, busy sequences as if the action were being filmed by characters with handheld cameras, buffeted and shaken by turbulence; some of his aerial-combat sequences were deliberately framed as if filmed by sky-diving cameramen in freefall (Hikawa 1999: 211).

Itano appears to have realised that limited animation, in turn, could favour a heightened sense of movement, not because it was 'limited' animation, but because truly swift movement eroded the gap between full and limited animation. As Chuck Jones recalled in the US:

> When we were doing *Rikki-Tikki-Tavi*, we had to study some film of a cobra striking so we could be accurate in showing a fight between a mongoose and a cobra. In one clip, the cobra actually struck the camera … . Now, apparently this cobra was eight feet away when he struck the camera – and yet there was only one frame between the two positions! He travelled eight feet in a twenty-fourth of a second! (Lewell 1982: 136)

The situation Jones describes also demonstrates one of anime's distinctive visual tropes in the making. Sheer speed, be it of darting swordplay or rocket-propelled action, can reach a level at which 'limited' animation is no longer limited, because even a 'full' rendering of the action would fail to capture it at twelve or even twenty-four images a second. Itano's signature device would soon become an explosive, multiple-launch missile attack, complete with curving contrails and devastating explosions, often from a perspective inside the action, such that the relative velocities of camera and launch vehicle caused some missiles to travel at different speeds to others, or even hang briefly in midair. The superabundant image of this 'Itano Circus' (Hikawa 1999: 211) accentuated the on-screen chaos, but also rewarded repeat viewings – another issue soon to become important with the advent of video.

TOMINO YOSHIYUKI AND 'REAL ROBOTS'

One director, Tomino Yoshiyuki, rejected the previous context-integrated simplicity of earlier shows, such as the directive he received (2002: 289) on *Yūsha Raideen* (1975, *Brave Raideen*), which tellingly utilises several English-language terms seemingly co-opted from the rituals of professional wrestling:

> You introduce a powerful opponent for Raideen, show them fighting the first *round*, and then show how Raideen polishes them off. That's the basic ingredient. Then you add a little story each episode. The most important thing is to show what weapons Raideen uses, and … you have to have lots of scenes which the kids will think are cool – showing his big *finish* move and *pose*.

Instead, Tomino's work throughout the late 1970s shows an ever-growing will to take the 'giant robot' shows more seriously, disregarding the vaguer, fantastical notions of children's entertainment, and attempting to inject more mature themes and explanations. Essentially, Tomino allowed his work to age with the generation that watched *Brave Raideen*, injecting elements more likely to appeal to more mature audiences. As his *Zambot 3* reached the end of its broadcast run in early 1978, Tomino shocked viewers by killing off several prominent cast members – at, it should be noted, no loss to a franchise that was already being shut down. The following year, in *Mobile Suit Gundam*, Tomino kept to the basic formulae of context-integrated toy shows, but offered a series of reasoned rationales for some of the counterintuitive tropes of modern anime.[12] Tomino, for example, found a reason for close combat in space between mechanical warriors, by positing 'Minovsky particles' that rendered radar inoperable (Schodt 1988: 88). He drew on the contemporary fame of Uri Geller to suggest a 'new breed' of children with psychic powers (Tomino 2002: 288), and invented straightforward logistical reasons to explain why teenage children got to be pilots in the first place. As Tanizaki Akira (1999: 163–4) observes, in the space of just a few years between the first episode of *Zambot 3* in October 1977 and the end of the original *Gundam* in January 1980, Tomino articulated a new response to the 'mecha' shows of previous seasons, creating a new genre of 'real robots', turning what was once an almost magical, fantastical icon (a *chōjin*, or 'superman' in Tanizaki's terms), into a simple, functional weapon or tool.

Despite low initial ratings, *Mobile Suit Gundam* (1979) has become one of the cash-cow franchises in modern anime

This focus on believability – on mecha that increasingly needed to obey at least some of the laws of physics – was, however, not a trope liable to endure long on television. In fact, the first *Gundam* series ended early, taken off air after a relatively low episode count of forty-three – its reception had been lacklustre, with initial ratings hovering unimpressively around the 5 per cent mark (Tada 2002: 29). However, its artistic heritage, rejuvenated by subsequent feature-length movie edits, and with repeats that gained it a 15 per cent audience share, would make it a pivotal event in the history of anime.

It was video, a new technology of distribution and exhibition, which allowed the *Brave Raideen* audience to remain with anime in the 1980s, long after earlier generations might have grown out of the medium. That same audience demonstrably had money to spend on spin-offs, with 4.4 million *Gundam* models sold in the two years after the release of the feature re-edit in cinemas (Tada 2002: 30).

The 'long' 1970s is often regarded as an intermediate period in the history of Japanese animation, separating the initial flourish of television of the 1960s from the sudden expansion of adult-oriented video in the 1980s. However, the apparent lack of incident, implied by the stability and endurance of *Sazae-san* and seasonal cinema events, belies a fervent series of technical and stylistic developments in the look and content of Japanese animation. The period saw deep changes in methods of production and practices of ownership, which in turn set the scene for what was arguably anime's greatest transformation, the arrival of commercial videotape in 1983, and its reception by a viewership that had grown up surrounded by the products of the medium now widely known as 'anime'.

NOTES

1. Literally, 'the union was opposed to a *meritocracy*' (*nōryokushugi*).
2. The most accessible written source for these is the Animage *Art of Animation II*, which contains data on each event for Tōei (1989: 47, 50, 52, 53, 55, 56, 58, 59, 60, 62, 63, 64, 67, 68, 69, 75, 81) and Tōhō (1989: 52, 553, 54, 55, 56, 57, 58, 59, 61, 62, 64, 65, 67, 69, 73).
3. Yamamoto (1989: 186) notes that the PTAs were far more approving of *Jungle Emperor*, the first TV programme to be *recommended* for children.
4. But see Wada-Marciano (2008: 63), who suggests that a very similar genre was part of Japanese film in the 1920s.
5. Ladd (Ladd with Deneroff 2009: 87) claims that this is what 'started' the Korean animation industry, seemingly unaware that his arrival came twelve years after the first broadcast work of Korean animation, itself made in response to the Korean release of Disney's *Peter Pan* (1953) (Yu 1999: 52).
6. Clements and Tamamuro (2003: 69).
7. Released in English as *Phantom Agents* – Clements and Tamamuro (2003: 237–8).
8. It is worth noting that experimentation was not solely the purview of Tatsunoko Pro. Many anecdotes recount the tricks and fudges common in the animation industry, such as Tsuji Masaki's claim (1996: 19) that the twinkling of the stars in the climax of *Jungle Emperor* was achieved by shooting through a silk stocking.

9. Filed as *Animentary: Critical Moments* in Clements and McCarthy (2006: 23) and many online sources, but as *Ketsudan* in Animage (1988: 37). The film will be referred to by its Japanese title, by which it is more typically known.

10. It could be argued that this attitude reflected that of the founder of the Hiroshima International Animation Festival, Kinoshita Renzō, who left Mushi Pro to start his own studio, and whose short films won numerous foreign accolades in the 1970s. As Clements and McCarthy (2006: 342) put it: 'before the post-*Akira* boom of the 1990s, Kinoshita was arguably the "official" face of Japanese animation abroad'.

11. *Mazinger Z* toys were initially made by another company called Popy, which was acquired by Bandai.

12. Sadamoto Yoshiyuki notes (Hotta 2005: 139) that what truly made Tomino a 'pro amongst pros' was his ability to deliver a product that satisfied the radically different demands of both sponsors and fans.

8 THE THIRD MEDIUM

The transformation of ownership and access 1977–96

In a period characterised by a booming Japanese economy (Kawai 1999: 81) and the increased availability of investment capital (Masuda 2007: 133–4), the advent of video led to a massive transformation in the nature of anime at the levels of ownership (studios and consumers), distribution and exhibition (video), and access (audiences). Such transformations, as noted by Barbara Klinger in *Beyond the Multiplex* (2006), affected all developed markets worldwide, with prospects not only for revenue from tape rentals and sales, but also in the potential for preserving artistic heritage long after initial TV broadcast or cinema exhibition. In Japan, this created a sudden segmentation of the anime market, preserving the pre-existing structure of children's entertainment, but also forming a new discourse among viewers who had been children in the 1960s and 1970s, now able to consume sequels and remakes with an adult sensibility. Tsugata (2011b: 30) has suggested that these changes truly created 'anime' as we know it today, distinct from the simpler 'Japanese animation industry' discussed in earlier chapters.

In terms of periodisation, this chapter spans the era from the widespread commercial availability of the video cassette recorder (VCR) to the impact of the DVD, cable broadcasting and other digital disruptions. It also considers the role of active fandom and magazine publishing in fostering a 'culture' of anime during the period, and hence begins in the watershed year of 1977 – when anime on TV first climbed above fifty titles in a single year.

The introduction of video created a new area of growth in the anime business. Combined sales of videos and laserdiscs (the 'videogram' market), intended either for rental or for direct retail, climbed for the next decade, with the quantifiable 'boom' years marked by the most rapid growth in 1985, another leap in 1989 and a third, smaller bump in 1995 (see Table 8.1).

TABLE 8.1: JAPANESE VIDEOGRAM ANIME SALES 1983–96

YEAR	SALES (IN BILLION YEN)
1983	2.7
1984	4.8
1985	8.2
1986	9.9
1987	12.3
1988	17.0
1989	28.4
1990	29.2
1991	31.5
1992	35.9
1993	41.5
1994	47.8
1995	61.0
1996	63.2

Source: Matsumoto (2011b: 185).

Of course, 'ownership' of movies was theoretically possible before the time of video, and Tezuka Osamu himself boasted (1997: 17–19) of his father's home projector and stash of expensive cartoon prints in the 1930s. We might also speculate as to the fate of the thousands of 16mm film projectors that were dumped on the Japanese public during the 1940s Occupation in order to facilitate the dissemination of 'information' films. It has always been possible for private individuals to 'own' films if they had the cash. Video, however, brought the prospect of owning a physical copy of a film, viewable on a whim, within the financial means of the wider public.

Technically, 'ownership' for consumers was, and still is, a fallacy. As the smallprint copyright notice diligently informs the viewer, the possession of a video cassette brings with it no rights to the intellectual property it contains. The possessor of a video cassette of *Akira* does not 'own' the film itself, but the right to watch that particular copy of it as often as he or she desires, in a private home (not a prison, oil rig or public hall), without charging admission, until such time as the tape wears out.

However, true ownership was a far more realistic prospect for animation companies, many of which had previously only worked on productions as labourers for hire. The arrival of video also brought true ownership within reach of those smaller production houses that were not vertically integrated into larger corporations. While it was still expensive to produce anime, a venture to make, say, a thirty-minute video original no longer entailed an investment of millions of yen in broadcast time-slots or theatrical bookings, but was now within the means of any investor prepared to remortgage an average-sized apartment. Whereas an angry distributor could have once killed a new work simply by refusing to release it (see, for example, the fate of *The King's Tail* in Chapter 4), video freed anime producers from the need to pander to such whims, as long as they did not mind the likelihood of smaller returns away from the cinema sector. Such a prospect encouraged many animation studios to leap from production into, at the very least, participation in a committee of investors in intellectual property that they themselves would control (Masuda 2007: 132). This, too, freed anime from many conservative constraints, and led to an era of wild experimentation, truncated failures and, eventually, successes in unexpected niches.

At the beginning of the period, most Japanese animation companies remained manufacturers with no claim on the intellectual property they produced as work for hire. Although some Japanese studios were undoubtedly simply grateful for any work, others baulked at their subaltern status, forced to continue their participation in the process solely at a production level, and within the constraints of budgets and parameters that necessitated limited animation. Masunari Kōji has noted that television production sets a minimum level of quality that also fast becomes a maximum level – in his case setting storyboard requirements at a notional 60–80 per cent of an animator's actual ability. Conversely in film production, there is no notional baseline for quality and no easy way of setting milestones, causing stress to animators who cannot assess their achievement until the entire film is complete (Kushida 2010: 98).

Fujioka Yutaka, the founder of Tokyo Movie, was reportedly annoyed at the imposition of limited animation on the medium, and deliberately sought coproduction deals in order to secure the higher funding that, he hoped, would ultimately allow him to bring his company's products to a notional pinnacle of 'full' animation (Yamazaki 2005: 188). However, the first fruits of his contacts with American studios merely amounted to more TV animation deals, with Tokyo Movie joining the ranks of below-the-line Japanese production houses (see Chapter 5), with subcontracted work on such American shows as *The Mighty Orbots* (1984).

Fujioka's attempt to involve Tokyo Movie in ownership and authorship, rather than mere production, had an unexpected side effect when negotiations with Disney turned sour. On an unspecified *Winnie the Pooh* cartoon project, a Japanese feint in order to secure more prominent involvement inadvertently kept the Japanese in subaltern status, but with significantly more money:

> Every single right that you can possibly think of, including the copyright for the work and the characters had to be solely owned by Disney. Otherwise they would not sign the contract. So we demanded 50 million yen as the production fee, which was accepted without problem. So we signed the contract, but …
> (Yamazaki 2005: 189)

A rise in the value of the yen immediately halved the effective amount of the deal, as it was to be paid in dollars that were now worth considerably less. Moreover, Fujioka's efforts were hampered by the erosion of the primacy of film itself, as independent exhibition events declined in favour of works that used the cinema to either cash in on pre-existing television properties, or advertise something that would shortly begin broadcast.

TABLE 8.2: ORIGINAL ANIME FILMS IN JAPANESE CINEMAS 1977–86

YEAR	ORIGINALS	SEQUELS OR TV RE-EDITS
1977	2	3
1978	4	8
1979	4	8
1980	4	14
1981	5	15
1982	5	16
1983	8	11
1984	6	13
1985	14	17
1986	19	20

Source: Animage (1989: 69–124).

By the late 1970s (see Table 8.2), television had largely colonised the world of Japanese cartoon film exhibition, with sequels or spin-offs from pre-existing television shows representing the majority of 'anime films' screened in Japanese cinemas. The percentage goes even higher if 'originals' based on fairy-tales are reassigned to the spin-off column, or if objects are counted by running time rather than title, since many of the 'originals' were short films, whereas the spin-offs were often cut together from many hours of TV footage. If we also count spin-offs from manga or live-action shows as 'sequels', then the number of originals during the period declines to only one or two a year. This, however, brings us closer to the 'media mix' (Steinberg 2012: 161–9), first discussed in Japan in the 1960s, but actively applied in numerous sectors of Japanese entertainment during the 1970s. In particular, Marc Steinberg notes (2012: 160, 165) the 'dissolution of the work into serial fragments' and the 'environmentalisation of media', turning access to anime from that of a creative work screened to an audience, to that of a constant oscillating 'media ecology' of TV viewing, cinemagoing, comic-reading, and active fandom.

There is an apparent upturn in 'original' works from 1983 onwards, although 'originality' here is often a moot point. We might, for example, note that *Penguin's Memory* (1985), while not technically a spin-off from a television series or a manga, had its origins in a series of animated TV commercials for Suntory Beer that ran throughout the previous year. Similarly, *Kamui no Ken* (1985, *Dagger of Kamui*) was an 'original' film without a television tie-in, but was based on a 1970 novel. More crucially, the mid- to late 1980s saw a rise in 'original' material in cinemas that was itself a spin-off from a new medium of distribution – the video cassette.

In the last days of 1983, a subsidiary of Bandai's video division released a thirty-minute episode of *Dallos*, a science-fiction anime by Studio Pierrot, an offshoot of Tatsunoko Pro. The work was obscure and almost impenetrable, since an accident of distribution had led the 'second' episode to be released almost a month ahead of the first. *Dallos* was written and directed, at least officially, by Toriumi Hisayuki, who had been a prominent animator in the 1960s and 1970s, and Oshii Mamoru, a younger director, also formerly of Tatsunoko, who had made his feature anime debut earlier that year with the acclaimed *Urusei Yatsura: Only You*.

Dallos has a special place in the history of Japanese animation because it was the 'first' work to be released straight to video. Potential viewers had to either buy the tapes or laserdiscs for themselves, or rent them. However, it does not hold up aesthetically as a work of note. Indeed, critics observed that it was 'badly served by hackneyed setups and execution by staff members who had yet to realise that the video audience would be slightly older than the viewership for TV serials' (Clements and McCarthy 2006: 129). Nevertheless, it heralded a transformation in the structure of the anime industry, wrenching distribution from the hands of studios and broadcasters, and delivering it into the hands of cornerstores, rental libraries and mail-order firms. This altered the level of exhibition, often turning a teenager's bedroom into a new screening venue, and hence encouraging genres more suitable to private viewing. Anime finally had a medium in which it could 'grow up', allowing the more mature thematic experiments of creators such as Tomino Yoshiyuki (see Chapter 7) to endure beyond the end of their particular season.

Misono Makoto (1999: 47) describes the arrival of video as the catalyst for an 'anime boom', but also for an 'age of confusion' (*konmei no jidai*), in which new forms of access and distribution presented unpredictable disruptions. Video offered new alternatives to the pre-existing media of cinema and television, leading to its swift recognition as a 'third medium' (Tokugi 1999: 307); however, there was also no clear consensus among producers and investors as to how video might be best exploited commercially, leading to chaotic experiments in content (Tokugi 1999: 310).

Traditionally, the video boom is articulated as a phenomenon that begins with the release of *Dallos* (Clements and McCarthy 2006: 646) and the subsequent rush of new works. Certainly, the number of new anime released straight to video doubled the number of titles in the anime market by the year 1986.[1] However, a concentration on the newest and most noticeable forms of anime in the period risks ignoring less visible changes elsewhere in the market. Video, after all, already existed in Japan in 1983, and had for some years offered viewers the chance to see older movies again or to record TV shows. Hence it did not merely introduce new themes and content to a dedicated audience, but also transformed the artistic heritage of its two 'rival' media.

Increasingly, cinema and television ceased to be unrepeatable 'events', but could be accessed by consumers long after their initial broadcast or theatrical release. To give but one example, a wartime obscurity such as Seo Mitsuyo's *Momotarō's Divine Sea Warriors*, once believed lost forever, was not only rediscovered but re-released on VHS, transforming its artistic heritage from mere rumour to a physical, accessible presence, available to any member of the public for a mere 3,800 yen (Takefuji 1993: 447). As a bonus extra, the *Momotarō* VHS tape also included Masaoka Kenzō's *The Spider and the Tulip*, transforming it from a hard-to-see print in a film library into a historical document available from any videostore. While the release of original content such as *Dallos* changed the nature of the anime market, the accessibility of older materials also offered the potential to change the discourse of anime for viewers, critics, historians and would-be animators – transforming the available archive of anime resources from an exclusive club into a mass-market phenomenon.

PRODUCTION: SCANIMATION AND LINE TESTING

Industrial videotape had been used in broadcast television since the 1950s (Clements and Tamamuro 2003: xv) and, although anime were still assembled frame by frame on film, videotape remained the default means of delivery to broadcasters. Tatsunoko Pro, a studio always prepared to experiment with new techniques (see Chapter 7),

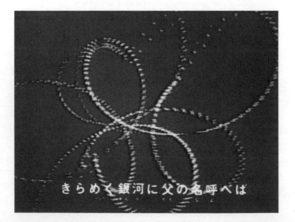

spiced up the opening credits of *Uchū no Kishi Tekkaman* (1975, *Space Knight Tekkaman*) with an effect whereby several images and credits vanished into harmonic waves.[2] This technique, referred to as 'scanimation' (Hikawa 1999: 203–4), used video playback to distort images into Lissajous curves, required the control of a digital circuit (a 'video synthesiser'), and hence arguably amounts to anime's first 'computer animation'. However, once the novelty of the new gimmick had worn off, the pulsating curves of scanimation were difficult to employ for any purpose other than decoration – they soon faded from

The opening sequence of *Space Knight Tekkaman* (1975) used video playback to create a harmonic wave effect

Tekkaman, but were retained as a recurring special effect in the same studio's *Time Bokan* (1975) to denote the operation of time-travel machinery.

Videotape found a more enduring application further back in the production process, when animators at several studios began to use on-site video cameras to shoot draft sequences of line drawings. This afforded animators the immediate opportunity to test timings, plot complex set-ups or even to make 'animatic' versions of their work in advance of actual shooting. Known in the English-speaking world as a 'line tester' (Taylor 2002: 11), these video camera set-ups were soon computer-controlled and referred to in Japan as Quick Action Recorders (QAR):

> Storyboards could be drawn in detail. By inputting the images and timings, if we replay them it is possible to study various problems during creation such as scene change, movement flow and whether timing was good. (Mochinaga 2006: 299)

Pioneered in Japan by the animation company NAC (AJA 2008 I: 88), QAR machines were presumably widespread by September 1983, when Mochinaga Tadahito travelled to China in order to demonstrate them to local subcontractors. Mochinaga (2006: 297) observes that his training assignment was preferable to previous attempts when Chinese animators had been sent to Japan for shorter training sessions, suggesting that the QAR was in use for a considerable period before his trip. However, he also notes that Chinese studios were liable to misuse the equipment, or at least fail to utilise its full potential. Once he had demonstrated the most basic applications of the machines, the Chinese animators would fail to attend further sessions. Mochinaga also sourly noted that the Chinese failed to maintain optimum conditions in the room where the QAR machine was kept:

> It was lucky that the machine had not broken down. When I mentioned this, a woman started to clean straight away. Excessive sanitary management would not hurt. [Even] Today in Japan some of these machines have trouble with their processors due to cockroaches that nest inside because of the warmth. So, cleaning is very important. So, too, is temperature control. The best results are when the temperature is between ten and thirty-five degrees and the humidity is between thirty and eighty per cent. Computers can go wrong if that is not maintained. (Mochinaga 2006: 298)

In many cases, the QAR machine was the first application of actual computing in the anime industry, but remained a specialised industrial tool rather than a commonplace desktop sight.

EXHIBITION: TIME-SHIFTING AND ARCHIVING

Video itself achieved far greater visibility among the anime audience, although neither software nor hardware was within the means of the average consumer until the late 1970s. Sony's Betamax and JVC's VHS formats were introduced in 1975 and 1976 respectively although, with initial costs exceeding 260,000 yen, they were still unaffordable in the mass market.

Nor did advertising make it immediately apparent what these 'video cassette recorders' were actually for. Japanese TV commercials in the 1970s featured a narrator listing Hollywood celebrities whose works were largely out of copyright in Japan, such as Charlie Chaplin and Marlene Dietrich, and cryptically adding that it was now possible 'to meet them whenever you want' with the aid of his Mac Lord VCR.[3] The chance to timeshift, but also to pause and review sporting events was another benefit cited in 1970s commercials, and soon advertising was highlighting the combination of VCR with personal video cameras. Until the early 1980s, the on-screen content visible in Japanese VCR commercials seemed deliberately restricted to sports, live events or indistinct nature images, as if the manufacturers dare not admit the VCR's application for watching copyrighted works.

They also occupied a legal grey area, particularly regarding their application for recording programmes from broadcast television. In the 'Betamax' case of Sony versus Universal City Studios, the US Supreme Court eventually ruled by a thin majority in Sony's favour, that videotaping for 'timeshifting' purposes constituted 'fair use' (Lobato 2012: 72):

time-shifting merely enables a viewer to see such a work which he had been invited to witness in its entirety free of charge, the fact … that the entire work is reproduced … does not have its ordinary effect of militating against a finding of fair use. (US Supreme Court 1984)

Only ten days after the Supreme Court's ruling, which established that VCR sales would be internationally uncontested, Sony launched a Japanese media campaign to assert the primacy of its Betamax format. Meanwhile, competitors using the rival VHS format began asserting more clearly that the VCR's functions included timeshifting – not merely coyly demonstrating the operation of the timer, but now also depicting programmes on screen, including children's cartoons, juxtaposed with the smiling face of a little girl who now, presumably, no longer missed her favourite show.

Misono (1999: 55) notes that television anime by 1986 exercised a 'broadening power' with shows such as *Dragon Ball*, *Maison Ikkoku* and *Gundam ZZ* all beginning their runs that year. However, his assessment seems to mix cause and effect. He identifies certain shows as having an enduring legacy within the tradition of anime fans, but surely the greatest contributing factor to this legacy is the fact that, thanks to videotape, they can now be remembered. VCR ownership in Japan by 1986 had reached the average private home. TV ownership continued to rise in the 1980s, and did not plateau until 1992, suggesting that some homes had multiple sets, and that a TV rating that showed a mainstream programme watched in the lounge, did not necessarily preclude the possibility that an entirely different programme was being watched simultaneously in another room (Clements and Tamamuro 2003: xv; Kawai 1999: 266).

The presence of videotapes, either pre-recorded or recorded from the television, finally allowed for the creation of an 'archive' of available anime, making it as accessible a hobby as, say, manga or science-fiction novels had previously been. The practice of being an anime fan hence now contained the prospect of a more active fandom. It was no longer merely a case of discussing one's favourite show; instead, it could be analysed, checked and rechecked and even shared with friends who might never have otherwise seen it. Nagayama Yasuo (2012: 238) likens this potential to the discovery of 'time travel', allowing viewers to revisit past events that had previously been unique and often unshared. A passion for anime was now easier to replicate, by the simple practice of helping others see it.

The widespread availability of video recorders not only made it possible for audiences to preserve and rewatch their favourite shows beyond the original intended broadcast. It also had an unforeseen industrial consequence, affording young animators the chance to spool in slow motion through the work of their elders. Hikawa Ryūsuke, for example, argues (1999: 306) that the sudden spread of the style of Kanada Yoshinori in the 1980s (see Chapter 7), was not merely a matter of aesthetics, but because trainee animators could now break down his sequences by watching them frame by frame. The kind of apprenticeship that was once only available to actual apprentices, or in extreme cases to enterprising artists who rifled through a studio's trash in search of discarded layouts (Ishiguro and Ohara 1980: 103), was now within the reach of would-be animators thanks to off-the-shelf consumer goods.

MATURING AUDIENCES, MAGAZINES AND CONVERGENT CONSUMPTION

These viewers in their teens in 1977, around the time of the violent ending of *Zambot 3*, formed the generation whose disposable income bought the first anime magazines and rented the first anime videos. Generational location was an important consideration in the period, which saw the coming of age of the post-war generation, and inevitable dissonance between it and the generation that preceded it.

Misono (1999: 44) suggests that at the production level, the animators entering the business in the early 1980s were the first generation to have grown up as consumers of television animation.[4] In other words, the reorientation of anime towards an implied 'fandom' was not merely a feature of technology, but also of attitudinal differences between the new generation and their predecessors.

However, his assertion is just as easily applied at the access level – the generation of children who had grown up watching cartoons as children, had now entered its teens. This inevitably brought some of them into contact with the long-established world of prose science-fiction fandom, where the sudden arrival of anime fans transformed many elements of science fiction's convention culture, leading to factional tensions and ultimately what Nagayama Yasuo calls (2012: 160) an 'otaku revolution'.

Nagahama Tadao, the director who had appealed to mature audiences with *Star of the Giants* said in 1978:

> What is missing from TV is anime aimed for junior and senior high-school kids. I want to give them something that gives impact on their heart. They want to, and feel they *ought* to read essays on life, but they have to study instead. But at least when they watch anime, they should be able to see earnest ideas on how to live. That is the kind of programme I would like to make (Misono 1999: 275)

Nagahama's comments allude to the possibility of anime aimed specifically at a viewership older than school-children. By the late 1970s, there were pioneers within the Japanese animation business who saw in this ageing, or rather, maturing, population of viewers new opportunities for a closed circle of consumption, such as magazines *about* Japanese animation (Tada 2002: 19), including its artwork, merchandise, voice actors and spin-offs, beginning with *OUT* in March 1977 (closed 1995), and soon followed by *Animage* (1978), *Animec* (1978–87), *The Anime* (1979–86), *My Anime* (1981–6), *B-Club* (1985–98)[5] and *Newtype* (1985).

OUT magazine, dedicated to movie subculture in general, was established in a year when the number of television broadcast anime climbed above fifty for the first time (AJA 2008 I: 37) – thirty new shows and almost as many repeats. This, combined with that year's handful of theatrical releases, seems to represent a tipping point in the number of objects required to create an 'archive' (Foucault 2002: 145) of items that could be studied, debated and discussed.

The number of anime accessible to the Japanese consumer has never diminished since that date. In fact, considering the arrival of video, the number of accessible anime has increased almost exponentially – not only in cinemas, but also on multiple television channels and from the new fixed sites of rental shops and retail stores. Arguably, 1977 was the first year in which 'anime' and anime fandom could assert a sense of itself as a culture, as a body of work with its own media of discourse, and its own developing sense of history. The first issue of *Animage* in July 1978, for example, was able to highlight the lingering popularity of *Space Cruiser Yamato*, but also the historical value of Takahata Isao's *Little Norse Prince*, the 'best' of current television animation, and a behind-the-scenes visit to the animation studio Tokyo Movie Shinsha. It also printed a focus on the career of the singer Mizuki Ichirō, and an interview with the voice actor Kamiya Akira (Animage 1998: 155). Already, there is evidence of the convergence of various fields of consumption – cinema, television and video (in the case of the reissue of *Little Norse Prince*), but also of tie-ins to theme songs and soundtrack albums; readers also received an exclusive poster of *Space Cruiser Yamato*, rewarding their support for the magazine with an image that both affirmed their fandom and put the magazine's own logo on their wall – what Marc Steinberg (2012: 167) calls an 'intensive expansion' into the readers' daily lives.

Moreover, although there had long been spin-offs or source materials in manga form for anime, 1977 also saw an early appearance of tie-in novels (Misono 1999: 30), with extensions of the *Space Cruiser Yamato* franchise into prose form, as well as events centred on the *Yamato* voice actors. Coupled with *OUT*'s monthly need to report 'anime news', the year arguably saw a noticeable conjunction of materials relating to anime – not only anime themselves both new and old, with the potential to rewatch at will, but also reportage, prose and audio. In all cases, such materials were clearly aimed not at the former children's audience, but at an implied readership of teenagers (Misono 1999: 31).

Answering punditry to the effect that 'the anime boom is actually an anime *character* boom', Ishiguro Noboru (Ishiguro and Ohara 1980: 235) once pointed out that the same could be said of the popularity of *Astro Boy* and *Qtarō the Ghost* a decade earlier. Although character merchandise was undeniably a contributing factor to the success of *Astro Boy*, precedents for such exploitation stretched back to the 1920s (Clements and McCarthy 2006: 166; Steinberg 2009: 117). Marc Steinberg (2012: 139) notes that although the term 'media mix' only entered common Japanese parlance in the 1980s, it often refashioned or refined ideas from the 1960s. It was in the 1960s, for example, that the power of television to function as a constant,

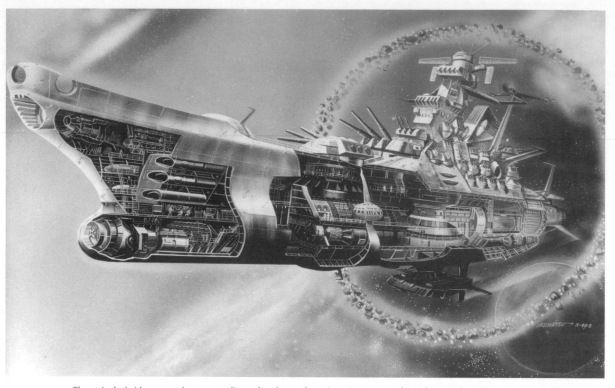

The arrival of video created a new medium of exchange for anime viewers, greatly prolonging the fandom for 1970s shows, and inspiring cinema sequels such as *Space Cruiser Yamato* (1977)

self-reinforcing brand identity began to make itself felt, with the first signs of awareness that spin-off merchandise could amount to more than mere stickers and decals. The theme song of 1969's *Attack No.1* sold 70,000 copies as a single during the two years that the volleyball series ran on Japanese television, with every broadcast amounting to a primetime commercial for the theme song itself (Yamazaki 2005: 121). Similar successes were noted at Mushi Pro, where an album of music from 1966's *Jungle Emperor*, the first of its kind, became a bestseller (Yamamoto 1989: 207–8) and led to heated arguments among the staff as to who should collect the fee for the lyrics, hastily dashed off in a forgotten lunch hour. However, in all such testimonials from the 1960s, the earning potential of such spin-offs is reported almost unintentionally, as if the owners have yet to see the available avenues of exploitation. Tsuji Masaki (1996: 37–8) notes that as a producer in the 1960s he was often beset by toy or card manufacturers wanting to license his product, but that he worked at a company ill equipped to manage such subcontracts.

Steinberg (2012: 149–53) cites Kadokawa Haruki, the publisher of *Newtype* magazine, as a pioneer in 'media-mix' strategies since the 1970s, not merely in anime, but in other media sectors such as pulp paperbacks, film novelisations and manga tie-ins. Steinberg also recognises the self-commemoration inherent in Kadokawa's own memoir; while Kadokawa himself (2005: 127, 133–5) makes these claims, he does so in a book that only half-playfully describes himself as a vainglorious, privileged corporate scion. It is certainly possible to point to Kadokawa as a pioneer in modern media, but this is to a great extent based on Kadokawa's ability to present the world with his autobiography: substantially easier for a millionaire who inherited a publishing company. Kadokawa's book, with its superb Annie Leibovitz cover depicting the author on a Tokyo overpass in knight's armour, is an argument for his role in the period, but is liable to overshadow the achievements of many less publicity-hungry entrepreneurs in the fields of, say, games, video, models or plush toys. There are sure to be other testimonials, as yet unwritten, that will present counterarguments to such an extraordinary bias.

We might also observe, as has been noted elsewhere (e.g. Gomery 2005: 173), that the mid- to late 1970s also represented a period of some transformation in Hollywood. Under the stewardship of Lew Wasserman, an overload of TV advertising was enlisted to push *Jaws* (1975) at the American market, creating the first paradigm for modern 'blockbuster' film-making. While *Yamato* did not follow this model precisely – nor could it in a smaller territory with a different product – it did nevertheless pursue the paradigm in miniature, converting a television audience's prolonged exposure to a 'free' product into exhibition capital by luring them back into cinemas. Kadokawa's own self-commemoration might lay a claim to his innovation in siting film within a media mix, but he was also arguably following a model that the American market was in the process of discovering.

Just as the first dedicated cinema theatres (see Chapter 1) were 'fixed sites' that created a demand for more content, *OUT* and its successors were soon scrambling to memorialise a newly conceived 'tradition' of what it meant to be an anime fan. This soon subsumed many steps in the ownership–access chain. In terms of ownership, vertically integrated companies began using their magazines as venues for new product – such as Miyazaki Hayao's *Kaze no Tani no Nausicaä* (*Nausicaä of the Valley of the Wind*), first published as a manga in *Animage* magazine from 1982, but also adapted into an anime film partway through its run in 1984.

In terms of production, exclusive offers of Behind the-scenes or Making of reports naturally favoured those works related to the journal through a shared investor or presence on the same committee. As competition increased between the magazines, corporations enforced a form of data enclosure, with, for example, Tokuma Shoten's *Animage* favouring Tokuma Shoten releases, Kadokawa's *Newtype* magazine becoming the most likely place for exclusives on Kadokawa productions and Bandai's *B-Club* pushing a view of anime that leaned heavily towards the robot shows that pushed Bandai products. We might note, here, the risk to the historian of relying on single sources from this period – as mentioned in the Introduction, the chances are high hereafter of corporate interests celebrating particular works because of their relationship to them, not necessarily because of any objective criteria of 'popularity'.

Distribution and exhibition also became exploitable, with magazines promoting their own dedicated or affiliated stores and exclusive access to cinema tickets or publicity events. And at the level of access, the magazines were able to alert their readers to video releases that could have otherwise entirely escaped their notice. The creation of a closed circle of consumption afforded the opportunity to sell tapes to an extremely limited group, but a targeted customer base that might contain the entire potential market – *Newtype*'s audited monthly print-run, for example, is 120,000,[6] a significant serviceable customer base for niche products, persuasively close to some estimates of the size of the entire otaku audience (Nomura Research Institute 2005: 52). Often overlooked in such discourse is the potential for the magazines to gain a degree of hegemony over artistic heritage. *Animage* magazine, for example, did not merely serve as the place of origin for *Nausicaä*, but became the main champion of *Nausicaä*'s attainments. Long after *Nausicaä*'s box-office returns might have faded into obscurity, its heroine continued to feature on covers and in her own ongoing manga serial in *Animage*, remaining one of the magazine's annual top-rated 'anime' characters for twenty years after her first appearance (Clements and McCarthy 2006: 445).

By the beginning of the 1980s, the convergence of production interests and the maturing of fandom, coupled with the archive of material, offered a degree of longevity to several anime objects – notably *Space Cruiser Yamato* and its ongoing sequels, *Gundam* and its ongoing sequels and the film *Nausicaä of the Valley of the Wind*. Yamaguchi Yasuo (2004: 110) calls this the 'maintenance of a core anime fandom' (*core anime fan no shiji*), and locates it specifically with the fans of the first 1974–5 season of *Space Cruiser Yamato*, who formed clubs during the original broadcast, and whose fandom was subsequently sustained by the reappearance of the franchise in reruns, a second and third season, movie theatres and on video. In any previous era, such artistic heritage would have swiftly dwindled, but the presence of a 'culture' already self-identifying as fandom permitted it to maintain momentum.

There is no consensus for a single tipping point for the recognition of an otaku culture, which is to say, a population of active fans sufficient to support an entire economy centred on anime consumption (Nomura Research Institute 2005: 80–1). However, one clear candidate is the Japanese release of the first spin-off movie from *Space Cruiser Yamato* (1977), for which the producer Nishizaki Yoshinobu recruited a number of fans as promoters. Publicised as a 'fan' initiative, but using materials supplied by Nishizaki himself, *Yamato* fans provided a sixty-page article for *OUT* magazine on the *Yamato* franchise. They were later recruited with the aid of a specially designed guerrilla marketing kit, which instructed them to flypost prominent locations, call radio stations to request the theme song and pester newspapers to run coverage – for which they were rewarded with animation cels and other production items. It was, according to Tim Eldred (2008a: 2), this performance of grassroots popularity that persuaded Tōei to show the film in its own chain of cinemas, vastly larger than the paltry four theatres of the Tōkyū chain originally planning to carry it. Tada Makoto (2002: 27) notes that the excitement over the *Yamato* movie was the first 'social manifestation' of anime fandom as culture, witnessed by the mainstream. Masuda Hiromichi (2011: 49–50) highlights not only ticket sales, but the public performance of fans queuing through the night.

The film's release was complemented by a week-long radio adaptation, a travelling exhibition of merchandise and the announcement by Nishizaki, as the furore finally died down, that he was founding an official fan club (Eldred 2008b: 1). As far as Tim Eldred is concerned, it was this marshalling of pre-existing fandom, and the application of those fans as shills and marketers, that allowed Nishizaki to persuade the mainstream that the *Space Cruiser Yamato* film was worthy of its notice. This concerted 'media mix' created a self-fulfilling prophecy of queues around the block, and resulted in 2.3 million ticket sales, and box-office revenue of 0.9 billion yen (Tada 2002: 28).

Yamato fandom's own self-commemoration claims that this set a 'box-office record' (Eldred 2008c), and anime-industry histories remember it as a 'great hit' (Seto *et al.* 2002: 173) or for its impact on mainstream media (Yamaguchi 2004: 111). However, while it broke records at particular theatres, particularly for that summer's domestic exhibition (Masuda 2011: 50), its overall takings were no recordbreaker in a year dominated by Hollywood imports such as *King Kong*, *The Enforcer* (*Dirty Harry III*), and *Rocky*. Tradition often confuses its success with that of its sequel, *Saraba Yamato* (1978, *Farewell Yamato*), which truly did break records and remains one of the all-time top-twenty anime at the Japanese box office (Tada 2002: 69).

Anime fandom put on a persuasive performance, alerting others to its existence and increasing the interest of publishers, distributors and viewers in anime content, but it was not a mainstream competitor with Hollywood films, Disney products or live-action movies. Nor was this fact unknown at the levels of exhibition and distribution, with figures from the Motion Picture Producers' Association of Japan plainly demonstrating that anime in the 1980s remained an occasional vacation diversion for audiences of children (see Table 8.3). The top-performing anime in the early 1980s were reiterations of the children's *Doraemon* franchise, often on a double bill with a live-action monster movie. Now, however, *Yamato* had demonstrated that anime fandom represented a discrete sector of new consumption that could be served or exploited through releasing more anime aimed not at children, but at teenagers.

TABLE 8.3: TOP ANIME BOX OFFICE 1980–3

YEAR	TITLE	TAKINGS IN BILLION YEN
1980	*Doraemon* film (plus others)	1.55
1980	*Yamato 3*	1.35
1981	*Doraemon* film (plus others)	1.75
1981	*Farewell Galaxy Express 999*	1.15
1982	*Doraemon* film (plus others)	1.22
1982	*Queen of a Thousand Years*	1.01
1983	*Doraemon* film (plus others)	1.00
1983	*Yamato 4*	1.35
1983	*Harmagedon*	1.06
1983	*Pro Yakyū o 10-bai Tanoshiku Miru Hōhō* (*How to Make Pro Baseball Ten Times More Exciting*)	1.08

Source: http://www.eiren.org/toukei/.

Doraemon the time-travelling cat remained a popular fixture at Japanese cinemas, despite failing to penetrate Anglophone markets

Doraemon, as part of children's double and triple bills that also included *Godzilla vs Mothra* (1964), and short anime spin-offs from *Ninja Hattori-kun* (1981) among others, generated good revenue in the 1980s, but the Motion Picture Producers' Association of Japan's figures for the same period (see Table 8.3) show what appears to be a new anime audience for more mature subjects, also spun off from television, but often presented as standalone features without double-bill enticements. These include several *Yamato* sequels, films based on the work of the *Yamato* designer Matsumoto Leiji, and two films based on popular books – one baseball-related and the other science fiction. In other words, on paper, the rise of anime fandom suggested that, by the beginning of the 1980s, there was a new market for anime, comprising an audience that would have previously been expected to tail off when it reached its teens. There was, undoubtedly, now an audience of core anime consumers, and some proportion of the 2.3 million ticketholders to the first *Space Cruiser Yamato* movie might be enticed back into theatres, book-shops and toy stores by other franchises, particularly during the early 1980s, when science fiction was an international growth market, still riding the success of the *Star Wars* films. However, Tada Makoto (2002: 28–9) cautions that there is also an element of self-fulfilling prophecy. *Yamato 2* (1978) earned 2.9 billion yen at the box office but was given three months to do so, making it something of a 'long hit' in his estimation, particularly since tickets bought by members of the public cost more than presold tickets bought by fans.

Tomino Yoshiyuki (2002: 24–5) writes in his memoirs of another tipping point, on the occasion of the premiere of the first *Gundam* movie on 22 February 1981. Even though the movie was little more than an edit of several TV episodes, Tomino found himself facing a riotous crowd far in excess of the cinema's capacity, in a crush of 15,000 people that threatened to attract police attention and turn the 'event' into a performance of social unrest rather than exuberant fandom. Nor is this claim limited to Tomino's own testimony, since it was commemorated nearly three decades later in a national newspaper as 'the day that anime changed' (Asahi Shinbun 2009).

Publicity for the *Gundam* event claimed it was a 'declaration of the new anime century' (*anime shinseiki sengon*), a reference to the dating chronology used in the *Gundam* series itself, but invested, then and now, with a deeper meaning by anime fandom. There is, perhaps, also a certain whimsical quality in proclaiming a new era at this point – viewers born in 1963, the year of *Astro Boy*, 'came of age' in 1981, perhaps encouraging fandom to map such an idea onto the anime medium itself.

'ORIGINAL ANIMATION VIDEOS', 'AFTER-MONO' AND 'MIDQUELS'

Tokugi (1999: 307) suggests there is a slight semantic distinction between the widespread acronyms OVA and OAV, claiming that 'original video animation' was an industrial term, introduced at the production level to differentiate between anime produced for film or television, and those works intended to go 'straight to video'. He sets this against the 'original animation video', which he regards as a marketing term, introduced at the level of distribution to make it clear that the object in question was not simply a repurposed work from film or television. However, such quibbles seem pointless – the acronyms have persisted interchangeably in English, one suspects, because monoglot pundits wish to brag that they can understand one element on a page of Japanese text.

Although not widely reported at the time, *Dallos* was not initially intended as the first 'original video anime'. To many of its makers, it was regarded instead as a 'failed' television project, dumped onto video in order to recoup development costs after proposals for a fifty-two-episode TV version were rejected (Hotta 2005: 424). Such a derogatory attitude seems to have been widespread among animators, who initially regarded video as a cheaper but less desirable alternative to the established media. Rintarō, for example, originally shrugged off video as nothing more than something with a lower budget than a movie, watched on a television screen – a bluntly technical assessment, issuing solely from a production perspective (Oguro 2009: 94). Tokugi (1999: 307) essentially agrees, refining his own assessment of the first video releases as little more than television specials which, for one reason or another, lack the element of TV distribution that would 'complete' them. Usually, the reason for this absence is aesthetic – an implied viewership too small for the mainstream, or content that would not be acceptable on broadcast media. It is only as the 1980s wore on that the animation industry appears to have appreciated that this very niche appeal could be video's great strength, offering the potential of a 'third medium' able to serve audiences far removed from the conservative viewers of television.

The early days of the video boom included a separate class of release, parsed in distinct terms by Tokugi (1999: 313) as *after-mono*, i.e. sequels to pre-existing franchises. Even if an anime was aimed at children on television, a video sequel could be engineered to age with the original audience, affording them a nostalgic revisitation of their childhood interests, possibly with more mature themes. Although the term after-mono appears to have fallen out of use by the turn of the twenty-first century, a sizeable proportion of anime videos to this day are not all-original *per se*, but continuations of earlier stories. In cases such as *Macross II* (1992), the release was originally conceived as both a continuation[7] and a commemoration, marking the tenth anniversary of the TV series with a six-part video special – a format more suited to the presumed age of the original audience, now in its late teens and early twenties. Video can also be the graveyard or retirement home for ageing franchises, whose ratings no longer justify a mainstream television broadcast, but nevertheless retain a significant smaller audience sector. Among such works we might include *Slayers* (1995), the TV broadcast of which was at first celebrated with theatrical cinema spin-offs, and then slowly laid to rest in video sequels as its audience tailed away (Clements and McCarthy 2006: 591).

A lesser, and often overlooked, form of anime video is the 'midquel', intended not as a standalone object but as an integral part of an ongoing franchise in another medium. Such items often formed the unsellable dross of foreign-rights deals in the 1990s, bundled into deals as 'bonuses', or picked up by rights buyers under the mistaken impression that they would make sense once translated. In the majority of cases, these items are related to untranslated novels, such as *Makū Senjō* (1991, *Dark Warrior*), released in Japan as a commemoration of its late author, but sold in the US market as an incoherent sci-fi B-movie, or *Vampire Wars* (1990), designed in Japan as an advert for the opening pages of a novel, but all but meaningless in foreign territories where the book was not available (Clements and McCarthy 2006: 133, 698–9). As Tokugi (1999: 313) observes, such works suggest that, although the quantity of new anime shot up in the mid- to late 1980s, the quality of the works being produced was wildly variable – Tokugi suggests only one in five releases during the period were any good, but offers no explanation as to how he reached this figure.

Arguably, the most worthwhile releases were those that began life as videos, but acquired enough of a following to justify their upgrade into TV serials and movies. Video hence also functioned both as a testing ground for new talent (Tokugi 1999: 311) but also for storylines, with the most notable successes of the period being the *Patlabor* (1988) and *Tenchi Muyō* (1992) franchises, both of which upgraded from video into the more established media. Crucially for many of the production houses, it also offered a unique new window of opportunity to participate in the ownership of anime objects.

There is a certain degree of confusion over what constituted 'video' releases. Since anime in the period were still assembled on film, regardless of the intended exhibition medium, several 1980s titles seem to exist in a liminal area. *Birth* (1984), cited as one of the key 'video' products of the era (Tokugi 1999: 308), was screened on an early-morning programme at the Tōkyū Pantheon cinema in July 1984, and hence also scrapes into histories of anime in the cinema (Animage 1989: 104). *Vampire Hunter D* (1985) was distributed as a film in Tōhō cinemas, but contains conspicuous moments of filler, as if a production originally intended for video

First released on video, then upgraded to television, and then to cinema movie events, the *Patlabor* series is one of the success stories of late twentieth-century anime

was suddenly bulked out to meet a suitable running time for theatrical exhibition. Other 'film' releases turn out, on closer inspection, to have received similarly extremely limited theatrical exposure, such as the early-morning screening of Oshii Mamoru's *Tenshi no Tamago* (1985, *Angel's Egg*) at the Tōei Hall in Tokyo, or *Ace o Nerae 2* (1988, *Aim for the Ace 2*), which is listed by Tokugi (1999: 313) as the epitome of 'video anime', but still received a theatrical 'premiere' at the Shōchiku Salon on 9 July 1988.[8]

Similar confusions attend some of the niche programmes whose own tradition and commemorations trumpet them as exclusive productions only available to a particular subscriber base of active fans. Although *Legend of the Galactic Heroes* is cited as a fan-led, subscription-only video release, it still appears on records of theatrical films in Japan, since its first episode was included on a double bill in Tokyo Classic cinemas in 1988 (Animage 1989: 131).

Such permeable boundaries, of course, are nothing new in the Japanese animation industry. We have already noted in previous chapters how *Momotarō's Sea Eagles* was shown to a captive audience, or how early films by Otogi Pro and Mushi Pro often put on a performance of theatrical exhibition. The endurance of such fudges into the video age owes some of its existence to the perennial value of marketing – in terms of the editorial methodology of many film magazines, an appearance of a cartoon in a movie theatre will suddenly qualify it for coverage, review and discussion, whereas the release of an obscure 'video' only to be found in the geeky section of a rental store, might otherwise escape the journalists' notice.

CONTENT AND THEMES: DEFINITIONS OF 'MATURITY'

'Maturity' of themes was also a mixed message. Tokugi (1999: 315–17) identifies several clear strands of 'adult' entertainment in the video anime of the 1980s, such as biker stories (*bike-mono*) – a number of violent tales that capitalise on the allure of bad boys on motorcycles, exploiting the hyperreality of Japanese animation to present stirring stunts and chase sequences that might be impossible to reproduce in a live-action feature. He also notes the blossoming of a small but significant subgenre of romance, such as *Machikado no Meruhen* (1984, *Street Corner Fairy Tales*), an MTV-influenced series of musical interludes, framing a story of young love. This, coupled with an implied male viewer in his mid-teens, soon led to concentrations in video anime on female characters, with the male-dominated casts of children's cartoons soon supplanted by female-dominated casts for teenagers, often competing for the affections of a single male. Kajishima Masaki, the creator of *Tenchi Muyō*, articulates the structure of such 'harem anime' in terms of the worldview of a frustrated, lonely, virginal boy between the ages of fifteen and eighteen (Oguro 2006: 104). In this, he refers not only to a lurid obsession with the female form, but a certain desperation that is prepared to consider, however briefly, sexual partners literally everywhere: fellow students, older students, teachers and office ladies. There is, certainly, an element in such anime of women as a great and beautiful mystery, and of the wish-fulfilment of such works, placing the viewer in the company of otherwise unattainable girls. However, the invisible cash cow of 1980s video animation was not romance, but pornography.

While *Dallos* might have just scraped the title of first video release, it did so only in a confusing scramble. The 'second' episode of *Dallos* was actually the first to be released, on 21 December 1983, a month ahead of the 'first' episode (Haraguchi 2000: 111). The first identifiable erotic anime video, a 'Lolita anime' in the *Wonder Kids* series (Haraguchi 2000: 153; Clements and McCarthy 2006: 376) was released on 21 February 1984, a year celebrated by historians as the first flourishing of science-fiction anime video, but actually dominated by paedophile erotica.

The pornographic sector was plainly much further ahead in embracing the innovations offered by video. *Wonder Kids*, *Lolita Anime* and the first instalments of the *Cream Lemon* series all followed in the same year, largely omitted from anime histories for reasons of understandable and wilful nescience and aesthetics. However, erotica soon flourished, capitalising on animation's facility in depicting scenes that would be prohibitively expensive or illegal to stage with real people.

Okada Toshio comments (2010: 190–1) that, while he regards the objectification of girls and young women in anime as benign, it places anime fans on a continuum that is inextricably connected to the activities of murderers and molesters. This was brought home by the arrest in 1989 of Miyazaki Tsutomu, a paedophile serial killer whose home was found to contain many works of violent pornography, including anime, and igniting a round of discussions of media uses and effects. The Miyazaki murders, or the Otaku Incident (Otaku Jiken) as the press unfortunately dubbed it, was one of two significant media 'events' that damned anime by association – the other being the 1995 Aum Shinrikyō gas attacks (Nagayama 2012: 246–7).

'Neither I, personally, nor my company has that element', notes Okada (2010: 191), 'but if we were to gather 10,000 anime fans or otaku, we would find five such people.' His phrasing is oddly similar to that of a reporter who noted that Miyazaki Tsutomu himself had been one of the 100,000 attendees at the manga convention Comiket (Nagayama 2012: 247) – both inadvertently imply that anime or manga fandom somehow nurtures such a sociopathic mindset, in a way that other arbitrary groups, such as 'people who ride on the train' or 'people who wear glasses' do not. It is, Okada concedes, a lunatic fringe, but just as the identification of fandom has created a discourse for appreciation of anime, it may also facilitate a discourse of deviance. We might also point to the corollary of cartoons for older viewers – although animation was clearly an 'adult' medium in many earlier periods (see, for example Chapters 2 and 3), the rise of entertainment animation since the 1950s had re-established it in the public eye as a 'children's' medium. In refashioning a 'children's' medium for adults, anime arguably makes a statement about wider applications for the art, but also risks appealing to an audience caught in arrested development, clinging to notions of infantilism. This, in turn, is often characterised in critiques of anime fandom with reference to a 'psychosocial moratorium', which is to say a proportion of the audience that favours cartoons, at least in part, as a means of rejecting or postponing the adult world of graduation, employment and adult human interactions (Pelliteri 2010: 179).

Anime erotica flourished in video rental – most distributors could be sure that Japan's 4,800 video-rental libraries were sure to take at least one copy of every release (Tada 2002: 46). Even in the mid-1990s, the average pornographic anime only sold an average of 13,000 units per title, compared, for example, to an average mainstream videogram sales figure of 15,000 per title, and occasional bestsellers such as the 110,000 units for *Neon Genesis Evangelion* (Clements 1998b: 84; Tada 2002: 46). However, since anime pornography was rented on average four times as often as other titles, it turned rental stores into a captive audience for tapes that retailed at up to 10,000 yen per unit. Such figures speak for themselves – pornography was a clear blue-chip strategy, with modest but firm returns in revenue.

It is, arguably, productive to regard developments in 'adult' Japanese animation in the 1980s and 1990s from the perspective of pornography not as a periphery, but as a core, to which other titles need to find some sort of stylistic connection. If it is financially 'safe' to include risqué elements that will appeal to the crowd who snap up the cash cows, then further development of the market invites some sort of refinement of this 'adult' content. In his history of video anime, Tokugi Yoshiharu regards (1999: 312) Kawajiri Yoshiaki's *Yōjū Toshi* (1987, *Wicked City*) as the commencement of a subgenre of violent, eroticised horror in Japanese animation, eschewing outright 'pornography' in favour of transgressive action and fantasy that would be prohibitively expensive for all but the most highly budgeted Hollywood competitors. Notably, Tokugi files *Wicked City* as a video work, even though it was one of those liminal titles intended for video but permitted the performance of theatrical exhibition (Animage 1989: 127). Kawajiri himself notes (Oguro *et al.* 2008: 58) that the project was planned as a half-hour video work, but upgraded to an eighty-minute feature when the potential of the material became apparent. Although such 'adult' video works only formed a subset of the production of the Japanese animation industry, outnumbered even in the 1980s by domestic television, children's stories and work for hire on foreign kids' shows, such stand-alone science-fiction or fantasy titles, with racy content that clearly established them as 'not for kids' would serve as the standard bearers for Japanese animation in many foreign territories in the 1990s. Tomino Yoshiyuki (2002: 322) suggests that television might have fostered 'adult' anime fans, but that video subsequently pandered to a solipsistic and diminishingly remunerative concentration on such fans: 'the foundation of show business is entertainment, not the expression of an autistic artistic consciousness'. There are indicators that his blunt assessment is mirrored elsewhere in the anime industry, in comments such as those by the producer Satō Hiroki that adult fans are not 'adult' so much as they are 'eternally fourteen years old' (Hotta 2005: 211–12) – a welcome replacement for a declining audience of real children, but still oddly ghettoised. Similarly, Okada Toshio (2010: 104–5) notes that mainstream journalists were deeply reluctant to even cover works that pandered to a fannish definition of 'realism', literally walking out in the middle of a press conference as soon as animators began discussing 'fan service'.

FAIR USE? FANDOM APPROPRIATES OWNERSHIP

The first specifically anime-related store in Japan was Yamato, opened in 1979 in Fukuoka, and subsequently renamed Animec. This was, however, regarded at the time as merely one more science-fiction shop, mostly specialising in manga, novels and foreign imports. The first science-fiction store to actively begin creating its own merchandise was General Products in Osaka, run by members of what would become the Gainax company (Takeda 2002: 106).[9] Takeda Yasuhiro (2002: 124) notes that the mindset of fandom found several innovative loopholes through copyright protection. In the case of the computer game *Dragon Quest* (1986) the characters and story were the property of the creators, but nobody had registered their equipment as intellectual property. Hence, there was no legal impediment to the sale of replica swords and armour resembling the items seen in the game – this in turn fed into the growing popularity of 'cosplay', in which fans participated in their chosen franchises by dressing up as their characters.

General Products was also one of the early companies to involve itself in 'garage kits' – unlicensed epoxy resin models, like Airfix kits but produced in small duplication runs with homemade moulds. Such user-generated materials were often, at least technically, in contravention of the intellectual property rights of the serials from which they drew inspiration, but General Products secured an innovative waiver scheme, the 'one-day licensing system, which allows amateur dealers to sell copyrighted materials only on the day of a particular event'

(Takeda 2002: 106). The companies who assented to this moratorium are not named, but it is implied that many did. The presence of such complex model kits also implies fans significantly older than the seven-year-old children once assumed to be anime's target market.

The General Products collective took its DIY attitude to extremes with the organisation of Daicon III, a science-fiction convention held in 1981 in Osaka, for which it even made a parody animation featuring many popular characters. The work was amateurish and haphazard, eschewing standard industry products by using, for example, shop-bought vinyl instead of standard cels (Takeda 2005: 50). Tellingly, the reception of the Daicon animation reflected the ambiguous contemporary attitude of copyright holders to parody – Tezuka Osamu actually complained that his characters were *not* in it (Okada 2010: 46). Notably, the five-minute *Daicon III* (1981) animation sequence also became a hidden forerunner of video anime, when its makers, 2 million yen ($9000) in debt from the convention, attempted to make good on their losses by offering tapes of their cartoon for sale (Takeda 2005: 105). *Daicon III* could never be sold through formal channels, as some intellectual property elements had not been cleared, but nevertheless constituted an informal precursor of the formal 'OAV' market.

We might discern in such activities a universal sense that fan activity is relatively benign. A five-minute parody video that happens to feature cameo elements from *Gundam* is not a threat to the *Gundam* series itself, but arguably an advertisement for it. Its existence presents no danger of 'loss of sales' to the owners and creators of *Gundam*, particularly when ownership of anime properties has moved away from single individuals towards 'production committees' of investors, and even artificial entities. In the case of *Gundam*, the original idea was partly credited to 'Yadate Hajime', a nonexistent entity designed to ensure that the studio, rather than the staff participants, retained ownership. It also suggests a mutual understanding, on the part of both fans and copyright owners, that fan activity was a small, artisanal venture that presented no threat to corporate revenues – the potential to industrialise fan activity to threatening levels will be addressed in Chapter 9.

More importantly, the existence of *Daicon III* points to a steadily growing group of would-be animators and creatives inspired by the products of the television era, but with an interest in pursuing their own material. Within four years of *Daicon III*, its makers had incorporated as the Gainax studio, and were already working on their first feature film, with investment capital from Bandai, now the owner of the *Gundam* studio, Sunrise. However, this sudden leap into a production capacity is not necessarily a sign of supreme ability, so much as a certain overconfidence in the spending power of the new anime audience.

We might also note that such a chronology of fans turning professional might reflect the self-commemoration of the Gainax studio. Although Gainax has now been an established corporation for a quarter of a century, its contemporary publicity still regularly returns to a self-image of a collective of fans made good. This can include self-figuration, as found in the mockumentary anime *Otaku no Video* (1991) that retells the fans' rise to fame in semifictional form, but also deep metatextual references – it is surely no coincidence that the title of *Neon Genesis Evangelion*, in Japanese *Shinseiki Evangelion*, forms a Greco-Japanese calque of Tomino Yoshiyuki's 1981 'proclamation of a new century' (*shinseiki sengon*), establishing *Evangelion* as a successor or response to *Gundam*. But at the level of testimonial credibility, we should be aware of the promotional value of persuading audiences that the film-makers are 'fans like them' – the establishment, in Allan Megill's terms (2007: 35), of a communal sense of tradition, inviting the indulgence of audiences, and their forgiveness for any short-comings. True enough, Gainax indeed comprised the youthful fans who found work in the anime world. But at the time they began work on *Honneamise no Tsubasa* (1987, *The Wings of Honneamise*), Yamaga Hiroyuki was a former film student with a body of amateur work ample enough to serve as anyone's showreel; Sadamoto Yoshiyuki was already a professionally published manga artist; and Anno Hideaki had already worked in a prominent position as an animator on *Nausicaä of the Valley of the Wind*.

THE WINGS OF HONNEAMISE: ISSUES IN DISTRIBUTION AND EXHIBITION

Ōritsu Uchūgun (*Royal Space Force*), as it was originally called, supposedly began production on Christmas Day 1984, the day that the Gainax corporation was registered as a holding company for the production's assets (Okada 2010: 140).

Members of the production committee of *The Wings of Honneamise* (1987) made several attempts to 'fix' it at the distribution stage, including meddling with the title and preparing misleading adverts

Royal Space Force was put into production at the very height of the first surge in video sales, when a studio's ownership of an all-new product, deeply ingrained in the newfound market of adult fans and active fandom, made 'by fans for fans', was immensely tempting. One imagines that investors hoped to bootstrap a new *Gundam* or a new *Yamato* out of nothing, which might have explained the enthusiasm during production for a possible movie sequel or television spin-off. However, as the footage of *Royal Space Force* neared completion in late 1986, and was found to be inconveniently free of many merchandising spin-off opportunities, there were signs among the investors and sponsors of cold feet. With authorship and production a *fait accompli*, Okada Toshio reports (2010: 77 8) outrageous attempts to 'fix' the ailing film project at the levels of distribution and exhibition, such as prolonged arguments over a sudden perceived need to retitle it.

Royal Space Force, it was determined, was 'not sexy enough'. Gainax refused to consider the suggested *Wings of Lequinni*, a retitling that would have refocused the entire film onto the character of a religious zealot who was merely conveniently female. Instead, the staff were lumbered with *The Wings of Honneamise*, a title that marketers hoped would evoke audience memories of *Nausicaä of the Valley of the Wind*, but which also contained the word 'wings' (approved by an airline sponsor), and which alluded to the otherwise unnamed kingdom in the film.

According to Okada, this was not merely a makework incident to justify the activities of the marketing department, but an intricately negotiated settlement in order to prevent certain investors from pulling out. Okada also maintains (2010: 75) that Bandai itself would have dropped its participation, to an immediate loss of 360 million yen, were it not for the fact that the company CEO had personally vouched for the project, and would have been forced to resign if it appeared to fail.

A further attempt to 'fix' the film at the distribution level was initiated by the advertising company Tōhō-Tōwa, tasked with selling a product increasingly regarded by its own investors as unlikely to break out of a small niche. With initiation costs of 800 million yen, the now-renamed *The Wings of Honneamise* would need to rank among the year's top ten domestic box-office releases merely to break even. With a certain grudging acknowledgement, Okada recalls (2010: 80) that Tōhō-Tōwa had only a single precedent – in terms of a successful 'original' anime feature, without a pre-existing TV audience – and that was *Nausicaä of the Valley of the Wind*. Accordingly, the promotions unit did everything in its power to make *Honneamise* appeal to precisely the same audience as *Nausicaä*, even if that meant misleading advertising.

As one example, Okada cites (2010: 80) the 'insect incident', in which the artist Sadamoto Yoshiyuki was commissioned to draw an image of a giant spider-beetle attacking the city from the film. The insect in question only appeared in the film as a finger-length child's pet, although the advert gave the impression that it would grow into a house-sized behemoth equivalent to the giant *ohmu* in *Nausicaä*. Okada was incensed, not only at the apparent conspiracy to mislead audiences about his film, but that the producers would assent to wasting the time of Sadamoto, who spent three days on the commission. Okada felt (2010: 81) that, if he had three days to spare, he could have better utilised the time by correcting several problematic scenes in the film itself.

The running time of *The Wings of Honneamise* was timed at precisely 119 minutes and fifty seconds, a hair's breadth under two hours, in initial documentation agreed to by all participants. It was only as investors panicked that producers began pressuring Gainax to reduce the length of the film, in order to squeeze in more potential returns on the investment.

Some animators have justified the bloated running times of certain anime movies, by arguing that it would be wasteful to discard a piece of completed animation even if its inclusion added little to audience enjoyment (Kushida 2010: 97). In both cel animation and digital animation, any cuts are best agreed at the script or storyboard stage when the only cost incurred is ink and a creative's time. Once assets are committed to animation itself, it is unlikely that producers would ever allow footage to be dropped. However, Okada Toshio notes (2010: 76) that an overly long film incurs not only unnecessary production costs, but inhibits its own ability to earn money at exhibition:

> A two-hour film can only be shown four times a day at the cinema. Four times a day would limit the box office revenue. An 80-minute film can be shown six times a day at the cinema. In Japan, a normal screening slot for a film is three weeks. Four times a day for three weeks means 4 x 21 = 84 screenings, but two more screenings a day gives 6 x 21 = 126 screenings. It means a 50 per cent sales increase and each cinema's profit goes up.

Certainly, when one looks at the running times of many of the films released in the 1980s, 'originals' usually clock in at lean running times just on the right side of feature length, while the majority of the two-hour animated movies are those assembled from pre-existing TV footage, such as *Gundam*, where quantity was favoured over quality. But as investment capital increases during the 'anime boom', we suddenly see running times of 131 minutes (*Harmagedon*), 130 minutes (*Crusher Joe*), 139 minutes (*Odin*). Notably, however, these originals are listed (Animage 1989) as standalone works, whereas many earlier, shorter works were intended to appear on double or triple bills. Several, such as Oshii Mamoru's *Angel's Egg*, also appear to have been exhibited only in early mornings or single-screen premieres, and hence did not have to compete for time-slots with the more usual afternoon and evening screenings at cinemas.

There are other considerations. Takeda Yasuhiro takes pundits to task who have claimed that *The Wings of Honneamise* was a box-office flop:

> It may not have been a huge hit, but it certainly wasn't a flop. Not a single theatre cancelled its run, and at some locations it actually had a longer run than initially planned. I think a false apprehension probably emerged because a few people voiced their own unfounded assumptions – that a story as complex and subtle as this couldn't possibly draw crowds, and from there the rumors just took on a life of their own. ... The budget scale meant that reclaiming all the production costs at the box office simply wasn't feasible. (Takeda 2005: 97)

In other words, *The Wings of Honneamise* was never intended to make its money back in cinemas, but was instead expected to monetise through licensing, video and merchandise – even though a theatrical release in 1987, its appearance in cinemas was now reframed as little more than a loss-leading advertisement for video sales. Such a claim, however, obscures to a certain degree the goldrush tensions of the period, when Japan's booming bubble economy arguably resulted in more investors than a film warranted. *The Wings of Honneamise* was originally mooted as a one-shot video release with a modest budget of 20 million yen (Hotta 2005: 148; Okada 2010: 64), which it might reasonably have expected to regain through standard sales. But by the time it entered production in the mid-1980s, amid a boom in anime's apparent popularity, it had accreted multiple interfering investors and sponsors, including the airline that insisted on the 'wings' in the title, a production now deemed to be a cinema release and a budget of 800 million yen (Okada 2010: 75–6).

Gainax was virtually bankrupted by the effort of producing *The Wings of Honneamise*, although Okada notes (2010: 98) that 'bankruptcy' is a sanctioned state that requires the managing director to recognise that the bills cannot be paid. Since he did not possess the business acumen to pronounce the company dead, it stumbled along, with mounting debts and increased disillusionment over the viability of the anime medium.

Okada notes (2010: 140) that staff on an anime production can draw different forms of capital from their participation. It is, in a sense, easier to expect directors and producers to be overworked or underpaid, since both stand to benefit from a production that is the better for their labours – either financially or in an augmented reputation that leads to subsequent projects. Moreover, a producer is usually able to work on several anime concurrently. However, '99.9% of an anime's staff is salaried. They are only paid per piece, per scene or per day. You cannot really ask them to over-strain' (Okada 2010: 141).

There may well have been connoisseurs of Japanese animation in the past, but it was only in the 1980s that audiences gained the means to retain their connoisseurship, to discuss it and pass it on, creating a discourse and an archive that could articulate 'anime' as an object of enquiry, appreciation and consumption. Thanks for the most part to video, but also to the new communities fostered by fandom events and magazine publishing, Japanese animation was able to experiment in the new area of material intended for 'adults', itself creating new forms of consumption.

Despite the sudden rise of fan-related products, the performance of new creators in the business often seems subject to the same issues in investment and finance management that troubled the earliest animators in the twentieth century (see Chapter 1). *The Wings of Honneamise* was, ultimately, a profitable object, that not only continues to generate revenue for its owners, but may reasonably be expected to do so for years to come. However, the creation of such cultural capital represented a huge risk for its investors, and threatened the health and well-being of many of its participants, particularly the low-echelon labourers alienated from the product of their labour – i.e. awaiting tardy salaries, with no further equity in the property.

As John Ruskin noted in *The Political Economy of Art* (1867: 57) enduring properties often require heavy front-end investment. This truth does not alter between media. Many 'original' anime videos of the 1980s are now forgotten, often because their quality does not hold up to the prolonged scrutiny of artistic heritage, or simply because their reception was time-sensitive.

Those anime from the period that remain prominent in today's public consciousness are often those that incurred higher production costs, and hence a more robust lifespan on video. However, a far more enduring aspect appears to be what Steinberg calls the 'media ecology' – it matters less to an intellectual property holder if, say, the original *Gundam* series is inaccessible to modern viewers. What matters is that the *Gundam* franchise – its world, its characters and its merchandise, is repurposable in sequels and in new formats, effectively using previous incarnations of the series as a form of brand identity to attract the attention of journalists, store shelvers and consumers. It is such a mindset that would transform anime once more in the 1990s, as the industry was colonised at the level of ownership by gaming investors, venture capitalists and carpetbaggers determined to co-opt anime as a catalyst for the 'contents' industry. The rise of this 'anime business', reshaping Japanese animation in hard-nosed, commodified terms, has been a prime feature of the industry in the digital age, and will be examined in the last two chapters.

NOTES

1. Indeed, it expanded to such an extent that the Keibunsha 'Complete Encyclopaedia …' series gave up attempting to cover Japanese animation after 1987 on the grounds that it was no longer possible to keep up with the field (Patten 2004: 65).
2. See http://www.youtube.com/watch?v=QgAbn9Dtd2o.
3. See http://youtu.be/A0m_jLCP4SU (Japanese VCR commercials 1977–93).
4. 'Generational location' here needs to encompass both will and means – Studio Nue, for example, was founded as the design studio Crystal Arts in 1972 but had to spend a decade below the line before gaining suitable creative capital to actively involve itself in production as one of the authors of the *Macross* saga. The Studio Nue staff was not quite of the generation Misono suggests, since its members' average age at the time of the first broadcast of *Astro Boy* would have been twelve.

5. Arguably, *B-Club*'s staff and readership migrated after its 'closure' to *Dengeki B-Magazine* (closed 1999), and thence to *Dengeki Animation Magazine* (closed 2001), and from there to *Dengeki Animaga*, which lasted until 2005. The reader is cautioned that magazines sometimes end because of low sales and declining audiences, but may also be simply rebranded or refocused to reflect changes in management or ownership.
6. The source for this is the Japanese Magazine Publishers Association, http://www.j-magazine.or.jp/data_002/c3.html#007.
7. Albeit intended as a continuation, the storyline of *Macross II* was contradicted by later episodes in the franchise, and it was subsequently edged out of the canon (Clements and McCarthy 2006: 387).
8. All the locations of exhibition are taken from Animage (1989: 112, 113, 134).
9. Watanabe Shigeru (Hotta 2005: 422) calls them the 'Daicon Group', parsing them as a fan community united by the convention, rather than the store. I refer to them as General Products, or as the 'future Gainax company' simply for convenience.

9 THE POKÉMON SHOCK
Anime goes global 1984–97, 1997–2006

On 16 December 1997, the thirty-eighth episode of the TV anime series *Pocket Monster*, more popularly known as *Pokémon*, featured a rapidly pulsing animation effect. The strobing sequence, appearing on almost 30 million Japanese television screens during primetime viewing, caused some 685 incidents of 'photo-paroxysmal response' in an audience chiefly comprising children. Although most viewers recovered en route to hospital, some 150 were admitted with symptoms of epileptic seizure, and two remained hospitalised for a fortnight (Takahashi and Tsukahara 1998: 631; Misono 1999: 85; Tsugata 2004: 198; Katsuno and Maret 2004: 80–1). The programme was taken off air for four months, and the Japanese TV industry subsequently agreed a set of guidelines on flashing effects, types of luminance and swift cutting in order to reduce the risk of a repeat incident.[1] However, the scandal of the 'Pokémon Shock' did nothing to curb the franchise's imminent emergence in overseas markets. If anything, the brief adverse publicity ensured that this latest incarnation of media-mix marketing achieved global brand recognition. In hindsight, we might consider it as the central 'event' of anime's overseas popularity, sitting at the midpoint of two different but interconnected categories of anime reception.

The history of Japanese animation often assumes a teleological aspect, focused implicitly through the gaze of the foreign viewer, as if everything must somehow build towards the viewer's first anime experience. One's first anime, be it *Akira* or *Sen to Chihiro no Kamikakushi* (2001, *Spirited Away*) or *Naruto* (2002), is framed as a moment of illumination, an end to anime prehistory, and all events before that moment are merely shadowy preparation – Megill (2007: 33) would call this an error of *memory* or *tradition*. Because of the sheer amount of Japanese animation available in translation, coverage of anime in languages other than Japanese favours the level of access, manifested as plot synopses, reviews or semiotic analyses. In academia and fan communities alike, it also tends to reflect viewers' own aesthetic bias, and often a fan-centred tradition that valorises the companies with the strongest publicity or convention presence. It is notable, for example, that so much ink is spilled on the works of otaku-focused companies such as Production IG and Madhouse, whereas Tōei Animation (makers of *One Piece*, 1999), Studio Pierrot (makers of *Naruto*) and Oriental Light and Magic (makers of *Pokémon*) dwarf them in sales.

Many writers are often apt to imagine that anime has magically appeared out of nowhere in the late 1980s, unaware of the precedence of 'hidden imports' in overseas markets during the previous decades. All too often, it is assumed that reaction and reception to anime in the author's homeland is a universal constant both there and in every other country, whereas, as Ernst Bloch once wrote, 'not all people live in the same Now' (Burke 2008: 24). Although there was a degree of transnational rationalisation in the globalised late 1990s and early 2000s, particularly after the introduction of the Digital Versatile Disc (DVD) made simultaneous, or near-simultaneous multiple-language releases of the same object much more likely, the narrative of anime history before the DVD is widely different from territory to territory. Sometimes, the reactions were less about the content than about its performative context, such as in Italy, where Marco Pelliteri (2010: 290–2) recalls a sudden, palpable influx of Japanese animation in the 1970s, seized on by broadcasters to fill airtime on newly expanding commercial channels. This, in turn, fed into an ongoing political situation in Italy, where the presence of certain Japanese shows on Italian television were cited as dangerous works promoting fascism, anti-Communism, violence and an unwelcome degree of realism in depicting war (Pelliteri 2010: 304–5). Such criticisms, of course, only applied to those objects that fitted Italian politicians' definition of 'Japanese' cartoons, such as the super-robot series known in Italy as *Goldrake* (1975, *UFO Robot Grendizer*) – there was, notably, no such criticism aimed at the gentle pastoral *Heidi*, which was no less a 'Japanese cartoon'.

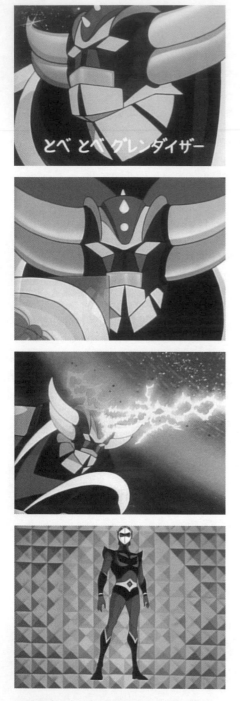

UFO Robot Grendizer (1975) enjoyed an entirely unexpected artistic heritage in Europe, where it became a favourite with schoolchildren and a bugbear of scandalised politicians

Soon afterwards, in France under the slightly different title *Goldorak, UFO Robot Grendizer* managed an even greater achievement, becoming the centre of a media backlash over a perceived 'cultural invasion' of Japanese products. As in Italy, *Goldorak* was a weapon in an unseen war among commercial television broadcasters to cram their airwaves with cheap content. During the silly season of summer-vacation broadcast, *Goldorak* achieved remarkable levels of popularity, and soon attracted the attention of adults. Masuda Hiromichi (2011: 59–60) notes with a degree of sly admiration that, if *Goldorak* truly were watched by as many French children as claimed, at a time when adults were likely to still be at work, it may have qualified in some sense as the most-watched anime of all time, achieving a notional TV rating in its time-slot of 100 per cent.

Goldorak's artistic heritage in France is usually parsed in terms of its enduring popularity (Clements and McCarthy 2006: 474), although there are other influences on its historiography. As a French-language programme, it was re-exported from France to Canada, hence gaining an additional opportunity to garner North American fans who had missed its broadcast in English. A notoriously 'violent' cultural product, it depicted massive destruction wrought by horned robots, with pilots spending their downtime on a counterproductively American-looking ranch (a red rag to French cultural theorists). It also caught the notice of two authors whose books helped to prolong its artistic heritage, through the effort of trying to deconstruct it. Liliane Lurçat's *A cinq ans, seul avec Goldorak: Le jeune enfant et la télévision* (1981) may well have been the first book ever written about anime outside Japan, although it is really about viewers' responses to something that happens to be anime – it does not even mention *Goldorak*'s Japanese origins, of which the infant interviewees are entirely ignorant. It remains a meticulously constructed work of psychological research, by a scientist testing children's reactions to popular television programmes. Thirty years on, Lurçat's measured, dispassionate approach to *Goldorak* still bears fruitful comparison with that of the politician Ségolène Royal, whose *Le Ras-le-bol des bébés zappeurs* (1989) remains a persuasive polemic about the harm caused by violence on television, and which singles out 'séries japonaises stupides et violentes' (1989: 45), both live action and animated, for particular vitriol. Like that of her Italian counterparts, Royal's reaction is part of a political discourse, choosing to access only the 'worst' of Japanese animation, and parsing it as a threat to domestic culture.

In a deliberate attempt to establish not only the multiple possible readings of Japanese animation, but also the multiplicity of viewer responses, Sakurai Takamasa (2009) visits anime events in such far-flung places as Saudi Arabia, Myanmar and the Czech Republic. Similarly, in a simple report of his own work on an educational film released in thirty-seven languages, Suzuki Shinichi (2008a: 4–24) alludes to the unexpected, and largely unchronicled success of 'Japanese animation' in such diverse territories as Laos, Nepal, Senegal and Uganda. Such evidence should serve to humble any attempt to tell the story of Japanese animation overseas by reference to any single language territory particularly when, as Fred Patten (2004: 23) notes, it would take an entire book to encompass merely the history of fandom in the United States, let alone issues of distribution, exhibition or production. A 2009 survey of twenty-three Japanese animation companies reported that 432 formal anime distribution licences were currently rented out to 138 countries around the globe, with only a few Central Asian republics and African states not participating (Masuda 2011: 167). Such figures, of course, exclude informal access such as piracy and fansubbing that presumably extends even further, leading Masuda Hiromichi to pronounce anime truly global.

Aesthetically, writers on anime are apt to fall for marketing hype that suggests anime is taking the world by storm – their assessment, as to whether this is a good thing or a bad thing often depends on whether they are celebrating an Oscar-winning movie or decrying straight-to-video pornography. However, to take the example of the United Kingdom, despite thousands of anime releases, 50 per cent of the UK industry's revenue for much of the 1990s was generated by just twenty titles, nineteen of them from a single distributor (Clements 2003: 21). Conversely, the worstselling anime in many territories sell so badly as to be outnumbered by the review copies sent out to the press (ANNcast 017 2009: 37) – despite the impressive media performance of bestsellers and headline-grabbing titles, median sales in the contemporary UK anime market are merely 1,300 copies. In other words, just as in Japan, anime's spread to the UK indicates a mass market of children, reaching several hundred thousand in the case of *Pokémon*, and a smaller, dedicated sector of older consumers buying 'fan-friendly' products. Such statistics also reflect Japan's confusion of several exclusive anime markets. For many participants, particularly latecomers unaware of the qualitative range of titles, it may not be immediately obvious that the million-plus sales figures for a nationwide Buena Vista release of a Studio Ghibli film like *Kiki's Delivery Service* (1989) has little bearing on the video release of an obscure late-night anime TV show, which barely scraped 4,000 sales in its home country, and is liable to achieve only a fraction of that number elsewhere.

A chapter such as this cannot do anything more than scratch the surface of anime's transnational fortunes. However, it can point the reader at common structures and possible errors of practice, which might be altered or adapted in other territories beyond the Anglophone world. And it may prove productive in focusing, however briefly, a discussion of anime's transnational success back to the context of its effect on the Japanese market.

Iwabuchi Kōichi (2004: 59) points specifically to the generation that grew up playing Japanese computer and console games, as the engine driving an overseas sense of 'Japan cool', but also notes that such a concept led to, in some cases, misguided triumphalism among Japanese producers, who mistook the admiration of a small niche of foreign fans for a general, worldwide acceptance of Japanese cultural products and norms. As a closer examination of the actual objects soon confirms, there were in fact at least two separate modes of consumption of Japanese animation, the confusion of which also complicates any narrative of anime history. Marco Pelliteri (2010: 5), somewhat fancifully, calls these modes the 'Dragon' (consumption of anime in celebration of its difference, such as the adult anime fans who like *Akira*), and the 'Dazzle' (consumption of anime because it has become an established norm, such as children who grew up with *Pokémon*). To which we might add other, unnamed categories, of family audiences who simply like films by Studio Ghibli, or disinterested channel surfers, who do not care where something comes from, but merely stumble across it on the television, where the revenue accruing to Japan has been paid by the exhibitor, rather than the viewer. Pelliteri suggests that one of his categories follows the other, but although that may be true in some cases, they also appear to persist concurrently, even in Japan.

In terms of the Japanese animation that found success in the Anglophone world, these contending groups of anime objects converged on the American market in the 1980s and 1990s. These included enduring structures, such as television shows made in Japan and localised for US television, often as part of a media-mix strategy to sell toys or games. Most conspicuously in the Anglophone market, anime for the mature and/or otaku audience became a recognisable niche in video sales, opening a category of 'adult' animation that recreated the rise of the Japanese otaku audience abroad. Notably, it was the mid- to late 1980s that brought this about, in part because of simple technological determinism, but also because of the availability of a greater 'archive' of material to choose from – the boom in available anime, and the 1980s rush of new products in Japan contributing to an interest in selling it elsewhere. It is for this reason that this chapter's subtitle offers two sets of dates roughly contiguous with Pelliteri's 'Dragon' and 'Dazzle' – 1984–97 for the growth of the 'otaku' market, and 1997–2006 for the far larger, mass-market phenomenon of mainstream titles such as *Pokémon*, prominent aesthetic milestones such as *Spirited Away*, and the continued otaku culture, which was contained within this second market, but often confused by its participants with the entirety of it.

Nausicaä of the Valley of the Wind (1983) was not a Studio Ghibli production, but created the talent base that would later form the award-winning studio

The American market's 'discovery' of specifically and proudly 'Japanese' animation came soon after the dissolution of ties below the line that had existed since the late 1950s. In particular, we might note the demise of Top Craft, a studio formed in 1972 by former Tōei animator Hara Tōru, which worked on many of the hidden imports of the following decade (see Chapter 5). After making the 'American' cartoon *The Last Unicorn* (1982), Top Craft evolved into two new units. One, Pacific Animation Corporation, continued to work below the line on 'American' projects until it was bought out and renamed Walt Disney Animation Japan. The other comprised animators who had worked on Top Craft's last project, *Nausicaä of the Valley of the Wind*. Watanabe Takashi (Oguro 2006: 415) observes that labour surpluses around this time enabled Top Craft to take a hard line with its staff, compelling many former key animators and layout artists to work as lowly inbetweeners. This may have been one of the factors that made *Nausicaä*'s animation so memorable, contributing both to the success of the film at the Japanese box office, and the subsequent renown of the animators responsible – the survivors of the hothouse *Nausicaä* production becoming part of the newly named, and far better-known, Studio Ghibli. *Nausicaä* itself, however, achieved a different, negative form of artistic heritage, adapted by American localisers into a shorter, bowdlerised video release called *Warriors of the Wind* (1986). The director of the original, Miyazaki Hayao, was aghast at the treatment his work received and his display represented a milestone in anime history, establishing the fact that the owners of anime might in future want some say in how it was localised. It is the reaction to *Warriors of the Wind* that initiates a new narrative in anime history, leading to post-production on *Princess Mononoke*, with Suzuki Toshio's presentation of a sword to Harvey Weinstein, attached to the message: 'No Cuts' (Clements and McCarthy 2006: 634). Arguably, Suzuki's famous sword stunt represents the culmination of the story begun with Mochinaga Tadahito's work on *The New Adventures of Pinocchio* – four decades after the American owners dictated to the Japanese production what to do, the Japanese owners now dictated conditions to the American localisers. A 'no cuts' clause was written into every Ghibli contract.

DISTRIBUTION AND PRODUCTION: FROM CULTURAL ODOUR TO CULTURAL FRAGRANCE

Anime's transnational discourse begins partway down the ownership–access chain, at the level of distribution, with business-to-business sales of anime objects from Japanese owners to foreign sublicensors. The value of such foreign deals has fluctuated wildly over the years, between a notional level of 100 per cent foreign revenue for the production money paid for *The New Adventures of Pinocchio*, to a level of zero foreign revenue for the many anime objects that fail to secure any foreign sale at all. Between these extreme poles, foreign revenue began at a level of around 30 per cent of production costs for *Astro Boy* in 1963, and was a vital factor in Tezuka Osamu's business plan in the 1960s (see Chapter 6). However, with the collapse of Mushi Pro at the beginning of the 1970s, anime's foreign revenue transformed into a periodic but unexpected bonus, for the most part removed from day-to-day planning at the level of Japanese production.

During the 1970s, anime's foreign sales diminished to around 8–10 per cent of total revenue, representing a small but significant part of its overall business (Funamoto 1998: 62). Critically, much of this revenue was invisible –

in sales of works that were, or *were made to be* lacking any aesthetic identification as 'Japanese'. This included science-fiction shows in 'denationalised' settings, but also World Masterpiece Theatre releases, set in demonstrably specific locales, but none of them Japan. An anecdote from Okada Toshio (2010: 107) suggests that, by the 1980s, many Japanese animators regarded World Masterpiece Theatre as the best kind of work – a worthy, export-focused labour in a long-established children's tradition, untainted by associations with otaku or media-mix marketing.

Iwabuchi Kōichi (2004: 57) notes that Japan's exports in consumer electronics, cars and other objects were long regarded as attempts to be 'culturally odourless'. We might recall Tezuka's drive to render *Astro Boy* 'denationalised' or 'placeless' (see Chapter 6), and observations by some foreign producers that characters or situations that appear 'too Japanese' are distracting and off-putting to the foreign viewer (Iwabuchi 2004: 68). However, Iwabuchi also affirms that a culture with a rising economic hegemony, as Japan experienced in the 1980s, could transform such cultural specificities from an unwelcome 'odour' into a more attractive 'fragrance', and that Japaneseness in the 1980s ceased to be something to be occluded, and became instead, something to be celebrated. Patten (2004: 33) cites Harmony Gold's pilot episode of *Macross* in 1984 as the first American release to openly celebrate anime for its Japanese origins. However, he also contends that this was a 'false dawn', and that the material's eventual mass-market release, on television the following year, was once more subsumed beneath a heavy rewrite and occluded origins, in the form of the TV series *Robotech*. Patten (2004: 37–9) instead identifies later events as indicative of the nascence of a true American otaku market – including the foundation of the magazines *Animag* (1987) and *Protoculture Addicts* (1988), and the distributors Streamline Pictures (1988), AnimEigo (1989), Central Park Media (1990) and ADV Films (1992). By the beginning of the 1990s, the US market was already generating an 'archive' of English-language subtitles and dubs of anime objects. Soon afterwards, titles from such pioneers were re-exported to form the substance of Manga Entertainment's initial push into the UK video market: *Akira*, *Hokuto no Ken* (1986, *Fist of the North Star*), *Dominion Tank Police* (1988) and *Urotsukidōji: Legend of the Overfiend* (1989).

Although some anime producers had aspired to overseas distribution as far back as the 1950s, many participants remained insular and focused entirely on the domestic audience. In some cases, this reflected a belief that limited animation was simply unsuitable for export, and best kept as a home industry. Takahata Isao argues (Ōtsuka 2001: 242) that lip-flaps, one of the corner-cutting devices of limited animation since *Astro Boy*, are only aesthetically convincing in Japanese, a language with restricted enunciation that made three mouth positions and a neutral fourth a relatively 'realistic' representation. 'In western languages', Takahata writes, 'at least eight positions are required for lip-flaps, since the muscles, tongue and oral cavity are used during speech.' However, regardless of Takahata's aesthetic objections, limited animation was still exported, including his own *Heidi*. Moreover, other animators allege that the relationship of lip-flaps to speech is variable even in Japanese, and that the better directors will match them more closely at times of important drama (Tomino 2002: 298).

Upon an anime object's sale at the distribution level, it returns to a new stage of production, in the hands of localisers. Localisation during the 'hidden import' period usually regarded Japanese animation as a raw material that needed to be honed into something suitable for the American market, typically without the approval or interference of the original owners. In a phenomenological sense, while Tezuka boasted of the sales of his *Tetsuwan Atomu* to American broadcasters (see Chapter 6), what was sold was actually *Astro Boy* – a semantically different work, created by the discourse between Tezuka's original and the limited access to its meaning gleaned by American producers watching it on fast-forward and making up the dialogue (Ladd with Deneroff 2009: 36).[2]

Akira (1988) spearheaded anime video labels in many countries, but cost substantially more than many contemporary productions

However, such a tradition ignores the parallel development of informal channels of production and distribution in the 1980s. The tradition of fandom holds that Japanese animation was dragged into the American market by the attention of fans. The US otaku market certainly displays a very similar paradigm to that of the growth of fandom in Japan – rooted in science fiction and film appreciation, expanding through university clubs and private meetings and growing significantly swiftly after the adoption of computers and the arrival of magazines as recurring sites of community and conversation. There are, however, also indicators that corporate interests courted the cooperation of American fans in much the same way that Nishizaki Yoshinobu put fans to work promoting the *Yamato* films in Japan. Asides in the history of American fandom (Patten 2004: 25–6, 29) point to Tezuka Osamu visiting Californian fans and Tōei Animation supplying the Los Angeles Cartoon/Fantasy Organisation (C/FO) with test merchandise to sell at conventions in 1978, followed by Tokyo Movie Shinsha furnishing a copy of *Castle of Cagliostro* for the video room at the 1980 Worldcon. In other words, while fandom did indeed grow, it did so with behind-the-scenes encouragement from the industry itself. In some cases, 'fan' video rooms at conventions not only screened videos provided by Japanese licence holders, but did so on hardware lent or donated by those same licence holders.

This, too, mirrors the model of Japanese expansion, aided in part by the compatibility of the American and Japanese NTSC TV systems, meaning that tapes recorded from Japanese TV could be played on American VCRs without additional conversion. Convention screenings of anime shows in America first began as raw, unsubtitled screenings, at which members were urged to 'shout out' if they could understand what was going on (Jenkins 1992: 76). However, this activity transformed over the following decade from the shared appreciation of otherwise unavailable foreign media, to an informal distribution network of unlicensed copies.

The nature of anime fandom, or rather the attitude of anime owners towards fan communities, changes in direct relation to the power of computers. At first, it is a simple message board of like-minded individuals, facilitating the organisation of fan groups and early conventions, but also the distribution of viewing guides to untranslated shows, and subsequently entire scripts. By the late 1980s, it was possible for, say, a Japanese speaker in Hawaii to send a translated anime script to a friend in California, who could create digital subtitles on an Amiga PC. These, in turn, could be synchronised to a laserdisc sent from Japan, creating a mastertape that could then be duplicated.

The tradition of fandom also holds that professionals are, by definition, not amateurs, and hence not fans. Thus fan tradition often ignores the function of fandom as a culture that nurtures the agents of anime's professional distribution. As American fans were continuing to swap tapes and dress up as anime characters, a few members were drifting into professional pursuits. Most notably Carl Macek, the owner of an animation gallery, moved into distribution with the founding of Streamline Pictures, a company seeking to bring the best of 1980s Japanese animation to the American mainstream.

For many, the citing of Macek within a 'fan' tradition would be controversial. He was, however, a pioneer of many of the tactics of the fan-friendly market, including the decision in the late 1980s to thwart piracy of the film *Akira* by offering a free anime cel with every cassette purchased. Macek remained resolutely and contentiously populist, replacing the original Japanese voice tracks and selecting only those films that he thought would work outside an otaku ghetto. He would soon attract rivals, such as US Renditions and ADV Films, whose practices led them to focus more on a 'fan-friendly' market, pandering to the demands of those within the American audience who identified themselves as 'anime fans', and who parsed this identification as one that required obscurer titles, odder niches and subtitled presentations with the original Japanese audio.

The tradition of anime fandom holds that the practices of Carl Macek, Fred Ladd and their fellows represent an outmoded, old-fashioned, perhaps even colonialist attitude towards Japanese animation, and that fan-oriented companies gradually replaced them with more faithful renditions of the scripts and plots. However, this claim often reflects the marketing of the new companies rather than objective reality. Clements (1998b: 88–90) observes that, while some overseas companies make sweeping and conspicuous changes to the language in their translations, others made equally influential alterations, while claiming to remain faithful to the original. At the other end of the scale, Stevenson (2010: 46–7) posits that it is a fallacy to assume that fan-made objects are guaranteed to be better or more exacting translations. The presence of subtitles does not necessarily guarantee a more faithful translation.[3] As argued by Katsuno and Maret (2004), even in the twenty-first century, anime franchises are subject to extensive changes with the consent of the Japanese owners, in order to secure a mass-market audience. And, according to Iwabuchi (2004: 69), producers do not make these decisions on a whim, but only after witnessing the fate of earlier titles in the mass market that had proved insufficiently denationalised.

All of which points to a true extension of the patterns of the Japanese market into anime's global expansion. Anime in foreign markets is both a mass market and a fan-niche phenomenon; it is both an invisible import and an acknowledged Japanese product, with its own subculture and discourse of magazines and conventions. Despite the self-commemoration of certain companies to the contrary, previous structures of anime continued – as limited film releases, small-interest fan niches and invisible imports – alongside the sudden mass-market expansion represented by the interests of Hollywood distributors. What changes recognisably during the period is the mass media's perception of anime, which varies in direct relation to the objects regarded at any particular time as epitomes. Anime in the last two decades has been variously cited as either an exciting teenage trend, *or* dangerous cartoon pornography, *or* a dangerously slipshod toy advert, *or* a fantastic investment *or* state-of-the-art Oscar-winning movies (Clements 2009a: 272–8). Such a confusion of reactions is explained in part by the sheer breadth of the medium, but also by the recurring fallacy among its commentators, that the performance of any single Japanese cartoon may be generalised as an indicator of the qualities of all others. See Table 9.1 for the Japanese films that proved most successful in the US.

TABLE 9.1. JAPANESE FILMS AT THE US BOX OFFICE – ALL-TIME TOP TEN

RANK	TITLE	YEAR	SCREENS	REVENUE ($ MILLION)
1	*Pokémon #1*	1999	3,043	85.7
2	*Pokémon #2*	2000	2,752	43.8
3	*Yu-gi-oh*	2004	2,411	19.8
4	*Pokémon #3*	2001	2,675	17.0
5	*Ponyo*	2009	927	15.0
6	*Spirited Away*	2002	714	10.0
7	*Digimon*	2000	1,825	9.6
8	*Shall We Dance?**	1997	268	9.5
9	*Howl's Moving Castle*	2005	202	4.7
10	*Ran**	1985	30	3.6

Note: *not animated.
Source: Masuda (2011: 67).

One may pick and choose the statistics one wishes. The number of American screens showing the first *Pokémon* movie (1999) is impressive when one considers accusations that 'foreign films are essentially excluded from the US' (Miller 2005: 190), occupying an average of just 0.75 per cent of available exhibition venues, whereas *Pokémon: The First Movie*, a demonstrably 'foreign' film, achieved a 9 per cent occupancy. However, it is equally possible to suggest that *Pokémon* underperformed screen for screen when compared with Kurosawa Akira's *Ran* (1985), appearing at a hundred times as many sites, but only generating twenty-eight times as much revenue. One might argue that the world of *Pokémon* fans in 1999 is very different from that of art-house filmgoers in 1985 – yes, it is, but surely *Pokémon* should therefore be more successful? While it is salutary to note that eight of the all-time top ten Japanese films at the American box office, including the top seven, are animated films (Masuda 2011: 67), of those box-office winners, three are related to a single franchise, *Pokémon*, while three others are the arguably unique and unrepeatable works of Miyazaki Hayao. Does this point to an anime boom or simply the accidental convergence of two singular successes? In fact, it points to a very limited, temporal success within the cinema exhibition community, only indirectly related to a significantly smaller 'boom' within the American fan community a decade earlier.

In *Shadow Economies of Cinema: Mapping Informal Film Distribution*, Ramon Lobato professes that an aesthetic bias within film studies has fostered an unwillingness to examine the role of informal elements of the film world – in which he includes straight-to-video Japanese animation. He notes (2012: 24) that even in America, 1980s video productions could go into profit with sales of just 15,000–20,000 units – as in the Japanese market discussed in Chapter 8, this was often possible solely on sales to rental stores. Lobato's catalogue of such informal works includes 'mediocre' cash-ins, 'mockbusters' that imitate a better-known mainstream film, edgy works of crime and erotica and material posing as video releases, but actually funded by cable TV companies and intended as channel filler. Such definitions are often cognate with the rise of video animation in Japan, and it should come as no surprise that they should fit so readily into the American market. In many cases, although certainly not all, an American release would also aesthetically reposition a Japanese work as something with both Japanese and American 'success', thereby increasing the chances of its re-export to other language territories.

However, the crucial elements here are the relatively low sales numbers, and the assumption that most of these sales will be to rental stores. Consider, then, the American distribution of the anime series *Trigun* (1998), brought to the US with a break-even sales point of 6,000 units. Eventually selling 30,000 units, it represented

a tidy profit to its American distributors (ANNcast 017 2009: 27'), and indicated a strong enough following in the Anglophone world to justify the production, largely for the overseas market, of a feature-film sequel in 2010. Such success stories represent an appreciable 'long tail' for the Japanese owners of anime. Sales to a foreign-language territory generally involve a minimum guarantee (i.e. an advance against sales) lasting for a set period of several years (Sevakis 2012b: 1). The labour in localising and selling the property is somebody else's problem, and at the end of the licence period, ownership returns to the Japanese, sometimes with the foreign-language production assets also forfeit. Repeated across a dozen language territories, as well as subsidiary regions such as UK or Australian rights for the Anglophone world, it is easy to see how such bonus monies could begin to skew the attitudes of Japanese producers. Unwilling to buy long-running shows, which require higher minimum guarantees and greater risks, foreign markets initially favoured standalone features or limited six-hour series (six OAVs, or a thirteen-episode TV show). It was only in the late 1990s, as AD Vision not only profited from the TV series *Evangelion*, but also began to buy similar serials as content for its own Anime Network, that American distributors began a similar battle for TV serials.

Instead of bidding on older shows with proven track records, the competition and bubble-market expansion of the American market led to companies bidding blindly on unmade shows, sometimes purely on the basis of staff resumés and a few pieces of artwork. Such a process turned the acquisition of Japanese products into an increasingly random lottery, with ever-climbing prices. Chad Kime, formerly of Geneon Entertainment,

Pretty Soldier Sailor Moon (1992) enjoyed a long artistic heritage in the form of sequel serials, repurposing old 'magical girl' tropes in a more commodified era illustrates the problem with the case of *Heat Guy J* (2002), a twenty-six-part TV series for which the company bid before it was even made, and for which Geneon paid far too much money, relative to its eventual sales potential. Moreover, the distribution of anime objects could often be skewed by political decisions back in Japan, such as the decision to 'bundle' several works in one deal (ANNcast 017 2009: 41'), forcing a foreign distributor to buy unsellable dross along with a desired title. The example Kime gives is *Akira*, a guaranteed high-return item in the American market, which was sold to him compulsorily attached to the mid-level video series *3x3 Eyes* (1991), as well as the children's show *Miffy*, entirely unsuitable for his customers:[4]

> It was like we were riding this gigantic glowing star that suddenly became a black hole. It was self-negatively reinforcing. We paid too much for the titles, which made us ship too much product, which made us get returns, which made us lose money, so we had to release more titles, but there was already a glut. So we had to try to make up the sales, but then we actually wound up selling less, so then we had to release more titles to make up for the sales, and thereby add to the problem. (ANNcast 017 2009: 43' 45")

The implosion of the American anime market bears many similarities to the collapse of Mushi Pro in Japan in the 1970s, with executives paying too much for products with uncertain saleability. The production of new anime in Japan drops dramatically after 2006, as the business rationalised along more sensible lines, and the flow of cash from overseas returned to 1990s levels. Companies such as Gonzo, which had come to rely on overseas funding, were forced to suspend production. Others showed a more resilient ability to weather the storm, thanks in part to balance sheets that showed the problem approaching from several years' distance. Toei's peak in overseas revenue, which is to say the peak in revenue from children's products, came in 2001, while Production IG's peak, which is to say the peak in revenue from adult products, came in 2006. The spacing of the data does rather imply that the consumers who pushed *Digimon: Digital Monsters* (1999), *Bishōjo senshi Sailor Moon* (1992, *Sailor Moon*) and *Yu-gi-oh* (2004) to their late 1990s heights are essentially the same people who came back five years later to buy *Ghost in the Shell: Stand Alone Complex* (2002). What we see in the early years of the twenty-first century is the ageing of the *Pokémon* generation, and the sudden removal of much of its buying power from the marketplace as it hits its late teens. In 2013, the remnants of the *Pokémon* generation are full fledged otaku in their twenties, but still dwindling.

OVERSEAS CAPITAL AND DOMESTIC MARKET SATURATION

In 1992, when overseas anime video sales were still in their infancy, Robert Woodhead of the fan-focused distributor AnimEigo predicted:

> In ten years, AnimEigo will probably be doing co-productions with the Japanese. I joke that in five years the Japanese will be doing their productions in English first, then in Japanese, because there are twice as many people in this country. The American end of the market will begin to drive the industry. (Woodhead, quoted in Sorfleet 1992: 11)

Woodhead's prophecy was not far off, although we might note that he seems unaware of the history of some American owners 'driving' Japanese production since *The New Adventures of Pinocchio*. Within three years of his words, the British company Manga Entertainment had contributed 30 per cent of the budget to the production of *Ghost in the Shell*, in order to pre-empt competition for foreign rights. By 2002, when Woodhead joked that the American market would drive Japanese production, the Japanese industry was in the midst of a massive increase in new television shows, mainly for a late-night audience (i.e. an 'adult' market). While supposedly intended for Japanese viewers, many such shows were produced to meet an implied demand from the US market. However, the American market, by equating *Pokémon*'s numbers with the future potential of 'adult' animation, had vastly overestimated the potential for anime this sector, and although there were undeniably some six-figure successes in the early twenty-first century, competition among American distributors

Manga Entertainment co-funded production of *Ghost in the Shell* (1995), in order to head off competition at the distribution stage

drove up the cost of new anime from manageable break-even points of 6,000 unit sales, to far riskier break-even points of 20,000 units and up (ANNcast 017 2009: 26′). Such amounts create new expenses of their own, in duplication fees and warehouse storage, and ultimately, in the size of the write-off required when unsold DVDs are returned in their thousands.

Even as conspicuous non-otaku successes like *Pokémon* and Studio Ghibli elevated anime's global currency, competition in the overseas otaku market pushed the price of foreign rights above a level where they were likely to earn back the cost of investment. Similarly, there are signs, even amid the breathless rush of anime's global popularity, of bad Japanese business decisions that also backfired. Tada Makoto (2002: 63–8) offers three poorly performing anime films as examples, each defeated by different aspects of the ownership–access chain. *Gundress* (1999) was released in Japanese theatres embarrassingly unfinished, a failure ultimately of production, but compounded by the immovable exhibition demands set up by ticket pre-sales. *Tonari no Yamada-kun* (1999, *My Neighbours the Yamadas*) generated reasonable box office, albeit a fraction of that expected for a Studio Ghibli film at the time, much to the annoyance of investors and sublicensors. This was parsed as a failure of authorship, because the subject matter proved unappealing to children, thereby rendering it unlikely to sell multiple tickets to entire families. The conglomerate Hitachi-Maxell attempted to enter the anime film market with *Kaze o Mita Shōnen* (2000, *The Boy Who Saw the Wind*), at a production cost of 700 million yen. Its subsequent box-office failure was blamed on poor marketing (i.e. distribution), but we might equally contend that its 'failure' came as a result of the unreal expectations placed upon it to earn a return on such a huge investment in just four weeks at the cinema. If Hitachi-Maxell had hoped to imitate the success of *Princess Mononoke*, it was presumably hoping to somehow do so without drawing upon the decade of brand-building undertaken by Studio Ghibli before *Princess Mononoke*'s release – even Ghibli's box-office returns started out small (Seto *et al.* 2002: 17). Such failures, however, do not appear to have troubled the Hollywood majors, which left the small American anime distributors to fight over fan-oriented product, video serials and most TV shows, while diligently grabbing the handful of proven market leaders.

TABLE 9.2: TOP SIX ANIME FILMS AT THE JAPANESE BOX OFFICE IN 1997

FILM	REVENUE (BILLION YEN)
Princess Mononoke	10.7
Doraemon: Nobita's Clockwork City Adventure	2.0
The End of Evangelion	1.5
Evangelion: Death and Rebirth	1.1
Hermes: Winds of Love	0.7
Boy Detective Conan: The Time-Bombed Skyscraper	0.6

Source: Funamoto (1998: 162)

Arguably, the greatest contribution to the concept of an 'anime boom' in Japan and the primacy of animation was brought about by the simplest of business facts – the revenue generated by certain big-name titles. Perusal of the titles of top-twenty films at the Japanese box office in the late 1990s tells its own story, of a convergence of several disparate streams of the anime industry – the old children's movies, the regular vacation roadshows (now called anime fairs), otaku-oriented special films and occasional wildcards. In cinemas, this reached its peak in 1997, a golden year for animation revenue, when six of the top ten movies at the Japanese box office were animated (see Table 9.2).

In 1997, an unprecedented 69.5 per cent of the revenue from the top twenty domestic films at the Japanese box office was generated by anime (Funamoto 1998: 163). However, it is never that simple – the singular success of Studio Ghibli's *Princess Mononoke* accounts for over half that total on its own, but represented the maturation of Studio Ghibli's family audience, which had been slowly building for the previous two decades. Ghibli films only broke even or made a modest profit throughout most of the 1980s. It was not until *Kiki's Delivery Service* that Ghibli films showed significant box-office returns. However, a breakdown of the Japanese audience demographics on Studio Ghibli films shows an overwhelming number of ticket buyers arriving in family groups, with 34.7 per cent of the audience comprising parents, but also an equal segment of friends or dating couples (Seto *et al.* 2002: 17). In other words, when a Ghibli film is truly popular, it can lure in entire family groups, vastly increasing its likely revenue when compared to films aimed at solo otaku.

If we couple the impressive Japanese box-office revenue for anime, with the mounting returns from foreign territories and the explosion of markets on cable, it is easy to see why the turn of the twenty-first century saw many Japanese pundits speaking of great profits and the rise of an 'anime business'. Mori Takeshi (Funamoto 1998: 57) notes that it was *Princess Mononoke* and *Evangelion* which were specifically responsible for public perception of a new 'anime boom', in particular *Evangelion*, since its merchandising and publishing tie-ins generated an income ten times greater than its box-office returns.

However, John Ellis points out (1992: 34) not only that Disney was the first to recognise the 'logical extension of the marketing of a particular film on the basis of narrative image', i.e. the use of tie-in products to augment a film's brand, but also that this was 'only possible with a relatively small number of films over any one period: the so-called blockbusters'. In terms of the truly mass market, particularly in the expectations and desires of a child consumer, there is only room for one *Cinderella*, or one *Lion King* (1994), or one *Pokémon* in the viewer's life at any one time.

Princess Mononoke (1997) generated 10.7 billion yen at the Japanese box office, outshining its nearest rival by a factor of five, and beating live-action competitors

Media-mix franchises might be able to persuade a hypothetical consumer to purchase a set of *Naruto* curtains, but he probably only has one window in which to hang them. For the duration of the product cycle and his interest in it, the *Naruto* curtains are the only ones he will have. While it might be possible to segment the market into a handful of big-name titles, there is still only a finite number of franchises before the market is entirely saturated. Moreover, Takeda Yasuhiro cautions (Hotta 2005: 37) that the same is true, albeit on a smaller scale, of the niche otaku market. It is also worth bearing in mind that anime does not exist in a racially homogenous vacuum – particularly in the eyes of children who simply see it as another cartoon, it is part of a global environment of animation. Just as in the 1950s (see Chapter 4), it faces foreign competition for viewers' attention, and in the children's animation market that means *Toy Story* (1995), *Cars* (2006) and Tokyo Disneyland. A child that takes the Disney shilling, self-identifying for familial gift-buying purposes as a fan of, say, *Beauty and the Beast* (1991) or *Mulan* (1948), may be essentially lost to anime tie-ins for the next couple of years. During the 1990s, Disney's *The Lion King* and *Aladdin* (1995) outperformed most *Doraemon* films and several Studio Ghibli releases at the Japanese box office, presenting a strong international rival to domestic franchises (Tada 2002: 69). Disney's titles and, subsequently, Pixar's have been even more dominant in the Japanese video market, where only the *Pokémon* franchise and Studio Ghibli have offered them any serious competition. Miyazaki's *Nausicaä* may have sold an impressive 200,000 copies on Japanese VHS, but Disney's *Aladdin* sold half as many again (Haraguchi 2000: 158).

Furthermore, a children's franchise, once established, can maintain its equilibrium for several years. *Pokémon* has been running since 1997; *Transformers* since 1984; *Dragon Ball* lasted for twelve years; *Sailor Moon* for seven; it is a much taller order to challenge the giants of the children's market than it is to carve out a small niche of 10 or 20,000 older otaku enthusiasts. Masuda (2007: 215) cautions that foreign competition and declining numbers of children both make entry into the children's animation market in Japan a risky proposition.

Not for the first time, some investors in the alleged 'anime boom' seem to have confused apples with oranges, assuming that the numbers were a repeatable, sustainable, expandable area. The upshot of all this data, however, is not necessarily an admission that the anime market has reached its maximum possible expansion. On the contrary, even for the most pessimistic of observers, the same statistics can point to a different conclusion, that the anime market may have reached its maximum possible expansion in Japan, a nation of just 127 million potential consumers, on a planet of 6 billion. During the 1980s and increasingly during the 1990s, a 'long tail' of sales to foreign territories could extend the potential earning power of certain anime objects far past the end of their natural lifespan in the home market. There had already been inklings of such a foreign engine of demand, not only in the continued below-the-line activities of animators working on foreign productions, but also in demands from abroad for more content. In the case of the TV show *Dirty Pair* (1985), an order arrived from the Italian market for thirty-six episodes of a show that had lasted for only twenty-six weeks. Accordingly, the Japanese made ten more, specifically for Italy, but ultimately sellable to any other territory, including back to Japan itself (Clements and McCarthy 2006: 146).

The size of the anime market, swelled by foreign revenue worth up to 50 per cent of annual income for some studios, reached an all-time peak in 2006 (AJA 2008 I: 37), from which it has since 'slumped'. However, a closer statistical analysis shows a number of factors at work. General figures for the industry as a whole show increased revenues during the period 1997–2005, but also increased numbers of titles. While *Pokémon* was a substantial contributor to foreign revenues in the period, it was by no means the sole source. Moreover, although *Pokémon* videos did indeed sell in their millions overseas (ANNcast017 2009: 33'), *Pokémon* is better considered less as a bestselling anime, more as an intermedial 'children's commodity … hardware, software, toys, TV, movies, card … one of the top-selling toys and games of all time' (Tobin 2004: 5), of which anime is merely a component. In the business sector, this was parsed in similar terms, as a realisation that anime, previously regarded as a subaltern sector of the Japanese media, was the nexus of a global business worth $6.59 billion per year (Kataoka 2011: 152). However, anime did not generate that income; it was merely its standard bearer.

DISTRIBUTION: ANIME IN THE US MASS MARKET

Foreign rights buyers pre-empting local competition and Japanese production committees in search of new markets combined the concerns of the otaku market and of the longstanding below-the-line participation of Japanese companies in foreign productions. By 2005, some newer Japanese studios regarded foreign markets as so essential that they would not initiate a new production unless half of it was paid for by foreign capital (Clements 2009a: 265). It is, it seems, this subset of productions that created the sudden spike in new, short anime serials in the middle of the first decade of the twenty-first century, as studios such as Madhouse and Gonzo allowed themselves to be steered directly by foreign concerns, as long as those concerns had money to spend.

Meanwhile, Hollywood's sudden interest in anime features in the 1990s might be parsed as a series of manoeuvres based on the politics of American distribution, itself inspired by the apparent, growing appeal of Japanese 'cultural fragrance' during the early 1990s. With American film distribution an oligopoly of only half a dozen companies (Gomery 2005: 175), we might reimagine ownership of an anime object as the latest fashion among such major players. Disney buys up the entire back catalogue of Studio Ghibli, and invests directly in *Spirited Away* – quite possibly influencing the conferral of an Academy Award upon it, which is usually seen as a 'Japanese' success. Warner Brothers distributes *The Animatrix* (2003) and the *Pokémon* movies, including the highest-earning Japanese film ever at the American box office, *Pokémon the Movie: Mewtwo's Counterattack* (1999). The same studio throws money into *Speed Racer* (2008), a live-action film based on a Japanese cartoon. Twentieth Century-Fox releases *Digimon*. On the periphery, Sony tries to turn anime *into* a Hollywood movie with *Final Fantasy: The Spirits Within*. Bringing up the rear, DreamWorks invests in anime as art-house, initiating an abortive attempt to snap up the works of Kon Satoshi, but also copies the Sony model in collusion with Paramount, by producing the live-action movie of *Transformers*. These moves not only presented a performance of Japanese animation as an important new trend, but also helped hide the fact that in the otaku market that had drawn the majors' attention to Japan in the first place, revenues were already declining.

Although anime's foreign appeal was, to some extent, ethnically signified, as a sign of Japaneseness, the nature to which anime might be said to be 'Japanese' in the twenty-first century is problematic. At the level of ownership, the capital invested in anime comes from multiple sources – it is 'globalised', just as likely to issue from African diamond mines as a Chinese tinsel factory or a Norwegian oil rig. But this has been the case since Videocraft hired Mochinaga Tadahito to make *The New Adventures of Pinocchio*. At the level of production, it is similarly transnational with, depending on how one counts, up to 66 per cent of the labour involved in making a 'Japanese' cartoon coming from overseas (Takahashi 2012). This, too, is merely a stage on a continuum dating back to the 1960s, with the offshoring of work on *Monster Man BEM* to Korea. Nor is it necessarily much of an issue to anime's owners, since all modern animation productions are transnational in nature. DreamWorks maintains an Indian subsidiary and Disney runs an Australian outpost, both of which contribute to films that, if they are assigned a nationality at all, are usually termed 'American'.

The difference with the anime business is that in many fields its Japaneseness has become its unique selling point to the otaku audience. Over the last twenty years Japanese origin or Japanese themes have created an orientalist 'value' for anime. Anime's appearance on the world stage, as a Japanese commodity around 1989, matched the boom of Japan's own economy, and the availability of Japanese capital to make idiosyncratic films like *Tonari no Totoro* (1988, *My Neighbour Totoro*) and *The Wings of Honneamise*. Foreign capital, at the time, was something of an afterthought, gradually gaining primacy through the 1990s as Japan's insular anime culture was found to have an unexpected afterlife overseas – particularly attractive to Japanese studios during Japan's long post-bubble recession. Foreign capital stripmined the adult-oriented anime of the video years, and when it exhausted that motherlode of gothic horror, SF and fantasy, returned as an investor in order to replicate more of it, beginning with Manga Entertainment's partial funding of *Ghost in the Shell*.

By the late 1990s, we see three interrelated strands of anime – the adult-oriented material characterised by *Ghost in the Shell*, the child-oriented material typified by *Pokémon* and Studio Ghibli's hybrid content, arguably with one foot in both the children's and adult market. All three, however, were influenced not only by foreign capital, but also by a transformative digitisation and computerisation of the Japanese animation industry, which is the subject of the final chapter.

NOTES

1. See http://www.tv-tokyo.co.jp/kouhou/guideenglish.htm.
2. This issue still occasionally arises in attempts by localisers to colonise the intellectual property of anime, with regrettable boasts found in some credits or on boxes that the English scripts have been 'written' by localisers whose functions are better described as editorial.
3. I would also note that there is a growing degree of nescience, or rather a mistaken tradition, among modern fansubbers, many of whom do not appear to realise how much of their practices originated in the releases of AnimEigo, an idiosyncratic but most definitely professional company.
4. Of course, companies are not obliged to release such unwanted shows. Often, they simply sit on the books as 'assets', and are either written off or shunted into the marketplace a few years later by new members of staff unaware of their mode of acquisition, or more trusting in their sales potential. It is, however, often difficult to explain to accountants that it is in the company's best interests not to release a property that has already been paid for.

10 THE DIGITAL ENGINE
New technologies and animation 1983–2012

Anime's digital era is framed by economic decline, with interest in computers beginning as an effort to save money during the early 1970s slump (or 'oil shocks'), and the industry's enthusiastic adoption of digital technology, reflecting the position of computers or games as one of the few growth areas during Japan's 1990s recession (Kawai 1999: 81). This chapter considers the boom years of the Japanese animation industry in terms of the radical changes brought to all levels of the ownership–access chain by new technologies, but also the swift growth in testimonials outside the usual areas of production and authorship, concentrating instead on issues of distribution and exhibition.

The most obvious aspect of the computerisation of the anime industry can be found at the production level. Masunari Kōji equates the impact of digital animation with a revolutionary change 'as essential as the discovery of fire' (Kamen 2012), referring not only to the alterations in the process, but to the sudden redundancy of entire skillsets, requirements for new skills, and an intake of new labour, forming the likely producers and directors of the next generation.

However, the most obvious application of computers, in 3D digital animation on works such as *Appleseed* (2004), is merely the most aesthetically obvious. In a revival of the rotoscoping debates of the 1950s (see Chapter 5), we might even argue that mapping new skins onto motion-captured footage is less 'animation' than it is a

mimetic 'special effect'. A perhaps greater transformation in production came within 2D animation in the same period, since digital technology not only replaced the cel-animation process in use since the 1930s, but often did so invisibly, while retaining the outward appearance, at the access level, of a continuity of cel-anime traditions and styles. One company in particular, Celsys, dominates production in the twenty-first century by providing the software platform on which much modern anime is made, and plays a similarly powerful role in the development of Japanese e-books and digitised comic publishing.

As Michael Gubbins argues (2012: 67), with reference to the film business as a whole, computers and digital media have also had a largely invisible, but equally far-reaching impact on all other sectors of the entertainment economy. In the case of Japanese animation, the booming market in gaming and consoles not only offered new work opportunities for existing studios, but led to substantial injections of investment capital from the gaming companies themselves, influencing the content and ownership of anime. Internet, cable TV and digital broadcasting have provided new structures of distribution that present radical changes and challenges to both formal and informal delivery systems – anime is debatably now easier to buy, but also easier

Shinji Aramaki's *Appleseed* (2004) makes much of its digital animation, although anime has been subtly integrating digital processes since the 1970s

to steal. Digitisation has also transformed technologies and conceptualisations of exhibition, not only in cinemas where hard-drives have replaced film reels, but through the creation of 'multilinear and mobile' access, on computer screens and mobile phones.

Digitisation has also transformed the audience's own concept of access, inviting not only simple viewership, but also ever more invasive participation in the creation and pseudo-creation of anime objects. Arguably, the digital age has lured many viewers into a reconsideration of their role in the chain, from passive end-users to active controllers of content, to such an extent that some even lay claim to the position at the opposite end of the chain, for the ownership of anime itself.

OWNERSHIP: THE EFFECT OF GAMING CAPITAL

According to Tsugata Nobuyuki (2004: 198) the English-language term '*anime business*' began to appear in the Japanese media in the 1990s as a result of the convergence between animation, computers and modern media. Whereas coverage of the anime industry had previously been production-, author- or access-focused, the implication of new revenue potential led to a new publishing subgenre concerning anime as a true business – in other words, as a discipline whose discourse centred on the production, management, buying and selling of objects. Initially, at least, a refreshing change from technical minutiae or cultural theorising, these books attempted a synoptic description of how the humble and largely overlooked Japanese animation business should suddenly bring in so much foreign money. Translations of typical book titles include *Anime's Future* (Funamoto 1998), *This Is the Anime Business* (Tada 2002), *Understanding the Anime Business* (Masuda 2007) and its sequel *Understanding the Anime Business More* (Masuda 2011). An even larger publishing niche concentrated on the 'contents industry' as the new term for what had previously been described as the 'media mix', with anime as a nexus for the related fields of manga, merchandising, toys and computer games.

Changes in the period were not merely a matter of finance, but of simple demographics. For those individuals in the industry who had stuck with the low returns and poor working conditions of anime in the Tezuka era, who had somehow evaded the worst side effects of 'anime syndrome' and remained working at Japanese studios, the 1990s saw them approaching retirement age. Men aged twenty during the big hiring bubbles of *Hakujaden* or *Astro Boy*, the most likely group to have attained management and executive positions at Japan's animation studios, would face the prospect of retirement, at the then-average age of fifty-five, somewhere between the years 1993 and 1998 (Whitehill 1991: 76). Takahashi Ryōsuke, in a personal communication, considers this issue to be the primary factor in several 1990s takeovers, such as that of the Sunrise animation studio by the Bandai toy company in 1994. Selling the studio that makes *Gundam* to its biggest client ensured that the ownership of the anime products remained in hands that best appreciated how to use it. Similar thinking may have underpinned changeovers at Studio Ghibli, around the sixtieth birthdays of Miyazaki Hayao (2001) and Suzuki Toshio (2008), with repeated attempts to pass on directorial and managerial responsibilities to a new generation.

Initially, gaming companies were little more than additional clients or production committee members, as opportunities arose for the use of animation either in games, or based on games. This was first apparent to the public at large on 20 July 1986, when the short anime films *Super Mario Brothers: The Battle to Rescue Princess Peach* and *Running Boy: Secrets of Star Soldier* were premiered in rival Shōchiku and Tōhō cinemas, each claiming to be the 'first' computer-game spin-off (Animage 1989: 119). Later years saw an ever-increasing presence of gaming capital in the animation sector, most notably on such franchises as *Street Fighter II: V* (1995) and *Pokémon*, both of which endured for significantly longer runs on television than all but the most popular anime shows. The 70mm computer-animated film *Space Boat* (1988) was made by Tōyō Links, and listed in the company's online filmography,[1] but could only be seen within the context of a particular, fixed event. This was because the footage formed the visual component of a 'ride' at the Seto Bridge Expo, one of many 'games' or events that apply animation or film to a novelty mode of exhibition.

However, anime companies had begun participating in the gaming sector significantly earlier. Digital data-storage formats, such as the laserdisc, allowed film footage to be accessed in a non-linear fashion – i.e. by skipping instantly to particular scenes instead of having to spool laboriously along a tape reel. Although this function is most often employed today simply for jumping between chapters on a DVD, it found its first application in the gaming world in computer arcades, where laserdiscs served to store animation footage for use in games. Sega's arcade machine *Astron Belt* (1983) featured a standard sprite-based shooting game, but with backgrounds incorporating video footage, stored on an internal laserdisc. This was later refined in games such as Taitō's *Time Gal* (1985), in which the player's actions did not move sprites on the screen but triggered branching storylines in full-motion video (FMV), in much the same fashion as the US arcade game *Dragon's Lair* (1983).

The video footage for *Time Gal* drew heavily on pre-existing talents – it was directed by Imazawa Tetsuo, animated at Tōei Dōga, and plainly drew inspiration for the heroine's design on the lead character from the popular series *Urusei Yatsura* (1981–6). Later in the decade, increasing numbers of animators would be drafted in to work on computer games, as the craze spread from limited arcade sites to home consoles and computers.

Okada Toshio cites (2010: 214) the year 1987 as a watershed in the capabilities of computer games, as widespread use of floppy disks allowed manufacturers to incorporate heavier graphic elements in their products for the home market. The increase of memory, both in terms of processing power and readable storage, periodically altered the nature of home computer games, from text-based games, to text-based games with bitmapped pictures, to text-based games with anime-style pictures and eventually photographs, full-motion video, and fully interactive environments. The technology of the games console similarly influenced the type of game with, for example, the three iterations of the Sony PlayStation bringing CD sound, then DVD video, then Blu-ray video into their presentations.

Somewhat idiosyncratically, Takahashi Ryōsuke regards (2011a: 53) many media staff as individuals who fail to attain their original goal but bring its tropes to their second-choice profession, with thwarted film directors becoming manga artists, thwarted manga artists becoming animators and thwarted animators finding employment in the computer-game sector. Such an assertion rather ignores the widespread hybridity between the anime and gaming worlds, and the richer rewards accruing from work for Sega, Sony or Nintendo. However, in Takahashi's defence, it is worth noting that the 'games sector' does not merely include lucrative multiple-year PlayStation contracts, but also the relatively low-rent, obscure work of dozens of production houses making niche-interest pornography, dating simulators and adventure games. Many such 'visual novels' retain the branching storyline paradigm of *Time Gal*, but dispense with its FMV and requirements for rapid hand–eye coordination in favour of yes/no questions rewarded by new still images. They utilise anime-style artwork, and might be regarded as the apotheosis of 'limited' animation, in which only a few hundred still images appear in the course of a story that lasts for several hours. This appears to have originally been a consequence of low memory capabilities – it being easier to store a 'realistic' anime-style bitmap image than a high-resolution photograph. However, the visual novels also seemed to favour the anime-style image in their distribution, possibly in the hope that by passing, even for a moment, for a previously unseen anime, the advert or box art might attract the eye of new consumers (Clements 1998d: 113).

Despite this, the digital animator Murahama Shōji essentially agrees with Takahashi, albeit with different emphasis, when he describes the advent of gaming commissions as a liberating explosion of opportunity for aspirant animators, previously excluded from the limited jobs available in a contracting anime market (Hotta 2005: 287). Murahama's perspective emphasises that the period saw the opening of a massive and largely unexpected frontier of new animation jobs, many of which were filled either by labourers from the old anime industry, but also by young digital animators with an entirely different skillset and approach. In one of the most celebrated examples, Sayama Yoshinori from Tōyō Links, when given the task of providing a medical monitor readout for *Macross Plus* (1994), chose not to animate it by hand, but instead digitised his own heartbeat to generate an actual signal (Clements 2009a: 369).

Tōyō Links was also one of the first companies to demonstrate that Tezuka Osamu's concept of an 'image bank' (see Chapter 6) could endure in the digital age, when the company repurposed a scanned image of a 3D plane model created for a *Macross Plus* trailer for reuse in the later *Macross 7* (1994). This, in turn, points to the growing primacy of digital animation, particularly in vertically integrated companies. As an increasing number of peripheral areas (model design, toy conceptualisation, games) required digital assets, an animation company that could also work digitally was sure to be favoured above one that clung to the old analogue working

Although praised as a quality anime, *Blue Submarine No. Six* (1998) was intended by its makers to advertise their services in the gaming world

methods. Notably, it was Tatsunoko Pro, a studio long associated with technical experimentation, which took the boldest step, authorising several employees to set up the digital-animation subsidiary IG Tatsunoko (now Production IG) in 1987.

The gaming sector offered rich rewards for designers and animators able to refashion their skills to work in the new area. In the case of Yoshizaki Takeshi, for example, whose company High Tech Lab Japan supplied the computer graphics for *Akira* in 1988, his involvement in straightforward animation was relatively minimal thereafter. Far more lucrative contracts awaited him in gaming, either making straightforward animation for the opening to the PlayStation game *Tōshinden 2* (1995), or assets for games such as *Starblade Alpha* (1996). Gaming capital was even influential by its mere prospect, with Murahama Shōji admitting that the Gonzo studio's anime *Blue Submarine No. Six* (1998) was made as an extended 'calling card' to advertise the animators' services to gaming companies (Hotta 2005: 288). Minami Masahiko notes (Oguro 2006: 15) that by 1992 gaming was offering better money and working conditions for animators than anime itself, leading to a palpable brain-drain of the best talent. Minami, then a young producer at Sunrise, instituted a policy that he hoped would retain the best talents for anime. He called this the Happiness Project (Shiawase Keikaku); although its precise implementation remains vague, its stated aim was to keep the workforce 'happy' by not pushing them to insane degrees of overwork, and affording them the opportunity to take pride in their achievements. The most conspicuous result of the scheme was the TV show *Cowboy Bebop* (1998). By the time the series was broadcast to wide acclaim, Minami had left Sunrise with several collaborators to form his own studio, Bones, which continued to work with Sunrise or Bandai on several later projects. In many cases, Bones would furnish footage for computer-game spin-offs – presumably part of the plan, as such commissions would keep gaming investment in the anime business, but prevent animators from defecting to the gaming sector.

Gaming sometimes simply offered new job opportunities in production on the games themselves. The early laserdisc games stored around twenty minutes of footage, roughly equivalent to a single 'original anime video'. Later formats, using DVD storage, were able to substantially increase their memory, with titles such as *Scandal* (2000), a PlayStation game that included three hours of animation from Production IG. At the next level, gaming companies often had money to spend on animation, involving anime companies at the production level, to make spin-off anime titles to essentially function as adverts for the games. The 'context integration' of the 1970s was now put to work for new owners, funnelling money into anime spin-offs promoting, among many others, *Fatal Fury* (1994), *Digimon*, *Tekken* (1990) and *Tōshinden*. By 1998, Tokyo TV ratings data reported sixty anime shows broadcast, of which only twenty were classified as 'children's' entertainment. Among the sponsors, 60 per cent were games companies and audiovisual equipment manufacturers (Funamoto 1998: 58).

PRODUCTION: 2D DIGITAL ANIMATION PROCESSES

When documenting the history of digital animation, the most common error of practice beyond simple nescience is likely to be that of aesthesis (Megill 2007: 33) – the most visible examples are not necessarily the 'first' or most significant. In the case of digital animation, the film *Golgo 13* (1983), with short sequences involving primitive 3D computer graphics, is most often cited as the harbinger of a new age. However, a far more significant milestone was reached the same year, seemingly without attracting any public notice, when the second episode of the World Masterpiece Theatre serial *The Yearling* was composited inside a computer, despite retaining the outward appearance of traditional 2D cel animation (Funamoto 1998: 189–90). Both these breakthroughs were the work of Kaneko Michiru's Japan Computer Graphics Laboratory (JCGL), but only the flashy, conspicuous disjuncture of *Golgo 13*'s 3D animation received widespread notice.

Although *Golgo 13* demonstrated a conspicuous use of computer graphics, its significance was also arguably trounced by a far shorter piece the same year. *Daicon IV*, Gainax's opening animation for the eponymous science-fiction convention included shots of 3D wireframe graphics, animated via the extremely limited capacities of the PC-9800. Although only a fraction of the length of *Golgo 13*'s more famous sequence, and seen by a comparatively tiny audience, its viewership comprised solely active fans, opinion formers and producers. Despite a performative action largely limited to a single screening, its artistic heritage and 'representative event' status has been demonstrable and enduring – contributing not only to Gainax's commission the following year to make *The Wings of Honneamise*, but also to Japanese fandom's commemoration of itself. Two decades later, the fan-focused live-action drama series *Densha Otoko* (2005, *Train Man*) featured an animated opening sequence by the Gonzo studio, affectionately pastiching *Daicon IV* for a new generation of otaku.

Errors of practice in tradition and commemoration have also skewed public perceptions of the development of digital animation. The production of Ōtomo Katsuhiro's *Akira* made extensive use of the Quick Action Recorder (see Chapter 8) to test complex sequences, but this was parsed in the film's own *Making of …* featurette as a revolutionary 'new' device. The QAR had been an industry standard for almost a decade, but was not commemorated until the release of *Akira* demanded objects of innovation to discuss.

Similarly, Oshii Mamoru's production of *Ghost in the Shell* composited digitally scanned foreground and background images, and employed an Avid non-linear editing suite – a relatively new piece of technology, but already adopted in many Hollywood studios. Oshii Mamoru's use of digital effects and non-linear editing on *Ghost in the Shell* was certainly a pioneering move in the anime industry, although it trailed behind Hollywood, and its 'revolutionary' artistic heritage is 'remembered' largely because of the animators' self-commemoration in their own documentary.

As noted by Suzuki Shinichi (2008a: 16), the adoption of computers was seen by some as a technological transformation that came from the bottom up. In other words, the upper 'authorship' echelon of designers, directors, writers and artists was the last to be affected. Whereas anime scripts were not even word-processed until the mid-1990s, and key animators continued to work with pencils, the lower levels of inbetweening, and, particularly, colouring, were swift to capitalise on the labour-saving functions of computers. Hence, on the international production of *Mina Smiles* (1993), Suzuki drew his storyboards in Japan with a pencil and paper – technology unchanged since the 1910s – but arrived at the subcontracting animation studio in Kuala Lumpur to discover that the facility was entirely computerised.

While *Ghost in the Shell* and its breathless *Making of …* got all the attention for 'being digital', asides elsewhere in industry accounts of the 1990s point to a swift, silent yet all-inclusive appropriation of digital technology by the Tōei Dōga studio at many levels of the production process. The potential of computers in animation had been recognised at Tōei as early as 1974, when the new president, Imada Chiaki, set up a study group to examine possible applications, in the hope that the untried technology might provide cost-saving solutions to the recession-hit studio (Funamoto 1998: 32, 189). The group's recommendations were eventually implemented in 1986, with the hiring of Fujitsū to set up the Computer Aided Tōei Animation System (CATAS), a server completed in 1991 (Yamaguchi 2004: 133). The name seems deliberately evocative of the Computer Assisted Production System (CAPS), a similar system developed by Disney during the same period (Telotte 2008: 200).

Subsequent adoptions at Tōei correlated to the falling prices of computer hardware, reflecting similar expansion in the gaming field, that saw games go from bespoke machines in arcades, to consoles monopolising the home television set, to PC games, to handheld electronics and apps. In animation, this progression saw computers evolve from being single, specialised machines with limited user access, to inclusion in departmental workstations and ultimately, ubiquity, with a machine on every desktop. Yoshimura Jirō, a former animator turned digital manager for Tōei, notes (Funamoto 1998: 38) that the tipping point came at the beginning of the

1990s, when both the price and power of desktop computers reached levels that favoured their mass appropriation. By 1995, the Tōei studio had computerised its 'tablework', hitching a PC to motors on multiplane cameras. Now zooms, tracking shots and basic parallax movements for multiplane backgrounds could be controlled in computerised increments, speeding up certain complex shots (Mikami 2011: 82).

In 1992, Tōei animators working on the anime-based game of *Fist of the North Star*, first used a beta edition of computer-animation tools to be released by the Celsys company under the umbrella name of the Revolutionary Engineering Total Animation System (RETAS). The RETAS suite integrated software that covered all the steps of the old analogue animation process – Stylos for creating digital 'pencil' images, Traceman for in-betweening, Paintman for colouring and Core RETAS for integrating and rendering the other elements. The Windows version of RETAS eventually included an additional program, Movie Edit Pro that allowed for the integration of limited effects (Yamaguchi 2004: 151). Employed sparingly on Tōei TV animation from 1993 onwards, the program offered an immediate 20 per cent saving on colouring costs alone (Masuda 2007: 172). Widely adopted throughout Tōei's subsidiaries and affiliates in 1997, it remains in general use in the 2D animation industry in Japan.

Once computing costs had fallen so that it was affordable to place a machine on every desktop, RETAS was rapidly adopted in the industry. Tōei began phasing out the old analogue cel process in 1997, with many of its titles thereafter, including *Doctor Slump* and *Spooky Kitarō*, now made entirely on computer. By 2002, Tōei's process was completely integrated into a system called Rabbit, with both on- and off-site computers linked through Internet connections to a central 1.4 Terabyte server, and thence to departmental compositor workstations and an Avid editing suite. This network extended to a wholly owned overseas subsidiary, Tōei Animation Philippines Inc., which used a frame relay running at 1.5 Mbps per second to upload artwork and assets directly to the Japanese headquarters (Yamaguchi 2004: 153; Mikami 2011: 90). Where once offshore work had to be delivered literally by hand, transported in a briefcase on a plane (see Chapter 6), it now materialised as if drawn in the next room, significantly increasing the efficiency of offshore subsidiaries.

Mikami Kōji notes (2011: 91) that, although the output product could resemble the old 2D cel animation, the change to computers required an alternate skillset. Until analogue artwork was replaced with fully digital drawing tablets, the old 'tracing' stage was replaced by 'scanning'. Digital colouring replaced the old forms of labour with an entirely different group of tasks, often deceptively simple. Whereas once colourists were required to mix and match paint tones, follow style guides and meticulously colour within the lines, digital colourists at least had fixed colour matching systems and the option of 'undoing' bad jobs. However, as Ōtomo Katsuhiro once complained during the production of *Steamboy* (2004), this very ease of alteration brought with it a distractingly wide range of options and gradations:

> Until now [1998] there was always a limit to the available colour palette. Now we can use sixteen million. That's enough to be functionally infinite, so the old standards for colour have been completely destroyed. And, of course, once something has been painted, it can be changed. If it's not exactly what you envisaged, you can pick away until you get it right. (quoted in Animage 1998b: 24)

As noted by Mikami (2011: 96), although computers themselves are relatively costly items of hardware, their price swiftly amortises with use, and while their maintenance is often a skilled job, their operation has been gradually proletarianised. Point-and-click operations have meant that many jobs in animation remain relatively low paid. However, there is still an operational cost and, while the lower stages of the process might remain low paid, expenses still accrue at the levels of character and environment design. Ōtomo Katsuhiro observed (Animage 1998b: 24) that, far from freeing artists from budgets and logistics, computers were just as likely to run up costs. In Ōtomo's case, a producer demanded that he include an intricate environment in the final cut of *Steamboy*, even though it had only been designed as an experiment – the cost of 'building' the virtual set had proved just as prohibitive as if it had been assembled in the real world (Animage 1998b: 24).

By 2007, the *Asahi Shinbun* was reporting that *Sazae-san* was the last anime to be made (Asahi Shinbun 2007) using the outmoded cel tradition, since only *Sazae-san* was still in production with staff too old to learn new techniques. The article implies not only that animators elsewhere have been forced to adapt or face the sack, but that Chinese outsourcing companies were also fully digital, and handling '20–30 per cent' of the workload of the 'Japanese' animation business. This assertion, however, cites a figure based on the number of processes handled offshore. In terms of actual manpower, vastly more labourers are employed in the lower echelons of colourists and inbetweeners than in the higher echelons of directors and key animators. As a result, in labour terms, the number of non-Japanese participants in the 'Japanese' animation industry is now more like 60–70 per cent of the overall workforce (Takahashi 2012).

PRODUCTION: 3D DIGITAL ANIMATION PROCESSES

3D computer graphics developed at a similar rate, pioneered by animators such as Kaneko Michiru, who established the Japan Computer Graphics Lab in 1981, after working for some time at its American forerunner, the Computer Graphics Lab at the New York Institute of Technology. A JCGL showreel[2] of materials from 1983–5 demonstrates the material available in a predictable series of extremely short contexts, particularly two-second corporate idents for Sony, Tōhō Video and several cable television companies. In much the same way as early cel animation was used for instructional purposes, JCGL animations can be seen in car adverts and documentaries, demonstrating the design of nuclear reactors and delving into the moving components of an automobile engine. There are, however, also obvious anime applications, with the company's work showcase adding dappled sunlight effects to the children's cartoon *The Yearling* as well as the work plainly regarded as its epitome in 1985, the opening credits to the feature-film version of the anime series *SF Shinseiki Lensman* (1984–5, *SF New Century Lensman*).

As noted above, the speed of digital adoption can be tied directly to the relative costs of computers and processing power. At the time of *Golgo 13* and *Lensman*, digital animation is a special effect, applied sparingly and in a limited context. It grows progressively throughout the 1990s from moments of animated logos or visualisations, to shorts, suitable for pop videos or adverts. Sunrise, for example, first subcontracted computer animation out to Tōyō Links for a sequence of a space colony in *Char no Gyakushu* (1988, *Char's Counterattack*), and increased its digital content thereafter. On the production of *Yūsha Ō GaoGaiGar* (1997, *King of Braves GaoGaiGar*), animators created a number of 'bank cuts', investing in expensive digital animation on sequences suitable for reuse in subsequent episodes. These included computer displays, energy readings and reflective effects, allowing the digital content of each episode to increase in increments (Funamoto 1998: 175). The close of the twentieth century saw several productions jostling for the chance to claim the cultural capital of being the 'first' fully digital anime – in the sense of being made with 3D rendered polygons. *Visitor* (1998) was intended as a video series, but premiered on the satellite channel WOWOW. It was then re-edited into a feature-length 'movie' edition, although *A.Li.Ce* (1999) beat it into cinemas. *Run=Dim* (2001), a Korean-Japanese coproduction, was a TV series that was fully 3D computer-animated – at thirteen episodes, roughly five hours of animation.

The application of 3D digital animation was not limited solely to the 'animation' industry. Far from it, in fact – 2D animation remained the medium of choice within the anime business, while 3D animation, in the form of 'Hollywood' tools such as Softimage, Lightwave, After Effects and Maya, were soon adopted by the Japanese film and games industry – even if animation sequences in *Virtua Fighter* (1996) resembled 2D anime, they were made using Softimage Toonz. Similarly, Omnibus Japan, a video post-production subsidiary of the film company Tōhoku Shinsha, took on several effects tasks on live-action productions such as *Mothra* (1996) and *Ultraman Zearth* (1996), and was subsequently drawn into Bandai's Digital Engine project, for work on games, commercials and other properties (Funamoto 1998: 179–80). This is notable because Omnibus Japan is a 'film' company, and hence not included in the traditional discourse of Japanese animation history. The fact that it was enlisting the same tools as 'animation' companies in the making of live-action works demonstrates the continuing hybridity of the animation and movie-making worlds; similar cross-pollination has been observed in Hollywood (Telotte 2008: 17).

Particularly in the early days of computer animation, form has driven content. When computer graphics remained conspicuously different from standard cel images, they found their best employment performing as computer graphics – appearing in science-fiction stories as heads-up displays, computer readouts and depictions of cyberspace. As the price and processing power of 3D computer animation reached a point where it could carry an entire half-hour or longer, its form continued to influence the content. Computer animators drew much of their skillset not from animation, but from puppetry and stop-motion, as many of the same issues returned in an age of digital assets. As in stop-motion, a 'set' was still a prolonged three-dimensional construction effort, and needed to see sufficient use once labour had gone into its creation. As in puppetry, ease of animation favoured shots that did not show characters or objects interacting with the ground, in order to avoid 'floaty contact', and animators tended to avoid close-up shots that showed characters' hands picking objects up or setting them down. Mecha of all kinds, robot or vehicular, usually comprised less complex artefacts than living creatures, favouring storylines of robot combat. Moreover, zero-gravity environments or futuristic hover vehicles removed all need for contact with surfaces, favouring plots that provided an excuse for such floating objects.

Several turn-of-the-century anime featured marine settings, as an underwater storyline not only validated the all-important 'floating' objects, but also allowed for largely barren, featureless backgrounds. In shows such as *Blue Submarine No. 6* (1998), a blue, watery filter on any image allowed for limited distance perception, saving money on backgrounds, and also helped hide the join between composited 2D and 3D elements (Brimmicombe-Wood and Tamamuro 1999: 38).

Watanabe Shinichi notes (Oguro 2006: 32) that the facility for digital video editing brought changes of its own to the tropes and stylistics of anime, through the sudden ease of single-handedly accomplishing tasks or experiments that would previously have required more intensive labour. A digital artefact, once created, could be resized, recoloured or cloned an infinite number of times, leading to a fad for vast identical robot armies. Conversely, a 3D model, once made, amortised its cost faster the more it was used, tempting some animators to let the camera linger a little too long on 'beauty passes' of spaceships, or even on any other shot. A recurring feature of early twenty-first-century anime was a certain unwillingness to leave any scene 'early', causing some anime to develop a dawdling narrative pace.

A fish-eye lens effect, a focus-pull or a contra-zoom, all of which would have once required intricate set-ups, or the drawing of sequentially deformed images, were now possible at the touch of a button. Some animators, notably Oshii and Ōtomo, experimented with digital effects that added imperfections – camera-shake, after-images, lens flares or splash effects that increased the naturalism of the image, creating the illusion that it had been filmed in a real-world environment (Funamoto 1998: 25). As Oshii noted at the time of *Ghost in the Shell*, digital animation afforded him the chance to engage some of the tricks of live-action camerawork:

Sori Fumihiko's *Vexille* (2007) is widely regarded as indicative of modern anime, although its director might also be described as a live-action film-maker working with 100 per cent special effects

Because the animated world only exists in two dimensions, your camerawork is normally limited. …
Digital animation makes it a lot easier to create visual tricks that give the illusion of three-dimensional
space, such as parallax, where objects in the foreground pass by 'faster' than those in the background, or
contra-zooms. (Newtype 1995: 16–17)

However the drift towards naturalism in anime seemed to hit a wall in the early 2000s, as animators revisited the old arguments over rotoscoping, now reformulated as a debate on the desirability of 'performance
capture'. Drawing to some extent on Mori Masahiro's (1975) arguments concerning the 'uncanny valley',
negative reviews for some of the earlier 3D anime, and most persuasively, the box-office flop of *Final Fantasy:
The Spirits Within* in 2001, some in the animation industry began to favour a withdrawal from the drift towards

Even Miyazaki Hayao, the champion of
analogue animation, would find uses for
digital animation techniques on his Academy
Award-winning *Spirited Away* (2001)

'naturalism' implied in the late-1990s computer world. *The Spirits Within* was not an anime film; it was made in the US with capital from the Japanese gaming company, so was 'Japanese' only at the level of ownership. Despite superb achievements in its animation, its characters were derided as 'eerie and unpleasant' (Clements 2009a: 374). Mori's 1975 model of a viewer's declining affinity for naturalistic, non-human characters as their appearance approached 'perfection' was well known in the Japanese entertainment industry, but usually discussed in terms of puppet shows (Clements 2009a: 374). After the public failure of *The Spirits Within*, with a shortfall on its earnings greatly in excess of the production expenditure of the entire anime business that year, Japanese animators largely gave up on the prospects of a continued aspiration towards 100 per cent naturalism. This move has been partly occluded by the publicity for the works of Sori Fumihiko, who came to animation from special effects and live-action film, and was soon to become Japan's most prominent 3D-digital feature creator, with a reputation attained first by *Appleseed* and then sealed by *Vexille* (2007). However, such films as his are debatably less 'animated' than they are shot live and then augmented with 100 per cent digital effects, altering backgrounds, foregrounds, characters and all but the basic data issuing from the captured performances.

The Japanese animation industry increasingly favoured the process known as 'cel shading' or 'toon shading', in which animation was made with 3D tools, but then processed to look as if it were 2D. The process was first used by Disney on *The Lion King* although its most prominent early appearance in anime was in Production IG's short film *Kai doh maru* (2001). As a result of toon shading, subsequent animated works from Japan demonstrate an increasingly enthusiastic grasp of 3D environments, and a palpably more 'solid' sense of their characters. Such processes first appeared in Japan within Miyazaki Hayao's 1997 *Princess Mononoke*, although they were subcontracted at the time to Tōyō Links (Funamoto 1998: 194; Sharp 2008: 128). Production IG's eight-minute animated sequence 'The Legend of O-Ren Ishii', included in Quentin Tarantino's *Kill Bill* (2003), knowingly imitated the scratchy xerography of 1970s cel cartoons, but was entirely based on motion-captured footage (Clements and McCarthy 2006: 337). There is an invisible corollary here, that the rise of such 3D facilities established a dominance and growing hegemony of 3D tools, both in their general use and in the favouring of those able to use them, crowding out the majority of animators skilled in the old 2D methods. In anticipation of such a prospect, or perhaps in a deliberate performance to highlight the threat, Miyazaki Hayao announced at the Japanese press conference for *Princess Mononoke* his intention to set up a 'Senior Ghibli' studio division that would continue to employ the old-fashioned methods as a form of living museum. However, Miyazaki's apprehensions appeared to have been allayed by the time of the production of his next film, *Spirited Away*, in which the ageing animator embraced 3D processes, at first with great reluctance, and then with increasing alacrity (Studio Ghibli 2002: 182).

Meanwhile, others have noticed that the Japanese industry's apparent desire to cling to 2D animation, or to 3D animation that looks like 2D, runs counterintuitive to international box-office statistics. Masuda (2007: 184) cautions that conspicuously 3D cartoons (from Pixar, Disney and DreamWorks) have consistently outperformed 2D cartoons in the international marketplace, even in competition against other works from the same parent studio. This suggests that the mainstream international audience favours 3D animation, to the extent that the anime industry may be building a new ghetto for itself in the 2010s. Jasper Sharp (2008: 122) observes that this is, at least in part, because 3D animation is not cheap, and requires significant 'manhours and technological innovations … to match the quality of the work of the frontrunners in the field'.

CONTENT: MUNDANE SETTINGS AND FANTASY FEMALES

Yamaga Hiroyuki suggests (Funamoto 1998: 154–5) that a drift towards realism, as opposed to naturalism, can be discerned in anime from the 1970s on, when it began to age with its audience. Anime gradually set aside the quasi-magical, unscientific rationales for plot and action, replacing them with ever more 'believable' storylines. While it might seem difficult to take Yamaga's pronouncement seriously in a field that still posits time travel, sex robots and teenage ninja, he is referring to 'realism' in its most literal sense, as a set of criteria for the internal consistency of on-screen events and motivations (Ellis 1992: 7). We can see elements of this, for example, in the drift from the godlike 'super robots' with their fairy-tale powers, to the meticulously designed and carefully limited qualities of the 'real robots' introduced by Tomino Yoshiyuki and Takahashi Ryōsuke.

There is a further step towards realism in the *nichijō* ('everyday', 'slice-of-life' or possibly 'mundane') subgenre of anime that focuses on down-to-earth dramas, and modern romances. An industry guidebook to the phenomenon suggests (Kinema Junpō Eiga Sōkō Kenkyū-sho 2011a: 28) it is a twenty-first-century innovation, but elements date back to the ever-present *Sazae-san*. Surreal or magic-realist romances, or comedies with science-fictional subplots, now compete with entirely 'mundane' stories that might as well have been shot as live action with real actors for all the difference animation makes. But, of course, animation does make a difference – it offers unprecedented degrees of control to film-makers. 'Mundane' anime drama has none of the overcast skies or compromised shooting schedules of live-action television. Its sunsets are always beautiful; its scenery always quintessentially seasonal; its framing always perfect. Even in its quest for realism, it renders the everyday hyperreal, particularly in its willingness to incorporate backgrounds and artefacts sourced from photographs, replicating the complexity of the real world to a degree that was previously costly for animators.

Furthermore, such a focus on 'reality' can represent a form of escapism for some sectors of the otaku audience, offering, for example, fantasies of the love or adoration of an unattainable other; a fresh-air rural antidote to cramped city life; a feisty but nurturing set of siblings; or a romanticised view of school or the workplace. There have long been elements of this in anime, ever since *Sazae-san*, but also in Miyazaki Hayao's *My Neighbour Totoro*, vouchsafing a virtual vacation for urban latch-key kids, and we can see it, too, in the yearning for playmates of the lonely children of *Bubu Chacha* (1999) or the glorification of simple friendship and human contact in *Colorful* (2010). As ever with the male otaku crowd, it is also intimated that this 'everyday' reality, of eavesdropping on the inner world of girls, is, in its way as fantastic a proposition as a ride on a rocketship.

An increased focus on female characters, for the benefit of an implied male viewer, had been a feature of Japanese animation since the video boom of the 1980s. It might also have been a negotiated reading of even earlier times, when male fans tuned in to see the semi-nude transformation scenes of *Cutey Honey* (1973), subverting a narrative supposedly designed for a female audience (Clements and McCarthy 2006: 121). The advent of computer games also saw an increased 'gamification' of female characters, and their objectification in narratives as prizes to be won or artefacts to be refined, a genre pioneered by the Gainax studio.[3]

According to Okada Toshio (2010: 214), Gainax's main advantages in the competition for consumer attention were quality of artwork and the ability to subvert their own characters. This was made clearest with *Dennō Gakuen 3* (1990, *Cyber Hi-School 3*), which featured the heroines from *Top o Nerae* (1988, *Gunbuster: Aim for the Top*) stripping and adopting sexually provocative poses. Gainax's subsequent *Princess Maker* (1991) adopted new strategy, presenting the development of a female character as the practice of the game itself – involving gameplay to determine what kind of 'princess' the player could rear from infancy to adulthood. Such a reduction of female characters into specific archetypes was soon reapplied in the 'dating simulation' subgenre of gaming. In its most basic form, a dating sim used a personality test, concealed within the choices made by the viewer of an interactive, branching narrative, to decide which of several love interests the player 'won' by the finale. This, in turn, played into statistical reports on toy sales that noted protagonists were far more likely to sell as merchandise than antagonists (Okada 2010: 99). Logically, the best possible character roster for an anime show would hence be a large number of female characters, each a possible love interest for the hero, but each also the possible basis of a collectible figurine or other such merchandise.

The toy company Bandai bought a controlling interest in the anime studio Sunrise in the late 1980s, and officially moved it under its corporate umbrella in 1994, an event parsed in different terms among animator testimonials. Takahashi Ryōsuke (personal communication) has described it as a sensible business move, in which the original founders of Sunrise, nearing retirement age, offloaded their shares to a major client, in order to ensure their staff's continued employment. However, Okada Toshio (2010: 98), then at the helm of his own struggling company, viewed the takeover as a hostile, ominous move sure to result in an increased commodification of the anime medium into multiple excuses for merchandising spin-offs, as soon happened with the announcement at Bandai of a media-convergence project, the Digital Engine, which sought to make anime the central focus of a matrix of games, toys and merchandising spin-offs (Funamoto 1998: 56).

The form this took outside the children's sector constitutes an epitome of modern anime for the 'otaku' market. Okada Toshio (2010: 99) points to toy market research that chronicled changing patterns of consumption among children, revealing that they favoured toys based on protagonists rather than antagonists.

> This was because statistical data had been showing that 'children do not spend their money on villains' for the previous ten years. If we release Ultraman and monster figures, hardly any children buy the monsters. They only buy Ultraman and the Ultra brothers. During the Shōwa era [up to 1989], both Ultraman and the monsters sold at the same rate. As for *Gundam*, [enemy] models sold better than the ones of the main character. However, since just before the change to the Heisei era [1989], consumer trends altered. Children projected themselves only onto the heroes and only bought the heroes and the main characters.

It is difficult to tell how much of this observation is cause and how much is effect – after all, this was the decade in which 'combination' toys (see Chapter 7) favoured the child who bought all five heroes, rather than a motley collection of their enemies. However, by the beginning of the 1990s, such observations from the world of children's battle-team shows and a few toy-advert anime had been applied across anime as a whole, leading to a rise in teams – Okada cites *Sailor Moon* as the primary example, with up to nine heroines (each with her own action figure) fighting a changing roster of foes. When applied to an audience outside the children's sector, most notably on the *Tenchi Muyō* franchise (1992–2005), the application of romantic or erotic themes to such an overpopulated cast came to be denoted by the cynical term 'harem anime' (Clements and McCarthy 2006: 649). Although *Tenchi Muyō*'s creator Kajishima Masaki is one of the most famous proponents of such themes, he was certainly not alone in their articulation. Kondō (1997) plots dozens of similar female anime characters on seven axes of personality; Clements (1998c) breaks down the female stereotypes of harem anime into just six distinct personalities, drawn not from observation, but from the programming code in dating-simulation games, suggesting in turn that their characteristics and relationship constitute a fundamental aspect of their creation.

DISTRIBUTION AND EXHIBITION: LATE-NIGHT TV AND THE OTAKU MARKET

Digital technology brought other changes to venues of access, reducing the importance of fixed site rental or retail stores. By the end of the first decade of the twenty-first century, online shopping accounted for 38.9 per cent of all Japanese DVD sales (Matsumoto 2011b: 191), while digital prints of films reduced shipping costs (and in some cases, the need for shipping at all) to cinemas. Perhaps even more important was the use of a digital signal in delivering content. The switchover of Japanese television, from analogue terrestrial broadcasting to a more diverse model of 'narrow-cast' niche-interest cable channels, satellite TV and subscription or pay-per-view, created an environment that favoured smaller niches. Primetime terrestrial television belonged, and still mainly belongs, to family- or child-oriented mainstream shows, often created as part of massive consumer drives to sell toys and other related products. However, the availability both of airtime to fill on new channels, and the increasing surety of being able to timeshift such shows to a more civil hour, with a VCR or TiVo, began to foster 'late-night' (*shin'ya*) anime intended for an adult audience (Masuda 2007: 131).

Simply broadcasting at midnight was not a new idea. The first 'late-night' anime was the unsuccessful *Village of the Immortals*, in the September of the first flush of *Astro Boy*'s success (Yamamoto 1989: 123; Animage 1988: 5). Many years later, its producer Sagisu Tadayasu alleged that its troubles were twofold – forced to compete in a market where Tezuka's cut-price production fees had yet to become apparent, and in a time-slot where no sane advertiser would be prepared to buy space (Misono 1999: 339). During the video boom of the 1980s, *Lemon Angel* (1987) was similarly broadcast on Fuji TV at 1 am, in five-minute segments in an attempt to drum up interest in the pop careers of its three stars. However, the true explosion of late-night anime did not take place until the proliferation of cable and satellite channels in the late 1990s created a new distribution site that would ultimately come to outweigh primetime in terms of the number of animated shows.

In the earliest days of late-night anime broadcasting, when recorders were likely to be analogue, and hence imperfect, the owners of anime were complicit in the trend for timeshifting. Magazines, produced by the same corporations that produced the anime themselves, published articles about setting video recorders, cautioning against rookie errors such as forgetting that one minute after midnight was actually a new day for timer purposes (Clements and McCarthy 2006: 646). Reading between the lines, such articles were an admission that these anime 'television series' hardly deserved the name. Although 'television' carried with it a certain aesthetic impact, and certainly sounded good to foreign-rights buyers, the late-night anime were arguably better parsed as new iterations of 'video', with costs slashed to such an extent that the price-point was zero, but the consumer was now expected to bring his own tape. Some were even presented not as complete works, but as works in progress, often lacking certain elements promised to be forthcoming in the inevitable video release.

Masuda Hiromichi (2007: 74) notes that the similarities and, to some extent, codependency of the videogram and late-night TV markets have created a fad for 'double transmission' (*niji hōei*), in which each regards the other as a secondary market for its products. This can take the form of small terrestrial affiliates granting airtime to obscure videos, or satellite premieres for video shows. It also allows scope for a certain hybridity of content, such as in the case of *Cowboy Bebop*, which existed in two broadcast versions. The terrestrial broadcast on TV Tokyo lasted for twelve episodes; the subsequent late-night satellite broadcast on WOWOW interpolated the twelve 'original' episodes with another fourteen that contained racier, more complex content (Clements and McCarthy 2006: 114).[1] In a phenomenological sense, the viewer who saw *Cowboy Bebop* on terrestrial television was watching a different show to the viewer who saw it on satellite. Moreover, the existence of an extended version incentivised viewers to seek out the full-length version on DVD, with the terrestrial broadcast of *Cowboy Bebop* serving as a loss-leader for a video version that was effectively twice as long.

Cowboy Bebop's dual formats reversed a situation common to television ever since 'TV versions' of films edited down certain forms of explicit content for a mass audience. Its success was palpable, particularly in an environment where racier shows were more likely to attract foreign sales, and hence turned late-night Japanese television into a dumping ground for hundreds of new, relatively cheap 'adult' shows, often lasting for only a single twelve-episode season.

By 2005, of ten listed Japanese TV markets and affiliates, only four bought anime for primetime or weekend-morning broadcast (i.e. for the children's and family market). The other six invested only in late-night anime, thereby favouring the kind of shows that appealed only to the small but lucrative niche of dedicated anime fans (Masuda 2007: 45). Coupled with satellite broadcasting, particularly on the WOWOW channel, viewers of anime on television enjoyed access to substantially more adult shows than in the past, albeit these were usually screened in the middle of the night when nobody was liable to be awake to watch them in real time. However, whereas low ratings would have been the kiss of death for a children's show, the relatively low viewership of late-night anime still proved to be significant, as long as the owners of the anime were able to lure the viewers into spending their money in different ways.

In 2002, Tada Makoto assessed the size of the Japanese 'fan' market as 400,000 viewers, each of whom could be expected to spend 10,000 yen (£80) a month on merchandise (Tada 2002: 63). Coupled with a small crossover into sales into the children's market of certain toys and goods, he calculated this as a gross annual revenue of 50 billion yen, of which, assuming a 5 per cent royalty, some 2.5 billion yen (£20 million) eventually returns to the coffers of anime's owners. Tada's viewer numbers, expressed in TV ratings terms, are worth only 0.4 per cent of national broadcasting, suggesting that even the viewership for a late-night TV show, screened at two in the morning for a mere handful of people, is still a significant population for the otaku market. Primetime children's cartoons might still live or die over ratings of 10 per cent, but the more adult shows could subsist on less than a twentieth of such viewers.

As Matsumoto Satoru argues (2011b: 188–91), the simple demographics of access to certain technologies, and their dominance in the distribution medium, fostered the growth of a particular audience sector. Ownership of a computer or PlayStation, and hence access to an independent, bedroom exhibition venue; ability to pay online; ownership of a programmable video device to record late-night shows; disposable income to pay, rather than relying on parental subsidy – all of these elements inevitably favour a viewer in his late teens or early twenties, which is to say, the otaku market. Matsumoto (2011b: 188) calls this the 'high target audience', and assesses its worth as 85–90 per cent of the Japanese animation market, largely owing to the high costs of bespoke 'collector's editions', the captive market of rental stores and the high mark-ups charged on special figurines or merchandise. While this figure might seem outrageously high at first glance, output of TV alone since 2005 suggests that the size of the total adult market almost matches that for children, before merchandise is even considered and that, while a smaller number of truly big-earning children's shows might endure for several years, the turnover of adult titles means many more 'new' adult anime each season (Masuda 2011: 88–9). Or to put it another way, while a one-shot children's movie might appear to deliver higher short-term returns in DVD sales, a late-night TV series with a limited edition box set, tie-in laptop, 'collectible' metal figurines and a subscription-based online game tie-in will sell fewer copies, but generate substantially more revenue from a single, notional consumer. Indeed, such a show needs to generate more revenue in more diverse sectors, in order to appease the multiple investors on its production committee. In the most extreme of examples, the primetime show *Evangelion* only lasted for twenty-six episodes on television, but its artistic heritage (or earning power) has persisted for almost two decades in reruns, re-edits, cinema spin-offs, games and over 3,000 merchandise items. As an inevitable corollary, adult shows tend to have a much shorter lifespan, and while some may return for a second season, most are gone in three months (Masuda 2011: 91).

Masuda Hiromichi (2007: 22–3) calls the fan/adult anime market 'Type 2' in his own statistics, in opposition to the 'Type 1' children's and family market.[5] In terms of output rather than revenue, he estimates that Type 2 is only worth 30 per cent of the market, but he is not counting the same statistical objects as Tada. Conflating the two analyses shows more billable production work for anime companies in children's shows but, unless they also happen to own shares in the toy company, there is greater potential revenue for them in the adult market. In other words, if an anime company wants to participate in anime at the level of ownership, the risk is far lower in the adult market than it would be in any attempt to take on the vast international toy and games conglomerates who control so much of children's consumption. However, there is still a hazard – Masuda (2011: 51) calls merchandising a 'high-risk, high-return' business model, since it requires the manufacture of objects without any immediate guarantee of a market for them. It is thus increasingly likely in the modern age that a franchise will be plotted as a multimedia commodity, but then market-tested as if it were merely a novel or manga, effectively soliciting fans as their own focus group before the merchandise phase is initiated. For this reason, it is increasingly a fallacy in the twenty-first century to claim that a new anime series or game is 'based on a manga' – usually, the manga element is merely the first to become apparent (Clements and McCarthy 2006: xvii).

The Nomura Research Institute (NRI) (2005: 52) assessed the anime otaku market in 2005 as a population of 110,000 Japanese, with an annual spending power of 20 billion yen (£163 million). This is a relatively small component of modern niche markets, dwarfed, for example, by the sector for domestic tourism. However, self-identification as an 'anime fan' places a consumer at the nexus of several other profitable fandoms, including manga (83 billion yen), and gaming (21 billion yen), firmly in the centre of the 'contents' category of niche consumption (NRI 2005: 54).

The NRI cautions (2005: 19–24) that, even within the anime sector, the 'otaku market' is not a single unified environment, but a convergence of several different consumer types. While the otaku mindset was often observed in early anime fans (Hotta 2005: 397; Masuda 2011: 49), otaku are not necessarily anime fans at all – it is possible to be a camera otaku, or a cat otaku or an otaku about any number of obsessions, although the NRI restricts its analysis of 'otaku marketing' to just twelve categories, of which anime is one. Nor is every 'otaku' a stereotypical, friendless shut-in – the NRI (2005: 22–3) allows, for example, for the existence of high-functioning 'social otaku' (*shakō hakyō otaku*), typically businessmen in their thirties with high disposable income and interest in a particular hobby. There are, similarly, 'fanzine girl' otaku (*dōjin joshi otaku*), the smallest of the listed anime categories comprising single women in their twenties with high disposable incomes and ample leisure time, sure to have been a consideration in the inauguration of Fuji TV late-night women's anime slot, 'Noitamina', which commenced broadcasting in 2005.

However, the NRI (2005: 27) concedes that there is a tangible difference in the means of marketing to otaku audiences, regardless of the category. Whereas traditional marketing emphasises the 'Four P's' of Product, Price, Promotion and Place, the NRI argues for an additional set of considerations. Appealing to otaku, claims the NRI, also requires a seller's integration of the 'Three C's' of Collection, Creativity and Community. With specific regard to anime, these break down into noticeable elements of the modern market:

Collection: DVD 'collector's boxes', peripheral character goods and merchandise, CD spin-offs.[6]
Creativity: self-made anime, *cosplay* (fancy dress), *dōjinshi* (fanzines and fan fiction).
Community: fan clubs, amateur associations, conventions.

(NRI 2005: 31)

Hence, while the structure of the anime market still supports casual viewers, occasional audiences and the children's market, a significant sector of the modern anime market can be expected to comprise viewers who do not merely watch the content, but commodify it, savour its arrangement in 'limited editions' and special boxes, and appropriate it for use in their own fan activities. Notably, although all of the above are 'activities' which may involve anime fans, not all of them monetise as products that can be sold to anime fans. This may lead to a new error of practice in commentary on the anime industry – a misplaced sense of tradition (Megill 2007: 35) that confuses certain 'suprapersonal' fan activities (e.g. cosplay) with revenue generation.

DISTRIBUTION: FORMAL AND INFORMAL DISRUPTIONS

The DVD (Digital Versatile Disc, sometimes Digital Video Disc) was released on the Japanese market in 1996 and found immediate support in the anime market, where it allowed for ease of storage, reduction in moving parts and limit of generation loss. It also offered an 'angle function' sometimes used in anime, permitting viewers to flip between the film itself and its original storyboards, access commentary tracks and choose between multiple language with switchable subtitles. Perhaps most crucially for the DVD, it was the chosen medium of storage for Sony's new PlayStation 2 game console in 2000, ensuring that 21 million gamers also bought themselves a DVD player. Annual sales of DVD anime in Japan climbed above 60 million in the year after the introduction of the PlayStation 2, and have not fallen below that level since (Kataoka 2011: 165). A format that appealed to anime fandom's love of alternative soundtracks and interactive extras, the DVD was a strong contributor to a rise in videogram sales in the early twenty-first century (Matsumoto 2011b: 185). However, it also represented a radical change in the nature of the objects 'owned' by fans. Assuming one could get around the copy protection, a DVD was a digitised signal that could be replicated without generation loss.

Kimura Makoto offers several competing models of anime distribution, beginning with the traditional Platform model (2011: 118), in which an anime is given away 'free', but financed by advertising revenue, generally aimed at selling related products to the viewers, some of which in turn generate licensing income. The popularity of the programme, as expressed in its TV ratings, sets the price for its advertising and hence the value of its related commodities. Such a model plainly describes anime on commercial television since *Astro Boy*. However, Kimura allows that not all anime exist in such a format, and that other types, particularly theatrical cinema anime, are distributed on a Windowing model (2011: 120) of ever-decreasing screen sizes in quarterly increments, from theatrical exhibition, to videogram release, to video on demand, to premium television broadcast, to an appearance on terrestrial broadcast. Modern anime of all forms is more likely to be a Goodwill model (2011: 126), in which the anime itself, be it film, television or straight-to-video, is an object created by a production committee, whose participants each have merchandise or spin-offs that they can sell to recoup their investment, and who expect a certain synergy from the presence of the other parties. Kimura also allows for a complex Ecosystem model (2011: 131) incorporating third-party licensees, but the effect is largely the same as his Goodwill model. However, writing long after the peak in anime revenues, he cautions (2011: 166–70) that any future business plan must expect a reduced income from 'packaged goods', meaning the physical objects of anime, on video or DVD. In other words, while anime remains a central component in the media mix, it is liable to return to the 1960s TV condition of being given away for 'free' in order to make money on related products. Masuda Hiromichi (2007: 71) used the term 'package' in 2007 to refer to the DVDs that formed a vital part of the market in anime goods – an item that could be rented, returned, bought, sold or attached to bonus items. Four years later, Masuda (2011: 160) was more explicit in pointing his readers to the precedents set by the music business, with consumers eschewing physical 'packaged' goods in favour of virtual downloads, which suggested that the potential for increased revenue on 'digital' products was greatly outweighed by the likely damage from piracy.

Digital sales offer a profit margin of 60–70 per cent, significantly more than the 20–30 per cent profits to be expected from the sales of DVDs or Blu-rays (Gubbins 2012: 81). That is, of course, already disruptive to traditional distribution, as the difference is created by the redundancy of disc duplicators, warehouse managers, bricks-and-mortar stores, rental libraries and possibly even foreign licensors. Such job losses are a lamentable but inevitable part of changes to what Ramon Lobato (2012: 4) calls the 'formal' network of distribution, which is to say, its legal, mainstream practice. More threatening to owners of anime intellectual property is the disruptive potential of the 'informal' network of distribution, which is to say, the illegal and grey markets for which digitisation also brings changes.

Digitisation turned timeshifting late-night anime from an innovative mode of formal exhibition into a hazardous component of informal distribution. A high-quality digital recording of an anime was little different from an officially sanctioned digital copy (Masuda 2007: 176). Unlike, say, the VHS copies of yesteryear, with ever-decreasing generational loss, drop-outs and breakable moving parts, a digital copy of an anime possesses an inconvenient immortality. Once it migrates to the Internet, it can effectively destroy the earning potential of any subsequent releases, in making itself available for 'free' to any downloader. The medium of reproduction, be it BitTorrent or file transfer, is less important than the fact of the reproduction, and the possible infinity of its replication.

EXHIBITION: PROJECTION ISSUES AND SCREEN-SIZES

The digitisation of production arrived hand-in-hand with the digitisation of exhibition, such as in the gradual adoption of Digital Light Projection (DLP) devices in Japanese cinemas. Kataama Mitsunori, formerly of Tōyō Links but subsequently hired by Studio Ghibli for its digital section, observes that Japan only had four cinemas in 1997 with DLP facilities, forcing even films made entirely digitally to be transferred onto traditional celluloid film for their cinema release. This, in turn, forced animators to create new programs that created 'noise' in the images to replicate the organic qualities of light saturation in celluloid film. In other words, the 'millions' of colours cited by Ōtomo Katsuhiro (above) were nowhere near as many as first thought.

> That sounds like a lot of colours, but it's actually quite minute. Celluloid film is very sensitive. When an image lights up on film, it doesn't turn white immediately but changes gradually … . There aren't enough gradations in 8-bit, so the colours jump … . The human eye is very sensitive to light and darkness, so it can detect the colour shift. (Kataama Mitsunori, quoted in Studio Ghibli 2002: 191)

However, this is only a minor issue when set against the declining potential for cinema releases to make any money at all. Anime remains a major earner at the Japanese box office, but only in a handful of identifiable brands (Masuda 2011: 112). There is no guarantee that audiences will return in similar numbers when those franchises fizzle out. Fortunately, statistically, cinema exhibition may not need to be self-funding in order to remain relevant in the modern media mix.

True theatrical exhibition in the modern age is a costly enterprise. While the production costs of a film are variable, a nationwide release incurs certain fixed costs of promotion and advertising, as well as a distributor's fee and the likelihood that 50 per cent of ticket sales will go to individual exhibitors. A film that earns 1 billion yen at the Japanese box office only returns an average of 100 million yen (£808,000) to its owners (Masuda 2007: 63; compare to US statistics in Vogel 2007: 191–3). A film that earns only 0.5 billion yen at the contemporary Japanese box office actually costs its owners 100 million yen in the shortfall on fees. Hence, although it is possible for a film to pay for itself on theatrical exhibition, it remains unlikely that theatrical exhibition itself will monetise anything but the most surefire box-office hits – such as *Pokémon*, *Doraemon* or a Studio Ghibli film.

However, theatrical exhibition has other benefits. In the case of the film *Zatch Bell: Attack of the Mekavulcan* (2005), its unimpressive 460 million yen cinema takings suggest that its owners were left with a shortfall of 100 million yen (Masuda 2007: 60). But such an expense included 300 million yen of promotion and advertising for the film, generating posters, advertising spots and merchandise, all of which pushed the brand, advertised the manga and game spin-offs and promoted the inevitable DVD release of the film. Meanwhile, the aesthetic identification of *Zatch Bell* as a 'film', rather than a humble TV series or manga, guaranteed it coverage outside normal venues, in cinema listings magazines and newspaper movie round-ups. To put it another way, the supposedly lacklustre performance of *Zatch Bell* at the box office might be reconceived as a massive saving of at least 200 million yen in terms of the marketing and advertising generated for the franchise as a whole, an expense that would itself be split between the members of the production committee. For the production committee participants who stand to sell more manga or more computer games as a result, the *Zatch Bell* film could be seen to be a superb economy of marketing. Moreover, despite its 'poor' performance, it still generated production fees for its animators, and an estimated 230 million yen for its exhibitors, 300 million yen for its distributors and 300 million yen of business for its advertisers (Masuda 2007: 63).

In terms of Allan Megill's errors of practice (2007: 33), calling *Zatch Bell* a failure would be a fallacy based on the tradition of the cinema business, rather than that of the 'contents' industry as a whole. In terms of Thomas Postlewait's compass of events (2009: 18), the reception of *Zatch Bell: Attack of the Mekavulcan* is for the most part irrelevant, except as an immediate income for its agents, and a new reminder of its artistic heritage in encouraging consumption in other media. This in turn prompts a consideration of what is actually being created and consumed. Itō Gō (2005: 120) talks of the disparity between a character with narrative substance, and a chara – diminutive shorthand that suggests, in the words of Marco Pelliteri (2010: 79), 'an icon devoted to commercial exploitation'. It hence brings us to the brink of a consideration of 'the anime industry' that ceases to regard it solely in terms of animation, and more as part of an integrated multimedia enterprise usually referred to as the 'contents industry'. We might also note the implications of such statistics – that the biggest risk of all in cinema anime in the twenty-first century would be to release an entirely original, standalone film. This brings with it a corollary, that the most likely anime films to be released will require that the audience be already familiar with the brand. Such a business model expects audiences to immerse themselves in such 'media ecologies', but also risks shutting down the anime cinema market to anyone who does not already identify themselves as a fan. This is perhaps nothing new – theatrical anime successes have been overwhelmingly tied to other media ever since *Saiyūki* in 1960.

However, the business analyst Masuda Hiromichi allows that such trends in theatrical exhibition only apply to those films that get a national release, in the expectation that they will monetise in the children's market. A 'cinema release' does not need to be national, and indeed in most cases it is regional, 'limited' or even a run in a single cinema, with concomitant drops in expenditure for promotion, advertising and distribution. Masuda notes (2007: 64) that even a film shown in a single cinema would need to sell 100 million yen's worth of tickets in order to generate a profit, but the same amortisation principles apply on a small scale as on the large. It is, arguably, less important for the forty-four-minute anime *Hotarubi no Mori e* (2011, *In the Forest of the Fireflies' Light*) that it is only screened in Japan in a single cinema, than it is for the cinema to serve as a venue for sales of DVDs, CDs and merchandise tied to the film, potentially doubling or tripling the owners' income from each ticket sold. Furthermore, the 'performance' or aesthesis of its theatrical exhibition is more likely to invite the attention of foreign film festivals and rights buyers for what a decade earlier would have surely been regarded as a forty-four-minute 'video' work.

The impact of the digital age is more clearly felt at the level of the 'small screen', although 'small' is a problematic term when audiovisual aficionados might have widescreen home televisions with advanced digital sound systems. To reach the home consumer, modern digital contents need not be 'broadcast' at all, but can be streamed or downloaded onto computers and mobile devices. Matsumoto Satoru further notes (2011b: 194) that the most lucrative and fastest-growing sector in the Japanese consumer market since 2006 has been mobile phones, many of whose providers offer media services that blanket-buy vast archives of 'content', including anime. These form new 'fixed sites' or captive audiences – a hypothetical twenty-first-century anime show need not necessarily be particularly popular, but can still be included in a bulk rights deal to a mobile-phone company. With video on demand direct to Japanese phones from 2010 (Masuda 2011: 151), Matsumoto predicts (2011b: 198) that iPhones and Android phones are poised to become the most popular medium of exhibition for all visual media. These, in turn, offer the potential for revenue in micropayments, but that itself is likely to be of small consolation in the relatively small 'adult' market.

ACCESS: PARTICIPATION AND 'HYPER-OWNERSHIP'

The Nomura Research Institute (NRI 2005: 42) repeats common wisdom from the world of marketing (e.g. Dibb and Simkin 1994: 211), that the best point to release a new product is at the cusp of its chances of acquiring a mainstream audience – i.e. after similar products have already gained the attention of early adopters, but before the market has been saturated with similar items and gone into decline. At the turn of the twenty-first century Misono Makoto predicted (1999: 405) that computers would transform the anime business, not only through their use in animation, but in their uptake *among* fans, particularly for communication between audience and owners. Okada Toshio suggests (2010: 214) that Gainax missed a window of opportunity, releasing its graphic striptease game *Cyber Hi-School* too late in the market for software of such a size and tone – three years earlier, and sales would have caught the crest of the early adopters and the swell of the mainstream market. Conversely, Gainax's Kamimura Yasuhiro suggests (Hotta 2005: 316–17) that the company's later anime series *Evangelion* was, more by luck than judgement, perfectly placed to capitalise on new communications technology, and that billboards and online forums, coupled with the inauguration of the Gainax company's website in 1995, had a palpable effect on the dissemination and popularising of *Evangelion*, creating a fixed site for community discussion and appreciation.

Where the first fan interactions, such as visits by enthusiasts to Studio Artland in the 1970s (see Chapter 7), were reported as literal face-to-face contacts, Kamimura Yasuhiro notes (Hotta 2005: 320) that the digitisation of communications and interactions has facilitated a boldness brought on by anonymity, and a bias in attention that favours the most passionate or contemptuous of reactions. This is negligible in the mass market, but a growing factor in the closed circle of otaku consumption, where sales are spread over a far smaller customer base.

Audiences in the twenty-first century do not merely have access to owners, but also to the production capabilities of animators. One of the 'chara' stars of the early twenty-first century is Hatsune Miku, a computer-generated singer who forms the end product of the Vocaloid software package. Although she is a playable character, manipulated by the owner of the software, she and her fellow virtual idols also appear in 'live' concerts, such as *Hatsune Miku Live Party*, themselves filmed and sold back to anime consumers. The implied buyer of a Hatsune Miku DVD may have paid several times for the same thing – becoming a fan of the software package, buying a ticket to the concert event and then buying the DVD of the same event.

Similarly, if someone wanted to buy the various components of a RETAS software package in 1998, it would have cost 540,000 yen (£4,400) – an expensive investment for a would-be animator (Funamoto 1998: 54). A decade later, the price of RETAS software had fallen by 95 per cent, making the full panoply of a Japanese animation studio affordable to any computer owner. Of course, merely owning RETAS would not turn the user into the next Tezuka, nor would running RETAS on a single machine lead to a swift production schedule.

However, animation software was now well within the means of the private consumer and animation hobbyist, leading to a surge in homemade animation, now with instant global distribution through the Internet.

The epitome of this modern hobbyist resurgence is Shinkai Makoto, a digital animator at a computer-games company, who made the twenty-five-minute short *Hoshi no Koe* (2002, *Voices of a Distant Star*) almost single-handedly, with off-the-shelf software. An elegiac tale reminiscent of Gainax's *Gunbuster*, *Voices* was an excellent demonstration of the many tricks available to the modern animator, such as photographs rendered as back-grounds. The performance of its construction became part of its marketing – by the time it reached the public, Shinkai's amateur work had been revoiced by professional actors and packaged by a professional company (Clements and McCarthy 2006: 710). Ironically, the growth of such amateur animators in Japan is vastly outweighed by the rise of trained professionals in China, where some 466,000 a year graduate from high-tech schools and colleges (Takahashi 2011b: 280). Even as the anime industry commodifies and exploits its own creation, sell-ing the tools and education for production, it continues to send most of the lower-echelon work offshore.

Now, as the trend in video formats drifts towards 'no format' – i.e. no physical copy of 'packaged goods' on a consumer's shelves – and the hosting of material on central servers, modern rights holders seek to redefine view-ers' sense of entitlement. To a degree, the trend towards online streaming and video on demand is an attempt to put the genie back in the bottle, as the companies that truly own anime urge viewers to return to a model that parses them as consumers rather than 'owners' in any sense. Meanwhile, a sector within anime fandom retali-ates with an addled notion of *hyper*-ownership, superseding that of the rights holders and sometimes even that of the original creators. In the rhetoric of the most fanatical fansubbers and video pirates, access should be mandatory and ownership should be universal, regardless of the intentions or obligations of the true owner, and irrespective of the adverse effect this might have on revenue.

A sector within anime fandom self-identifies with notions of what Bourdieu (1986: 47) calls embodied or lin-guistic capital, seeking the institutional capital of other fans' gratitude and respect by illegally appropriating elements of ownership. Some even claim that they do so out of a sense of duty to a higher power within anime: its dissemination into new quarters. But the rhetoric of fansubbing began in the days of VHS, when tapes were sure to be poor copies, and multiple generation loss suggested a form of built-in obsolescence. Once an illegal digital copy is made, no matter how well intentioned, it can reproduce and spread with viral intensity and counterproductive immortality. Matsumoto Satoru (2011b: 197) points out that, in a borderless age, it is now possible for an informal fanmade English subtitled version of a new anime show to be online within hours of the original broadcast. As Chris Anderson (2009: 71) notes:

> The reason that piracy is a special class of theft is that the costs to the rightful owner are intangible.
> If you make a music album that is then pirated, the pirates haven't taken something you own, they have *reproduced* something you own. This is an important distinction, which boils down to the reality that you don't suffer a loss, but rather a *lesser gain*.

Masuda (2011: 168–9) believes that the rise of piracy or unsanctioned informal access presents anime's owners with an ongoing dilemma. An experimental 'fingerprinting' of twenty-one new anime titles, about thirty hours of content, released between 1 October 2009 and 31 January 2010, has revealed the truly massive extent of 'infor-mal' viewing. The objects were duplicated over 25,000 times, and viewed 28.7 million times, exclusive of online streaming sites such as Nico Nico Douga or YouTube, which supplied no data (Masuda 2011: 168). As Masuda himself observes, if every one of those viewers were paying a mere 100 yen (£0.81) each to watch the same content, the revenue from the anime business would be twenty or thirty times larger than it is – 'Heaven for the viewers', he writes, 'but hell for the creators.'

> Popularity, of course, does not necessarily equal profit.
> So from the consumer's perspective, there is a huge difference between cheap and free. Give a product away, and it can go viral. Charge a single cent for it, and you're in an entirely different business, one of clawing and scratching for every customer. (Anderson 2009: 62)

The dilemma faced by modern anime producers is that their product appears to be immensely popular, but only for as long as people do not have to pay for it. Anime were previously given away at a price point of zero, or sold as cinema events for the price of a ticket. Even if all anime access were formalised overnight, how much would it actually be worth?

Although such appropriation violates the moral rights of anime's true owners to decide when and where (or if) they give it away for free, some have suggested (Tanaka 2011) that anime, particularly anime that demands an access fee of some sort, benefits from a free preview medium, so viewers can try before they buy. If anime clings to the Windowing model (Kimura 2011: 119), it is likely to be doomed to decreasing returns and increasing piracy. But if it embraces the Goodwill model (Kimura 2011: 125), there is the potential for anime to be given away 'free' in order to generate other income elsewhere. In such a scenario, anime ceases to become the product, and becomes instead the advert for the product. This would amount to a reconceptualisation of the thirty years after 1983 as an anomaly, although for the bulk of anime's history, and for the majority of its thousands of hours of content, it *has* been given away, for 'free' to consumers in exchange for advertising messages about chocolate, or product placement and context-integration selling robot toys. Table 10.1 charts connections between the anime and digital worlds.

TABLE 10.1: ANIME–DIGITAL CONNECTIONS 1974–2012

YEAR	EVENT
1974	Tōei Dōga sets up work group to investigate applications of computers
1978	*Mah Jong Game* (arcade)
1979	*Space Invaders* (arcade)
1980	*Pacman* (arcade)
1981	First Japanese personal computer (NEC PC-8801)
	Japan Computer Graphics Lab (3D animation) founded
1982	Tōyō Links (later Links Digiworks) founded
1983	*Golgo 13* uses 3D computer animation by Tōyō Links
1985	*Time Gal* (arcade) stores animation on a laserdisc
	Super Mario Brothers (console)
1986	Fujitsū commences work on CATAS for Tōei
	Second Love (strip mah jong game with anime-style characters)
	Super Mario Brothers game-based anime (20 July)
	Running Boy game-based anime (20 July)
1987	Widespread use of floppy discs increases graphic component of PC games
	Ys (PC-8801)
1988	*Super Real Mah Jong III* (first animated striptease)
	Softimage Creative Environment (3D animation software – US)
	Videoscape rendering and modelling (3D animation software – US)
1989	*Cyber Hi-School* (Gainax)
1990	*Cyber Hi-School 3* (***Gunbuster*** characters)
	IBM introduces DOS to Japan
	Tōei Dōga acquires its first digital server
	Videoscape renamed LightWave 3D (US)
1991	*Princess Maker* (Gainax – first 'life simulation')
1992	*Dōkyūsei* (first dating sim)
	Fist of the North Star game includes animation made with RETAS beta version
1993	Celsys releases TraceMan, PaintMan and CoreRETAS software, bundled as RETAS!Pro 1.0

YEAR   EVENT
1994   *Dōkyūsei* OAV
        Sony PlayStation also plays audio CDs
        Disney's **The Lion King** (US) is the first cartoon to employ cel-shading
1995   **Ghost in the Shell** features digitally scanned cels and Avid non-linear editing
        Tōei Dōga using computer-controlled multiplane cameras
1996   Japanese release of the Digital Versatile Disc (DVD)
1997   Tōei Dōga adopts digital layouts and colouring using RETAS 3.0
        Dr Slump and **Spooky Kitaro** now made entirely on computers
        Home Internet access for 10 per cent of the Japanese population
        Bandai initiates Digital Engine media-convergence project
1998   **Visitor** made entirely with 3D computer graphics (video)
        Broadband Internet introduced in Japan
        Digital Media Mart (DMM) begins download content service
        Full RETAS animation software package retails for 540,000 yen (£4,400)
1999   **A.Li.Ce** made entirely with 3D computer graphics (feature)
2000   *Scandal* (Production IG game, contains three hours of animation)
        Sony PlayStation 2 also plays DVDs
        NHK commences digital satellite broadcasting
        Nippon Animation forms coproduction partnership Nippon Animedia with Takara, Epoch and Agatsuma
2001   **Kai Doh Maru** uses 'toon shading' to make digital animation look like cels
2002   Home Internet access for 50 per cent of the Japanese population
        Voices of a Distant Star – 'homemade' anime sells 100,000 DVDs
2003   NHK commences digital terrestrial TV broadcasting
        Japanese test-marketing of the Blu-ray disc
2004   mixi (most popular Japanese social network) begins
2005   Sega acquires a majority stake in Tokyo Movie Shinsha
        Plateau in Japanese PC sales
        Historical peak in domestic anime videogram sales (97.1 billion yen)
        iTunes service begins in Japan
        YouTube starts
2006   Sony PlayStation 3 also plays Blu-rays
        Crunchyroll begins as video-sharing website
2006   Japanese cellphone sales exceed PCs
        Niconico Dōga video-sharing website begins
2007   **Sazae-san** is the 'last' cel anime
2008   RETAS Studio all-in-one production package retails for 30,000 yen (£245)
        NHK On Demand service begins
        Crunchyroll becomes legitimate licensor of video content
2009   38.9 per cent of Japanese DVD sales now online
        Home Internet access for 80 per cent of the Japanese population
        Tōhō, Tōei, Shōchiku, Nikkatsu and Kadokawa launch the video-on-demand service Maru Maru Eiga
2011   Niconico Dōga and Funimation form Funico for streaming US content
2012   Bandai suspends all new packaged goods in the American market
        Japanese TV switches over to full digital – end of analogue signal

Notes: Game titles in plain italics; animated titles in bold italics
Sources: Funamoto (1998: 54, 189–195); Clements (1998d); Yamaguchi (2004: 152); NRI (2005: 5, 120); Clements and McCarthy (2006: 217–19); Asahi Shinbun (2007); Sharp (2008); Dittbrenner (2008); Koyama-Richard (2010: 97); Matsumoto (2011b: 185–7); Mikami (2011); Tada (2002: 89); Cunningham and Silver (2012); Masuda (2011: 153).

NOTES

1. See http://www.linksdw.com/jb2_1.html.
2. See http://www.youtube.com/watch?v=_WlAnrdtGmg.
3. Pelliteri (2010: 109) observes that similar subversion is at work within supposedly 'male' shows, many of which include cloyingly cute mascot characters designed for negotiated readings by female viewers.
4. The gimmick had also been essayed in the video age, when *Blue Seed* (1994–5), a twenty-six-episode series on both television and video, delivered 'bonus' content (mostly extra nudity and violence) in its video incarnation (Clements and McCarthy 2006: 66).
5. In a sequel that seemed even keener on coining new terminology, such as 'MD' for 'merchandising', Masuda (2011: 85) reformulated these categories as A-type (Adult) and KF-type (Kids/Family).
6. The NRI adds 'cel art', with the caveat (2005: 35, n.7) that these are rarities in a digital age.

EPILOGUE
The end of anime's first century

In the final chapter to his book on historical epistemology, Allan Megill (2007: 210) asks what the tasks of history are. He concludes that they are:

· identifying
· evangelising
· entertaining
· being useful.

To draw an analogy with animation itself – like the imparting of the illusion of life to artificial images, history is a fictive process that requires omission and elision. It is what we leave out that makes history readable, concepts comprehensible, examples relevant and books finishable. Much of the achievement of this work lies in the marshalling of thousands of pages of Japanese documentation, opening windows on primary source material, and highlighting not only the values, but also the potential pitfalls, of Japanese-language testimonials on the anime industry.

The nature of the 'anime industry' has transformed radically several times since its inception. Changes in technology, not only in production, but also in other aspects of the ownership–access chain, have steered the abilities and aims of creators, and also the expectations of audiences. If we ask 'what we talk about when we talk about anime', the answer in 1958 is very different from that in 1963, or 1983, or 1997 or 2013. The modern discourse of an 'anime industry' encompasses several overlapping structures. New technologies, talents and tastes are less likely to destroy old structures than they are to create new ones alongside the former paradigms, leading to a situation today in which family feature films can still resemble features of the 1950s, alongside TV shows created along models developed in the 1970s and 1980s, and 'adult' shows across multiple formats, intended for an audience that would be barely recognisable to the pioneers of anime's early days. Digital animation wiped out cels, although since *Sazae-san* was still made the old-fashioned way until 2013, even that structure persisted into the twenty-first century. It is vital for any researcher who hopes to make sense of 'anime' to realise that anime is not a monolithic entity, but a palimpsest of many legacies of technology or taste.

Anime today faces a crisis, but responses to various previous crises have created 'anime' as we know it. The modern dilemmas over the 'value' of anime, and the opportunity or threat presented by foreign access, both formal and informal, represent a new crisis. But it pales in comparison with the sudden slump of the market for Japanese animation in 1945 or 1972, or the drastic reformulation of working practices caused by the adoption of limited animation in 1962. Japanese animation's form will doubtless be transformed again, and exist alongside the vestiges of its previous paradigms. Perhaps unsurprisingly, we might frame this assessment as 'farce' in the terminology of Hayden White (1987: 79), rejecting any claims of a golden age of anime from which we now drop away, or towards which we now climb. There is still a chance that 'anime' as we know it may be entirely destroyed in the next decade, diluted out of all recognition by globalisation, or rendered extinct by lack of revenue. But at some level of the ownership–access chain, there will still be something that we might describe as a Japanese animation industry.

For a history of anime to be useful, it must have some relevance to the present day, and perhaps even tomorrow. Studies of Japanese animation outside Japan have had the potential to 'be useful' ever since foreign distributors began to buy anime as objects to sell. In history, as in animation itself, true style and true meaning can only become apparent by what we leave out, and hence those elements we choose to accentuate and highlight.

Gainax's Takeda Yasuhiro notes that character goods themselves are not a market with infinite potential, but one already approaching saturation (Hotta 2005: 46–7). He likens anime's consumer peripherals business to a scorched-earth policy in customers' wallets, which will soon precipitate a 'market reset' and a drastic reduction in the number of supportable franchises. If the anime market reaches such a point, then even the 'otaku' sector may become one of the legacy strands of Japanese animation, enduring, like *Sazae-san* or Tōei kids' movies or Studio Ghibli films, as an epitome of a model that worked in the past, but only for a limited number of market leaders. It has even been mooted that the otaku market of the late twentieth century represents a one-time convergence of technology and generational location, and that it will not replace itself. This, in turn has led to suggestions, only partly tongue in cheek, of an approaching phenomenon of 'Silver Anime', in which merchandise and tie-ins are largely targeted at an ever-ageing audience of *Yamato* and *Gundam* fans, now entering their fifties (Masuda 2007: 209).

In an overview of the contemporary anime marketplace, the producer Kataoka Yoshirō (2011: 173–80) offers a breakdown of the greatest threats facing modern anime, and some pointers towards 'fixing' such issues. Kataoka's solutions can be summarised as follows:

· reduced reliance on terrestrial TV as a preview medium
· shifted focus from TV onto theatrical films
· prioritised clampdowns on illegal streaming/download sites
· applied use of events [e.g. signings, Q&As, concerts]
· revitalisation of anime in overseas markets
· return to creator-oriented works.

Kataoka recognises that there are participants in the modern anime market whose products need no fixing – Studio Ghibli's films continue to pay for themselves at the box office, for now; *Pokémon* continues to generate revenue from its 'media ecology'; *Sazae-san* continues to occupy primetime, unchallenged; 'otaku' niches like *Death Note* (2006–7) continue to monetise, despite being broadcast after midnight. Kataoka's proposals are designed more for everybody else – those who would seek to carve new niches for themselves in the anime industry, without directly competing with those who are already there.

EXHIBITION AND ACCESS: NEW MEDIA AND HYPER-OWNERSHIP
Masuda Hiromichi (2007: 120) returns to Tsugata's model of new waves in anime's popularity, and notes that similar factors seem to attend them. Each is remembered to have been initiated by a single landmark work, or a handful of similar landmark works released in a limited period. The work in question temporarily increases anime's appeal outside a limited niche, generating new avenues of income for participants in the market. But he also points to an element of technological determinism, in the sense that the accessibility or mass-market availability of a new medium also accompanies these events – widespread TV ownership for *Astro Boy*, widespread VCR ownership for *Nausicaä*, game consoles for *Pokémon* and digital access for the successes of the early twenty-first century.

The year 2006 marked the first time that the sales revenue from mobile phones outstripped the sales revenue from personal computers in Japan (Matsumoto 2011b: 194) – a change in consumption habits that saw the Japanese market acquiring platforms that facilitated e-books and the viewing of anime, along with other media, on the new format of a handheld screen.

Like all other elements of the film business, anime is heavily influenced by its source of revenue, and the nature of 'advertising', 'public relations,' or to use a word that has since gained negative connotations, 'propaganda', has exerted a remarkably strong pull on the nature of Japanese animation. While formats and workers may come and go, the need for revenue remains a constant in the film business. Advertising arguably reached its transformational apotheosis in the early 1970s, when certain new TV anime, even of a fictional narrative form, were conceived as glorified advertisements for the spin-off merchandise. Some scholars regard this development as so crucial to the understanding of the medium, that they are even prepared to consider dating the origin of 'true' anime from the commencement of this media mix (Tsugata 2011a: 6).

By the 1980s, the arrival of the home-video format permitted this advertising machine to penetrate a new market. As well as serving a new generation of children, it targeted the older generation for whom 'children's cartoons' were no longer acceptable, driving up the age of the implied viewer, and further entrenching the anime business in merchandising – not necessarily of toys, but of spin-off music, tickets to public events, gadgets, decorations and figurines. Much anime effectively became a marketing machine for itself, as part of a revenue-generation system that required the symbiotic, and arguably, sanitising or homogenising influence of a multimember 'production committee' rather than a single, driving creator's vision.

'Generational location' is one issue. The middle managers of the Mushi Pro era, who went on to form the start-up anime companies of the 1970s that arguably learned from Mushi's mistakes, were all approaching retirement by the 1990s. Many sold their interests to toy or game companies, creating even deeper commercial and marketing-oriented holds on the 'creative' nature of Japanese animation (Takahashi 2012).

As the end of Japanese animation's first century approaches, it is apparent that all these issues exert a powerful influence on the medium. As VHS, DVD and Blu-ray are replaced by online hosting, anime loses its physical presence – in industry terms, the 'packaged goods' for which distributors can charge a price (Kataoka 2011: 166–7). Contemporary distributors can be seen searching for a new means of monetising their property, each related in some way to previous paradigms. They can give it away free to advertise other products – a solution redolent of TV of the 1970s but also of advertising in the decades preceding. They can package it as an exclusive event, designed to attract a bespoke audience – a solution redolent of the fan-focused activities of the 1980s and 1990s. They can cling to a cinema distribution model, which has worked for Studio Ghibli, although even Ghibli's big-name creators are retiring or on the verge of retiring. Perhaps they can seek to subsume animation into another medium, as part of the process of creating a computer game – a solution that sustained many parts of the business in the 1990s. In the 2000s, an identifiable subset of the industry has abandoned anime itself in favour of teaching others how to make it – either in the academic sector or on the convention circuit – selling the tools and the expertise, rather than the final product.

For those in the anime sector who cling to the sales of 'packaged goods' as a means of making money, piracy and illegal downloads represent a far greater threat. Chris Anderson (2009: 68) has argued that only an outmoded paradigm is under threat, and that intellectual property owners might consider reconceiving piracy as a form of new marketing, eventually creating legal consumers:

As Steve Jobs famously pointed out, if you download music from peer-to-peer services, you're likely to deal with problematic file formats, missing album information, and the chance that it's the wrong song or a poor quality version. The time it takes to avoid paying means 'you're working for minimum wage,' he noted. Nevertheless, if you're time-rich and money-poor, that makes sense. Free is the right price for you.

But as you get older, the equation reverses and $0.99 here and there no longer seems like a big deal. You migrate into a paying customer, the premium user in the freemium equation.

The problem with such a 'freemium' model for anime is that it assumes a level plateau of demand. Anderson's hypothetical teenage consumer will scrimp and fiddle with the Internet to obtain a free Eminem album when he has nothing better to do, but transform, like a butterfly, into a legal consumer when he gets a little older and decides he cannot be bothered to waste so much time. There is, however, no guarantee that an anime consumer will still want anime two years later. Product cycles in anime are swift, 'classics' are rare and viewer attention is limited. Cartoons, despite the protestations of their apologists, still tend to be a childhood (or teenage) obsession that most consumers grow out of. By the time most anime fans are old enough to monetise Anderson's business model, they have either lost interest in that anime, or in anime altogether. Ironically, the only areas that can sustain it are the ones that are already cash cows – the lucrative market in quality children's entertainment, which is paid for by adults, and the niche market of self-involved, solipsistic titles for obsessive fans.

Arguably, the problem lies not with the collapse of 'packaged goods', but of an industry-wide, and relatively recent, 'tradition' that perceives packaged goods as the primary source of revenue. The idea that private individuals pay for Japanese animation is largely a creation of the video age; we might just as easily contend that the period 1983–2012 was an anomaly, and that the bulk of Japanese animation, for the majority of its existence, has been funded by sponsors, advertisers and educational bodies, with the end consumer experiencing it for 'free'. Online access is only an issue if it is illegal – in other words, if it is an assertion of hyper-ownership against the wishes of the true owners. It has been suggested (Tanaka 2011) that a preview medium is a vital contributor to a user's decision to spend money on anime, and that hence it is in the interests of anime companies to make parts of their products available for free in new media formats. However, crucially, such a paradigm calls for formal access – controlled by the owner, not by the viewer.

DISTRIBUTION: FOREIGN MARKETS

While there is an identifiable 2006 peak in the size of the anime industry (Kataoka 2011: 153), from which successive years have shown a slow decline, 2006 itself boasted an uncharacteristically high number of anime productions. If we break down the figures between continuations of pre-existing shows and new shows, we see that the real difference between 2006 and the years on either side was the sheer number of new shows put into production. In the year 2006, the Japanese animation business produced 135,530 minutes of new animation, some 20,000 minutes more than the previous year, with the difference entirely comprising all-new franchises with no previous track records – i.e. new shows and films rather than continuations of pre-existing franchises, sequels or remakes (Kataoka 2011: 159). It is this sudden upward jolt in original productions that has been 'halted' by the apparent slump ever since. A wider, longer-term perspective on the figures from, say, 2005–9 suggests that the anime business has displayed a general trend towards a plateau or a slow growth, and that the only true anomaly is the 2006 'peak' from which subsequent years have been assumed to decline.

But if the 2006 peak is unusual, what caused it? It surely represents the returns from the worldwide spike in interest in Japanese animation following the Oscar-winning success of Studio Ghibli, as well as the maturation of several long-term franchises in the children's market. In other words, it suggests a domestic windfall occasioned by the foreign investors' interest in Japanese cartoons. The middle of the first decade of the twenty-first century saw numerous American firms attempting to outmanoeuvre each other on rights by entering coproduction deals with Japanese companies. Far from reflecting a doomsday scenario for the Japanese animation business, this interpretation instead suggests that it was foreign interest that was oversubscribed, and that the Japanese animation industry continues on as before, perhaps retrenched somewhat in favour of its domestic audience.

One reason for the proliferation of new serials is that few seem to last beyond an initial season of thirteen episodes. Only a tiny handful of shows – such as *Naruto*, *Bleach* and *Pokémon* – continue for long story arcs and renewed seasons. We might use the four- or five-year lifespan of *Eureka Seven: Ao* (2012–) as an example of the anime product cycle at work (Kimura 2011: 146), but *Eureka Seven*'s four seasons were something of an anomaly. The majority of modern anime are still gone in three months.

Kataoka's reiteration of the importance of the foreign market might seem, at first, a throwback. The glory days of foreign anime were 1997–2003, when *Pokémon* videos sold in America in the millions, and when the pent-up archive of Studio Ghibli was unleashed on foreign markets. The massive rise in foreign revenue, climbing from 8–10 per cent of the anime industry's income in 1995 to a peak of 45–50 per cent around 2002 (Clements 2009a: 265; Osmond 2012b) before collapsing to its 1995 levels once more, represents a shift in new media, but also the interest and maturation of the *Pokémon* generation. It would seem reasonable to suggest that while foreign interest in anime was a sudden bubble, it was a very lucrative one. Like all bubbles, it had its roots in an actual commodity, a commodity that can still be sold. As argued by Masuda Hiromichi, whose 2011 book on anime devoted substantially more space to the international animation market than its 2007 predecessor, Japanese animation should give up on its potential as a global commodity. The fact that many investments in the early twenty-first century turned out to be misplaced does not mean that anime has no potential in foreign markets.

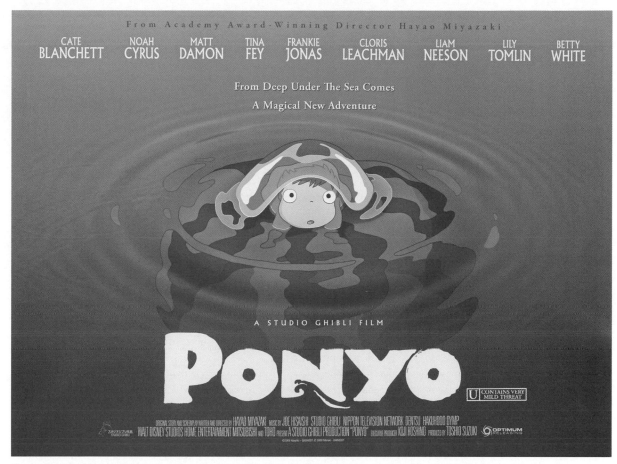

Ponyo (2008) listed no job titles in its end credits, opting instead for an alphabetical list of everyone involved in the production

To take a lesson from the Hollywood animation business, it does not seem to have bothered American investors that 60.7 per cent of the revenue from *Finding Nemo* (2003), and 58.6 per cent of the revenue for *The Incredibles* (2004) came from outside the US (Masuda 2007: 212). Any single domestic population is vastly outnumbered by viewers in foreign territories, many of which may be exploitable. Nor should we forget a common error of our own practice, in equating the foreign market solely with 'us' – there are many foreign markets. Tellingly, when Japanese researchers 'fingerprinted' digital files to follow their path to informal viewers online, the majority of the illegal host servers and downloads appeared to originate in China (Masuda 2011: 168).

Ushiki (2011: 242–3) observes that 'Japanese animation' is exiled from primetime in China, and must compete in the Chinese cinema marketplace for space in an import quota of only thirty-five foreign films a year, against Hollywood blockbusters and Pixar movies. However, it is surely not much of a leap to argue that Chinese participation on some anime productions is already significant enough to qualify them as 'Chinese animation', making such works immensely more competitive by allowing them to enter the marketplace outside the quota restrictions.[1] As noted by Nunokawa Yūji (Takahashi and Nunokawa 2011: 307), the expectation that China will switch over to a digital broadcast signal in 2016 may point to a sudden expansion of channels requiring content. The smart money in Japan may already be considering China, not a return to America, as the holy grail of anime in the next ten years. However, Japan's fortunes in China are vulnerable – when Japanese cars are attacked by mobs in Chinese cities because of sabre-rattling over the Senkaku Islands, what stable future is there for Japanese cultural products?

ACCESS AND PRODUCTION: EVENTS AND ADDED VALUE
The Nomura Research Institute suggests (NRI 2005: 35) that any otaku 'culture', be it trainspotters, gamers or anime fans, places value on particular types of experience – parsed somewhat whimsically as Events, Holy Lands and Legends. In anime terms, these experiences can take the form of:

- **Events:** conventions, comic marts, group DVD shopping, voice-actor concerts, anime all-nighters, film festivals.
- **Holy Lands:** Akihabara (shopping), Tokyo Big Site (convention venue); particular anime locations or sites.
- **Legends:** physical interactions with anime-industry celebrities, signings, photo opportunities, onstage Q&As.

The 'virtual pop idol' Hatsune Miku is, in one sense, the quintessence of modern anime. She is an inheritor of the fan-centred commodity culture of the 1980s and of the do-it-yourself home-brew animators of the 2000s. In both her appearances and the events that replay them in cinemas around the world, she is also a fine ambassador for the 'dreams of export'. While it might be possible to find illegal copies of her concert footage, the subtext of her concert videos presents a superb challenge to a modern audience – that to appreciate or even assess her fully, one must attend a concert in person: the ultimate antidote to piracy. But is she 'animated'? Arguably, Hatsune Miku is less an animated cartoon than she is a 'special effect' – a modern-day trick-film sideshow that makes the same promises of spectacle and wonder once bellowed by sideshow hucksters and 1910s cinema managers. As an onstage device that captures the performance of an unseen actress, she perhaps owes more to the puppet tradition than to animation itself. But, as noted on several occasions in this history, puppetry and animation have long been close cousins.

More importantly, her concerts are events, like any form of live appearance by participants in an anime – voice actors, singers, bands or creators. At the most basic level, Kataoka (2011: 175) suggests that TV is no place for a modern anime owner to make money, although TV companies may well pay him to make anime for them. Despite the dispiriting figures for box-office returns on even moderately successful anime films (Masuda 2007: 63), Kataoka suggests that limited theatrical release still offers an opportunity to accrue income directly from an audience by establishing a fixed site where fans can congregate and consume. This fact appears to have already been recognised by Tōei, ever the quiet innovator of Japanese animation, which has already grown money from 'events' to 2.9 per cent of its annual income (Masuda 2011: 213). Similarly, Tada Makoto (2002: 139) notes, for example, that an estimated 2,400 people each daily pay 1,000 yen to enter the Studio Ghibli Museum. They hence generate roughly £20,000 per day of revenue simply by turning up, and that is before they eat in the restaurant or buy souvenirs at the gift shop. Such regular, blue-chip income is only possible with a powerful, established brand, reducing the risk of constructing such a location in the first place, and in ensuring that the customers will continue to attend in a steady stream.

Kataoka further argues (2011: 176–7) that the culture of conventions, film festivals and concerts is ripe for further exploitation by the anime industry, which should be integrating itself even deeper into fandom in order to profit directly from its manifestations. Masuda (2011: 144–5) reports that the Japanese music industry since 2006 has shown a sharp upward trend in both the number of concerts, and the number of attendees. As live events with income accruing directly to the performers, concerts offer a means of earning money that is not only unaffected by the decline in packaged goods, but may even benefit from the increased availability of 'free' samples, even if illegal.

Moreover, as Kataoka (2011: 179) specifically highlights, foreign events may also offer the best means of monetising interest in anime among overseas fans – the 44,000 attendees at California's Anime Expo, the 50,000 at Anime Festival Asia in Singapore or the 58,000 at Barcelona's Salon del Manga. These, in turn, represent huge potential for sales in a closed circle of consumption, corralling consumers into captive audiences for days at a time. Of course, for many such attendees, presence at such events often involves 'suprapersonal' (Megill 2007: 35) fan activity, from which no money at all may accrue to anime's makers, but Masuda's point is that anime's makers ought to change that. It should also be noted that there is a degree of nescience concerning legalities, even among earnest, good-hearted fans – an observer from the Japanese Society for Rights of Authors, Composers and Publishers (JASRAC) reported that the DVDs on sale in the dealers' room at one Italian convention were all pirate copies (Masuda 2011: 168).

The 'event' paradigm may also be applicable to anime in terms of production, such as worldwide simulcast 'premieres' to thwart piracy, although thus far the anime industry seems reluctant to embrace other technical innovations such as stereoscopic 3D presentations. The first 3D anime, in the sense of stereoscopic vision, was *Ie Naki Ko* (1978, *Nobody's Boy*), screened in some Japanese cinemas in a 1980 movie edit that involved a 'stereochrome' process – presumably the spectral separation process that uses polarised lenses to differentiate images between the eyes. A fourteen-minute *Qtarō the Ghost* 'movie' in 1986 was released with a 3D process using the anaglyph process of red/blue lenses (Animage 1989: 115; Haraguchi 2000: 62). Neither of these gimmicks – and they were indeed gimmicks, rather than new media of expression – appear to have caught on. Yet.

OWNERSHIP AND AUTHORSHIP: RESPECT FOR TRUE CREATIVITY

Meanwhile, the anime industry continues to find new ways to strip itself bare. In successive moves, it has exhorted viewers to subsidise their own entertainment in the 1980s with the advent of video, and to bring their own storage media in the 1990s with the advent of late-night anime. A cynic might argue that the Vocaloid phenomenon of Hatsune Miku in the twenty-first century, along with the continuing subgenre of how-to manuals, software and education, is yet another level of attrition, with some anime viewers now being asked to provide their own content. However, this is not necessarily a bad thing. It is yet another subset of the crisis and response of the animation industry, and one which does not cause other forms of Japanese animation to disappear. If anything, the much-touted success of Shinkai Makoto has encouraged do-it-yourself projects among fans exploiting new tools and technologies – itself an effective return of Japanese animation to its hobbyist roots of a century earlier. Such participation need not only be at the level of production – another future development might involve taking 'hyper-ownership' to its logical conclusion, either at the distribution level by crowd-sourcing the funding for legal translations, or even at the level of ownership, by turning high-spending fans into giant 'committees' of producers.

Kataoka's final suggestion (2011: 180) is also the hardest to implement. In a single closing paragraph, he obliquely deconstructs and undermines the last twenty years of writings on the 'anime business', by reminding the reader that it is only a business because businessmen tell us it is. Although Okada Toshio puts on a performance of being the money-minded executive in charge of the Gainax company, there are moments in his memoirs where the mask slips (Okada 2010: 140), and he reveals an ongoing creative tension in the anime workplace, between those for whom it is merely a job, and those for whom it is a vocation. Okada alludes (2010: 77) to a standoff between petulant, 'childish' creatives and stern, 'grown-up' producers, while Kataoka essentially calls for the 'children' to be put back in charge. Of the top ten anime films of all time at the Japanese box office, only three in the lower ranks were *Pokémon* movies, resulting from focus groups, business plans and production committees (Masuda 2011: 112). The biggest earners, and hence, Kataoka implies, the models most worth emulating, were the films of Studio Ghibli, which values the creative freedom of a small group of artists, whose leader, Miyazaki Hayao, can be found in twentieth-century accounts as a younger man, arguing for better working conditions at Tōei, criticising the rise of context-integrated TV shows and refusing to accept anything but the best treatment for his works in foreign territories.

There is, perhaps, something salutary to be discerned in the market's reliance on sudden, unpredictable works of quality. Anime's revenues in 1997 were entirely skewed by just one film, Miyazaki's *Princess Mononoke*. In 2001, they were skewed once again by his Oscar-winning *Spirited Away*, which took the most money of any anime feature in Japan, 30.9 billion yen at the domestic box office. Despite many attempts in the anime industry to replicate Miyazaki's attitude, working methods and even stylistic interests, no company seems able to replicate his triumphs, not even his own Studio Ghibli, which struggles to match his box office without him in the director's role. In fact, subsequent films from Ghibli have attempted to establish the studio itself, and even the name 'Miyazaki' as a brand that can exist without Miyazaki Hayao's presence, most notably

The digitally animated *Astro Boy* (2009) could be an early example of 'post-anime', using Japanese intellectual property, but made in the US and Hong Kong

in the commissioning of his son, Gorō, to direct recent features. The closing credits of Miyazaki's *Ponyo* (2008) simultaneously commemorate everybody and nobody, discarding all job titles and ranks in favour of simply listing the names of all participants in the production. This is a fascinating performance – its performative action is of a truly egalitarian collaborative effort; its representative event is far more likely to ensure that the only name anyone ever associates with the production is Miyazaki's own. Repeated on the later *Arrietty* (2010), this gimmick may have served an even more devious purpose, ensuring not only that Miyazaki's name was associated with it, but occluding the fact that he was not its director.

Miyazaki Hayao is arguably a one-off genius like Tezuka, which helps explain his studio's unwillingness to admit he is fully retired, even after his official resignation in 2013. But a notional search for a 'new Miyazaki' cannot be conducted in business schools, toy companies or accountancy firms. It needs to be conducted among artists and animators, the very interest group in Japan that is being eroded by anime's drift offshore. Kataoka's fixes may help preserve anime as an industry and a business in the second decade of the twenty-first century, but the future of anime as an art form, and as a thing of enduring value, still rests as it did at the time of its inception, in the hands of artists and artisans with vision.

NOTE

1. Ushiki actually says 'roughly 50' films, implying that he already regards the official number as a rather permeable barrier, quite possibly for reasons such as this. But see also Aosaka *et al.* (2007: 184) for discussions of possible geographical variance of anime preferences within China, and Endō (2008: 81–92, 144, 162) for discussion of the relative success of 'informal' distribution of Japanese media in China.

BIBLIOGRAPHY

Acuff, Daniel with Robert Reiher, *What Kids Buy and Why: The Psychology of Marketing to Kids* (New York: Free Press, 1997).

AJA [Association of Japanese Animations (sic) and Tokyo Bureau of Industrial and Labour Affairs], *Anime no Text; Anime Gyōkai o Mokushisu Hito no Tame ni [Anime Text: For Those Aiming for the Japanese Animation Industry]*, 3 vols and DVD (Tokyo: AJA, 2008).

Akita Takahiro, 'Manga Eiga no Warai to Eiyū: Momotarō to Sensō' ['Laughter and Heroes in Cartoon Films: Momotarō and the War'], in Iwamoto Kenji (ed.), *Eiga to Dai Tō-A Kyōeiken [Film and the Greater East Asia Co-prosperity Sphere]* (Tokyo: Shinwasha, 2004), pp. 255–68.

Allison, Anne, 'Cuteness as Japan's Millennial Product', in Joseph Tobin (ed.), *Pikachu's Global Adventure: The Rise and Fall of Pokémon* (Durham, NC: Duke University Press, 2004), pp. 34–49.

_____ *Millennial Monsters: Japanese Toys and the Global Imagination* (Berkeley: University of California Press, 2006).

Altman, Rick, *Sound Theory/Sound Practice* (New York: Routledge, 1992).

Anderson, Chris, *Free: How Today's Smartest Businesses Profit by Giving Something for Nothing* (New York: Random House, 2009).

Animage, *The Art of Japanese Animation I: 25 Years of Television Cartoons* (Tokyo: Tokuma Shoten, 1988).

_____ *The Art of Japanese Animation II: 70 Years of Theatrical Films* (Tokyo: Tokuma Shoten, 1989).

_____ *Best of Animage: 20th Anniversary* (Tokyo: Tokuma Shoten, 1998).

_____ 'Bandai Visual's 2001 A Space Odyssey', *Animage* vol. 235 (January 1998b), pp. 18–31.

ANNcast 017 [Interview with Chad Kime], http://www.animenewsnetwork.com/anncast/2009-12-03, 13 December 2009.

_____ 023 [Interview with Carl Macek], http://www.animenewsnetwork.com/anncast/2010-01-14, 14 January 2010.

Annett, Sandra, 'Animating Transcultural Communities: Animation Fandom in North America and East Asia from 1906–2010', PhD dissertation, University of Manitoba, 2011.

[Anon], 'Pioneer Announces End of LaserDisc Player Products', http://www.pioneer.eu/uk/newsroom/news/news/endoflaserdiscplayer/index.html, 15 January 2009.

Anthony, Scott *et al.*, *If War Should Come (The GPO Film Unit Collection Volume Three)* (London: BFI, 2009).

Aosaka Tomoyuki *et al.*, *Contents Business in China: Hendō suru Shijō, Taitō suru Sangyō [Contents Business in China: Fluctuating Markets, Emerging Industry]* (Tokyo: Shōeisha, 2007).

Asahi Shinbun, 'Kieru TV Anime no Cel-ga, Nokoru no wa Sazae-san dake' ['As Cel Imagery Disappears from TV Anime, Sazae-san Is All That's Left'], *Asahi Shinbun*, http://www.asahi.com/komimi/TKY200708290098.html, 29 August 2007.

_____ 'Ano toki anime ga kawatta: 1981 Anime Shinseiki Sengon' ['The Time Anime Changed: 1981 Proclamation of a New Anime Century'], *Asahi Shinbun*, http://www.asahi.com/showbiz/manga/TKY200910170173.html, 17 October 2009.

Ashbaugh, William, 'Contesting Traumatic War Narratives: Space Battleship Yamato and Mobile Suit Gundam', in David Stahl and Mark Williams (eds), *Imag(in)ing the War in Japan: Representing and Responding to Trauma in Postwar Literature and Film* (Leiden: Brill, 2010), pp. 327–54.

Balio, Tino, *Grand Design: Hollywood as a Modern Business Enterprise, 1930–1939* (Berkeley: University of California Press, 1993).

Ban Toshio and Tezuka Productions, *Tezuka Osamu Monogatari: Manga no Yume, Anime no Yume 1960–1989 [The Tezuka Osamu Story: Dreams of Manga, Dreams of Anime 1960–1989]* (Tokyo: Asahi Shinbunsha, 1992).

Baricordi, Andrea *et al.*, *Cartoonia Anime: guida al cinema d'animazione giapponese* (Bologna: Granata Press, 1991).

Barnouw, Erik, *Tube of Plenty: The Evolution of American Television*, 2nd rev. edn (Oxford: Oxford University Press, 1990).

Barrier, Michael, *Hollywood Cartoons: American Animation in Its Golden Age* (New York: Oxford University Press, 1999).

_____ and Bill Spicer, 'An Interview with Chuck Jones', *Funnyworld* vol. 13 (1971), reprinted online at http://www.michaelbarrier.com/Funnyworld/Jones/interview_chuck_jones.htm.

Baskett, Michael, *The Attractive Empire: Transnational Film Culture in Imperial Japan* (Honolulu: University of Hawaii, 2008).

Beier, Carl, 'Film Briefing of Air Crews', *Hollywood Quarterly* vol. 1 no. 2 (January 1946), pp. 236–7.

Bernardi, Joanne, *Writing in Light: The Silent Scenario and the Japanese Pure Film Movement* (Detroit, MI: Wayne University Press, 2001).

Bernays, Edward, *Propaganda* (New York: Ig Publishing, 2005) [reprint of 1928 edition].

Berndt, Jaqueline (ed.), *Global Manga Studies #1 – Comics Worlds and the Worlds of Comics: Towards Scholarship on a Global Scale* (Kyoto: Seika University International Manga Research Center, 2010).

Bevir, George, 'Quake Threatens Tape Supply: Broadcasters Plan Emergency Delivery Methods as Disaster in Japan Forces Factories to Close', *Broadcast*, 25 March 2011, p. 1.

Bock, Audie, 'Kon Ichikawa', in James Quandt (ed.), *Kon Ichikawa* (Ontario: Cinematheque Ontario, 2001), pp. 37–51.

van Bogart, John, 'Mag Life Tape Expectancy 10–30 Years' (Pittsburgh, PA: Foundation of the American Institute for Conservation, 1995), http://cool.conservation-us.org/bytopic/electronic-records/electronic-storage-media/bogart.html.

_____'General Comments on the Stability of Videotape', in *Study of the Current State of American Television and Video Preservation* (Washington, DC: Library of Congress, 1996), pp. 299–304, http://www.loc.gov/film/pdfs/tvvanbogart.pdf.

Bordwell, David, Janet Staiger and Kristin Thompson, *The Classical Hollywood Cinema: Film Style & Mode of Production to 1960* (London: Routledge, 1985).

_____ and Noël Carroll, *Post-film: Reconstructing Film Studies* (Madison: University of Wisconsin Press, 1996).

Bourdieu, Pierre, 'Forms of Capital', in J. G. Richardson (ed.), *Handbook of Theory and Research for the Sociology of Education* (Westwood, CT: Greenwood Press, 1986), pp. 46–58.

Brimmicombe-Wood, Lee and Tamamuro Motoko, 'Deep Six', *Manga Max* no. 12 (November 1999), pp. 34–8.

Bryce, Mio, Christie Barber, James Kelly, Siris Kunwar and Amy Plumb, 'Fluidity and Hybridity in Global Imagery', *Electronic Journal of Contemporary Japanese Studies*, 29 January 2010.

Burke, Peter, *History and Social Theory*, 2nd edn (Cambridge: Polity, 2005).

_____ *What Is Cultural History?*, 2nd edn (Cambridge: Polity, 2008).

Burkman, Thomas (ed.), *The Occupation of Japan: Arts and Culture: The Proceedings of a Symposium at Norfolk, Virginia 18–19 October 1984* (Norfolk: General Douglas MacArthur Foundation, 1988).

Butsch, Richard, *The Making of American Audiences: From Stage to Television, 1750–1990* (Cambridge: Cambridge University Press, 2000).

Canemaker, John, 'Winsor McCay', in Maureen Furniss (ed.), *Animation – Art and Industry* (New Barnet: John Libbey, 2009), pp. 93–104.

Casey, Bernadette, Neil Casey, Ben Calvert, Liam French and Justin Lewis, *Television Studies: The Key Concepts* (London: Routledge, 2008).

China Daily, 'Nihon Saiko? Meiji Jidai no Anime Film Kyōto de Haiken' ['Japan's Oldest? Meiji Era Anime Film Discovered in Kyōto'], *People's Daily*, online edition, http://j.people.com.cn/2005/08/01/jp20050801_52250.html, 1 August 2005.

Chun, Jayson, *"A Nation of a Hundred Million Idiots"? A Social History of Japanese Television 1953–1973* (New York: Routledge: 2007).

Clements, Jonathan, 'The Mechanics of the US Anime and Manga Industry', *Foundation: The Review of Science Fiction* no. 64 (Summer 1995), pp. 32–44.

_____ 'View from the Inside: The Mechanics of Anime Pornography', in Helen McCarthy and Jonathan Clements, *The Erotic Anime Movie Guide* (London: Titan Books, 1998a), pp. 16–21.

_____ '"Snuff Out These Sick Cartoons": Anime Goes West', in Helen McCarthy and Jonathan Clements, *The Erotic Anime Movie Guide* (London: Titan Books, 1998b), pp. 82–93.

_____ 'Sex with the Girl Next Door: The Roots of the Anime Erotic', in Helen McCarthy and Jonathan Clements, *The Erotic Anime Movie Guide* (London: Titan Books, 1998c), pp. 94–111.

_____ 'Cruise Controls: Interactive Erotica and Digital Dating', in Helen McCarthy and Jonathan Clements, *The Erotic Anime Movie Guide* (London: Titan Books, 1998d), pp. 112–17.

_____ *The Development of the UK Anime and Manga Market* (London: Muramasa Industries, 2003).

_____ *Schoolgirl Milky Crisis: Adventures in the Anime and Manga Trade* (London: Titan Books, 2009a).

_____ 'Grown-ups' [interview with Yamaga Hiroyuki], *Neo* no. 67 (2009b), p. 17.

_____ 'Living Happily Never After in Women's Manga', in Josef Steiff and Adam Barkman (eds), *Manga and Philosophy* (Chicago, IL: Open Court, 2010a), pp. 93–109.

_____ 'Yoshinobu Nishizaki 1934–2010' (obituary), http://schoolgirlmilkycrisis.com/blog/?p=1976, 7 November 2010 [cited as 2010b].

_____ 'Umanosuke Iida 1961–2010' (obituary), http://schoolgirlmilkycrisis.com/blog/?p=2020, 26 November 2010 [cited as 2010c].

_____ 'The Curious Case of the Dog in Primetime', in Joseph Steiff (ed.), *Sherlock Holmes and Philosophy* (Chicago, IL: Open Court, 2011a), pp. 307–15.

_____ 'Milky Crisis', *SFX Ultimate Guide to Anime* (SFX Specials no. 50) (2011b), pp. 50–1.

_____ 'The Ties That Bind', *Neo* no. 89 (2011c), p. 17.

_____ 'Manga Snapshot: WAai Boys in Skirts', *Neo* no. 92 (2011d), pp. 32–5.

_____ 'Scotland Loves Anime', *Neo* no. 92 (2011e), pp. 36–8.

_____ and Barry Ip, 'The Shadow Staff: Japanese Animators in the Tōhō Aviation Education Materials Production Office 1939–1945', *Animation: An Interdisciplinary Journal* vol. 7 no. 2 (July 2012), pp. 189–204.

_____ and David Langford, 'Mecha', in *The Encyclopedia of Science Fiction*, online edition, http://www.sf-encyclopedia.com/entry/mecha, 2012.

_____ and Helen McCarthy, *The Anime Encyclopedia: A Guide to Japanese Animation since 1917*, rev. and expanded edn (San Francisco, CA: Stone Bridge Press, 2006).

_____ and Tamamuro Motoko, *The Dorama Encyclopedia: A Guide to Japanese TV Drama since 1953* (San Francisco, CA: Stone Bridge Press, 2003).

Cohen, Karl, *Forbidden Animation: Censored Cartoons and Blacklisted Animators in America* (Jefferson, NC: McFarland, 1997).

Condry, Ian, 'Anime Creativity: Characters and Premises in the Quest for Cool Japan', *Theory, Culture & Society* no. 26 (2009), pp. 139–63.

_____ *The Soul of Anime: Collaborative Creativity and Japan's Media Success Story* (Durham, NC: Duke University Press, 2013).

Crafton, Donald, *Before Mickey: The Animated Film 1898–1928* (Cambridge, MA: MIT Press, 1982) [paperback edition 1984].

_____ *The Talkies: American Cinema's Transition to Sound 1926–1931* (Berkeley: University of California Press, 1997).

Cunningham, Stuart and Jon Silver, 'Timeline – On-line Distribution of Feature Films', in Dina Iordanova and Stuart Cunningham (eds), *Digital Disruption: Cinema Moves On-Line* (St Andrews: St Andrews Film Studies, 2012), pp. 189–94.

Davis, Darrell and Emilie Yueh-yu Yeh, *East Asian Screen Industries* (London: BFI, 2008).

Deneroff, Harvey, '"We Can't Get Much Spinach!" The Organization and Implementation of the Fleischer Animation Strike', *Film History* vol. 1 (1987), pp. 1–14.

Denison, Rayna, 'Anime Tourism: Discursive Construction and Reception of the Studio Ghibli Art Museum', *Japan Forum* vol. 22 nos 3–4 (2010), pp. 545–63.

Denzin, Norman, *Interpretive Biography* (Newbury Park, CA: Sage Publications, 1989).

Dibb, Sally and Lyndon Simkin, *The Marketing Casebook: Cases and Concepts* (London: Routledge, 1994).

Dittbrenner, Nils, 'Anime Interactive: Video Games and Manga Culture', in Martha-Christine Menzel *et al.* (eds), *Ga Netchū: The Manga Anime Syndrome* (Frankfurt: Deutsche Filmmuseum, 2008), pp. 134–43.

Dobson, Sebastian, 'Reflections of Conflict: Japanese Photographers and the Russo-Japanese War', in Frederic A. Sharf, Anne Nishimura Morse and Sebastian Dobson, *A Much Recorded War: The Russo-Japanese War in History and Imagery* (Boston, MA: Museum of Fine Arts, 2005), pp. 52–83.

Domenig, Roland, 'Review: Kenji Iwamoto: Gentō no seiki. Eiga zenya no shikaku bunkashi' ('Centuries of Magic Lanterns in Japan: A History of Visual Culture on the Eve of Cinema'), *Animation* no. 6 (2011), pp. 193–6.

Dower, John, *Embracing Defeat: Japan in the Aftermath of World War II* (Harmondsworth: Penguin, 1999).

Driscoll, Mark, 'From Kino-Eye to Anime-eye/ai: The Filmed and the Animated in Imamura Taihei's Media Theory', *Japan Forum* vol. 14 no. 2 (September 2002), pp. 269–96.

Dym, Jeffrey, 'Tokugawa Musei: A Portrait Sketch of One of Japan's Great Narrative Artists', in Aaron Gerow and Mark Nornes (eds), *In Praise of Film Studies: Essays in Honor of Makino Mamoru* (Yokohama: Kinema Club, 2001), pp. 139–57.

Ehrlich, David with Jin Tianyi, 'Animation in China', in John Lent (ed.), *Animation in Asia and the Pacific* (New Barnet: John Libbey, 2001), pp. 7–32.

Eldred, Tim, 'Yoshinori "Iko" Kanada, 1952–2009', http://www.starblazers.com, 2009.

_____ 'Out of the Darkness …: An Overview of Yamato Fan History', http://www.starblazers.com/, 2008a.

_____ 'As Large as Life: Yamato Events of the Production Years', http://www.starblazers.com, 2008b.

_____ 'Space Battleship Yamato Timeline' http://www.starblazers.com, 2008c.

Ellis, John M., *Against Deconstruction* (Princeton, NJ: Princeton University Press, 1989).

Ellis, John, *Visible Fictions – Cinema: Television: Video*, rev. edn (London: Routledge, 1992).

_____ *TV FAQ: Uncommon Answers to Common Questions about TV* (London: I. B. Tauris, 2007).

Elsaesser, Thomas, *Early Cinema: Space, Frame, Narrative* (London: BFI, 1990).

Endō Homare, *Chūgoku Dōman Shinjinrui: Nihon no Anime to Manga ga Chūgoku o udokasu [The New Breed of Chinese 'Dongman': Japanese Cartoons and Comics Animate China]* (Tokyo: Nikkei BP, 2008).

Ezra, Elizabeth, *Georges Méliès: The Birth of the Auteur* (Manchester: Manchester University Press, 2000).

Fiske, John, *Television Culture*, 2nd edn (London: Routledge, 2011).

Fling, Fred, *The Writing of History: An Introduction to Historical Method* (New Haven, CT: Yale University Press, 1920).

Foucault, Michel, *The Archaeology of Knowledge* (London: Routledge, 2002) [reprint of 1972 translation of 1969 French original].

Francks, Penelope, *Japanese Economic Development: Theory and Practice* (London: Routledge/Nissan Institute, 1999).

_____ *The Japanese Consumer: An Alternative Economic History of Modern Japan* (Cambridge: Cambridge University Press, 2009).

Fu Poshek, 'The Ambiguity of Entertainment: Chinese Cinema in Japanese-occupied Shanghai, 1941 to 1945', *Cinema Journal* vol. 37 no. 1 (Fall 1997), pp. 66–84.

Fujiki Hideaki, 'Benshi as Stars: The Irony of the Popularity and Respectability of Voice Performers in Japanese Cinema', *Cinema Journal* vol. 45 no. 2 (2006), pp. 68–84.

Fujiko Fujio A, *Manga no Michi [The Manga Road]* (Tokyo: Chuo Bunko Comics, 1996) [in 14 volumes].

_____ and Fujiko F. Fujio, *Fujiko Fujio A to Fujiko F. Fujio: Futari de Shōnen Manga Bakari Kaitekita [Two People Who Only Drew Boys' Comics]* (Tokyo: Nippon Tosho Centre, 2010).

Fujita Junichi, 'Kanren Nenpyō' ['Related Chronology'], in Iwamoto Kenji (ed.), *Nippon Eiga no Tanjō [The Birth of Japanese Film]* (Tokyo: Shinwasha, 2011), pp. 393–401.

Funamoto Susumu (ed.), *Anime no Mirai o Shiru: Post-Japanimation Keyword wa Sekaishi + Digital [Understanding the Future of Anime: Post Japanimation the Keywords Are Global + Digital]* (Tokyo, Ten Books, 1998).

Furniss, Maureen (ed.), *Animation – Art and Industry* (New Barnet: John Libbey, 2009).

Furuya Tōru, *Hero no Koe: Hyūma to Amuro to Boku no Seiyū Jinsei [Hero's Voice: Hyūma, Amuro and My Voice-acting Life]* (Tokyo: Kadokawa Shoten, 2009).

Galbraith, Stuart, *The Toho Studios Story: A History and Complete Filmography* (Lanham, MD: Scarecrow Press, 2008).

Gan Sheuo Hui, 'To Be or Not to Be: The Controversy in Japan over the "Anime" Label', *Animation Studies* vol. 4 (2009), pp. 35–44.

Gao Weijin, 'Minzhu Dongbei de Shezhi' ['The Production of *Democracy North-East*'], http://www.cndfilm.com/20090604/107544.shtml, online extract from *Zhongguo Xinwen Jilu Dianying Shi [A History of Chinese Documentary Film]* (Beijing: Zhongyang Wenxian, 2003).

Gay, Peter, *Style in History* (New York: W. W. Norton, 1988) [reprint of 1974 edition].

Gerow, Aaron, 'The Industrial Ichikawa: Kon Ichikawa after 1976', in James Quandt (ed.), *Kon Ichikawa* (Ontario: Cinematheque Ontario, 2001), pp. 385–97.

_____ 'Film Notes', *The Roots of Japanese Anime [sic] until the End of WW II*, liner notes to the DVD (Tokyo: Zakka Films, 2008), pp. 5–11.

_____ *Visions of Japanese Modernity: Articulations of Cinema, Nation, and Spectatorship, 1895–1925* (Berkeley: University of California Press, 2010).

_____ and Mark Nornes, *In Praise of Film Studies: Essays in Honor of Makino Mamoru* (Yokohama: Kinema Club, 2001).

Gerteis, Christopher, *Gender Struggles: Wage-earning Women and Male-dominated Unions in Postwar Japan* (Harvard, MA: University Center East Asian Monographs, 2009).

Gfader, Verina, *Adventure-Landing: A Compendium of Animation* (Berlin: Revolver Publishing, 2011).

Gill, Tom, 'Transformational Magic: Some Japanese Super-heroes and Monsters', in D. P. Martinez (ed.), *The Worlds of Japanese Popular Culture: Gender, Shifting Boundaries and Global Cultures* (Cambridge: Cambridge University Press, 1998), pp. 33–55.

Goldschmidt, Rick, *The Enchanted World of Rankin/Bass: A Portfolio* (Issaquah, WA: Tiger Mountain Press, 1997).

Gomery, Douglas, 'Economic and Institutional Analysis: Hollywood as Monopoly Capitalism', in Mike Wayne (ed.), *Understanding Film: Marxist Perspectives* (London: Pluto Press, 2005), pp. 168–81.

Grainge, Paul, Mark Jancovich and Sharon Monteith, *Film Histories: An Introduction and Reader* (Edinburgh: Edinburgh University Press, 2007).

Grassmuck, Volker, 'Otaku: Japanese Kids Colonize the Realm of Information and Media', in *Mediamatic* 1991, archived at http://www.mediamatic.net/11784/en/otaku.

Green, Jonathon, *The Cassell Dictionary of Slang* (London: Cassell, 1998).

Greenberg, Larry, 'The Arrival of Cinema in Japan', in Friends of Silent Films Association and Matsuda Film Productions (eds), *The Benshi – Japanese Silent Film Narrators* (Tokyo: Urban Connections, 2001), pp. 6–12.

Greenberg, Raz, 'The Animated Text: Definition', *Journal of Film and Video* vol. 63 no. 2 (Summer 2011), pp. 3–10.

Grieveson, Lee, 'Why the Audience Mattered in Chicago in 1907', in Paul Grainge, Mark Jancovich and Sharon Monteith (eds), *Film Histories: An Introduction and Reader* (Edinburgh: Edinburgh University Press, 2007 [1999]).

Gubbins, Michael, 'Digital Revolution: Active Audiences and Fragmented Consumption', in Dina Iordanova and Stuart Cunningham (eds), *Digital Disruption: Cinema Moves On-line* (St Andrews: St Andrews Film Studies, 2012), pp. 67–100.

Guilford, J. P. and P. C. Smith, 'A System of Color Preferences', *American Journal of Psychology* vol. 73 no. 4 (1959), pp. 487–502.

Gunning, Tom, 'The Cinema of Attractions: Early Film, Its Spectator and the Avant-garde', in Thomas Elsaesser (ed.), *Early Cinema: Space, Frame, Narrative* (London: BFI: 1990), pp. 56–62.

Guttman, Allen and Lee Thompson, *Japanese Sports: A History* (Honolulu: University of Hawaii Press, 2001).

Hamano Yasuki (ed.), *Animation Kantoku Hara Keiichi [Animation Director Hara Keiichi]* (Tokyo: Shōbunsha, 2005).

Haoyang Songwei (ed.), *Shootmen* (California (location not specified): Louvy Corporation, 2005).

Haraguchi Masahiro (ed.), *Animage Pocket Data Notes*, Annual (Tokyo: Tokuma Shoten, 1989–2000).

Hartwell, David, *Age of Wonders: Exploring the World of Science Fiction* (New York: Tor Books, 1996).

Hase Masato, *Eiga to Iu Technology Keiken [Cinema and Technological Experience]* (Tokyo: Seikyūsha, 2010).

Hatakeyama Kenji and Kubo Masakazu, *Pokémon Story* (Tokyo: Nikkei BP, 2000).

Heinze, Ulrich, 'Radio and Television Consumption in Japan: A Trilateral Intercultural Comparison with the UK and Germany', *Electronic Journal of Contemporary Japanese Studies*, http://www.japanesestudies.org.uk/articles/2011/Heinze.html.

High, Peter, *The Imperial Screen: Japanese Film Culture in the Fifteen Years' War 1931–1945* (Madison: University of Wisconsin Press, 2003).

Hikawa Ryūsuke, 'Anime Tokushu Gihō no Hensen' [Alterations of Anime Special Techniques], in Misono Makoto (ed.), *Zusetsu Terebi Anime Zensho [Complete Book of TV Animation: Illustrated]* (Tokyo: Hara Shobō, 1999), pp. 181–214.

Hiramatsu Keiichirō (ed.), *Terebi 50-nen in TV Guide: The TV History of 50 Years* (Tokyo: Tokyo News Tsūshinsha, 2000).

Hirano Kyōko, 'The Occupation and Japanese Cinema', in Thomas Burkman (ed.), *The Occupation of Japan: Arts and Culture: The Proceedings of a Symposium at Norfolk, Virginia 18–19 October 1984* (Norfolk: General Douglas MacArthur Foundation, 1988), pp. 141–54.

_____ *Mr. Smith Goes to Tokyo: Japanese Cinema under the American Occupation, 1945–1952* (Washington, DC: Smithsonian Institute, 1992).

Horibuchi Seiji and Iiboshi Manami, *Moeru America: Beikokujin wa Ikanishite Manga o Yomuyō ni natta ka [Turning America On: Was It Possible for Americans to Somehow Become Manga Readers?]* (Tokyo: Nikkei BP, 2006).

Hoshiyama Hiroyuki, *Hoshiyama Hiroyuki no Anime Scenario Kyōshitsu [Hoshiyama Hiroyuki's Anime Screenplay Classroom]* (Tokyo: Raichōsha, 2007).

Hotta Junji, *Gainax Interviews* (Tokyo: Kōdansha, 2005).

Hu Tze-yue, 'The Animated Resurrection of the Legend of the White Snake in Japan', *Animation* vol. 2 (March 2007), pp. 44–61.

_____ 'Dare no Mukete no Animation ka: Shusen Chokugo no Animation Eiga' [Animating for Whom in the Aftermath of a World War], in Iwamoto Kenji (ed.),

Senryoka no Eiga: Kaihō to Kenetsu [Film under the Occupations: Emancipation and Censorship] (Tokyo: Shinwasha, 2009), pp. 243–67.

_____ *Frames of Anime: Culture and Image-building* (Hong Kong: Hong Kong University Press, 2010).

Hughes-Warrington, Marnie, *Fifty Key Thinkers on History*, 2nd edn (London: Routledge, 2008).

Ichikawa Kon and Mori Yuki, 'Beginnings', in James Quandt (ed.), *Kon Ichikawa* (Ontario: Cinematheque Ontario, 2001), pp. 21–35.

Ikeda Kōichi, *Char e no Chinkonka: Waga Seishun no Akai Suisei [A Requiem for Char Aznable: My Youth as the Red Comet]* (Tokyo: Wani Books, 2007).

Ikeda Noriaki and Itō Hideaki, *Renzoku Ningyōgeki no Subete [All about NHK Puppet Serials]* (Tokyo: Enterbrain, 2003).

Ingulsrud, John and Kate Allen, *Reading Japan Cool: Patterns of Manga Literacy and Discourse* (Lanham, MD: Lexington Books, 2009).

Inomata Kenji, 'Teikoku no Zan'ei to Gojira Eiga' ['The Relics of Imperial Cinema and the Godzilla Movies'], *Jinbun Kagaku Kenkyū* [Niigata University Studies in Humanities] no. 120 (2007), pp. 79–102.

Inoue Akito, *Gamification: Game ga Business o Kaeru [Gamification: How Games Are Changing Business]* (Tokyo: NHK Shuppan, 2012).

Inoue Manabu (ed.), *Ikinari Saishūkai [Sudden Endings]* (Tokyo: Takarajima-sha, 1995) (Bessatsu Takarajima no. 235).

Inoue Shinichiro (ed.), *Anime DVD Kanzen [Complete] Catalogue* (Tokyo: Kadokawa Shoten, 2000) (cited as Inoue 2000a).

Inoue Takeo, *Nijū Seiki Anime Daizen [Encyclopaedia of 20th Century Animation]* (Tokyo: Futabasha, 2000) (cited as Inoue 2000b).

Inui Naoaki, *That's TV Graffiti: Gaikoku Terebi Eiga Sanjūgonen no Subete [All about 35 Years of Foreign TV and Films]* (Tokyo: Film Art-sha, 1988).

Ishiguro Noboru and Ohara Noriko, *Terebi Anime Saizensen: Shisetsu Anime 17 Nenshi [The Frontline of Television Animation: A Personal History of 17 Years in Animation]* (Tokyo: Yamato Shobō, 1980).

Ishikawa Mitsuhisa, *Animation Gyōkai, Itanji Producer no Genjōriki Kakumei [The Animation Industry and a Non-conformist Producer's On-the-spot Revolution]* (Tokyo: KK Bestsellers, 2009).

Itatsu Yuko, 'Japan's Hollywood Boycott Movement of 1924', *Historical Journal of Film, Radio and Television* vol. 28 no. 3 (August 2008), pp. 353–69.

Itō Gō, *Tezuka Is Dead: Hirakareta Manga Hyōgenron e [Tezuka Is Dead: Postmodernist and Modernist Approaches to Japanese Manga]* (Tokyo: NTT Shuppan, 2005). Wording of title translation thus in Japanese edition.

Iwabuchi Kōichi, *Recentering Globalization: Popular Culture and Japanese Transnationalism* (Durham, NC: Duke University Press, 2002).

_____ *Feeling Asian Modernities: Transnational Consumption of Japanese TV Dramas* (Hong Kong: Hong Kong University Press, 2003).

_____ 'How "Japanese" Is *Pokémon*?', in Joseph Tobin (ed.), *Pikachu's Global Adventure: The Rise and Fall of Pokémon* (Durham, NC: Duke University Press, 2004), pp. 53–79.

Iwamoto Kenji (ed.), *Nippon Eiga no Tanjō [The Birth of Japanese Film]* (Tokyo: Shinwasha, 2011).

Iwasaki Yoshikazu *et al.* (eds), *Osamu Tezuka* (Tokyo: National Museum of Modern Art, 1990).

Jenkins, Henry, *Textual Poachers: Television Fans and Participatory Culture* (New York: Routledge, 1992).

Kadokawa Haruki, *Waga Tōsō: Furyō Seinen wa Sekai o Mezasu [My Struggle: A Delinquent Youth Aims for the World]* (Tokyo: East Press, 2005).

Kajiyama Sumiko, *Suzuki Toshio no Ghibli Book* (Tokyo: Nikkei Business Bunko, 2009).

Kamen, Matt, 'Space Showman' [interview with Masunari Kōji] in *Manga UK*, http://www.mangauk.com/?p=4644, 30 June 2012.

Kanō Seiji, *Nippon no Animation o Kizuita Hitobito [The People Who Built Japanese Animation]* (Tokyo: Wakakusa Shobō, 2004).

Kataoka Yoshirō, 'Nippon no Anime Shijō' ['The Japanese Animation Marketplace'], in Takahashi Mitsuteru and Tsugata Nobuyuki (eds), *Anime-gaku [Anime Studies]* (Tokyo: NTT Shuppan, 2011), pp. 152–83.

Katō Akiko, *Nihon no Ningyōgeki 1867–2007 [Japanese Puppet Theatre 1867–2007]* (Tokyo: Hōsei Daigaku, 2007).

Katō Mikiro, *Eigakan to Kankyaku no Bunka Shi [A Cultural History of Cinema and Audience]* (Tokyo: Chūō Kōron Shinsha, 2006).

_____ *Animation no Eiga-gaku (Animation Film Studies)* (Kyoto: Rinsen Shoten, 2009).

Katsuno Hirofumi and Jeffrey Maret, 'Localizing the Pokémon TV Series for the American Market', in Joseph Tobin (ed.), *Pikachu's Global Adventure: The Rise and Fall of Pokémon* (Durham, NC: Duke University Press, 2004), pp. 80–107.

Kawai Nobukazu (ed.), *Japan Almanac 2000* (Tokyo: Asahi Shinbun-sha, 1999).

Kawai Ryū, 'Saigo no Shōnintachi' ['The Last Witnesses'], in Shibayama Tatsuo and Kobayashi Shūji *et al.* (eds), *Mushi Pro Tenamonya: Dare mo Shiranai Tezuka Osamu [Mushi Pro Maverick: The Tezuka Osamu That Nobody Knows]* (Tokyo: Kuraki-sha Bijutsu, 2009), pp. 12–13.

Kawamoto Kihachirō, 'Mochinaga Tadahito Sensei no Omoide' ['Memories of My Teacher Mochinaga Tadahito'], in Tadahito Mochinaga, *Animation Nitchū Kōryūki [A Chronicle of Sino-Japanese Animation Interchange]* (Tokyo: Tōhō Shoten, 2006), pp. 339–41.

Keene, Donald, *Emperor of Japan: Meiji and His World, 1852–1912* (New York: Columbia University Press, 2002).

Kimura Makoto, 'Anime Business no Kihon Model' ['A Basic Model of the Anime Business'], in Takahashi Mitsuteru and Tsugata Nobuyuki (eds), *Anime-gaku [Anime Studies]* (Tokyo: NTT Shuppan, 2011), pp. 115–51.

Kinema Junpō Eiga Sōkō Kenkyū-sho [Kinema Junpo Film Integration Research Office], *'Nichijōkei Anime' Hit no Hōsoku [The Rules for Making a Hit 'Mundane Anime']* (Tokyo: Kinema Junpō-sha, 2011a).

_____ *Anime Producer no Shigoto-ron [On the Profession of the Anime Producer]* (Tokyo: Kinema Junpō-sha, 2011b).

Kinokuniya, *Animation no Senkakusha Ōfuji Noburō: Kokō no Genius [Animation Pioneer Ōfuji Noburo: Isolated Genius]* (DVD) (Tokyo: Kinokuniya, 2010).

Kinsella, Sharon, *Adult Manga: Culture and Power in Contemporary Japanese Society* (Richmond: Curzon Press, 2000).

Kitamura Hiroshi, *Screening Enlightenment: Hollywood and the Cultural Reconstruction of Defeated Japan* (Ithaca, NY: Cornell University Press, 2010).

Kitano Taiitsu, *Nippon Anime Shigaku Kenkyū Josetsu [An Introduction to the Historical Study of Japanese Animation]* (Tokyo: Hachiman Shoten, 1998).

Kitaoka Shinobu, *Morikawa Kazuyo ga Ikita Kyū-'Manshū' Sono Jidai: Kakumei to Senka o Kakenuketa Seishunki [The Time That Morikawa Kazuyo Lived in the Former 'Manchuria': A Youth amid Revolution and Warfare]* (Tokyo: Bungei-sha, 2009).

Kitayama Seitarō, 'Sen-Eiga no Tsukurikata' [How to Make Animated Films], in Zen Nihon Katsuei Kyōiku Kenkyūkai, *Eiga no Kiso Chishiki [Basic Facts for Film Education]* (Tokyo: Kyōiku Shokan, 1930), pp. 321–41.

Klinger, Barbara, 'Film History Terminable and Interminable: Recovering the Past in Reception Studies', *Screen* vol. 38 no. 2 (Summer 1997), pp. 107–28.

_____ *Beyond the Multiplex: Cinema, New Technologies and the Home* (Berkeley: University of California Press, 2006).

Kobayashi Shūji *et al.*, *Mushi Pro Tenamonya: Dare mo Shiranai Tezuka Osamu [Mushi Pro Maverick: The Tezuka Osamu That Nobody Knows]* (Tokyo: Kuraki-sha Bijutsu, 2009).

Koga Futoshi, 'Méliès wa Itsu kara Shirarete ita no ka: Nihon ni Okeru Méliès Kotohajime' ['When Did Méliès Come to Be Known? The Beginnings of Méliès in Japan'], in Iwamoto Kenji (ed.), *Nippon Eiga no Tanjō [The Birth of Japanese Film]* (Tokyo: Shinwasha, 2011), pp. 44–62.

Komaki Masanobu, *Animec no Goro [My Time at Animec]* (Tokyo: NTT Shuppan, 2009).

Komatsuzawa Hajime, 'Momotaro's Sea Eagle', In Mark Nornes and Fukushima Yukio (eds), *The Japan/America Film Wars: World War II Propaganda and Its Cultural Contexts* (Langhorne, PA: Harwood Academic Publishers, 1994), pp. 191–5.

_____ 'Princess Iron Fan (Saiyūki)', in Mark Nornes and Fukushima Yukio (eds), *The Japan/America Film Wars: World War II Propaganda and Its Cultural Contexts* (Langhorne, PA: Harwood Academic Publishers, 1994), pp. 225–9 [cited as Komatsuzawa 1994b].

Kon Satoshi, *Kon's Tone: Sennen Joyū e no Michi [Kon's Tone: The Road to Millennium Actress]* (Tokyo: Shōbunsha, 2002).

Kondō Takashi, *Kusō Bishōjo Yomihon [The Guide of Fantastic Beauties]* (Tokyo: Bessatsu Takarajima-sha, 1997).

Kōuchi Junichi, 'Gendai Manga Eiga ni Tsuite' ['Concerning Contemporary Cartoon Film'], *Tōyō*, October 1936, pp. 101–3.

Koyama-Richard, Brigitte, *Japanese Animation: From Painted Scrolls to Pokémon* (Paris: Flammarion, 2010).

Kurosawa Akira, *Something like an Autobiography* (New York: Vintage Books, 1983).

Kurosawa Kiyoshi, Yohota Inuhiko *et al.*, *Anime wa Ekkyō suru [Anime in Transition]* (Tokyo: Iwanami Shoten, 2010).

Kushida Makoto, *Ani Kuri 15 DVD x Materials* (Tokyo: Ichijinsha, 2009).

_____ (ed.), *Welcome to the Space Show: Official Guide Book* (Tokyo: Ichijinsha, 2010).

Kushner, Barak, *The Thought War: Japanese Imperial Propaganda* (Honolulu: University of Hawaii Press, 2006).

Kuwahara Keisuke, 'Animation ni Okeru Oto to Ugoki no Hyogen: Tetsuwan Atomu no Chūshin ni' ['The Appearance of Sound and Movement in Animation: Astro Boy'], *Japanese Journal of Animation Studies* vol. 9 no. 1 (2008), pp. 25–32.

Kwon Jae-woong, *The Development of Digital Cultural Products in the Age of Globalization: Focusing on the Korean Digitalized Animation Industry*, PhD dissertation, Temple University, 2006.

Ladd, Fred, with Harvey Deneroff, *Astro Boy and Anime Come to the Americas: An Insider's View of the Birth of a Pop Culture Phenomenon* (Jefferson, NC: McFarland, 2009).

Lamarre, Thomas, *The Anime Machine: A Media Theory of Animation* (Minneapolis: University of Minnesota Press, 2009).

Lebas, Elizabeth, *Forgotten Futures: British Municipal Cinema 1920–1980* (London: Black Dog Publishing, 2011).

Ledoux, Trish (ed.), *Anime Interviews: The First Five Years of Animerica Anime and Manga Monthly* (San Francisco, CA: Cadence Books, 1997).

Lent, John, 'Animation in Asia: Appropriation, Reinterpretation, and Adoption or Adaptation', *Screening the Past* no. 11 (2000), http://www.latrobe.edu.au/www/screeningthepast/firstrelease/fr1100/jlfr11c.htm.

_____ (ed.), *Animation in Asia and the Pacific* (New Barnet: John Libbey, 2001).

_____ and Xu Ying, 'China's Animation Beginnings: The Roles of the Wan Brothers and Others', in *Asian Cinema*, Spring/Summer 2003, pp. 56–69.

Lewell, John, 'The Art of Chuck Jones', in Maureen Furniss (ed.), *Animation – Art and Industry* (New Barnet: John Libbey, 2009), pp. 131–44. [Reprinted from *Films and Filming* vol. 336 (September 1982), pp. 12–20].

Lie, John, 'Sociology of Contemporary Japan', *Current Sociology* vol. 44 no. 1 (1996), pp. 1–95.

Linsenmaier, Timo, 'Why Animation Historiography?', *Animation Studies* vol. 3 (2008), pp. 51–9.

Litten, Frederick, 'Starving the Elephants: The Slaughter of Animals in Wartime Tokyo's Ueno Zoo', *Asia-Pacific Journal* vol. 38–3–09 (21 September 2009).

_____ 'On the Earliest (Foreign) Animation Films Shown in Japanese Cinemas', 2013, http://litten.de/fulltext/nipper.pdf.

Lobato, Ramon, *Shadow Economies of Cinema: Mapping Informal Film Distribution* (London: BFI/Palgrave Macmillan, 2012).

Lurçat, Liliane, *À cinq ans, seul avec Goldorak: le jeune enfant et la télévision* (Paris: Éditions Syros, 1981).

Lutz, Edwin G., *Animated Cartoons: How They Are Made, Their Origin and Development* (Bedford, MA: Applewood Books, not dated) [reprint facsimile of 1920 edition originally published by Charles Scribner's Sons].

MacWilliams, Mark (ed.), *Japanese Visual Culture: Explorations in the World of Manga and Anime* (Armonk, NY: M. E. Sharpe, 2008).

Makino Mamoru, 'Rethinking the Emergence of the Proletarian Film League of Japan (Prokino)', in Aaron Gerow and Mark Nornes (eds), *In Praise of Film Studies* (qv), pp. 15–45 (2001a).

_____ 'On the Conditions of Film Censorship in Japan before Its Systemization', in Aaron Gerow and Mark Nornes (eds), *In Praise of Film Studies* (qv), pp. 46–67 (2001b).

_____ 'The Establishment of the Study of Visual Philology', in Aaron Gerow and Mark Nornes (eds), *In Praise of Film Studies* (qv), pp. 74–103 (2001c).

Mandel, Ernest, *An Introduction to Marxist Economic Theory* (New York: Pathfinder Press, 1973).

Mannoni, Laurent, *The Great Art of Light and Shadow: Archaeology of the Cinema* (Exeter: University of Exeter Press, 2000).

Masuda Hiromichi, *Anime Business ga Wakaru [Understanding the Animation Business]* (Tokyo: NTT Shuppan, 2007).

_____ *Motto Wakaru Anime Business [Understanding the Anime Business More]* (Tokyo: NTT Shuppan, 2011).

Matsubashi Hironobu *et al.*, *Pia Cinema Club Gaikoku Eigaban [Guide to Foreign Films Released in Japan]* (Tokyo: Pia, 2005).

Matsumoto Natsuki, 'Eiga Torai Zengo no Katei-yō Eizō Kiki: Gentō, Animation, Gangu Eiga' ['Domestic Imaging Appliances during the Advent of Film: Magic Lanterns, Animation and Toy Films'], in Iwamoto Kenji (ed.), *Nippon Eiga no Tanjō [The Birth of Japanese Film]* (Tokyo: Shinwasha, 2011a), pp. 95–128.

Matsumoto Satoru, 'Digital Jidai no Anime Ryūtsū' ['Anime Distribution for the Digital Age'], in Takahashi Mitsuteru and Tsugata Nobuyuki (eds), *Anime-gaku [Anime Studies]* (Tokyo: NTT Shuppan, 2011b), pp. 184–98.

McCarthy, Helen, *Hayao Miyazaki: Master of Japanese Animation* (Berkeley, CA: Stone Bridge Press, 1999).

_____ *The Art of Osamu Tezuka: God of Manga* (Lewes: Ilex Press, 2009).

Megill, Allan, *Historical Knowledge, Historical Error: A Contemporary Guide to Practice* (Chicago, IL: University of Chicago Press, 2007).

Meyer, Leonard B., *Style and Music: Theory, History and Ideology* (Chicago, IL: Chigaco University Press, 1996).

Mikami Kōji, 'Anime Seisaku Shuhō to Gijutsu' ['Anime Production Methods and Techniques'], in Takahashi Mitsuteru and Tsugata Nobuyuki (eds), *Anime-gaku [Anime Studies]* (Tokyo: NTT Shuppan, 2011), pp. 70–112.

Miller, Toby, 'Hollywood, Cultural Policy Citadel', in Mike Wayne (ed.), *Understanding Film: Marxist Perspectives* (London: Pluto Press, 2005), pp. 182–93.

Minakawa Yūka, *Nippon Dōga no Kōbōshi: Shōsetsu Tezuka Gakkō [The Rise and Fall of Japanese Animation: The Story of the Tezuka School]* 2 vols (Tokyo: Kōdansha, 2009) [volumes cited as 2009a and 2009b].

Misono Makoto (ed.), *Zusetsu Terebi Anime Zensho [Complete Book of TV Animation: Illustrated]* (Tokyo: Hara Shobō, 1999).

Mittell, Jason, 'A Cultural Approach to Television Genre Theory', *Cinema Journal* vol. 40 no. 3 (Spring 2001), pp. 3–24.

Miyao Daisuke, 'Before Anime: Animation and the Pure Film Movement in Pre-war Japan', *Japan Forum* vol. 14 no. 2 (2002), pp. 191–209.

Miyazaki Hayao, *Orikaeshiten [Halfway Point: 1997–2008]* (Tokyo: Iwanami Shoten, 2008).

_____ *Starting Point: 1979–1996* (San Francisco, CA: Viz Media, 2009).

Miyoshi Hiroshi, 'Nihon no Animation Studio Shi' ['A History of Japanese Animation Studios'], in Tokuma Memorial Cultural Foundation for Animation, *Annual Report 2006–2007* (Tokyo: Tokuma Memorial Cultural Foundation for Animation, 2007), pp. 12–17.

Mochinaga Tadahito, *Animation Nitchū Kōryūki [A Chronicle of Sino-Japanese Animation Interchange]* (Tokyo: Tōhō Shoten, 2006).

Mori Masahiro, 'The Uncanny Valley', *Automaton*, http://spectrum.ieee.org/automaton/robotics/humanoids/the-uncanny-valley, 12 June 2012 [translation of 'Bukimi no Tani', *Energy* no. 7 (1975), pp. 33–5].

Mori Yasuji, *Mogura no Uta: Animator no Jiden [The Mole's Song: An Animator's Autobiography]* (Tokyo: Animage Bunko V, 1984).

_____ 'Atogaki' [Afterword] to Tezuka Osamu, *Boku no Manga Jinsei [My Manga Life]* (Tokyo: Iwanami Shinsho, 1997), pp. 221–3.

Murasawa Masataka, 'Anime Gakumon Bunsū' ['The Diversification of Anime Scholarship'], in Takahashi Mitsuteru and Tsugata Nobuyuki (eds), *Anime-gaku [Anime Studies]* (Tokyo: NTT Shuppan, 2011), pp. 285–306.

Nagayama Yasuo, *Sengo SF Jiken Shi: Nihonteki Sōzōryoku no 70-nen [An Event History of Postwar SF: 70 Years of Japanese Imaginative Power]* (Tokyo: Kawade Books, 2012).

Nakai Kōichi, *Nihon Kōkoku Hyōgen Gijutsu-shi: Kōkoku Hyōgen no 120-nen o Katta Creator-tachi [A Technical History of Japanese Advertising Imagery: The Creators Who Shouldered 120 Years of Advertising Imagery]* (Tokyo: Genkōsha, 1991).

Napier, Susan, *Anime from Akira to Howl's Moving Castle: Experiencing Contemporary Japanese Animation* (New York: Palgrave Macmillan, 2006).

Narita Yūta, 'Nihon Eiga to Koe Benshi: Katsudō Benshi o Tsūjita Nihon Eiga Shi Saikō no Kokoromi' ['Japanese Film and the Voice Benshi: A Trial Reconsideration of the Movie Benshi in Japanese Film History'], in Iwamoto Kenji (ed.), *Nippon Eiga no Tanjō [The Birth of Japanese Film]* (Tokyo: Shinwasha, 2011), pp. 273–301.

Nash, Eric, *Manga Kamishibai: The Art of Japanese Paper Theater* (New York: Abrams, 2009).

Nelson, Andrew, *The Modern Reader's Japanese–English Kanji Dictionary*, 2nd rev. edn (Rutland, VT: Charles E. Tuttle Company, 1974).

Neuwirth, Allan, *Makin' Toons: Inside the Most Popular Animated TV Shows and Movies* (New York: Allworth Press, 2003).

Newtype, 'Cybernetic City: Ghost in the Shell' [Interview with Oshii Mamoru], *Newtype*, November 1995, pp. 16–17.

NHK Hōsō Bunka Kenkyūsho, *Terebi Shichō 50-nen [50 Years of Television Ratings]* (Tokyo: NHK Shuppan, 2003).

Nichigai Associates, *Mangaka Anime Sakka Jinmei Jiten [Writers of Comics in Japan: A Biographical Dictionary]* (Tokyo: Nichigai Associates, 1997).

Nippon Animation, *25 Shūnen Kinen Nippon Animation Zensakuhinshū [25th Anniversary Memorial: Nippon Animation Complete Works Compendium]* (Tokyo: Planet Publishing, 2001).

Nishizaki Yoshinobu, 'My Anime Life: Yamato ni Itaru made, Yamato ni Ketsubetsu suru made' ['My Anime Life: Until Yamato Arrives, until Yamato Departs'], *My Anime* no. 1 (1981), pp. 100–4.

Nomura Research Institute (NRI), *Otaku Shijō no Kenkyū [Research in the Otaku Marketplace]* (Tokyo: Tōyō Keizai, 2005).

Nornes, Abe Mark (Markus), *Japanese Documentary Film: The Meiji Era through Hiroshima* (Minneapolis: University of Minnesota Press, 2003).

_____ and Fukushima Yukio (eds), *The Japan/America Film Wars: World War II Propaganda and Its Cultural Contexts* (Langhorne, PA: Harwood Academic Publishers, 1994).

_____ and Aaron Gerow, *Research Guide to Japanese Film Studies* (Ann Arbor: University of Michigan Center for Japanese Studies, 2009).

Ogata Emiko, *Animation no Senkakusha Ōfuji Noburō: Kokō no Genius [Animation Pioneer Ōfuji Noburō: Isolated Genius]* (Tokyo: Kinokuniya, 2010) [sleeve notes to the DVD of the same name].

Ogilvy, David, *Confessions of an Advertising Man* (London: Southbank Publishing, 2004).

Oguro Yuichirō, 'Tōei Chōhen Kenkyū: Shirakawa Daisaku Interview' ['Tōei Extensive Research: Shirakawa Daisaku Interview'] at *Web Anime Style*, http://www.style.fm/log/02_topics_m.html, 9 November–20 December 2004 [cited as Oguro 2004a].

_____ 'Tōei Chōhen Kenkyū: Nagasawa Makoto Interview' ['Tōei Extensive Research: Nagasawa Makoto Interview'], at *Web Anime Style*, http://www.style.fm/log/02_topics_m.html, 24 September–29 October 2004, in seven parts [cited as Oguro 2004b].

_____ 'Tōei Chōhen Kenkyū: Serikawa Yūgo' ['Tōei Extensive Research: Serikawa Yūgo'], at *Web Anime Style*, http://www.style.fm/log/02_topics_m.html, 13–17 September 2004 [cited as Oguro 2004c].

_____ *Anime Professional no Shigoto: Kono Hito no Hanashi o Kikitai 1998–2001 [Anime Professionals' Occupation: I Want to Listen to This Person's Story]* (Tokyo: Asuka Shinsha Animestyle Archive, 2006).

_____ et al., *Plus Madhouse 02: Kawajiri Yoshiaki* (Tokyo: Kinema Junpō-sha, 2008).

_____ et al., *Plus Madhouse 04: Rintarō* (Tokyo: Kinema Junpō-sha, 2009).

_____ *Anime Creator Interviews: Kono Hito no Hanashi o Kikitai 2001–2002 [Anime Creator Interviews: I Want to Listen to This Person's Story]* (Tokyo: Kōdansha, 2011).

Okada Toshio, *Otakugaku Nyūmon [An Introduction to Otakuology]* (Tokyo: Ōta Shuppan, 1996).

_____ *Yuigon [Testament]* (Tokyo: Chikuma Shobō, 2010).

Okamoto Rei, 'Portrayal of the War and Enemy in Japanese Wartime Cartoons', *Journal of Asian Pacific Communication* vol. 7 nos 1 and 2 (1996), pp. 5–17.

Ōkawa, Hiroshi, *Kono Ichiban no Jinsei [This Number One Life]* (Tokyo: Jitsugyō no Nipponsha, 1963).

Ōkubo Ryō, 'Utsushi-e kara Eiga e: Eizō to Katari no Keifu' ['From Reflected Pictures to Film: A Genealogy of Image and Speech'], in Iwamoto Kenji (ed.), *Nippon Eiga no Tanjō [The Birth of Japanese Film]* (Tokyo: Shinwasha, 2011), pp. 64–94.

Ono Kosei, 'Tadahito Mochinaga: The Animator Who Lived in Two Worlds', *Animation World Magazine* vol. 4 no. 9 (December 1999), www.awn.com.

Oshii Mamoru, *Tariki Hongan Shigoto de Makenai Nanatsu no Chikara [Salvation through Outside Help: Seven Powers for Work That Does Not Fail]* (Tokyo: Gentōsha, 2008).

Osmond, Andrew, 'Jimmy Murakami's Five Decades of Animation', in *Animation World Network*, 19 December 2001, http://www.awn.com/articles/people/jimmy-murakamis-five-decades-animation.

_____ *Satoshi Kon: The Illusionist* (San Francisco, CA: Stone Bridge Press, 2009).

_____ 'A Ton of Work' [Jimmy Murakami interview], *Manga UK*, 4 March 2012a, http://www.mangauk.com/?p=3656.

_____ 'Toon Titan', in *SFX Ultimate Guide to Anime*, 2012b, pp. 54–61.

Ōtomo Katsuhiro, *Kaba: Otomo Katsuhiro Artwork* (Tokyo: Kōdansha, 1989).

Ōtsuka Eiji and Ozawa Nobuaki, *Japanimation wa Naze Yabureru ka [Why Does Japanimation Fail?]* (Tokyo: Kadokawa, 2005).

Ōtsuka Yasuo, *Sakuga Asemamire [Sweating over Animation]*, rev. and expanded edn (Tokyo: Tokuma Shoten, 2001).

_____ *Little Nemo no Yabō [The Prospect of Little Nemo]* (Tokyo: Studio Ghibli, 2004).

_____ and Mori Yūki, *Ōtsuka Yasuo Interview: Animation Juō Mujin [Ōtsuka Yasuo Interview: Animation Rush of Business]* (Tokyo: Jitsugyō no Nipponsha, 2006).

Ōwada Hideki, *Kidō Senshi Gundam-san Itsutsu-me no Maki: Gundam Sōsei [Mobile Suit Mr Gundam #5: The Genesis of Gundam]* (Tokyo: Kadokawa Shoten, 2009).

Ōyama Kumao and Hayashi Nobuyuki (eds), *Animation Kantoku Dezaki Osamu no Sekai [The World of Animation Director Dezaki Osamu]* (Tokyo: Kawade Shobō Shinsha, 2012).

Painter, Andrew, *The Creation of Japanese Television and Culture*, PhD dissertation, University of Michigan, 1992.

Patten, Fred, *Watching Anime, Reading Manga: 25 Years of Essays and Reviews* (Berkeley, CA: Stone Bridge Press, 2004).

Pelliteri, Marco, *The Dragon and the Dazzle: Models, Strategies and Identities of Japanese Imagination, A European Perspective* (Latina: Tunué, 2010).

Postlewait, Thomas, *The Cambridge Introduction to Theatre Historiography* (Cambridge: Cambridge University Press, 2009).

Power, Natsu, *God of Comics: Osamu Tezuka and the Creation of Post-World War II Manga* (Jackson: University of Mississippi Press, 2009).

Quiquemelle, Marie-Claire, 'The Wan Brothers and Sixty Years of Animated Film in China', in Chris Berry (ed.), *Perspectives on Chinese Cinema* (London: BFI, 1991), pp. 175–86.

Ragone, August, *Eiji Tsuburaya: Master of Monsters* (San Francisco, CA: Chronicle Books, 2007).

Raskar, Ramesh *et al.*, 'Visualizing Photons in Motion at a Trillion Frames per Second', at MIT Media Lab website, December 2011, http://web.media.mit.edu/~raskar//trillionfps/.

Richie, Donald, *The Image Factory: Fads and Fashions in Japan* (London: Reaktion Books, 2003).

Royal, Ségolène, *Le Ras-le-bol des bébés zappeurs* (Paris: Éditions Robert Laffont, 1989).

Ruh, Brian, *Stray Dog of Anime: The Films of Mamoru Oshii* (New York: Palgrave Macmillan, 2004).

Ruskin, John, *The Political Economy of Art* (London: Smith, Elder & Co., 1867).

Saitō Takao, *Kajiwara Ikki Den [Biography of Kajiwara Ikki]* (Tokyo: Shinchōsha, 1995).

_____ *Kajiwara Ikki: Yūyake o Miteita Otoko [Kajiwara Ikki: The Man Watching the Sunset]* (Tokyo: Bungei Bunko, 2005).

Sakurai Takamasa, *Anime Bunka Gaikō [Anime Cultural Diplomacy]* (Tokyo: Chikuma Shinsho, 2009).

_____ *Nippon wa Anime de Saikō suru: Kuruma to Ieden ga Gaika o Kasegu Jidai wa Owatta [Japan Renewed by Anime: The Age of Income from Cars and Electronics Has Ended]* (Tokyo: Ascii Shinsho, 2010).

Salt, Barry, *Film Style and Technology: History and Analysis*, 3rd edn (London: Starword, 2009).

Sata Masunori and Hirahara Hideo, *A History of Japanese Television Drama* (Tokyo: Japanese Association of Broadcasting Art, 1991).

Satō Tadao, *Kinema to Hōsei: Nitchū Eiga Zenshi [Cinema and Gunshots: A Prehistory of Sino-Japanese Films]* (Tokyo: Iwanami Shoten, 2004).

Saunders, Frances Stonor, *Who Paid the Piper? The CIA and the Cultural Cold War* (London: Granta Books, 2000) [reprint of 1999 edition].

Schatz, Thomas, *Boom and Bust: American Cinema in the 1940s* (Berkeley: University of California Press, 1997).

Schilling, Mark, *Contemporary Japanese Film* (New York: Weatherhill, 1999).

Schodt, Frederik L., *Inside the Robot Kingdom: Japan, Mechatronics and the Coming Robotopia* (Tokyo: Kodansha International, 1988).

_____ *The Astro Boy Essays: Osamu Tezuka, Mighty Atom, Manga/Anime Revolution* (San Francisco, CA: Stone Bridge Press, 2007).

Seto Tatsuya *et al.*, *Nippon no Anime [All about Japan Anime]* (Tokyo: Takarajima-sha (Bessatsu Takarajima #638), 2002).

Sevakis, Justin, 'The Anime Economy', on *Anime News Network*, http://www.animenewsnetwork.co.uk/feature/2012-03-05 [in three parts, cited as Sevakis 2012a].

_____ 'All about Licensing', on *Anime News Network*, http://www.animenewsnetwork.com/feature/2012-06-11 [in three parts, cited as Sevakis 2012b].

Sharp, Jasper, 'Between Dimensions: 3D Computer Generated Animation in Anime', in Martha-Christine Menzel *et al.* (eds), *Ga Netchū: The Manga Anime Syndrome* (Frankfurt: Deutsche Filmmuseum, 2008), pp. 120–33.

_____ *Historical Dictionary of Japanese Cinema* (Lanham, MD: Scarecrow Press, 2011).

Sheldrake, John, *Management Theory: From Taylorism to Japanization* (London: International Thomson Business Press, 1996).

Shibata Masaru, 'Eiga o Omo to shita Watashi no Jijoden' ['My Autobiography with a Focus on Film'], *Eiga-shi Kenkyū* no. 3 (1974), pp. 45–59.

Shibayama Tatsuo and Kobayashi Shūji *et al.*, *Mushi Pro Tenamonya: Dare mo Shiranai Tezuka Osamu [Mushi Pro Maverick: The Tezuka Osamu That Nobody Knows]* (Tokyo: Kuraki-sha Bijutsu, 2009).

Shimokawa Oten, 'Nihon Saisho no Manga Eiga Seisaku no Omoide' ['Recollections of the First Cartoon Film Production in Japan'], *Eiga Hyōron* no. 3 (1974), p. 39.

Shiota Tokitoshi, 'Anime Kirai mo Osoreru Kawajiri Yoshiaki: 80-nendai Video Boom ni Saita Eros no Hana' ['Kawajiri Yoshiaki's Fear and Loathing Anime: The Glorious Flourishing of Eros in the 1980s Video Boom'], in Oguro Yuichirō *et al.*, *Plus Madhouse 02: Kawajiri Yoshiaki* (Tokyo: Kinema Junpō-sha, 2008), pp. 110–13.

Shull, Michael and David Wilt, *Doing Their Bit: Wartime American Animated Short Films 1939–1945* (Jefferson, NC: McFarland, 2004).

Sodei Rinjirō, 'Satire under the Occupation: The Case of Political Cartoons', in T. Burkman (ed.), *The Occupation of Japan: Arts and Culture: The Proceedings of a Symposium at Norfolk, Virginia 18–19 October 1984* (Norfolk: General Douglas MacArthur Foundation, 1988), pp. 93–106.

Solomon, Charles, 'The Disney Studio at War', in Maureen Furniss (ed.), *Animation – Art and Industry* (New Barnet: John Libbey, 2009), pp. 145–50 [reprint from *Walt Disney: An Intimate History of the Man and His Magic*, 1998].

Sorfleet, Winston, 'Interview with Robert Woodhead', *Protoculture Addicts* no. 20 (1992), pp. 10–16.

Stahl, David, 'Victimization and "Response-ability": Remembering, Representing, and Working through Trauma in Grave of the Fireflies', in David Stahl and Mark Williams (eds), *Imag(in)ing the War in Japan: Representing and Responding to Trauma in Postwar Literature and Film* (Leiden: Brill, 2010), pp. 161–202.

Staiger, Janet, 'The Hollywood Mode of Production to 1930', in David Bordwell, Janet Staiger and Kristin Thompson (eds), *The Classical Hollywood Cinema: Film Style & Mode of Production to 1960* (London: Routledge, 1985), pp. 85–154.

_____ *Interpreting Films: Studies in the Historical Reception of American Cinema* (Princeton, NJ: Princeton University Press, 1992).

Standish, Isolde, *A New History of Japanese Cinema: A Century of Narrative Film* (London: Continuum, 2005).

Steinberg, Marc, 'Immobile Sections and Trans-series Movement: Astroboy and the Emergence of Anime', *Animation* vol. 1 (November 2006), pp. 190–206.

_____ 'Anytime, Anywhere: Tetsuwan Atomu Stickers and the Emergence of Character Merchandizing', *Theory, Culture & Society* no. 26 (2009), pp. 113–38.

_____ *Anime's Media Mix: Franchising Toys and Characters in Japan* (Minneapolis: University of Minnesota Press, 2012).

Stevenson, Richard, *Degrees of Freedom: The Influence of Fansubbing on Mainstream Subtitling Practices*, MSc dissertation, University of Edinburgh, 2010.

Stingray and Nichigai Associates (eds), *Anime Sakuhin Jiten [Dictionary of Animation Works]* (Tokyo: Nichigai Associates, 2010).

Stringer, Julian, 'Japan 1951–1970: National Cinema as Cultural Currency', in Dina Iordanova and Ruby Cheung (eds), *Film Festival Yearbook 3: Film Festivals and East Asia* (St Andrews: St Andrews University Press, 2011), pp. 62–80.

Studio Ghibli, 'Utilizing Digital Technology to Create "Beautiful Images", in *The Art of Miyazaki's Spirited Away* (San Francisco, CA: Viz LLC, 2002) [trans. of 2001 Japanese edn], pp. 182–92.

Sugiyama Taku, 'Terebi Anime no Zenshi: Tōei Chōhen Anime no Jidai' ['The Prehistory of TV Anime: The Era of Tōei Long-form Animation'], in Misono Makoto (ed.), *Zusetsu Terebi Anime Zensho [Complete Book of TV Animation: Illustrated]* (Tokyo: Hara Shobō, 1999), pp. 91–120.

Sunrise, *Sunrise Anime Super Data File* (Tokyo: Tatsumi Shuppan, 1997).

Suzuki Shinichi, *Anime ga Sekai o Tsunagu [Anime Connects the World]* (Tokyo: Iwanami Junior Shinsho, 2008) [Suzuki 2008a in citations].

Suzuki Toshio, *Eiga Dōraku [Film Hobby]* (Tokyo: Pia, 2005).

_____ *Shigoto Dōraku: Studio Ghibli no Genjō [Work Hobby: On the Spot at Studio Ghibli]* (Tokyo: Iwanami Shinsho, 2008) [Suzuki 2008b in citations].

Suzuki Yoshitaka, *Japanese Management Structures 1920–80* (New York: St Martin's Press, 1991).

Sweet, Matthew, 'Too Late, We Realise That Silence Was Golden in the Cinema', *Daily Telegraph*, 10 December 2011, http://www.telegraph.co.uk/culture/film/8948327/Too-late-we-realise-that-silence-was-golden-in-the-cinema.html.

Tada Makoto, *Kore ga Anime Business da [This Is the Anime Business]* (Tokyo: Kōsaidō, 2002).

Takada Akinori, *Anime no Samenai Mahō [Anime's Unwoken Magic]* (Tokyo: PHP Kenkyūsho, 1995).

Takahashi Makiko, 'The Development of Japanese Television Broadcasting and Imported Television Programs', MA thesis, Michigan State University, 1992.

Takahashi Mitsuteru and Tsugata Nobuyuki (eds), *Anime-gaku [Anime Studies]* (Tokyo: NTT Shuppan, 2011).

_____ 'Animation ni Okeru Jinsai Ikusei' [The Training of Capable Personnel for Animation'], in Takahashi Mitsuteru and Tsugata Nobuyuki (eds), *Anime-gaku [Anime Studies]* (Tokyo: NTT Shuppan, 2011), pp. 253–84 [Takahashi 2011b in citations].

_____ and Nunokawa Yūji, 'Nihon Anime no Genjō to Mirai' ['The Current and Future Condition of Japanese Animation'], in Takahashi Mitsuteru and Tsugata Nobuyuki (eds), *Anime-gaku [Anime Studies]* (Tokyo: NTT Shuppan, 2011), pp. 307–17.

Takahashi Ryōsuke, 'Tōkichirō o Kidotte' ['Sensing Tōkichirō'], in Shibayama Tatsuo and Kobayashi Shūji et al. (eds), *Mushi Pro Tenamonya: Dare mo Shiranai Tezuka Osamu [Mushi Pro Maverick: The Tezuka Osamu That Nobody Knows]* (Tokyo: Kuraki-sha Bijutsu, 2009), pp. 60–3.

_____ 'Anime Enshutsu-ron: Anime ni Okeru Enshutsu, mata Kantoku to wa' ['On Anime Production: Concerning Anime Production and Direction'], in Takahashi Mitsuteru and Tsugata Nobuyuki (eds), *Anime-gaku [Anime Studies]* (Tokyo: NTT Shuppan, 2011a), pp. 47–69.

_____ 'Sleeping with Tezuka: Ryōsuke Takahashi on the Golden Age of Anime', http://www.mangauk.com/?p=sleeping-with-tezuka, 2012.

Takahashi Takeo and Tsukahara Yasuo, 'Pocket Monster Incident and Low Luminance Visual Stimuli', *Pediatrics International* vol. 40 no. 6 (1998), pp. 631–7.

Takahashi Toshie, *Audience Studies: A Japanese Perspective* (London: Routledge, 2010).

Takahata Isao, *Eiga o Tsukuri-nagara Kangaeta Koto [Thoughts while Making Movies]* (Tokyo: Tokuma Shoten, 1991).

_____ *1991–1999 Eiga o Tsukuri-nagara Kangaeta Koto II [Thoughts while Making Movies II]* (Tokyo: Tokuma Shoten, 1999).

Takamoto Iwao with Michael Mallory, *Iwao Takamoto: My Life with a Thousand Characters* (Jackson: University Press of Mississippi, 2009).

Takeda Yasuhiro, *The Notenki Memoirs: Studio Gainax and the Men Who Created Evangelion* (Houston, TX: AD Vision, 2005).

Takefuji Tetsurō, *Animesoft Kanzen Catalogue* (Tokyo: Kadokawa Shoten, 1993).

Takemura Mana, *Majyokko Days [Magical Girl Days]* (Tokyo: Bug News Network, 2009).

Takeuchi Osamu et al., *Gendai Manga Bijutsukan [The Encyclopaedia of Contemporary Manga 1945–2005]* (Tokyo: Shōgakukan, 2006).

Tanaka Tatsuo, 'Net-jo Chosaku Kenhogo Chōka wa Hitsuyō ka – Anime Dōga Haishin o Jirei Toshite ['Is It Necessary to Strengthen Intellectual Property Rights on the Net? – With Reference to Precedents in Animation Distribution'] (Tokyo: Research Institute of Economy Trade and Industry, *RIETI Discussion Paper Series* 11-J-010, 2011).

Tanizaki Akira, 'Anime Mechanic Hensen Shi' ['The Historical Transformation of Anime Mechanics'], in Misono Makoto (ed.), *Zusetsu Terebi Anime Zensho [Complete Book of TV Animation: Illustrated]* (Tokyo: Hara Shobō, 1999), pp. 155–82.

Tartikoff, Brandon and Charles Leerhsen, *The Last Great Ride* (New York: Turtle Bay Books, 1992).

Tatsunoko, *Tatsunoko Pro Anime Super Data File* (Tokyo: Tatsumi Shuppan, 1999).

Taylor, Philip, *Munitions of the Mind: A History of Propaganda from the Ancient World to the Present Day*, 3rd edn (Manchester: Manchester University Press, 2003).

Taylor, Richard, *The Encyclopedia of Animation Techniques* (Oxford: Focal Press, 2002) [reprint of 1996 edition].

Te Wei and Chang Songling, 'Wasuregatai Fang Ming Tongzhi' ['Unforgettable Comrade Fang Ming'], dated 20 May 2005, Afterword to T. Mochinaga, *Animation Nitchū Kōryūki [A Chronicle of Sino-Japanese Animation Interchange]* (Tokyo: Tōhō Shoten, 2006), pp. 344–7.

Telotte, J. P., *The Mouse Machine: Disney and Technology* (Urbana: University of Illinois Press, 2008).

Tezuka Osamu, *Boku no Manga Jinsei [My Manga Life]* (Tokyo: Iwanami Shinsho, 1997).

_____ *Boku wa Manga ka [I Am a Comic Artist]* (Tokyo: Nihon Tosho Centre, 1999).

Tezuka Productions, *Tezuka Osamu Gekijō [The Animation Filmography of Osamu Tezuka]* (Tokyo: Tezuka Productions, 1991).

Tinios, Ellis, *Japanese Prints: Ukiyo-e in Edo 1700–1900* (London: British Museum Press, 2010).

Tobin, Joseph (ed.), *Pikachu's Global Adventure: The Rise and Fall of Pokémon* (Durham, NC: Duke University Press, 2004).

Tokugi Yoshiharu, 'OVA no Jūgonen' ['Fifteen Years of Original Video Animation'], in Misono Makoto (ed.), *Zusetsu Terebi Anime Zensho [Complete Book of TV Animation: Illustrated]* (Tokyo: Hara Shobō, 1999), pp. 305–30.

Tokyo Movie Shinsha, *TMS Anime Super Data File* (Tokyo: Tatsumi Shuppan, 1999).

Tomino Yoshiyuki, *Dakara Boku wa ... Gundam e no Michi [And So I ... The Road to Gundam]* (Tokyo: Kadokawa Sneaker Bunko, 2002) [reprint of Tokuma Shoten edn, 1981, with new Afterword].

_____ *Tomino ni Kike! [Ask Tomino!]* (Tokyo: Animage Bunko, 2010).

Tompkins, Jane (ed.), *Reader-Response Criticism: From Formalism to Post-structuralism* (Baltimore, MD: Johns Hopkins University Press, 1980).

Toriumi, Jinzō, *Anime Scenario Nyūmon [An Introduction to Anime Screenwriting]* (Tokyo: Eijinsha, 1987).

Tsuchiya, Yuka, 'Imagined America in Occupied Japan: (Re)Educational Films Shown by the U.S. Occupational Forces to the Japanese, 1948–52', *Japanese Journal of American Studies* no. 13 (2002), pp. 193–213.

Tsugata Nobuyuki, 'Research on the Achievements of Japan's First Three Animators', *Asian Cinema* vol. 14 no. 1 (2003), pp. 13–27.

_____ *Nihon Animation no Chikara: Hachijūgo-nen no Rekishi o Tsuranuku Futatsu no Jiku [The Power of Japanese Animation: Two Axes Running through an 85-year History]* (Tokyo: NTT Shuppan, 2004).

_____ *Animation-gaku Nyūmon [An Introduction to Animation Studies]* (Tokyo: Heibonsha, 2005).

_____ *Nihon Hatsu no Animation Sakka Kitayama Seitarō [Japan's First Animation Creator: Kitayama Seitarō]* (Kyoto: Rinsen Shoten, 2007a).

_____ *Anime Sakka toshite no Tezuka Osamu: Sono Kiseki to Honshitsu [Tezuka Osamu as an Anime Auteur: His Locus and Substance]* (Tokyo: NTT Shuppan, 2007b).

_____ 'Ōfuji Noburō Sakuhin List' ['Filmography of Ōfuji Noburō'], in *Animation no Senkakusha Ōfuji Noburō: Kokō no Genius [Animation Pioneer Ōfuji Noburō: Isolated Genius]* (Tokyo: Kinokuniya, 2010) [sleeve notes to the DVD of the same name].

_____ 'Nihon no Shoki Animation no Shosō to Hattatsu' ['Aspects and Development of Early Animation in Japan'], in Kurosawa Kiyoshi, Yohota Inuhiko *et al.*, *Anime wa Ekkyō suru [Anime in Transition]* (Tokyo: Iwanami Shoten, 2010), pp. 9–30 [listed in citations as Tsugata 2010b].

_____ 'Anime to wa Nani ka' ['What Is Anime?'], in Takahashi Mitsuteru and Tsugata Nobuyuki (eds), *Anime-gaku [Anime Studies]* (Tokyo: NTT Shuppan, 2011), pp. 3–23 [Tsugata 2011a in citations].

_____ 'Anime no Rekishi' ['The History of Anime'], in Takahashi Mitsuteru and Tsugata Nobuyuki (eds), *Anime-gaku [Anime Studies]* (Tokyo: NTT Shuppan, 2011), pp. 24–44 [Tsugata 2011b in citations].

_____ *Terebi Anime Yoake Mae: Shirarezaru Kansai-ken Animation Kōbōshi [Before the Dawn of TV Anime: A History of the Rise and Fall of Forgotten Kansai-area Animation]* (Tokyo: Nakanishiya, 2012).

Tsukada Hiro'o (ed.), *Nippon Onseisaku Sakusha Meikan [Directory of Japanese Audio Production]* (Tokyo: Shōgakukan, 2004).

Tsuji Masaki, *TV Anime no Seishunki [The Early Days of TV Anime]* (Tokyo: Jitsugyō no Nipponsha, 1996).

_____ *Bokutachi no Anime Shi [Our Anime History]* (Tokyo: Iwanami Junior Shinsho, 2008).

Tsutsui, William, 'W. Edwards Deming and the Origin of Quality Control in Japan', *Journal of Japanese Studies* vol. 22 no. 2 (Summer 1996), pp. 295–325.

Tungate, Mark, *Ad Land: A Global History of Advertising* (London: Kogan Page, 2007).

Ubukata Tow, *Ubukata-shiki Anime & Manga Sōsaku-juku [The Ubukata-method Anime & Manga Story Cram School]* (Tokyo: Takarajima-sha, 2009).

Uchikawa Yoshimi (ed.), *Nihon Kōkoku Hattatsu Shi [A History of the Development of Japanese Advertising]* (Tokyo: Dentsū, 1980).

Uchiyama Takashi, 'Nihon to Kaigai no Anime Seisaku' ['Animation Policy in Japan and Overseas'], in Takahashi Mitsuteru and Tsugata Nobuyuki (eds), *Anime-gaku [Anime Studies]* (Tokyo: NTT Shuppan, 2011), pp. 230–50.

[US Supreme Court] *Sony Corp.* vs. *Universal City Studios* – 464 U.S. 417 (17 January 1984), https://supreme.justia.com/cases/federal/us/464/417/case.html.

Ushiki Riichi, 'Anime to Chiteki Zaisan Hō' ['Anime and Intellectual Property Law'], in Takahashi Mitsuteru and Tsugata Nobuyuki (eds), *Anime-gaku [Anime Studies]* (Tokyo: NTT Shuppan, 2011), pp. 201–29.

Ushio Sōji, *Yume wa Ōzora o Kakemeguru: Onshi Tsuburaya Eiji Den [Dreams Bustling in a Big Sky: The Life of My Mentor Tsuburaya Eiji]* (Tokyo: Kadokawa Shoten, 2001).

_____ *Tezuka Osamu to Boku [Tezuka Osamu and I]* (Tokyo: Sōshisha, 2007).

Vogel, Harold, *Entertainment Industry Economics: A Guide for Financial Analysis*, 7th edn (Cambridge: Cambridge University Press, 2007).

Wada-Marciano, Mitsuyo, *Nippon Modern: Japanese Cinema of the 1920s and 1930s* (Honolulu: University of Hawaii Press, 2008).

Wakisaka Akira, 'Women at Work', in Sato Mari and Sato Hiroki (eds), *Japanese Labour and Management in Transition: Diversity, Flexibility and Participation* (London: Routledge, 1997), pp. 131–50.

Webster, Leonard and Patricie Mertova, *Using Narrative Inquiry as a Research Method: An Introduction to Using Critical Event Narrative Analysis in Research on Learning and Teaching* (London: Routledge, 2007).

Wells, Brian, 'Frame of Reference: Toward a Definition of Animation', *Animation Practice, Process & Production* vol. 1 no. 1 (2011), pp. 11–32.

Wells, Paul, *The Fundamentals of Animation* (Lausanne: AVA Publishing, 2006).

_____ 'From Sunnyside to Soccer: Reading Up on Animation', *Animation Practice, Process & Production* vol. 1 no. 1 (January 2011), pp. 3–9.

White, Hayden, *The Content of the Form: Narrative Discourse and Historical Representation* (Baltimore, MD: Johns Hopkins University Press, 1987).

Whitehill, Arthur, *Japanese Management: Tradition and Transition* (London: Routledge, 1991).

Williams, Raymond, *Television: Technology and Cultural Form*. 2nd edn with new Preface (London: Routledge, 1990) [originally 1975].

Yamada Shōichi, *Bunka toshite no Terebi Commercial [Cultural Perspectives on TV Commercials]* (Kyoto: Sekai Shisōsha, 2007).

Yamaguchi Katsunori and Watanabe Yasushi, *Nihon Animation Eiga Shi [The History of Japanese Animated Films]* (Osaka: Yūbunsha, 1977).

Yamaguchi Takeshi, *Maboroshi no Kinema Man-Ei: Amakasu Masahiko to Katsudōya Gunzō [The Dream of Man-Ei Cinema: Amakasu Masahiko and the Activist Group]* (Tokyo: Heibonsha, 2006).

Yamaguchi Yasuō (ed.), *Nippon no Anime Zenshi [Complete History of Japanese Animation]* (Tokyo: Ten Books, 2004).

Yamamoto Eiichi, *Mushi Pro no Kōbōki: Ani Meita no Seishun [The Rise and Fall of Mushi Production: The Youth of 'A. Nimator']* (Tokyo: Shinchōsha, 1989).

Yamamoto Kikuo, *Nippon Eiga ni okeru Gaikoku Eiga no Fikyō: Hikaku Eiga Shi Kenkyū [The Influence of Foreign Films on Japanese Films: Research in Comparative Film History]* (Tokyo: Waseda Daigaku, 1983).

Yamamoto Y. and Katō Mikirō, 'Selective Animation to iu Gainen Gihō' ['Conceptual Techniques in Selective Animation'], in Katō Mikirō, *Animation no Eiga-gaku [Animation Film Studies]* (Kyoto: Rinsen Shoten, 2009).

Yamamura Kōji, *Animation no Sekai e Yōkoso [Welcome to the World of Animation]* (Tokyo: Iwanami Shoten, 2006).

Yamazaki Keishi, *Terebi Anime Damashi [Spirit of TV Anime]* (Tokyo: Kōdansha Gendai Shinsha, 2005).

Yokota Masao, 'The Japanese Puppet Animation Master: Kihachiro Kawamoto', *Asian Cinema* vol. 14 no. 1 (2003), pp. 28–44.

Yokoyama Ryūichi, *Yokoyama Ryūichi: Waga Yūgiteki Jinsei [Yokoyama Ryūichi: My Playful Life]* (Tokyo: Nippon Tosho Centre, 1997).

Yoon Hyejin, 'The Animation Industry: Technological Changes, Production Challenges, and Global Shifts', PhD dissertation, Ohio State University, 2008.

Young, Louise, *Japan's Total Empire: Manchuria and the Culture of Wartime Imperialism* (Berkeley: University of California Press, 1998).

Yu Kie-un, 'The Development of the Korean Animation Industry: Historical, Economic and Cultural Perspectives', PhD dissertation, Temple University, 1999.

Zakka Films, *The Roots of Japanese Anime until the End of WWII* (DVD) (Tokyo: Zakka Films, 2008).

FILMOGRAPHY

The prefix 'JCD' denotes a film's serial number in the Agency for Cultural Affairs Japanese Cinema Database (Bunkachō Nihon Eiga Jōhō System), which I have used as the default location for any film data in cases of hard-to-find films in the early chapters. Japanese-language details for each film can be called up by adding the serial number to the web address http://www.japanese-cinema-db.jp/details/.

For example, JCD 34498 denotes Ashida Iwao's propaganda film *Hi no Maru Tarō: Musha Jugyō* (1936, *Rising Sun Tarō: Warrior Training*), data on which may be found online at http://www.japanese-cinema-db.jp/details/34498.

This straightforward numerical system is immensely easier than the use of transliterations or Japanese characters. At the time of writing, the JCD is pedantically exacting with search terms, demands precise Japanese spelling and punctuation, even to the extent of variant kanji, and simply returns a blank entry in the event of a single discrepancy. On those occasions where a film does not show up in the JCD, I revert to the Stingray and Nichigai *Dictionary of Animation Works*, denoted by DAW and a page number. For example *Poppoya-san* (DAW 724) denotes the page of the *Dictionary of Animation Works* where details of Kumagawa Masao's *Poppoya-san* series can be found.

INDEX

Page numbers in **bold** indicate detailed analysis; those in *italic* denote illustrations; *n* = endnote.

LIST OF ILLUSTRATIONS

While considerable effort has been made to correctly identify the copyright holders, this has not been possible in all cases. We apologise for any apparent negligence and any omissions or corrections brought to our attention will be remedied in any future editions.

Snow White and the Seven Dwarfs, © Walt Disney Productions; *Hatsune Miku Live Party*, © 2011 Crypton Future Media, Inc.; *The Phantom Ship*, Chiyogami Eiga-sha; *Baguda-jo no Tozoku* (*The Thief of Baguda Castle*), Jiyū Eiga Kenkyū-jo; *Mabo's Great Race*, Satō Eiga Seisaku-sho; *Black Cat*, Chiyogami Eiga-sha; *National Anthem*, Chiyogami Eiga-sha; *Katsura-hime*, Chiyogami Eiga-sha; *Song of Spring*, Chiyogami Eiga-sha; *Benkei tai Ushiwaka*, © 2008 Zakka Films; *The Plane Cabby's Lucky Day*, Kyoryoku Eiga-sha; *Momotarō of the Sky*, Yokohama Cinema Shōkai; *Sky Eagles*, Chiyogami Eiga-sha; *The Aerial Battle Over Shanghai*, Sankichi News; *Mabo as Kinoshita Tokichiro*, Satō Eiga Seisaku-sho; *Momotarō's Sea Eagles*, © 2008 Zakka Films; *Gulliver's Great Activities*, Kindai Eiga-sha; Rohto Pharmaceuticals advert from ACC advertising CM showreel dvd IOBD-21064) © 1961 Dentsū, 2010 Avex; *Au Fou!* (1967), Kuri Jikken Manga Kobo; *A Poet's Life*, © 1974 Kawamoto Production Ltd; *I Am Two*, © 1962 Kadokawa Herald; Pentax camera ad from ACC advertising CM showreel dvd IOBD-21064, © 1964 Asatsū DK, Pentax; *Hakujaden*, Tōei Dōga; *Magic Boy*, Tōei Dōga; *Rudolph the Red-Nosed Reindeer*, Rankin/Bass Productions/Videocraft International; *Saiyūki*, © 1960 Tōei Dōga; *Tales from a Certain Street Corner*, © 1961 Tezuka Production Co. Ltd/Mushi Production Co., Ltd; *Astro Boy*, © 1963 Tezuka Production Co. Ltd/Mushi Production Co., Ltd; *Tetsujin 28*, TCJ Animation Center; *Jungle Emperor* (*Kimba the White Lion*), © 1965 Tezuka Production Co. Ltd/Mushi Production Co., Ltd; *1001 Nights*, © 1969 Tezuka Production Co. Ltd/Mushi Production Co., Ltd; *Panda Go Panda*, © 1971 TMS; *Dog of Flanders*, 1975 Nippon Animation; *Star of the Giants*, © 1968 Kajiwara Ikki/Kawasaki Noboru/TMS; *Battle of the Planets*, © 1972 Tatsunoko Pro; *Heidi*, © 1974 ZUIYO; *Mazinger Z*, © 1972 Dynamic Planning/Tōei Dōga; *Mobile Suit Gundam*, © 1979 Sotsū Agency/Bandai; *Space Knight Tekkaman*, © 1975 Tatsunoko Pro; *Space Cruiser Yamato*, © 1977 Westcape Corporation; *Doraemon the time-travelling cat*, © Fujiko Pro/Shōgakukan/TV Asahi/ADK; *Patlabor* series, © Headgear/Bandai Visual/Tohoku Shinsha; *Wings of Honneamise*, © 1987/1995 Bandai Visual; *UFO Robo Grendizer*, © 1975 Dynamic Planning/Tōei Dōga; *Nausicäa of the Valley of the Wind*, © 1984 Nibariki/Tokuma Shoten; *Akira*, © 1988 Akira Production Committee; *Pretty Soldier Sailor Moon*, © 1992 Naoko Takeuchi/ PNP/Tōei Dōga; *Ghost in the Shell*, © 1995 Masamune Shirow/Kodansha Ltd/Bandai Visual Co. Ltd/Manga Entertainment; *Princess Mononoke*, © 1997 Nibariki/TDNG; *Appleseed*, © 2004 Masamune Shirow/Seishinsha/Appleseed Film Partners; *Blue Submarine No. Six*, © 1998 Satoru Ozawa/Bandai Visual/Toshiba EMI/Gonzo; *Vexille*, © 2008 Vexille Production Committee; *Spirited Away*, ©2001 Nibariki/TGNDDTM; *Ponyo*, © 2008 Nibariki, GNDHDDT; *Astro Boy*, © 2009 Imagi Crystal Ltd., Tezuka Productions; *Perfect Blue*, Mad House/Rex Entertainment; *Jin-roh: The Wolf Brigade*, Bandai Visual Productions/Production I.G.; *Afro Samurai*, © Kouta Hirano/Shonen Gahosha Co. Ltd/Hellsing K.G.; *Hellsing*, © 2006 Kouta Hirano/Shonen Gahosha Co. Ltd/Wild Geese; *The Girl Who Leapt Through Time*, © Tokikake Film Partners; *Summer Wars*, © Summer Wars Film Partners; *Tales From Earthsea*, © Nibariki – GNDHDDT; *Last Exile*, © 2011 Gonzo/Fam Partners.